Stephen Hetherington on Epistemology

Also available from Bloomsbury

The Philosophy of Knowledge: A History, edited by Stephen Hetherington
Epistemology: The Key Thinkers, edited by Stephen Hetherington
A History and Philosophy of Expertise, by Jamie Carlin Watson
Knowledge, Number and Reality, edited by Nils Kürbis, Bahram Assadian and Jonathan Nassim

Stephen Hetherington on Epistemology

Knowing, More or Less

Stephen Hetherington

Edited by
Jeremiah Joven Joaquin and Mark Anthony Dacela

BLOOMSBURY ACADEMIC
LONDON • NEW YORK • OXFORD • NEW DELHI • SYDNEY

BLOOMSBURY ACADEMIC

Bloomsbury Publishing Plc, 50 Bedford Square, London, WC1B 3DP, UK
Bloomsbury Publishing Inc, 1359 Broadway, 12th Floor, New York, NY 10018, USA
Bloomsbury Publishing Ireland, 29 Earlsfort Terrace, Dublin 2, D02 AY28, Ireland

BLOOMSBURY, BLOOMSBURY ACADEMIC and the Diana logo are
trademarks of Bloomsbury Publishing Plc

First published in Great Britain 2024
This paperback edition published 2026

Copyright © Stephen Hetherington, Jeremiah Joven Joaquin and
Mark Anthony Dacela 2024

Stephen Hetherington has asserted his right under the Copyright,
Designs and Patents Act, 1988, to be identified as Author of this work.

Jeremiah Joven Joaquin and Mark Anthony Dacela have asserted their right under the
Copyright, Designs and Patents Act, 1988, to be identified as Editors of this work.

For legal purposes the Permissions and publication details on pp. ix–x constitute
an extension of this copyright page.

Cover image: 'Going, Going' by Parveen Seehra; courtesy of the artist

All rights reserved. No part of this publication may be: i) reproduced or transmitted in
any form, electronic or mechanical, including photocopying, recording or by means of
any information storage or retrieval system without prior permission in writing from
the publishers; or ii) used or reproduced in any way for the training, development or
operation of artificial intelligence (AI) technologies, including generative AI technologies.
The rights holders expressly reserve this publication from the text and data mining
exception as per Article 4(3) of the Digital Single Market Directive (EU) 2019/790.

Bloomsbury Publishing Inc does not have any control over, or responsibility for,
any third-party websites referred to or in this book. All internet addresses given
in this book were correct at the time of going to press. The author and publisher
regret any inconvenience caused if addresses have changed or sites have
ceased to exist, but can accept no responsibility for any such changes.

A catalogue record for this book is available from the British Library.

ISBN: HB: 978-1-3503-4474-7
PB: 978-1-3503-4495-2
ePDF: 978-1-3503-4475-4
eBook: 978-1-3503-4476-1

Typeset by Integra Software Services Pvt. Ltd.

For product safety related questions contact productsafety@bloomsbury.com.

To find out more about our authors and books visit www.bloomsbury.com
and sign up for our newsletters.

Contents

Author's preface		vi
Foreword		viii
Permissions and publication details		ix
Editors' introduction		1
1	Epistemic internalism's dilemma	5
2	Is epistemically adequate epistemology possible?	15
3	Elusive epistemological justification	23
4	Gettieristic scepticism	41
5	Epistemic disaster averted	57
6	Knowing failably and knowing imperfectly	63
7	Sceptical possibilities? No worries	77
8	Knowledge that works: A tale of two conceptual models	101
9	Knowledge as potential for action	121
10	Sceptical challenges and knowing actions	141
11	Some fallibilist knowledge: Questioning knowledge-attributions and open knowledge	161
12	The luck/knowledge incompatibility thesis	179
13	The redundancy problem: From knowledge-infallibilism to knowledge-minimalism	193
14	And next?	215
15	A life in philosophy	227
Index		243

Author's preface

In 2021, JJ Joaquin and Mark Dacela, from De La Salle University in Manila, Philippines, asked me if I was interested in their editing a selection of my published epistemology writing. I already knew JJ and Mark, especially from visiting DLSU at their invitation in 2013. They were fine hosts, both academically and personally. I was indeed interested in their generous and gracious proposal – if we were to publish with a good publisher with whom we would be happy.

Immediately, I suggested Bloomsbury. I had worked with their philosophy editor, Colleen Coalter, on a few projects, dating back to 2011, including my general-editing the 2019 four-volume *The Philosophy of Knowledge: A History*. I greatly respect Colleen – her philosophical sensibility and range, professionalism and friendliness. She is an *excellent* commissioning editor. And she was supportive of this book from the outset, for which I was very grateful. I also welcomed the enthusiastic and helpful comments by Bloomsbury's anonymous referees. JJ and Mark then oversaw the editing of the book-to-be, making the process enjoyable and rewarding.

The book includes several published papers, beginning with my first epistemology publication, from 1990. There are also excerpts from my *Good Knowledge, Bad Knowledge* (Oxford University Press, 2001), along with two newly written chapters gesturing at ideas from *Epistemology's Paradox* (Rowman & Littlefield, 1992), *Knowledge and the Gettier Problem* (Cambridge University Press, 2016) and *What Is Epistemology?* (Polity Press, 2019).

May I comment on the spirit with which I might be thought to approach epistemology's challenges? I recall a moment from my PhD dissertation defence at the University of Pittsburgh. An examining committee member asked me whether I was worried that no one would *agree* with what I was saying. I was slightly surprised at the question, not having thought about the issue. So my unworldly reply was a naïvely unperturbed 'No'. And that was that. It did not worry me then. But it does not worry me even now, reflecting *less* naïvely upon my career. We tend to encourage students to follow arguments through to wherever these might lead. How a student reacts to finding herself in that place is a separate matter. But at least she will not have prematurely abandoned the search. I have always *tried* not to step away from where I was being led by various lines of epistemological thought, no matter that the result has at times been a not-so-easily believed thesis. My *aim* has never been to produce theses with that character. It has simply happened.

This book is a mixture of arguments and proposals, clustering around several pivotal epistemological themes. Some of those arguments and proposals are more contentious, some less so. Which are more likely to be true? I leave such assessments to others. To me, each of the arguments seems good. To me, each of the proposals seems true. But *fallibilism* happens to be among those proposals: I readily accept that whatever seems true might be false, even when it rests upon what seems to be a good argument. Being *told* how unorthodox some of one's views are (as has often occurred to me, including by anonymous referees) can reinforce that first-personal sense of fallibility.

For what it is worth, it has never felt to me that all epistemologists share that sense of their epistemological moments. Some do, and I am among them. But philosophy is so ancient and varied that, it always strikes me, *we might all now be deeply mistaken*, even in our generally shared professional assumptions about what should be taken for granted within metaphysics, epistemology and so on. Philosophy's deep vulnerability *even to itself* has always been, for me, part of what makes it both appealing and difficult. This sensibility has grown stronger within me over the past two-plus years, when reading more widely within classical Greek, Chinese, Arabic and Indian philosophy, particularly – all of this for my *Defining Knowledge* (Cambridge University Press, 2022) and *Being Philosophical* (Polity Press, forthcoming 2024).

I end this preface with a less-than-fully-serious question about what *sort* of book this is. I have written a few philosophy *mono*graphs. The prefix 'mono' is used in describing such books because each of them, supposedly, is a sustained single argument (even when built upon smaller ones) for a single main thesis. In which case, what should a book such as this be called? It is a collection of many (smaller) arguments, for many theses (some larger, some smaller). Is it a *poly*graph?

Perhaps notoriously, that term is already featured in circles far removed – thankfully – from philosophy. Still, with one eye watching warily that existing use of the term, may I offer this book as a record of my own answers – attempts at truth-telling – to several interweaving laneways of epistemological questioning? I do so in a fallibilist tone of voice, of course.

Stephen Hetherington
Sydney, Australia
June 2023

Foreword

Stephen Hetherington has been a distinctive voice in analytic epistemology for more than three decades. Over that time, he has investigated and defended a range of controversial theses about knowledge:

1. *Minimalism*: Knowing is true believing.
2. *Gradualism*: Knowing is sometimes better, sometimes worse: with respect to particular propositions, there are degrees or grades of knowing
3. *Practicalism*: Knowing-that is a form of knowing-how
4. *Fallibilism*: Knowing has the potential to be not knowing: any of the components of a particular failable knowing might not have been present.

Moreover, he has been a keen observer and critic of our tendencies to project our ways of thinking onto others and to rest content with easy appeals to intuition.

This book provides an excellent entry to, and synopsis of, Stephen's writings on topics in epistemology. Some of the chapters draw on central journal articles, including 'Knowing failably' (*Journal of Philosophy*, 1999) and 'Sceptical Challenges and Knowing Actions' (*Philosophical Issues*, 2013). Other chapters are drawn from his books: *Epistemology's Paradox* (1992); *Knowledge Puzzles: An Introduction to Epistemology* (1996); *Good Knowledge, Bad Knowledge* (2001); *Epistemology Futures* (ed.) (2006); *How to Know: A Practicalist Conception of Knowledge* (2011); *Knowledge and the Gettier Problem* (2016); *The Philosophy of Knowledge: A History* (ed.) (2019); *What Is Knowledge* (2019); *Defining Knowledge* (2022); and *Being Philosophical* (2023). The final chapter is an interview conducted with Stephen by the editors of this volume.

I know Stephen best for his work as editor of the *Australasian Journal of Philosophy*, from Issue 92.1 to Issue 100.1. Over those eight years, I was able to observe the same qualities that are evident in Stephen's epistemological writings: meticulous attention to detail, an extraordinary capacity for hard work, an unlimited willingness to follow lines of Enquiry wherever they may lead, and a determination to do what is right and fair for the discipline of philosophy. In that time, I also discovered other things that are revealed in the concluding interview, including our shared passion for cricket. I hope that Stephen gets to lead the philosophical good life for many years to come.

Graham Oppy

Permissions and publication details

Chapter 1, 'Epistemic Internalism's Dilemma', was Stephen Hetherington's first epistemology publication: *American Philosophical Quarterly* 27 (1990), 245–51. It is reprinted with permission from the University of Illinois Press.

Chapter 2 is newly written. It conveys something of the challenge developed in *Epistemology's Paradox: Is a Theory of Knowledge Possible?* (Savage, MD: Rowman & Littlefield, 1992).

Chapter 3, 'Elusive Epistemological Justification', is from *Synthese* 174 (2010), 315–30. It is a revision of a 1992 UNSW talk that was cited by David Lewis at the outset of 'Elusive knowledge', *Australasian Journal of Philosophy* 74 (1996), 549–67. It is reprinted with permission from Springer Nature.

Chapter 4, 'Gettieristic Scepticism', is from *Australasian Journal of Philosophy* 74 (1996), 83–97. It is reprinted with permission from Taylor & Francis.

Chapter 5, 'Epistemic Disaster Averted', is from *Analysis* 59 (1999), 194–200. It is reprinted with permission from Oxford University Press.

Chapter 6, 'Knowing failably and knowing imperfectly', has two parts. Section 6.1 is the first half of 'Knowing failably', from *The Journal of Philosophy* 96 (1999), 565–87. It is reprinted with permission from *The Journal of Philosophy*. Sections 6.2 and 6.3 are, respectively, Section 2.6 ('Knowing failably and sceptical possibilities') and Section 2.10 ('Imperfect knowledge') from Hetherington's *Good Knowledge, Bad Knowledge: On Two Dogmas of Epistemology* (Oxford: Clarendon Press, 2001). These sections are reprinted with permission from Oxford University Press.

Chapter 7, 'Sceptical Possibilities? No Worries', is from *Synthese* 168 (2009), 97–118. It is reprinted with permission from Springer Nature.

Chapter 8, 'Knowledge That Works: A Tale of Two Conceptual Models', is from *Aspects of Knowing: Epistemological Essays* (ed.) S. Hetherington (Oxford: Elsevier, 2006), 219–40. It is reprinted with permission from Elsevier.

Chapter 9, 'Knowledge as Potential for Action', is from *European Journal of Pragmatism and American Philosophy* 9 (2017), at http://journals.openedition.org/ejpap/1070. It is reprinted with permission from the *European Journal of Pragmatism and American Philosophy*.

Chapter 10 was published as 'Skeptical Challenges and Knowing Actions', in *Philosophical Issues* 23 (2013), 18–39. It is reprinted with permission from John Wiley and Sons.

Chapter 11, 'Some Fallibilist Knowledge: Questioning Knowledge-attributions and Open Knowledge', is from *Synthese* 198 (2021), 2083–99. It is reprinted with permission from Springer Nature.

Chapter 12, 'The Luck/Knowledge Incompatibility Thesis', is from *The Routledge Handbook of the Philosophy and Psychology of Luck*, 1st edition by (eds.) I.M. Church and R.J. Hartman, Copyright 2019 by Imprint. Reproduced by permission of Taylor & Francis Group.

Chapter 13, 'The Redundancy Problem: From Knowledge-infallibilism to Knowledge-minimalism', is from *Synthese* 195 (2018), 4683–702. It is reprinted with permission from Springer Nature.

Chapter 14, 'And Next?', is newly written. It offers brief versions of ideas from two of Hetherington's books – *Knowledge and the Gettier Problem* (Cambridge: Cambridge University Press, 2016) and *What Is Epistemology?* (Cambridge: Polity Press, 2019).

Chapter 15, 'A Life in Philosophy', is an interview that provides insight into the life and work of Stephen Hetherington, and his views about philosophy in general, and epistemology, in particular.

Editors' introduction

In his 2022 parting words as editor of the *Australasian Journal of Philosophy*, Stephen Hetherington ('*AJP* – 100*', *AJP* 100: 1–2) briefly reflects on how the years have *flown* like a hummingbird 'hovering, wings faster than fast can see – an illusion of mid-air immobility'. Although the thirty years or so of his prominent philosophical career may have similarly *flown*, this collection proves that Stephen's mobility of thought is far from illusory.

We met Stephen at the 2012 Australasian Association of Philosophy in Wollongong, Australia. Right before lunchtime in Room 302, we listened to Stephen as he carefully explained why the Gettier problem is an infallibilist confusion. After his talk, we mustered the courage to approach him, but our initial introductions were full of awkwardness. Thankfully, our dear friend, Alan Hájek, whom we previously hosted at De La Salle University, our home university, was there to nudge us out of such a state. We invited Stephen to the Philippines for a talk a year later, and the rest, as they say, is history.

This book celebrates the many *chance* encounters we had with Stephen. It is not every day that you get to call a philosopher like Stephen a friend. But our friendship was founded on luck: the lucky circumstances that led us to Wollongong in 2012, and to meet and be friends with him. We are lucky that the friendship we started a decade ago has been going strong a decade after.

This book is our way of expressing our gratitude to Stephen for accommodating our fallible selves, tapping up our degree of knowledge by a notch or two, and inspiring us to become better professional philosophers. But most of all, this book is a celebration of his life as a philosopher and an epistemologist extraordinaire. The hovering wings of a hummingbird stretch over several pages. We now have a chance to appreciate its flight!

This is the first collection that brings Stephen's *heterodox* views on knowledge, justification, scepticism and the Gettier Problem. This includes eleven of his published papers, two sections from *Good Knowledge, Bad Knowledge: On Two Dogmas of Epistemology* (2001), two new essays, and an interview we had with him. The works that were reprinted have been originally published from 1990 to 2021 in various academic journals. Stephen's freshly written materials describe the key ideas in his *Epistemology's Paradox: Is a Theory of Knowledge Possible?* (1992), *Knowledge and the Gettier Problem* (2016) and *What Is Epistemology* (2019). These materials will give readers a more holistic appreciation of Stephen's thinking and his original perspective on some of philosophy's central questions about knowledge.

The collection fittingly starts with Stephen's first published epistemology paper, 'Epistemic internalism's dilemma'. The first chapter sets the tone for the whole collection as it argues that epistemic internalism at its core must confront a dilemma that either commits the internalist to a vicious infinite regress or externalism. When Stephen compares the internal condition of justified belief to a horizon that you can only 'reach what *was* never what *is*', he could very well have been talking about the fate of the epistemologist who attempts to understand a 'reachable horizon' that can never be truly grasped.

Chapter 2, 'Is epistemically adequate epistemology possible?', explores this idea further as Stephen examines what it is to think as an epistemologist and what it is to *be* epistemological. An original piece written for this collection, this chapter describes the key ideas in Stephen's first book, *Epistemology's Paradox*, where he proposes to treat the epistemologizing efforts as tools that should themselves be evaluated epistemically. In effect, Stephen turns epistemology on itself and calls out epistemologists for projecting their own epistemic standards onto *non*-epistemological subjects, failing to do justice to the complexity involved in evaluating epistemic situations given varied perspectives and incommensurable contexts between the epistemologist and the non-epistemological subject.

In Chapter 3, 'Elusive Epistemological Justification', Stephen explains how this complexity makes epistemological thinking susceptible to meta-epistemological scepticism. The title of this chapter is of course an allusion to David Lewis's 'Elusive Knowledge' (1996), which Stephen admires but of which he is also critical. Stephen here argues that, since justifying epistemological thinking leads to a vicious infinite regress, and, given that non-epistemological and epistemological thinking are intertwined, no one *ever* has good epistemic justification for what they are saying or thinking when doing this *as* a philosophical enquirer.

The next five chapters further extend this meta-epistemological scepticism to traditional ways of thinking about the Gettier problem, justification, knowledge and scepticism itself. In Chapter 4, 'Gettieristic Scepticism', Stephen links the orthodox view of Gettier cases with orthodox sceptical reasoning and radical scepticism. In Chapter 5, 'Epistemic Disaster Averted', he challenges the infallibilist conceptions of justification, arguing that justification is nothing if not truth-conducive. Chapter 6, 'Knowing Failably and Knowing Imperfectly' is divided into two parts. The first is 'Knowing Failably', where Stephen re-introduces the concept of *failable* knowledge. The second comprises Sections 2.6 and 2.10 of *Good Knowledge, Bad Knowledge: On Two Dogmas of Epistemology* (2001), where he demonstrates how failability can defuse traditional sceptical arguments that depend on an absolutist conception of knowing. In Chapter 7, 'Sceptical Possibilities? No Worries', Stephen reflects on sceptical doubting itself and describes how sceptical challenges are dialectically self-defeating; and thus do not pose an actual epistemic threat. Finally, in Chapter 8, 'Knowledge That Works: A Tale of Two Conceptual Models', Stephen challenges us to free ourselves from a philosophical habit that commits us to infallibilism. As an alternative, he describes the *Working Knowledge Model* as a way of thinking about knowledge that accepts fallibility and gradualism. The arguments and ideas discussed in these five chapters provide the groundwork for his well-known views on knowledge-practicalism and knowledge-fallibilism.

The chapters that follow offer a succinct account of Stephen's knowledge-practicalism and knowledge-fallibilism, and their subsequent applications to traditional ways of thinking about scepticism, epistemic luck, justification and the Gettier cases. In Chapter 9, 'Knowledge as Potential for Action', Stephen discusses the history and underlying philosophy of knowledge-practicalism – the view that knowledge is an ability that is manifested by various knowing actions. In Chapter 10, 'Sceptical Challenges and Knowing Actions', he describes how knowledge-practicalism frees epistemology from the metaphysics of a Rylean intellectualism, which then undermines sceptical challenges. In Chapter 11, 'Some Fallibilist Knowledge: Questioning Knowledge-Attributions and Open Knowledge', he defends fallibilism by introducing a kind of knowledge attribution that acknowledges the epistemically significant possibility of mistakes and a way of knowing that is self-questioning. In Chapter 12, 'The Luck/Knowledge Incompatibility Thesis', he applies his thinking about fallibilism and how it relates to the problem of epistemic luck. In Chapter 13, 'The Redundancy Problem: From Knowledge-Infallibilism to Knowledge-Minimalism', Stephen advocates fallibilism and knowledge-minimalism as alternatives to infallibilism. Finally, in Chapter 14, 'And Next?', another newly written piece, Stephen revisits the arguments in *Knowledge and the Gettier Problem* (2016), and argues that, among other potential failings, epistemologist are being infallibilist when they appeal to intuitions in their assessments of Gettiered beliefs. Then he sketches a 'burrowing' conception of knowledge, an idea he presented in *How to Know* (2011) and *What Is Epistemology?* (2019), which treats knowing as always a matter of knowing a fact or state of affairs – by knowing more or fewer further details *within* that fact or state of affairs.

We close the collection with Chapter 15, 'A Life in Philosophy', a transcript of our discussion with Stephen, where he talks candidly about his life and work, influences and motivations, and contributions and possible legacy.

Stephen 'would welcome' being remembered as someone who argued strongly for a 'few odd epistemological ideas'. And we hope that this collection contributes to this end. But we also hope that readers may find in these chapters how a fallible mind has tried to have a glimpse of the 'reachable horizon' of what it means to know … more or less.

Jeremiah Joven Joaquin and Mark Anthony Dacela
De La Salle University, Manila, Philippines
7 June 2023

1

Epistemic internalism's dilemma

1.1 The dilemma

Suppose some epistemic internalist believes that you have a justified belief.[1] At least part of what he or she thinks is that *some* aspect A of your circumstances is epistemically internal to you and is at least *part* of what makes you justified.[2] In thinking that A is epistemically internal to you, the epistemic internalist is presumably crediting you with some *grasp* of A.[3]

But what does this 'grasp' involve? For a start, the internalist *should* not just be assuming that A is *mentally* internal to you (in the sense that if you *have* a belief it is mentally internal to you). Being mentally internal, say, should not be seen as sufficient for being epistemically internal.[4] The same is true of your being aware *that* the item is mentally internal (e.g. your being aware that you have the belief in question): even this should not be viewed as sufficient to make the item epistemically internal. For example, let A be a belief of yours that an epistemologist could think helps justify some other belief B of yours, and suppose you grasp A, in that you grasp its *presence*. But suppose, too, that you have no idea that A plays a role in making B justified. I suggest that, in such a case, A is no more *epistemically* internal to the *epistemic* situation constituted by A helping to justify B than is any *other* belief C you realise you have – where an epistemologist looking on might see C as *irrelevant* to B's being justified. C is just as mentally internal to you, say, as is A; but this should hardly be sufficient for its being epistemically internal. If I am right, then, the epistemic internalist should conclude that A is *not* epistemically internal to you (even though it is mentally internal to you). For then the following structure is instantiated:

> (E) Something is helping you have justification, even though you have no idea, awareness, or appreciation that it is doing so.

Instantiating (E) should be viewed as what *makes* the contemporary paradigms of epistemic externalism epistemically externalist. Thus, someone like Alvin Goldman (1979) would insist that part of what makes your belief justified can be its being held as the result of a *reliable* belief-forming process – even when you have no idea *that* this is true of your belief. (E) is thereby instantiated; an epistemically externalist condition of justified belief is present.[5]

Equally, what makes Descartes the traditional paradigm epistemic internalist should be seen as the fact that his view of something's contributing to your certainty does *not* instantiate (E). He asks not only that your idea *be* clear and distinct, for instance; he wants you to appreciate *that* it is. And in his fourth *Meditation* he asks that you be continually *aware* of the principle that a clear and distinct idea is true; the *truth* of this principle is not enough. God can supposedly make a clear and distinct idea be true, but God does not determine what judgements Descartes has. Descartes's search for true judgements involves his appreciating the role of clarity and distinctness in attaining that end. It also requires that he not simply rely on the *truth* of the belief that God exists and is not a deceiver; he thinks he needs to be aware *that* God exists and is not deceiving him.

Central to epistemic internalism, therefore, is the view that A is epistemically internal to you only if you can appreciate it as such. Even if A is internal to you in, say, a mental sense, it still might not be *epistemically* internal to you. The epistemic *internalist* might purport to describe your situation, from his or her epistemological perspective, as including your epistemically internalising A – but unless *you* appreciate A as helping you have justification, A will *not* be epistemically internal to you. (It depends on you; it is *your* epistemic Within, so to speak.) If A can contribute in way W to your being justified,[6] without your being aware *that* it is doing so, then A instantiates (E): it is, like the fact of your belief being – or not being – reliably formed, epistemically external to you.

A necessary condition, therefore, of some given A being epistemically internal to you is your appreciating *that* it is contributing to your being justified. But what about this appreciating, this being aware, of A's contributing? If it is necessary to A's-being-epistemically-internal-to-your-being-justified, then it plays some role, too, in your being justified. (For example, if A's-being-epistemically-internal-to-your-being-justified is necessary to your being justified, then, by the transitivity of necessary conditions, your appreciating of A as epistemically internal is itself necessary to your being justified.) Then, however, we must again ask whether (E) applies to the situation. Your appreciating-that-A-is-contributing-to-your-being-justified is contributing to your being justified; need you in turn appreciate *that* it is doing so? What the epistemic internalist should say is that you must. Otherwise, by its instantiating (E), your appreciating-that-A-is-contributing-to-your-being-justified is itself epistemically external to your being justified. Yet a necessary condition of A's being epistemically internal to you was your appreciating *that* it is contributing to your being justified. And if the latter aspect of your situation is epistemically *ex*ternal to your being justified, then no doubt the former is too.[7] The epistemic internalist therefore must confront a dilemma, as follows.

The Dilemma's First Horn. If A is to be epistemically internal to you, then you must appreciate *that* A is contributing to your being justified. But then you must appreciate that this appreciating is itself contributing to your being justified. And hence, by analogous reasoning, the same is true of the *new* appreciating. This pattern recurs, and the epistemic internalist therefore faces the prospect of an infinite regress of appreciatings, one I assume to be vicious.[8] The regress, (R), is this.

According to epistemic internalism about a condition A of your having a justified belief,

(1) A contributes to your justification

only if

(2) You appreciate that A contributes to yow justification

only if

(3) You appreciate that your-appreciating-that-A-contributes-to-your-justification (i.e. the appreciating which is (2)) contributes to your justification

only if

(4) You appreciate that the appreciating which is (3) contributes to your justification

only if

(5) You appreciate that the appreciating which is (4) contributes to your justification

only if

…. And so on.

Note that this does not entail that *you* appreciate the 'only if' connections; arguably, epistemic internalists themselves must appreciate these, but you need not. Hence, you need not appreciate *that* there is an infinite regress either. Nevertheless, I assume that the epistemic internalist's thinking that (R) will be *true* of you (even if you are unaware that it is) will make *him or her* want to avoid (R). He or she should therefore wish to evade The Dilemma's First Horn too.

The Dilemma's Second Horn. On the other hand, if any member of (R) is allowed to be epistemically *external* to you, then A is epistemically external to you also. If, say, (2) is false of you, then so is (1), according, at any rate, to epistemic internalism. Hence the epistemic internalist will decide that A does *not* contribute internalistically to your justification. The epistemic internalist will therefore be conceding the fight over A's epistemic role to the epistemic externalist. A necessary condition of an epistemic internalism about A's role in your having justified belief is therefore that each of (1), (2), (3), etc. obtain of you. That is, epistemic internalism returns to The Dilemma's First Horn. But The First Horn *also* implies that A will not be epistemically internal to you. On either The First Horn *or* The Second Horn, then, A fails to be epistemically internal to you as a justified believer. I call this Epistemic Internalism's Dilemma.

The Dilemma says, in effect, that once you begin epistemically internalising, you are logically committed to never *stopping*. The Dilemma is that, since A is epistemically internal to you only if you appreciate *that* it is, this commits you to a regress of iterated appreciatings, *unless* one of these appreciatings is epistemically external to you. The only way this pattern of appreciating can avoid regress is if some part of it also avoids being what it was originally supposed to be – namely, part of what made *A* epistemically internal to you. Epistemic internalism must give way to epistemic externalism, and therefore it must be an empty concept. Necessarily, there are no epistemically internal conditions of justified belief.

The Dilemma conjures up an interesting picture of the epistemically internal. It suggests that *A* is epistemically internal only if your appreciating *A* as epistemically internal entails that *A* is therefore *not* epistemically internal. Its being epistemically internal requires your appreciating it as such, but the very appreciating of it as such *destroys* it as such. It might not be destroyed in every sense (it might continue to be mentally within you), but it will cease to play an independent *epistemic* role. *In the very act of being appreciated as epistemically internal*, the purportedly epistemically internal *A* dies, becoming the appreciating-of-*A*-as-epistemically-internal.[9] A *non*-epistemically internal *A* might remain (again, for instance, you might still have a belief *A*), but it cannot be simultaneously internal and *epistemic*.

The concept of an epistemically internal condition of justified belief is therefore like the concept of a reachable horizon. It is necessarily empty. Its being *non*-empty requires that some aspect *A* of your situation be subjected to irreconcilable demands. For the concept of something being epistemically internal to you is *non*-empty only if you focus your thought on *A* in a way which makes that concept empty. (Now you see it; therefore you do not! Now you are at the horizon; therefore you are not! You can only reach what *was* the horizon, never what *is* the horizon.)

1.2 Some historical intimations of the dilemma

The last section develops the Dilemma in full generality. *A* was *any* aspect of your circumstances which *some* internalistically inclined epistemologist might claim plays *some* role in your having a justified belief. I think it also reveals how simple the Dilemma is. It is therefore rather puzzling why epistemic internalism seems so attractive to so many good epistemologists, such as BonJour (1985) and Chisholm (1989: ch. 8). This puzzlement should be reinforced by the realisation that (i) views which discuss what a contemporary epistemic internalist could plausibly endorse as possible instances of *A* have a significant philosophical pedigree, and that (ii) *worries* about those possible instances of the epistemic internalist's *A* – worries which do not require much modification in order to be seen as instances of the Dilemma – have an equally significant philosophical lineage.

In this section, I will discuss four examples which exemplify (i) and (ii), all from early part of the twentieth century. In Wittgenstein's attack on private language, Russell's views on the epistemic accessibility of logical particulars, Sellars's critique of the Given, and a worry raised by Ayer about basic statements, I see more specific voicings of objections which, when adapted to the concept of the epistemically internal, instantiate the Dilemma.[10]

1.2.1 Wittgenstein on private language

Let us consider Ludwig Wittgenstein's criticism in his *Philosophical Investigations* of the idea of someone attempting to use a private language. At present there is a great deal of debate about just how to interpret Wittgenstein's argument, and I will not attempt to settle that matter here.[11] I will quickly sketch, instead, how Wittgenstein's argument might be made to play a role in an argument against the possibility of your being able to epistemically internalise a sensation. That latter argument will be seen to instantiate the Dilemma.

Suppose you are a putative private language user: you claim that you can use language to refer to some internal aspect of you (such as a sensation S), about which no one *else* can know (Wittgenstein 1958: sec. 243). Now, such use is certainly not sufficient for your epistemically internalising S: your using a private name to refer to a private sensation S does not imply your being aware of S's role in your having a justified belief. So S's being privately referred to is not identical with S's being epistemically internal, and Wittgenstein's private language argument is not automatically an argument against epistemic internalism. However, we can ask whether, when you *are* aware of S playing a role in your having a justified belief (as epistemic internalism might require of you), your awareness includes your use of a private name for S. If it does, then the tension Wittgenstein notices would be part of the tension the Dilemma captures, as I will now show.

On one interpretation of Wittgenstein (Kripke 1982), the objection to your ability to use a private name for your sensation is that this must presuppose the existence of other persons sharing your language, in which case your use of the language is not private after all. On another interpretation (McGinn 1984: 89–90), the objection is that you will have to presuppose the use of the language at other *times*, in which case your present use of the language is not private after all. (So, on the former interpretation, privacy is privacy from other *people*, while, on the latter interpretation, privacy is temporal momentariness.) Either way, the structure of the worry portrays the concept of a private language to be flawed much as that of a reachable horizon is. For (says the worry) the attempt to refer to what is private is impossible: a necessary condition of referring to it is that, insofar as it is referred to, it is not private. And therefore, *if* S's being epistemically internal to you requires that you have a private, linguistic, grasp of S, then part of your instantiating the Dilemma is your instantiating a Wittgensteinian kind of objection.[12] Once again, nothing can be internal and epistemic.

1.2.2 Russell on logical particulars

One of Bertrand Russell's interests at one time was, of course, the notion of a logical particular (1918: 55–60). A logical particular is a very short-lived sense-datum, which can be an immediate object of awareness (or, in Russell's terminology, acquaintance). Russell's own motivation for introducing the concept is part of a quest more for a logically perfect language than for an account of justified belief. Still, just as part of one way to possibly instantiate the Dilemma is to consider a Wittgensteinian worry about your epistemically internalising a private sensation by, in part, privately naming it, I will briefly show why I think Russell would endorse the application of Epistemic Internalism's Dilemma to logical particulars. Suppose you think that you can epistemically internalise a Russellian logical particular. Russell says something which suggests that, on grounds similar to mine, he would think you could *not* do so.

If you can epistemically internalise a logical particular, it is only by mentally stepping back from it, appreciating *that* it is internal to you and *that* it can play a justificatory role for you. But when Russell talks of your being acquainted with a logical particular, he clearly precludes your knowing (as he puts it; but we could speak, more generally, of your being aware of) any propositions *about* the particular (Pears 1981: 153). Interacting with complete propositions in this way would bar your interacting with just the logical particulars within those propositions. Epistemically internalising a logical particular would be a more complex understanding than the Russellian acquaintance with the particular by itself would be.

Why would this greater complexity 'bar' your interacting just with the logical particular, though? You *can* interact with the particular, after all; you can be acquainted with it. Still (from the end of the previous paragraph), this acquaintance will not include your being aware of its epistemic role. For *that* awareness could only be *of* a proposition, not a particular. Even if the particular is part of the proposition, the acquaintance with the particular itself would not be part of the *understanding* of its justificatory role which would be what the epistemic internalist sees as justificatorily relevant. The acquaintance with the particular would drop out of the picture as epistemically irrelevant. The more complex understanding would take its place, as far as the epistemic internalist is concerned. For epistemic purposes, therefore, the understanding of the particular would supplant the particular. The logical particular can remain internal to you, but it could not be *epistemically* internal to you.[13]

1.2.3 Sellars on the given

At the beginning of his well-known critique of the classic foundationalist view of sense-data as the foundations of knowledge (as epistemic givens), Wilfrid Sellars (1963) apparently echoes Russell's thinking.[14] If you have a sense-datum, then you sense a particular (1963: 128). If this is an understanding, or a knowing, of the particular, it is a kind of knowledge that is at least analogous to being *acquainted* with the particular, to use the Russellian term (1963: 130). However, the epistemic *foundationalist's* purpose in using the sensory given is to ground all propositional empirical knowledge – all empirical knowledge that such and such is the case, all knowledge of empirical *facts* (1963: 128). And that can be done only if the grounds are themselves cases of propositional knowledge (1963: 128–9, 131–2). Hence, it is only empirical knowledge of facts, not of particulars, that could be epistemically basic. And, says Sellars, this is why it is a confusion to think 'that a sensation of a red triangle is the very paradigm of empirical knowledge' (1963: 134).

And this thinking, when it is applied to the concept of the epistemically internal, instantiates the Dilemma. Let the putatively foundational grounds of empirical knowledge be conscious *awarenesses* that the sensation is present and epistemically relevant; that is, let them *not* instantiate (E), and therefore let them be epistemically internal to you. The problem is that, when the sensation is grasped by you in a way that could be appropriate for grounding your empirical knowledge, it ceases to be relevant *as* a particular. At that moment, all that is epistemically operative is the *propositional* awareness. The sensation might be *in* you, but it will not be an *epistemic* part of you. It might be internal, but it could not be *epistemically* internal.

1.2.4 Ayer on basic statements

In what is presumably his best-known book (1946), A.J. Ayer also employed such thinking. His early positivist's quest for the verifiable led him to what he called *basic* propositions, ones which 'refer solely to the content of a single experience' (1946: 13). And these, he notes, while possessing the apparent virtue of being irrefutable, forfeit this advantage by seemingly committing the sin of not saying anything either:

> [These ostensive propositions] are supposed to be purely demonstrative in character, and so incapable of being refuted by any subsequent experience [...] [But] the notion of an ostensive proposition appears to involve a contradiction in terms. It implies that there could be a sentence which consisted of purely demonstrative symbols and was at the same time intelligible. And this is not even a logical possibility [...] The fact is that one cannot in language point to an object without describing it.
>
> (1946: 120–1)

Ayer's Introduction (1946: 14) to the second edition of *Language, Truth and Logic* is less impressed by this first edition reasoning. Nevertheless, it seems right to me, at least when we ask (much as we did for Wittgenstein's private language user) whether an epistemic internalist could coherently conceptualise you as using basic statements to linguistically articulate something's being epistemically internal to you. Thus, consider these remarks of Ayer's:

> the form of words that is used to express a basic proposition may be understood to express something that is informative both to another person and to oneself, but when it is so understood it no longer expresses a basic proposition.
>
> (1946: 120–1)

Those comments suggest that Ayer would agree with the following. If a basic proposition of yours is to refer to some basic experience that is *epistemically* internal to you right now, then you must be able to appreciate, right now, *that* the experience is internal to you and *that* it is contributing to your being justified. However, to have the latter appreciation right now is to supplement the basic experience in a way that effectively *eliminates* it from the epistemic state of affairs. For your experience right now is therefore partly constituted by your mentally stepping back from the supposedly basic experience and using, not the mere *fact* of the basic experience, but your *awareness* of it. The *epistemic* internalising of a basic proposition implies that the basic proposition itself plays no epistemically internalist role.[15]

Notes

1. Epistemic internalists usually discuss justification, not knowledge. The main difference between these two notions is, of course, typically taken to be that knowledge does, whereas justification does not, imply truth. Truth is generally assumed to be an epistemically *external* factor, see, e.g., Audi (1988: 113–16). For an overview of the epistemological community's treatment of the epistemic internalism/externalism distinction, see Alston (1986). For a slightly non-standard view of epistemic internalism, see Fumerton (1988).

2. I say 'at least *part*' because, for generality's sake, I am happy to allow that an epistemically internalist condition could be necessary, sufficient, or even something looser still. I am interested in whether something could be epistemically internal by being *at all* relevant to your having justified belief in some particular context.

3. By 'grasp' (or by 'appreciate' or 'be aware', terms I will use interchangeably) I mean whatever conscious mental operation the epistemic internalist requires you to undergo, in order for you to epistemically internalise A. This operation might be more – it might be less – cognitively sophisticated. BonJour (1987) would also talk of grasping A (1987: 297), as well as of having an 'inkling' of A (1987: 303) and of whether A is your *reason* (1987: 297, 303, 312n2).

4. Conversely, it should not be taken to be necessary either: A's being epistemically internal should not be seen as entailing A's being mentally internal. When I say that A is some aspect of your circumstances, I *mean* this – in all its apparent generality. Your grasp of A will presumably be mentally internal (see fn. 3), but A itself need not be. Most epistemologists would prefer that it be mental, of course; the examples I will discuss in Section 1.2 are all like that. I am only noting that A itself need not be. I suspect that it is by forgetting this – and so not properly separating the epistemically internal and, for instance, the mentally internal – that epistemic internalists have given us a view which falls prey to my Dilemma. (I suspect, too, that when an epistemic internalist's view *apparently* avoids my Dilemma, it is because the theorist has not properly distinguished what makes something mentally internal, say, from what makes it epistemically internal. Something can be mentally internal, yet epistemically external, as I am about to argue.)

5. Since I am discussing only justification *conditions* (see fn. 2), not *theories*, deciding that some condition of your having justification is epistemically internal does not entail that justification as a whole is epistemically internal. (Presumably, though, if *all* the conditions of justification are epistemically internal, then justification is too.)

6. Strictly, this 'in way W' is redundant. Some instance of A contributing in way W is itself an instance of A. (So, it will transpire, epistemic internalism asks that you appreciate not only *that* A is contributing to your justification, but *how* it is doing so. For if A contributes, it does so in *some way* W: A-contributing-in-way-W is therefore contributing too. Epistemic internalists, I presume, will not *want* to admit that their view asks this of you: see, for example, Audi (1988: 112) But, as I argued above, they *should* do so. Either that, or they should become epistemic *externalists*.)

7. Or, at least, if the latter aspect if epistemically external, then the former one will not be wholly internal. But I will assume that a condition (as against a theory: see fn. 5) is either wholly internal or wholly external.

8 My assumption is based on the following plausibility consideration. Each member of the sequence *depends*, for its status as epistemically internal, on the next member. Moreover, this dependence is not merely identity. In general, your appreciating that A contributes to your being justified is not the same as your appreciating *that* the former appreciating contributes to your being justified.

9 And, in the spirit of fn. 6, notice that if we let the appreciating-of-A^*-as-epistemically-internal (for some given instance A^* of A) be an instance of A itself, then this result recurs. In the very act of being appreciated as epistemically internal, the purportedly epistemically internal appreciating-of-A^*-as-epistemically-internal dies, becoming the appreciating-of-this-appreciating-of-A^*-as-epistemically-internal-as-itself-epistemically-internal. In other words, we encounter The Dilemma's First Horn.

10 All four of my examples will be more obviously applicable to non-inferential, than to inferential, justification. But the Dilemma still applies to both types of justification. It is simply easier to find historically important candidates for the epistemically internal among accounts of non-inferential justification. (One of the implications of the Dilemma is that this should not be easier, of course. Whether A is an immediate sensing or whether it is a logical relation between propositional contents, the Dilemma is equally relevant.)

11 See, e.g., Fogelin (1987), Kripke (1982), McGinn (1984), and Baker and Hacker (1984). I discuss one aspect of the debate elsewhere (Hetherington 1991).

12 S's being epistemically internal to you does require that you have a grasp of S (of S's contributing to your justification). But is this grasp private, in that no one else *has* it? If not, we might argue that no one else could know of S's justificatory role in the way you can, and hence that S (or its justificatory role) is in that sense private to you. In this chapter I remain agnostic as to whether your private grasp would be linguistic (a use of language, in order to be aware of S's justificatory role, which no one else could employ as you do). Hence, I am not *assuming* that Wittgenstein's private language argument implies the Dilemma. Again, my conclusion is that *if* S's being epistemically internal to you implies your using a private language to grasp S's justificatory role, *then* Wittgenstein's private language argument applying to you is one aspect of the Dilemma applying to you.

13 For Russell, a logical particular is complete and self-subsistent (in Frege's terms, it is saturated). But for it to be epistemically internal you have to treat it as *in*complete, as *un*saturated, as needing to be *appreciated* by you, as needing to be described by you in a special way. And to treat something complete as incomplete is to deny its being what it is.

14 It is not clear that Sellars is offering just one criticism of that view. I will outline one part of his thinking, a part which is particularly relevant to my discussion.

15 Ayer's own worry, in the second indented passage I quote from him, questions whether the basic proposition could even be *non*-epistemically internal (by being thought, for example, and hence being mentally, though not epistemically, internal). He seemingly believes that the basic proposition would be eliminated from the *entire* state of affairs, not just the *epistemic* state of affairs, since he is apparently implying that there can *be* no basic proposition for you to believe. I will not address that issue here, though.

References

Alston, W.P. (1986), 'Internalism and Externalism in Epistemology', *Philosophical Topics*, 14: 179–221.
Audi, R. (1988), *Belief, Justification, and Knowledge*, Belmont, CA: Wadsworth.
Ayer, A.J. (1946), *Language, Truth and Logic*, 2nd edn, New York: Pelican.
Baker, G.P. and Hacker, P.M.S. (1984), *Scepticism, Rules and Language*, Oxford: Blackwell.
BonJour, L. (1985), *The Structure of Empirical Knowledge*, Cambridge, MA: Harvard University Press.
BonJour, L. (1987), 'Nozick, Externalism, and Skepticism', in S. Luper-Foy (ed.), *The Possibility of Knowing*, 297–313, Savage, MD: Rowman & Littlefield.
Chisholm, R.M. (1989), *Theory of Knowledge*, 3rd edn, Englewood Cliffs, NJ: Prentice-Hall.
Fogelin, R.J. (1987), *Wittgenstein*, 2nd edn, London: Routledge & Kegan Paul.
Fumerton, R. (1988), 'The Internalism/Externalism Controversy', *Philosophical Perspectives*, 2: 443–59.
Goldman, A.I. (1979), 'What Is Justified Belief?' in G.S. Pappas (ed.), *Justification and Knowledge*, 1–23, Dordrecht: D. Reidel.
Hetherington, S. (1991), 'Kripke and McGinn on Wittgensteinian Rule-Following', *Philosophia*, 21: 89–100.
Kripke, S.A. (1982), *Wittgenstein on Rules and Private Language*, Cambridge, MA: Harvard University Press.
McGinn, C. (1984), *Wittgenstein on Meaning*, Oxford: Blackwell.
Pears, D. (1981), 'The Function of Acquaintance in Russell's Philosophy', *Synthese*, 46: 149–66.
Russell, B. (1918), 'The Philosophy of Logical Atomism', reprinted in D. Pears (ed.), *Russell's Logical Atomism*, 1972, 31–142, London: Fontana.
Sellars, W.F. (1963), 'Empiricism and the Philosophy of Mind', in *Science, Perception, and Reality*, 127–96, London: Routledge & Kegan Paul.
Wittgenstein, L. (1958), *Philosophical Investigations*, trans. G.E.M., Anscombe, Oxford: Blackwell.

2

Is epistemically adequate epistemology possible?

2.1 Background

I am far from the first epistemologist to ask whether epistemology can succeed in its central aims. That question has motivated much of my epistemological writing. It sparked my 1987 PhD dissertation, leading to my *Epistemology's Paradox* (1992). That book offered a transcendental reason why any attempt to understand someone's either having, *or* lacking, either knowledge *or* justification, say, must fail. The reason was transcendental, by focusing on what it is for someone *to be thinking epistemologically at all*. The failure was epistemic: in particular, there is no epistemological knowledge or justification. This chapter conveys a sense of that reason and that failure.

The dissertation sprang from a suspicion (extended in the book). The suspicion was that much epistemological thinking unwittingly exemplifies a form of *projection*. For example, can we understand knowledge's nature if we rely on terms apt only for what knowing would be like *for* an epistemological thinker? No one sees themselves as doing this. Yet witness such recurring themes as ideal knowledge, 'real' knowledge, knowing that one knows, reflective knowledge, *knowledge* (italicized!), etc. When *being* epistemological, it is difficult not to feel their allure. But might this be due to projecting, albeit unconsciously, a standard apt for an epistemologically reflective epistemic subject or agent? That would certainly lessen epistemology's worth. Misreading its own reach, epistemology would fail to be about everyone.

For example, I argued that the famous/infamous 'Gettier cases' are easily read as situations where the knowledge being challenged, all things considered, *is* knowledge satisfying a demand reasonably imposed only upon an epistemological perspective on the case. The epistemic subject Smith, within Gettier's (1963) cases, is denied knowledge due to failing a justificatory standard aptly imposed only on any epistemologist evaluating the case. Smith fails to be aware of what we, as epistemological readers, see about his situation. If he *was* to have that awareness, he would not remain justified in his final belief. Since he is actually a *non*-epistemological epistemic subject, though, we should consider the possibility of his having a *non*-epistemological form of knowledge.

That is not an interpretation reflecting what epistemologists, relying on 'intuitions', routinely say about such cases. But I do provide an argument; I am not merely 'trading intuitions'. When epistemologists assure us of how 'intuitively clear' it is that Smith lacks knowledge, does this entail his lacking the knowledge in question? Not unless those epistemological perspectives are infallible regarding the epistemic status of someone lacking such a perspective. And are they?[1]

2.2 A structural question

Accordingly, *Epistemology's Paradox* explored how epistemology's prospects might depend on distinguishing an epistemological epistemic subject from a non-epistemological one.

Consider an enquirer, E, being epistemological about epistemic subject S. E might be asking any of the following (and/or other) questions, for some 'p'. Does S know that p? Does S fail to know that p? Does S have a justified belief that p? Does S lack a justified belief that p? Such questions fuel everyday epistemological inquiry. E's answer might meet good *professional* standards of philosophical thinking. But what makes her answer *epistemically* good?

For specificity, let E ask how S fares epistemically within S's setting: 'Does S know that p?' Replies by fellow philosophers reach E; publication occurs; job done; which is where *Epistemology's Paradox* enters. E's goal in talking about S is to evaluate (in any of many possible ways) some epistemic principle P, such as a partial or full condition for knowing. As epistemologists, though, we should also welcome evaluating the epistemic fortunes of our *own* evaluations of others' epistemic fortunes. So (I ask), *what true epistemic principle, if any, does E's reasoning about S and P meet?* Does E have knowledge, for example, in pronouncing upon S and thereby P? Is E's view of S and thereby P at least justified?

I am asking how E can be a successful epistemic subject *while* epistemologically discussing S. To be a successful epistemic subject *is* to instantiate a true (and apt) epistemic principle.[2] Even so, a delicate balancing act must be accomplished if such a principle is to be satisfied by an *epistemological* epistemic subject. Can this be done?

First, being epistemological about S requires some sort of *detachment from S* and her setting. This I interpret as one's needing to have in mind *something* (of immediate epistemic relevance) about S and her setting that is *not* also in S's mind. One is reflecting *on* S, in a way – an epistemological way – that is not S's. (Even if S is being epistemological, she is not occupying E's specific perspective on her at that moment.)[3]

However (and second), having epistemic success while being epistemological about S requires an ability to *identify with S* within her setting. This could take different forms. One way to gesture at the basic point is this: one needs to be able to reflect *with* (not only *on*) S within her setting, if one is fully to understand *how it is for S* there. In this sense, one needs to be able to have in mind *nothing* (of immediate epistemic relevance) about S and her setting that is not in S's mind there.

And those two needs are jointly incompatible. One cannot simultaneously both detach from, *and* identify with, S in those ways. Yet doing so is vital, I argued, to thinking epistemologically about S in her setting *while* also having epistemic success in so doing.[4]

Those contrary needs might not be how *E feels* about herself at that moment, or even what constraints she *acknowledges* when being epistemological. I am describing two contrary directions in which *E should* be pulled, though. Perhaps the most challenging word in the previous paragraph is 'simultaneously'. *E* might object that she can think epistemologically about *S*, and can *then* think as *S* is doing ('of course I can imagine being in *S*'s situation'), and can *then* continue being epistemological, while now holding in mind how *S* was thinking: 'I can clearly move back and forth between those perspectives.' And she *can* do so. But does she have *transferrable* epistemic success in so doing? *E* cannot still be thinking epistemologically about *S while* (even passingly, in imagination) being non-epistemological in whatever way *S* is being. *E* cannot reflect epistemologically on *S* while also (even in imagination and temporarily) being or functioning as *S*. Two modes of *epistemic being* are involved here. One is epistemological, about *S* and *P* at that time. The other is non-epistemological about *S* and *P* at that time.

2.3 Contexts and David Lewis

That hidden clash between perspectives amounts also to an incommensurability of contexts. We can understand the clash better, and its potential significance, by comparing it with perhaps its closest neighbour, arising in David Lewis's (1999) contextualism about knowledge-attributions.

Epistemologists rarely, it seems, treat themselves as epistemic subjects of their favoured epistemic principles and theories. This is what *Epistemology's Paradox* did. It was also a notable element in Lewis's contextualism. Can one have knowledge when being epistemological? Can one have it when thinking philosophically *about* knowledge? That is one instance (a welcome Lewisian one) of my general challenge. But I will explain why, in two respects, Lewis's response was too simple.

Let us recall what he said about contexts where one is thinking epistemologically (being *E* about some *S*). This is his Rule of Attention:

> a possibility not ignored at all is *ipso facto* not properly ignored […] No matter how far-fetched a certain possibility may be, […] if in *this* context we are not in fact ignoring it but attending to it, then for us now it is a relevant alternative.
> (Lewis 1999: 434)

This rule matters because, for Lewis, knowing that *p* is a matter *of* eliminating all not-*p* possibilities not properly ignored. He then reasons thus:

> Do some epistemology. Let your fantasies rip. Find uneliminated possibilities of error everywhere. Now that you are attending to them, […] you are no longer ignoring them, properly or otherwise. So you have landed in a context with an enormously rich domain of potential counter-examples to ascriptions of knowledge. In such an extraordinary context, […] it never can happen (well, hardly ever) that an ascription of knowledge is true. […] This is how epistemology destroys

knowledge. But it does so only temporarily. The pastime of epistemology does not plunge us forevermore into its special context.

(1999: 434)

That is a bold story, and I agree with some of it. Still, it is too simple to deliver its claimed result about all epistemology.

First, doing epistemology does not automatically open one, even on Lewis's account, to sceptical possibilities. Doing epistemology need not include attending to those details. Nor is epistemology always about knowledge-ascriptions. Lewis infers a thesis, about epistemological thinking in general, to which he is not entitled, even given his Rule of Attention.

There *is* insight in that rule, and *Epistemology's Paradox* was centred upon an instance of it.[5] But the book did not presume that being epistemological always includes attending to sceptical possibilities. My argument sought greater generality, in both its conclusion (concerning more than *knowledge*, let alone *knowledge-ascriptions*) and its premises (not presuming the epistemological thinker's attending to *sceptical* possibilities). Thus, the book's argument was directed at someone's being epistemological by attending *to some epistemic P* (maybe along with test cases) – where *P*, although epistemic in content, might not be about sceptical possibilities. Must even *this* thinking – hence, *any* epistemological thinking – fail epistemically, such as by falling short of knowledge? This is a more challenging question than what arises when we assume (with Lewis) that all epistemological thinking attends to sceptical possibilities. So, Lewis set himself a misleadingly easy challenge. He was right to see that there is something distinctive about an epistemological context, and that this 'something' could be a threat to knowing, *and* that this threat might not persist in non-epistemological contexts. But his argument for this picture was inadequate.[6]

Another inadequacy is even more revealing. It also reflects Lewis's overly simple conception of epistemological contexts. We have noted that they need not include any attending to sceptical possibilities. We must do justice, too, to what the epistemologist *should* be attending to when thinking about her epistemic subject.

Suppose that you are reflecting epistemologically on whether some (non-epistemological) *S* knows that *p*. Maybe you attend to a sceptical possibility. For Lewis, you thereby *lack* knowledge of *S*'s knowing that *p*. But (Lewis allows) you might then *leave* your epistemological context, perhaps 'moving to' *S*'s; whereupon – magic! – you might even proceed to know that *p*. You could be there, alongside *S*, knowing, much as she does, that *p* – now that you have 'stepped out of' your epistemological context.

However, there is an unfortunate respect (as follows) in which that Lewisian picture elides some of the implicit complexity in your epistemological context.

Unlike you, your epistemic subject *S* is inside a non-epistemological context. You are asking, in an epistemological way, whether she knows that *p*. But can you 'see infallibly into' her non-epistemological context, 'from within' your epistemological one? You cannot, and so a necessary condition of your knowing whether *S* knows that *p* is that, somehow, you need to *blend* the two contexts: either you 'step into' her context *while still inside* your epistemological one, or you 'bring S into' your context *while she remains inside her* non-epistemological one. The point in each case is for you to be able to understand and do justice to *what it is to be* her, with her non-epistemological perspective – if your epistemological perspective is to evaluate fairly whether, within her own perspective, she knows that *p*.

But this cannot be done, as we saw with the structural problem mentioned briefly in Section 2.2, and as is shown at length in *Epistemology's Paradox*. When *E* is being epistemological in relation to *P*, *E* is reflecting on some epistemic subject(s) in relation to *P*.[7] Rightly, Lewis acknowledges that epistemological contexts discussed by him can concern knowledge-ascriptions either to oneself (one's 'present self or [one's] earlier self, untainted by epistemology') or 'to others' (1999: 434). When *E* asks epistemologically whether *S* knows that *p*, this is one perspective being directed at another. And the epistemological perspective needs to be able to *embed or encompass the non-epistemological one within* it, if an adequate epistemic status is to be present for the epistemological one. When asking epistemologically (as we are doing) whether, for example, *E* knows whether *S* knows that *p*, we are asking, in part, whether *E*'s perspective on *S* understands *S*'s perspective well enough. (And remember that we require *E*'s perspective not to be projecting itself onto *S*'s. It needs to 'try on' *S*'s perspective 'from within', free of *E*'s epistemological preconceptions.) Again, therefore, we are evaluating a perspective, *E*'s, that should be *blended with* the non-epistemological one, in the sense of being able to enter into, before somehow seeing beyond, that other perspective and whatever insights or limitations it might have – *en route* to an epistemological evaluation of the non-epistemological perspective, an evaluation that attains a worthy epistemic status, thanks partly *to* its 'empathetic' understanding, not only of some P, but of how it is for *S* in relation to *P*.[8]

Epistemology's Paradox sought to do justice to that complexity, as does the next chapter. Their shared verdict is unencouraging for the epistemic past, present, *or* future of epistemology.

Notes

1. I describe how this explains the appeal in Kaplan's (1985) argument against 'the Gettier problem' being a real problem (Hetherington 1987, 1992). Rightly, Kaplan takes seriously the fact that, from the perspective of the 'Gettiered' epistemic subject, nothing more can sensibly be asked of her inquiring. Her justification need not be supplemented, either through awareness or through deed, by appropriate recognition and defusing of the 'Gettier circumstance' that, from an onlooking epistemological perspective, seems incompatible with knowing. Kaplan infers that knowing is unimportant for inquirers. My interpretation is different. I distinguish between two kinds of inquirer and their respective epistemic needs. I distinguish between what knowledge would be for a non-epistemological epistemic subject and what it would be for an epistemological one (such as someone presenting a Gettier case).
2. In theory, this can occur even when a principle does not highlight its applicability to epistemological inquirers. Epistemic principles are standardly about *any* epistemic subject.
3. What *is* it to be epistemological? I did not try to determine this. The dissertation (1987) built on Alston's (1989: ch. 6) distinction between *epistemic levels*, treating an

epistemological perspective as one for which being justified requires being justified in being justified, or for which knowing requires knowing that one knows, or, more generally, as one that is *being reflective about* some epistemic principle. *Epistemology's Paradox* (1992) made life more difficult for me by generalizing that simple approach. When E is testing epistemic principle P (for having, or for lacking, some partial or complete epistemic status), I asked only that E *not fail* P at that moment, as a necessary condition of E's not failing epistemically at that moment. I was being interpretationally charitable, wishing not to commit E to meeting an epistemic standard about which E is not *being actively epistemological* at that moment. I am now content to rely mainly on the dissertation's simpler criteria – as we find in the next chapter ('Elusive Epistemological Justification').

4   For an application of such thinking to sceptical thinking, specifically, see Hetherington (1994).

5   My more general 'rule' was that, when E is attending to P, there is a P-related problem for E's having knowledge or justification, or whatever epistemic status P concerns.

6   There was related correspondence between Lewis and me about his paper: see Beebee and Fisher (2020: xx–xxi, 504–6, 508–9, 511–13). I should also mention another limitation on his argument. He relies on a contextualist theory of knowledge(-ascriptions); I sought not to impose a specific theory of knowledge upon my hypothesized epistemological thinkers. My aim was to work with whatever epistemic principle (or theory) a particular E was *being epistemological about* at the time in question. Being epistemological about one principle need not include being epistemological about any others at that time. (See fns 3 and 5.)

7   E might be reflecting on a clearly non-epistemological S, or an S being epistemological about another principle, P^* (or more than one of those possible instances of 'S'). Could E be reflecting on *herself* at that moment? (Think of Descartes, while being epistemological, asking whether he knows at that moment.) This would be at least E's reflecting on E's reflecting on E, all in relation to P. Even this does not escape my argument: see Hetherington (1992: ch. 1).

8   Like Lewis, by the way, I allow that there might be knowledge that p within the non-epistemological context, even if the epistemological context is empty of knowledge. Naturally, the knowledge in the non-epistemological context would be non-epistemological in nature: S might know that p by satisfying a true account P of knowledge, doing so in a *non*-epistemological way, not needing also to be reflecting on P.

References

Alston, W.P. (1989), *Epistemic Justification: Essays in the Theory of Knowledge*, Ithaca, NY: Cornell University Press.

Beebee, H. and Fisher, A.R.J. (eds) (2020), *Philosophical Letters of David K. Lewis, Volume 2: Mind, Language, Epistemology*, Oxford: Oxford University Press.

Gettier, E.L. (1963), 'Is Justified True Belief Knowledge?' *Analysis*, 23: 121–3.

Hetherington, S. (1987), *Narcissistic Epistemology*, PhD dissertation, University of Pittsburgh.

Hetherington, S. (1992), *Epistemology's Paradox: Is a Theory of Knowledge Possible?* Savage, MD: Rowman & Littlefield.
Hetherington, S. (1994), 'Sceptical Insulation and Sceptical Objectivity', *Australasian Journal of Philosophy*, 72: 411–25.
Kaplan, M. (1985), 'It's Not What You Know That Counts', *The Journal of Philosophy*, 82: 350–63.
Lewis, D. (1999), 'Elusive Knowledge', in his *Papers in Metaphysics and Epistemology*, 418–45, Cambridge: Cambridge University Press.

3

Elusive epistemological justification

What does it take for some epistemological thinking to be epistemically justified? Indeed, is that outcome even possible? I argue that it is not possible: no epistemological thinking *can* ever be epistemically justified. A vicious infinite regress of epistemological reflection is the price that would have to be paid for having some such justification. Clearly, that price would be too high.

3.1 A meta-epistemological question

Epistemological practice includes, essentially, people making assessments of knowledge, justification, or cognate epistemic features. It is routine to hear instances of thinking like this: 'Imagine these circumstances .... Would the belief that p, formed in such circumstances, be knowledge? I believe so [or: I do not believe so]'. Confidence is generally high at these moments. Data thereby arise, fodder for supposedly fecund epistemological theorizing. Theories are tested, advocated, or discarded. Epistemological life proceeds.

But it rarely includes much reflection upon the epistemic status of its own pronouncements. What makes an *epistemological* claim justified or unjustified, knowledge or not knowledge? When arguing on behalf of some theory of justification or knowledge, must our supporting claims satisfy that theory – if any at all? Presumably so (we will say), if the theory claims to describe *all* justification; otherwise, perhaps not. Yet is that *all* we can say about this issue?

Far from it. Long ago, I developed some sceptical thoughts about it (Hetherington 1992).[1] Later, David Lewis (1996) did likewise. My main goal was to reflect upon epistemological reflection; Lewis's was not. Still, he argued that when one engages in epistemology, one's mind is opened to sceptical possibilities; at which point, one loses whatever knowledge one previously possessed.[2] On different grounds, I had also argued for epistemological reflection's having that sort of effect upon itself.[3] And this chapter includes some related reasoning for the following meta-epistemological conclusion.

> No epistemological thoughts are ever epistemically justified. *By* having an epistemological thought, one lacks epistemic justification for it. (For example, no one has justification for an epistemological attribution of justification.)[4]

Naturally, this is not a thesis I hope is true; I welcome refutation of it. As we may say, adapting some famous remarks by David Hume,

> [even if] reason is incapable of dispelling these clouds, nature herself suffices to that purpose, and cures me of this philosophical melancholy and delirium, either by relaxing this bent of mind, or by some avocation [such as everyday epistemology], and lively impression of my senses [and intuitions], which obliterate all these chimeras. I dine, I play a game of back-gammon, I converse [with other epistemologists], and am merry with my friends [including my epistemological ones]; and when, after three or four hour's amusement, I wou'd return to these speculations, they appear so cold, and strain'd, and ridiculous, that I cannot find in my heart to enter into them any farther.
>
> (1978 [1739–40]: 269)

Whenever I turn away from this chapter's reasoning, even if to other philosophical pursuits, I find myself blithely confident that some epistemological positions are justified, while others are not, that some amount to knowledge, while others do not. Am I correct at those moments? Not if this chapter is correct.

3.2 An informal preview

Here is a preliminary sense, a brief and less formal one, of my main argument.

> Having justification as an epistemological thinker requires *too much* epistemological thought (either impossibly lengthy or impossibly complex epistemological reflection). This is because no epistemological thinker can have justification, via an apt principle of justification, without reflecting upon doing so – and because the need for this self-reflectiveness never ends. (Whenever it seems to do so, this reflects a confusion between being non-epistemological and being epistemological.)

Why is all of that so? What *is* epistemological reflection? And in what way, exactly, must it be self-reflective if it is to be epistemically justified? How does it then become *too* lengthy or complex ever to be epistemically justified? I will develop detailed answers to these questions.

3.3 Being epistemological

What is it to think epistemologically? First, one must be theorizing. Epistemology is officially 'theory of knowledge', sometimes in effect 'theory of justification'. We are not being epistemological simply in describing Paula as knowing her name. We could be epistemological in saying that she knows it through testimony and her senses.

I propose that someone is thinking epistemologically if and only if she is thinking about some epistemic theory or principle – its truth and/or its epistemic status and/ or its explanatory role in accounting for her and/or someone else's knowledge and/ or justification, etc.[5] I will say that the person is being epistemological *in relation to*, or *about*, that principle. To be epistemological at a time is to be thinking epistemologically. To do this is to be thinking about some given epistemic principle. Hence, at a particular time, one *is* epistemological only in relation to the epistemic principle about which one is *being* epistemological.

That relativisation to a specific principle matters. If a person is not thinking about a particular epistemic principle, she is not being epistemological in relation to, or about, that principle. At different times, she may be epistemological about different epistemic principles, by turning her attention from one to the other.[6] So, a person's being epistemological *simpliciter* is her being epistemological relationally – in relation to one or more epistemic principles or theories, about which she is thinking.

What is an epistemic theory or principle? Here is a representative suggestion. Each such principle articulates a condition C of an epistemic concept's applicability. For simplicity, I will talk only of principles concerning justification, and ones where C is a putatively *sufficient* condition. (It could instead be a putatively necessary condition, or even a confessedly weaker indication, of justification's presence.) A putatively sufficient epistemic principle may take this form:

J   For any epistemic subject x and time t: if x satisfies condition C at t, then (other things being equal) x is justified at t in believing that p (for any p whose content is appropriately connected with the nature of C).[7]

For instance, one principle might specify what kinds and amounts of data justify predictions about the weather. Another could describe what is sufficient for having justified beliefs about one's physical surrounds. If a given principle's condition C is *not* putatively sufficient, that principle says that justification is to only some extent, and in some way, constituted by condition C.[8]

3.4 Two kinds of epistemic subject

What would it be to have justification as someone theorizing about what it is to have justification? In general, to have justification is to satisfy a true and sufficient principle of it[9]:

JSat   For any epistemic subject x and time t: x has justification at t if and only if at t there is some true and sufficient epistemic principle P (one instantiating J, the generic form of epistemic principle mentioned above, in Section 3.3), whose contained antecedent x satisfies, and hence whose contained consequent x satisfies. (This constitutes her having justification *via P* at t for her belief that p.)

JSat is a generic account of what it is to have justification. I will argue, however, that there is a category of epistemic subjects who fail even *JSat*'s generic condition. Those epistemic subjects are all and only epistemological thinkers.[10]

Let us distinguish, then, between epistemic subjects who are, and those who are not, epistemological. Recall that to be epistemological at time t is to be epistemological in relation to some epistemic principle P at t. This requires one to be thinking at t about P. Someone who is epistemological in that way, in relation to P at t, would be an epistemological *epistemic subject* of P at t.[11] She is to be distinguished from what we may call a *standard* epistemic subject of P at t – who is not thinking at t about P.[12]

Standard epistemic subjects are the more standard epistemological fare. Epistemologists enjoin each other not to endorse epistemic principles that accord knowledge or justification only to epistemic subjects who display marked intellectual sophistication (such as an epistemological focus). But those same epistemologists tend to assume that the resulting epistemic principles are true of *all* epistemic subjects if true of some. However, an epistemic subject is only ever an epistemic subject of a given epistemic principle at a given time.[13] Someone could be a standard epistemic subject of a particular epistemic principle at one time, yet an epistemological epistemic subject of that same principle at another time.

We may rewrite *JSat* with that distinction in mind.

> *JSat** For any epistemic subject x and time t: x has justification at t if and only if at t there is some true and sufficient epistemic principle P (instantiating *J*) such that (1) x is either a standard, or an epistemological, epistemic subject of P at t, and (2) x satisfies P's contained antecedent (hence P's contained consequent) as the kind of epistemic subject of P at t which, by (1), she is. That is, (2_S) if x is a *standard* epistemic subject of P at t, she satisfies P's contained antecedent (hence P's contained consequent) without thinking about P. And (2_E) if x is an *epistemological* epistemic subject of P at t, she satisfies P's contained antecedent (hence P's contained consequent) while thinking about P.

Now let us abstract from *JSat** what will be needed, in Section 3.5, for my main argument.

To have epistemological justification is to have justification as an epistemological epistemic subject. By *JSat**, this is to satisfy a true and sufficient epistemic principle P's contained antecedent while also being epistemological in relation to P. An epistemic subject (call her *Sub*) would thereby have that justification as an epistemological epistemic subject *of P*.

P's contained antecedent requires *Sub* to be in some circumstance C; and we may assume that she is indeed in C. But if *Sub* is not simultaneously thinking about P, then in relation to P at that time she is not being *epistemological*. Nor, therefore, is she being an epistemological *epistemic subject* of P. In which case, *Sub* is not in C *as an epistemological epistemic subject of P*. Thus, she is not having justification via P as an epistemological epistemic subject at that time.

So, to have justification as an epistemological epistemic subject is to have it via the epistemic principle in relation to which one is being that epistemological thinker. Correlatively, to be epistemological in relation to P (by thinking about it), while having justification via some other principle P^* (about which one is not thinking), is to have justification only as a *standard* epistemic subject – a standard epistemic subject in relation to P^*. And to have justification as a standard epistemic subject is not to do so as an epistemological epistemic subject. (I will return to this distinction in Section 3.6.)

3.5 A meta-epistemological scepticism

From the previous section, a necessary condition of our epistemological epistemic subject Sub's having justification via an epistemic principle is that she be reflecting on that principle. But that requirement entails her having *no* justification as an epistemological epistemic subject. This section derives that meta-epistemologically sceptical result.

I begin by refining Section 3.4's main point. Suppose that Sub is thinking about epistemic principle P. (She might be reflecting on whether P is true, or on whether it is justified.) But suppose that Sub has no views at that time on P's *helping her* to have justification. In that event, her relationship *to* P's applying to her is not itself epistemological. Therefore, P is not applying to her *qua* epistemological epistemic subject. Accordingly, if Sub is to have epistemological justification via P, she must also be thinking about the connection between P and her belief's justificatory status at that time.

So, we have this thesis – an extension of $JSat^*(2_E)$ – about epistemological justification:

> *EJ* For any putatively sufficient epistemic principle P, time t, and epistemological epistemic subject x: x has justification for her belief that p, via P at t, only if at t she is thinking about P – including P's applying to her at t.[14]

There are different ways to satisfy *EJ*'s contained consequent. Sub might think about whether P is true of her. She could reflect upon how, in her view, P is true of her. But in each case, I will now argue, she has no epistemological justification via P.

The basic reason is that no one can do *enough* epistemological thinking to have justification via a given P. No matter what P's contained antecedent asks Sub to do, *EJ* requires that she also be thinking *about* her doing it. Again, this could be her considering whether doing what is required by that contained antecedent suffices for having justification, and whether its doing so applies to her own case. Or she may be thinking that doing what is required by P's contained antecedent *does* suffice for having justification, and that it is a condition which *is* satisfied in her own case. In any event, if Sub is to have justification as an epistemologist via P, this will be because she has it via a principle like this:

> P1 For any epistemological epistemic subject *x* and time *t*: if, at *t*, *x* satisfies *P*'s contained antecedent, and, at *t*, *x* is thinking about how and/or whether she satisfies that contained antecedent, then (other things being equal) she has justification at *t* for her belief that *p*. (She does so via *this* putatively sufficient principle, *P1*.)

Why is that so? From where has *P1* appeared? It is needed in our account of *Sub*'s having justification via *P*, simply because her relationship to *P*'s applying to her is to be epistemological. (1) In order to satisfy *P*'s contained antecedent *as* an epistemological epistemic subject, *Sub* has to do more than whatever that antecedent specifies. From *EJ*, she must reflect, too, upon her satisfying *P*'s contained antecedent.[15] (2) However, by engaging in such reflection, she is doing what the *further* epistemic principle *P1* asks her to do, in order that she have justification. *P1* specifies what *Sub* must be doing in addition to whatever *P* specifies – so that, in doing whatever *P* specifies, she is doing it *as* an epistemological epistemic subject of *P*.

Yet even that is not enough. We needed to call on *P1* because *Sub*'s doing only whatever *P* asks her to do is not enough to give her justification *as* an epistemologist. But that same problem applies to *P1* no less than to *P*: *Sub* is unable to have justification as an epistemological epistemic subject by satisfying only *P1*'s contained antecedent. The reason for this is as follows.

If *P1* is needed in order to account for *Sub*'s having justification via *P* as an epistemological epistemic subject, this makes *Sub* an epistemological epistemic subject *of P1* at that time. By *EJ*, however, *Sub* has justification via *P1* as an epistemological thinker only if *P1* is true of her as someone thinking about how and/or whether it is true of her. Yet if *Sub* is thinking about *P1* in that way, she is doing *more* than *P1*'s contained antecedent specifies as sufficing for justification. A *further* putatively sufficient epistemic principle's intervention is therefore needed. *Sub* would have justification as that epistemological epistemic subject only because this further principle, *P2*, is true of her – where *P2* stands to *P1* as *P1* did to *P*. That is, *P2* specifies what more is needed if *Sub* is to satisfy *P1* as an *epistemological* epistemic subject:

> P2 For any epistemological epistemic subject *x* and time *t*: if, at *t*, *x* satisfies P1's contained antecedent, and, at *t*, *x* is thinking about how and/or whether she satisfies that contained antecedent, then (other things being equal) she has some correlative justification at t. (She does so via this putatively sufficient principle, *P2*.)

Nor does this sequence end with *P2*. *Mutatis mutandis*, the same reasoning as introduced *P2* into this tale now leads us to acknowledge a *new* putatively sufficient principle, *P3* – standing to *P2* as *P2* does to *P1* and as *P1* does to *P*. This pattern continues without end, relying next upon *Sub*'s thinking about *P3*'s applying to her, then upon her thinking about *P4*'s applying to her (where *P4* stands to *P3* as *P3* did to *P2*), then upon ..., etc. The upshot is as follows.

(1) Someone has justification via a true and sufficient epistemic principle *P* as an epistemological thinker at time *t*, only if, at *t*, she is thinking about the

applicability to her of *P1*, of *P2*, of *P3*, and so on, *ad infinitum*. This is her thinking about the applicability to her either of an infinite number of principles individually or of an infinitely large principle.[16]
(2) She cannot accomplish this task, be it infinitely extended or be it infinitely complex.[17]
(3) Hence (by *modus tollens*, from 1 and 2), no one can have justification via a true and sufficient epistemic principle *P* as an epistemological thinker. Epistemic success is unattainable for anyone as an epistemological thinker.[18]

This result applies even to epistemic principles *purporting* to be about epistemological epistemic subjects. Even for a principle that calls for an epistemological epistemic subject to be thinking about its own applicability to her, there is a truth about how and/or whether it is applying to her. By *EJ*, however, that truth cannot apply to her as an epistemological epistemic subject unless its doing so is being thought about by her. (The fact that it is itself about epistemological-thinking-about-itself does not change this point.) So, the epistemological thinking which that truth is about must be nested within further epistemological thinking (then more, and more again, etc.). Our sceptical conclusion thus remains intact: there is no epistemological justification.[19]

3.6 Disarming a non-reflectivist suggestion

It is a non-trivial inferential leap from (A) to (B):

(A) There is no true and sufficient epistemic principle, via which some epistemologist has justification while thinking about doing so;
(B) There is no true and sufficient epistemic principle, via which some epistemologist has justification.

But Section 3.5's regress argument made that leap. Should it have done so?

In endorsing *EJ*, I was denying what I have previously called non-reflectivism – epistemic externalism, directed at epistemological justification (Hetherington 1992: ch. 6). For I was denying that someone can (i) be thinking at *t* about the putative justificatory link between an epistemic principle *P** and herself at that time, (ii) fail to have justification via *P** at *t*, (iii) possess justification at *t* via a true and sufficient epistemic principle *P* about which she is *not* thinking, yet (iv) possess the latter justification *as* the epistemological thinker about *P** that she is at *t*.

Was that denial correct? Or should we reject *EJ*? Must epistemologists be as endlessly reflective as I am requiring, if justification is to come their way? Non-reflectivism allows that an epistemological thinker can have justification via a true and sufficient epistemic principle even when not reflecting upon whether it is true of her. Non-reflectivism may allow, for example, that an epistemological thinker's development of a theory of empirical justification could be justified *a priori*.[20]

That non-reflectivist objection to my argument might also be formulated in terms of epistemic levels.[21] Even for an epistemological epistemic subject, could there be different levels of epistemic justification? Minimally, to have epistemological justification at a particular epistemic level is to satisfy a true and sufficient principle *P about* justification at that level. But the regress argument requires our epistemological *Sub* also to *reflect on* her having justification via *P*. And surely (continues the objection) this further reflection is needed only if *Sub* is to have justification for the *higher-level belief that* she has justification via *P*. This is so, no matter what level of justification *P* describes. Hence (concludes the objection), *EJ* is wrong: an epistemologist can have justification via a true and sufficient *P* without thinking about doing so – even while being epistemological by thinking about a distinct *P** instead. She could have justification via *P* while lacking what would have been higher-level justification via *P*+, a principle *about P*-justification.

That objection fails. I noted in Section 3.4 that someone is a standard – or is an epistemological – epistemic subject, only *relative* to a given epistemic principle and a given time. Relative to a given *P* and *t*, a person can be either an epistemological epistemic subject or a standard epistemic subject – not both – depending on whether she is thinking at *t* about *P*'s applicability to her. Now, the objection from epistemic levels posits someone, *Sub*, as thinking about *P** – while having justification via *P*, a true and sufficient principle about which she is not thinking. (For example, she is pondering the nature of empirical justification for beliefs about the external world. And these thoughts of hers are said to be justified *a priori*.) However, the objection does not describe *Sub*'s having *epistemological* justification via *P*. At most, it describes what *would* be epistemological justification via *P*, if (for a start) *Sub* was being epistemological in relation to *P*. Relative to a true and sufficient principle *P* of *a priori* justification, say, *Sub* is being epistemically successful – but not also epistemological.

In contrast, relative to a true and sufficient principle *P** of empirical justification *Sub* is being epistemological – but not also epistemically successful. So, the posited case does not describe someone's attaining epistemic success via a true and sufficient epistemic principle insofar as she is being an epistemological epistemic subject *of* that principle. Although it claims to describe her – a single entity – both as being an epistemological epistemic subject and as having epistemic success, it does not show that a single *epistemic subject* is satisfying both of these descriptions. The posited objection wondered whether my argument was confusing epistemic levels; the objection confuses types of epistemic subject.

Moreover, it is possibly *because* the objection confuses types of epistemic subject that it presses its point about epistemic levels.[22] For an epistemological epistemic subject of a principle *P*, justification *does* require higher-level justification via *P* (and, as it transpires, an infinitude either of other principles or of complexity in the overall justification-licensing principle). It is only for *standard* epistemic subjects of *P* that such a requirement should be rejected. Epistemologists are right not to require higher-level justification of standard epistemic subjects – but wrong to exempt themselves from that requirement.[23]

3.7 False epistemic principles

I am saying that no epistemological thinker can have justification via a true and sufficient epistemic principle (and, given *JSat**, there is no other way to have it). Yet this tells us that there are *no* true and sufficient epistemic principles – unless we cease expecting them to quantify univocally over all epistemic subjects.

For example, suppose that *Sub* is in a Chisholmian self-presenting state of seeming to see red – a circumstance which, if she were a standard epistemic subject, would suffice for her being justified in believing that she sees something red.[24] Suppose also that she is reflecting epistemologically upon her having such justification in that way. Section 3.5's regress argument entails that she thereby *fails* to have such justification in that way. Her epistemological thinking 'gets in the way' of having justification as that epistemological thinker.

Accordingly, no epistemological epistemic subject can have justification by being in anything like a self-presenting state. One would have to be reflecting at that time on being in that self-presenting state and on thereby having that justification. But being in a self-presenting state precludes one's simultaneously reflecting on being in it. If we take seriously the distinction between epistemological and standard epistemic subjects, therefore, we should accept that if there is immediate justification, it is available only to *standard* epistemic subjects. Any associated Chisholmian foundationalism is unavailable for epistemological epistemic subjects.

And that example may be generalized. Standardly, epistemologists seek both universality and univocality when theorizing. Their epistemic principles quantify over all epistemic subjects at once, offering a univocal account – of what it is for *any* epistemic subject to have a given kind of justification. But if my point in this chapter is right, they should do that no more.

First, epistemological epistemic subjects and standard epistemic subjects must satisfy respectively different conditions if they are to have justification. An epistemological epistemic subject of a putatively sufficient epistemic principle needs to be thinking about its applying to her (if it is to do this successfully); whereas no standard epistemic subject of that principle need do so.[25]

Moreover, any epistemic principle is false insofar as it does include epistemological epistemic subjects within its univocal scope; for none of these *can* have justification via it. No putatively sufficient epistemic principle is a true account of how epistemological epistemic subjects can have justification.[26]

Of course, we could decompose any putatively sufficient epistemic principle P into two sub-principles, P_S and P_E. P_S applies to standard epistemic subjects. P_E is restricted to epistemological epistemic subjects. I have argued neither for nor against any standard kinds of scepticism – each being about standard epistemic subjects having some form of justification.[27] But each P_E has been found to be wholly false – false for *all* of its (epistemological) epistemic subjects.

3.8 Persons

Our sceptical result obtains even for principles that seem as if they *ought* to be about all epistemic subjects. Consider again a principle purporting to describe a simple sort of perceptual justification. Seemingly, such a principle can be about everyone, because all of us employ our senses in forming or supporting many beliefs. Even epistemological thinkers do so.

Well, that is not quite so. A principle about a simple kind of perceptual justification might indeed be true of all *persons* – yet probably only because each person is at least sometimes a *standard* epistemic subject. That epistemic principle is not thereby true of all epistemic subjects. Not every epistemic subject has perceptual justification, since no epistemological epistemic subject does. Although an epistemological epistemic subject may be using her senses, our regress argument shows that this never suffices for her having justification as an epistemological epistemic subject. Too much extra reflection is required of her, in addition to her sensing, if she is to have perceptual justification as an epistemological epistemic subject.

Resistance to that conclusion might nonetheless linger, along the following lines.

Suppose that a person, Percy, is sensing in a way described by a true and sufficient P's contained antecedent as sufficing for perceptual justification. Suppose also that Percy is doing more besides, by thinking about his sensing. But the 'more besides', by coexisting with the sensing, does not *undo* the sensing's justificatory work. Percy is sensing in a way that, were he not thinking epistemologically, would (according to P) give him justification as a standard epistemic subject. Hence, he retains that justification even when thinking epistemologically. He can have the perceptual justification when being epistemological, even if not *by* being epistemological.

The flaw in such reasoning is that (as Section 3.5 explained) the 'more besides' does deprive an epistemological thinker of justification. The 'more besides' coexists with the sensing within the person, but not within any epistemic subject. Percy is using his senses epistemologically, as it were. He therefore fails to use them in a way that gives him justification (an outcome categorially available only *to* an epistemic subject). The regress to which the 'more besides' commits Percy leaves him too mired in epistemological thinking (about his sensing) for his sensing to give him justification. He cannot have any standardly perceptual justification as an epistemological thinker.

Standard forms of scepticism aside, maybe Percy has other kinds of justification at that time. Yet he would do so only as a standard epistemic subject, by satisfying true and sufficient epistemic principles about which he is not thinking. He might, for instance, be using his senses reliably and non-epistemologically (that is, standardly), relative to another true and sufficient principle about perceptual justification. But he would not thereby acquire perceptual justification *in* his capacity as the epistemological thinker he is at that time, about a particular principle of perceptual justification.

The temptation to think otherwise confuses significantly different epistemic modes of the one person. The concepts of a person and an epistemic subject are not identical.[28] Even if the one person is perceiving reliably and thinking epistemologically about doing so, this does not entail that the one epistemic subject is doing so. And epistemic principles quantify over epistemic subjects, not (strictly speaking) over persons. Even when a principle claims to be talking about people, it cannot quite succeed: a person *qua* object-of-an-epistemic-principle's-focus is *ipso facto* an epistemic subject.

And a person *qua* epistemic subject need not be an epistemic subject *qua* person. Epistemology is, first and foremost, about epistemic subjects. It talks about persons only *qua* epistemic subjects.

3.9 Being impurely epistemological

Seemingly, this chapter confronts us with a stark choice: either lack all epistemic justification as an epistemological thinker; or never *be* an epistemological thinker. But we may wonder whether that choice is needlessly stark. In particular, is it possible to think epistemologically, and to gain epistemic justification in doing so, by being *less purely* epistemological?

The picture in this chapter has been one of epistemological inquiry (if it is to produce justified conclusions) as needing to possess, *per impossibile*, an unending relentlessness, a crystalline purity – unceasingly pondering pertinent epistemic principles. Maybe, however, epistemological thinking is not like that. Perhaps it is never so purely or extremely epistemological. Might I have been analysing the epistemic power only of an unrealistically exaggerated conception of what it is to be epistemological?

Certainly in practice, that could seem so. It is undeniable that people, when thinking epistemologically, will often not satisfy *only* my conception of epistemological inquiry. For instance, even while reflecting upon an epistemic principle, you may also be evaluating related observations or scientific data. You would be combining epistemological thinking with non-epistemological thinking. Maybe epistemological thinking is always accompanied by some non-epistemological thinking.

Yet even this would not allow it to evade our meta-epistemological scepticism. The strictly epistemological part of your thinking would still be failing to provide you with epistemic justification – irrespective of whether your non-epistemological thinking, when accompanying that epistemological thinking, could be at all justified. We may put this point more strongly: Within any quest for epistemically justified views, any strictly epistemological thinking is a liability. No purely epistemological presence contributes justified views itself. So, if epistemological thinking as we practise it *is* epistemological by having a strictly epistemological core, then it is unjustified insofar *as* it is epistemological, strictly speaking.[29]

Still, might our sceptical regress argument show that there never *is* a purely epistemological core within any attempts at thinking epistemologically? We may formulate that idea like this: Epistemological thinking is only ever *messily* epistemological, never purely so. At any rate, it is like that if it is ever to provide justification. In other words, we can regard epistemological thinking non-sceptically only if we characterize it as being partly non-epistemological.

But care is needed here. The previous-but-one paragraph explained why we could not evade the sceptical result by conceiving of our actual episodes of epistemological thinking as mere sums of (i) epistemological thinking, independently characterisable as epistemological, plus (ii) non-epistemological thinking, independently characterisable as non-epistemological. Instances of (i)-plus-(ii) would *not* portray epistemological thinking as being present only messily (in the intended sense of 'messily'). That is because in principle the epistemological part of an instance of (i)-plus-(ii) is separable from the non-epistemological part. The sum, (i)-plus-(ii), is therefore a combination of two conceptually independent elements – the epistemological and the non-epistemological. And, we have seen, the epistemological element provides only unjustified views.

What the present suggestion needs, then, is a conception of our episodes of epistemological thinking as including both epistemological and non-epistemological elements – but with these *not* being characterisable, as respectively epistemological and non-epistemological, independently of each other. In every relevant way, they would be ineliminably intertwined. No epistemological thinking would be only epistemological. And this would be so, no matter how finely we 'slice' the epistemological thinking: it would be partly non-epistemological, 'all the way down'. Not only 'everyday' epistemological thinking would be partly non-epistemological. Even the most 'conceptually pure' epistemological thinking would remain partly non-epistemological.[30]

We must wonder, however, whether that is really possible. Insofar as there would still be *some* difference between epistemological thinking and non-epistemological thinking, something constitutes that difference. What would do so? The criterion I have used in this chapter for characterizing epistemological thought – namely, reflection upon an epistemic principle – remains the most apt. Maybe each 'unit', no matter how small, of epistemological thought also includes some non-epistemological thought. Even so, some aspect of that unit includes reflection upon an epistemic principle; else, it is not even a minimally epistemological aspect of some thinking. We have seen, however, why *that* aspect of any such minimal unit of only-mixedly-epistemological thought would contribute no justification. The point remains, therefore, that if some justification is available, this is only because of the *non*-epistemological aspect of whatever minimal mixture is being hypothesized to be epistemological-(although-only-mixedly-so). Even for that minimal unit, then, unless we relinquish the category of the epistemological altogether, we continue to be susceptible to this chapter's meta-epistemological scepticism.[31]

Notes

1   For some recent thoughts, see Hetherington (2006a).
2   Lewis's news was not wholly gloomy. He allowed that one might regain one's former knowledge, once the epistemological moment is past.
3   My argument was more general, in part by not relying upon the highly contestable assumption – which Lewis clearly employed – that epistemological reflection includes attention to sceptical possibilities.
4   My argument will also apply, *mutatis mutandis*, to epistemological theorizing about knowledge. But this application will not be made explicit throughout this chapter.
5   More than this can be involved in particular cases: the person could be reflecting upon more than one epistemic theory, for example. But our generic description captures a *core* conception of what it is to be thinking epistemologically. We may

6 'What if she is thinking about two such principles over a sustained period, back and forth, comparing them?' Then she is epistemological during that extended period about both principles, even if there are times within it when she is epistemological only about one of the two. For simplicity (and because I believe that my argument is generalisable to these more complex cases), I will continue talking just about the simpler case, of reflection upon a single principle.

7 For simplicity, I talk here of believing. But my discussion also applies, *mutatis mutandis*, to acceptance and awareness, say.

8 Footnote 3 adverted to Lewis's 'highly contestable assumption [...] that epistemological reflection includes attention to sceptical possibilities'. It may be objected that my characterisation of epistemological reflection – as involving attention to an epistemic principle – is no less contestable. Notably, particularism might be cited – as an epistemological practice of assessing the presence or absence of knowledge or justification without doing so by applying a principle or theory of knowledge of justification. But particularism does this so as to *test* or *support* a principle or theory of knowledge or justification. Consequently, even it accords with my criterion of epistemological reflection upon some such principle or theory.

9 (i) I will use the phrase 'true and sufficient' when talking of a principle whose condition is both putatively sufficient in form and actually sufficient in effect. Whenever I am not assuming a principle's truth, therefore, I speak only of its being 'putatively sufficient'. (ii) As Section 3.3 allowed, some epistemic conditions are not even putatively sufficient. (They are putatively necessary, or confessedly weaker still.) Nevertheless, one actually has justification by satisfying a particular principle only if it is both putatively and actually sufficient in its description of that kind of justification.

10 The terms 'epistemologist' and 'epistemological thinker' are being used to designate someone only when she is being epistemological. In this sense, a professional epistemologist is not always an epistemologist.

11 This is so, provided that she is an epistemic subject *at all* of P at t. What is required for this prior condition to be true of her? We may treat 'epistemic subject of P' as short for 'potential subject of P', meaning only to indicate a *categorial* aptness for being described more specifically as satisfying P. (See also fn. 28.)

12 Here, too, see the previous footnote.

13 I have urged elsewhere that we should focus epistemological analysis upon epistemic agents, not epistemic subjects (Hetherington 2006b: sec. 10). This is especially apt when discussing *epistemological* epistemic subjects/agents, because to be epistemological is to be thinking in what is presumably an agentive way. I will continue writing in this chapter of epistemic subjects, including epistemological ones. But we may take it that they are agentive subjects. This point will matter in fn. 20.

14 Would a similar constraint apply to epistemological *beliefs* as such – not only to *justified* epistemological beliefs? It would, if a genuinely epistemological belief must either be (i) accompanied by reflection upon some principle P that specifies a sufficient condition of the belief's being epistemological, or (ii) justified simply in order to be epistemological. The former need would obtain if epistemological belief – justified or not – is always suitably self-reflective. The latter need would obtain if

epistemological belief is nothing – literally nonexistent – if not justified. Here, I take no stand on either of these independently interesting ideas.

15 In arguing against what he calls meta-justificatory foundationalism, Jeremy Fantl (2003) calls upon similar reasoning to mine. In his terms: For any feature F that makes a foundational belief justified, the epistemic agent's having reason to believe that a belief has F makes the belief *more* justified than the fact of its having F would make it.

16 One may reply, 'Surely no such regress could really develop. After ... five? six? how many? ... iterations, no real sense could be made of them. (Would we lack the words even to formulate these iterations after that while?) So, externalism is true of epistemological justification – if there is to be any. And why, therefore, should there *not* be any – obtaining in some externalist way, bypassing this section's internalist strictures?' However, if internalism is *ever* to be aptly applied, epistemological epistemic subjects in particular are those to whom it would be aptly applied. It is they (if anyone) who are aware of, and who muse upon, their epistemic practice and epistemic principles. Notice, also, how many recurrent aspects of epistemological focus reflect internalist ideas – for example, that of 'stepping back' from an inquiry so as to think about it, even contemplating all of an inquiry's presumptions.

17 Fantl (2003) defends a moderate version of Peter Klein's infinitism. (See Klein (2005) for a more recent statement of his views.) Fantl's aim is to avoid the implication 'that humans must have the ability to actually entertain an infinite series of reasons' (2003: 560). He does this by accepting that propositions can be justified well *enough* for knowledge, even without being *completely* justified (2003: 560). But although I wish Fantl's approach well, it does not save epistemological thinkers from the present sceptical reasoning. For this reasoning commits such thinkers, if they are to have (epistemological) justification *at all*, to perpetually continued reflection upon the associated epistemic principle(s).

18 One may ask, 'Could there be propositional epistemological justification even if – courtesy of this section's regress argument – there is no doxastic epistemological justification?' Propositional epistemological justification would include propositions 'reflecting' upon other propositions in epistemological ways. Yet then (by this section's form of reasoning) there would be an infinity of further propositions 'reflecting' in such theoretical ways. Indeed, it is even clearer for propositional than for doxastic justification that an infinity of theoretical propositions would be implicated in some such vicious regress.

19 A clarification: This sceptical conclusion is not saying that, even at best, epistemological thinking can be only *somewhat* justified, or justified only *fallibly*. Our regress argument applies to any amount, and any standard, of epistemological justification. Our sceptical worry is structural. It pertains to the relationship of applicability between (i) any putatively true and sufficient epistemic principle of *any* form and strength of justification, and (ii) any would-be *epistemological* epistemic subject of that principle. Even to claim that some merely *moderate* amount of merely *fallibilist* justification is present for an epistemological view is still to imply that the support for the view in question satisfies a true and sufficient principle, one *about* that lesser amount, and that fallibilist form, of justification. In other words, even when the amount and form of justification are less impressive, some true and sufficient principle describes what is required for possessing precisely *that* amount and form of justification.

20 Might non-reflectivism even allow that the epistemological thinker's theory of empirical justification is justified *contextually*? By this, I mean that it is justified through resting upon a basis that is not itself justified – because it is taken for granted, simply not questioned – within this context of inquiry. For such a view of justification, see Annis (1978) and Williams (2001: ch. 14). But that contextualist proposal is itself a principle of how justification is to be present. Even a contextualist principle saying that justification can be contextual (by resting upon some contextually unjustified and unquestioned beliefs) is itself an epistemic principle P telling us what suffices for the presence of some justification. Thus, it does not escape the scope of this chapter's argument: to end an epistemological inquiry (*qua* search for epistemological justification) by pointing to some contextually unjustified beliefs is to cease *being* epistemological at that time. It is to seek to ground what is epistemologically justified on what is not only not justified (and not questioned) in that setting, but what is non-epistemological. For once inquiry ends by taking some thesis for granted, epistemology is no longer being pursued, at least in relation to that thesis. An epistemological moment includes inquiry, reflection upon epistemic ideas – not a cessation of inquiry, a taking-for-granted. More precisely: although one *will* take much for granted when being epistemological, one is not thereby being epistemological *about*, or in *relation* to, that which is being taken for granted. Regardless of whether or not justification can be grounded in non-justification (as contextualism claims), no *epistemological* justification is grounded in *non*-epistemological justification. I return to this issue in Section 3.9.

21 On this notion, see Alston (1989: ch. 6).

22 Or perhaps instead the confusion arises because the concept of a *person* is being substituted for that of an epistemic subject. This could occur because, seemingly, a single person at the one time is both (i) the epistemological epistemic subject (not gaining justification in that capacity) in relation to P^* and (ii) the standard epistemic subject in relation to P (being claimed to have justification by satisfying P). I will discuss this issue in Section 3.8.

23 The inclination to accord an epistemological epistemic subject justification via a P about which she is not thinking should also be allayed if we adopt fn. 13's recommendation. We would think of an epistemological x as first and foremost an epistemic agent. We would realize that at t she is such an agent only in relation to some P. Then if we accept that she would have justification only as an epistemic agent, we will infer that, at t, she has justification *qua* epistemological epistemic agent only via P – the lone principle in relation to which, at t, she is actively being epistemological.

24 See Chisholm (1989: 18–20).

25 This complexity in how we must conceive of epistemic subjects is the reason why *JSat* needed to be replaced by *JSat**.

26 One might wonder whether this is so when the epistemic principle in question is about a form of justification which (unlike Chisholmian self-presentation) has the potential to be comparatively reflective and self-aware, such as coherence. Suppose that someone is reflecting upon a coherentist principle *CJ* which her reflections at that time also seem to satisfy: 'My musings upon *CJ* and coherentist justification are themselves coherent. How apt.' Yet even these reflections are not thereby justified epistemologically, unless she is reflecting *upon* how her reflections satisfy *CJ*: 'These epistemological claims of mine about *CJ* and coherentist justification are justified by satisfying *CJ* itself'. In making this assessment, however,

she would be mistaken. She could have this epistemological justification only by satisfying, not *CJ*, but instead a *further* principle. For simplicity and charity, let us assume that this new principle (call it *CJ+*) would also be coherentist. It will describe *meta-*coherence – the coherence of (i) a belief about one's having coherentist justification for beliefs $b_1, ..., b_n$ via *CJ*, with (ii) those mutually coherent-via-*CJ* beliefs $b_1, ..., b_n$. But then this sort of need will continue *ad infinitum*. Now it applies to *CJ+* – thereby generating a need for a new principle *CJ++* to enter the story – as previously it did to *CJ*. On and on, this pattern proceeds. Hence, even here, this thinker will not be justified epistemologically. A vicious infinite regress sees to that. Although she may believe that her beliefs $b_1, ..., b_n$ at that moment are justified in a coherentist way, this meta-belief of hers is not itself both justified and epistemological. Nor, therefore, are her beliefs $b_1, ..., b_n$ – no matter their content.

27 Equally, when arguing in Section 3.6 against non-reflectivism (externalism about epistemological epistemic subjects), I was arguing neither for nor against standard epistemic externalism (about standard epistemic subjects). For the standard distinction between epistemic externalism and epistemic internalism, see Hetherington (1996: chs 14–15).

28 Although here I have not discussed the full relationship between those two concepts, here is a brief suggestion. The concept of an epistemic subject is an epistemologist's way of thinking of something as being the subject of an epistemic principle. The 'something' might, or might not, always be a person; I take no stand on whether animals are ever epistemic subjects. In any event, the thing's being an epistemic subject would be its having an epistemic property or mode of being. To be an epistemological epistemic subject is to have a different property from whatever makes one a standard epistemic subject. If my argument in this chapter is sound, a belief's instantiating the property of being justified depends, in part, on which of these other properties the belief or believer has at that time.

29 Moreover, it can distract you from pursuing alternative thinking which would provide some justification (albeit standard – not-strictly-epistemological – justification).

30 Williamson (2008) argues that much philosophical thinking does not draw upon any special faculty, such as of intuition. Instead, it applies a comparatively ordinary capacity to gain knowledge of counterfactual truths (and thereby modal truths, in particular). Epistemological thinking is clearly intended by Williamson to be subsumed under this characterisation.

31 But see Hetherington (2008) for some further thoughts – non-sceptical ones – on the nature of philosophical knowledge. A significant re-conceptualization of such knowledge might be needed here.

References

Alston, W.P. (1989), *Epistemic Justification: Essays in the Theory of Knowledge*, Ithaca, NY: Cornell University Press.

Annis, D.B. (1978), 'A Contextualist Theory of Epistemic Justification', *American Philosophical Quarterly*, 15: 213–19.

Chisholm, R.M. (1989), *Theory of Knowledge*, 3rd edn, Englewood Cliffs, NJ: Prentice-Hall.

Fantl, J. (2003), 'Modest Foundationalism', *Canadian Journal of Philosophy*, 33: 537–62.
Hetherington, S. (1992), *Epistemology's Paradox: Is a Theory of Knowledge Possible?* Savage, MD: Rowman & Littlefield.
Hetherington, S. (2006a), 'Introduction: Epistemological Progress', in S. Hetherington (ed.), *Epistemology Futures*, 1–9, Oxford: Clarendon Press.
Hetherington, S. (2006b), 'How to Know (That Knowledge-That Is Knowledge-How)', in S. Hetherington (ed.), *Epistemology Futures*, 71–94, Oxford: Clarendon Press.
Hetherington, S. (2008), 'Knowing-That, Knowing-How, and Knowing Philosophically', *Grazer Philosophische Studien*, 77: 307–24.
Hume, D. (1978 [1739–40]), *A Treatise of Human Nature*, 2nd edn, P.H. Nidditch (ed.), Oxford: Clarendon Press.
Klein, P. (2005), 'Infinitism and the Solution to the Regress Problem', in M. Steup and E. Sosa (eds), *Contemporary Debates in Epistemology*, 131–40, Malden, MA: Blackwell.
Lewis, D. (1996), 'Elusive Knowledge', *Australasian Journal of Philosophy*, 74: 549–67.
Williams, M. (2001), *Problems of Knowledge: A Critical Introduction to Epistemology*, Oxford: Oxford University Press.
Williamson, T. (2008), *The Philosophy of Philosophy*, Malden, MA: Blackwell.

4

Gettieristic scepticism

4.1 Introduction

I believe that epistemologists are yet to appreciate the full epistemological potential of so-called Gettier cases. Such cases are only ever interpreted as establishing the following thesis – that which Gettier (1963) himself took his cases to support:

(*) Not every justified true belief is knowledge.

Nevertheless, arguing for that thesis is not the only use an epistemologist can make of Gettier cases. As I will demonstrate, he might also use them *sceptically*.[1] Not only can he agree with the standard interpretation of them as supporting (*); he could see in them a new way of arguing for (!):

(!) There is no knowledge.

That is, Gettier cases might fuel a radical scepticism on his part. And my aim in this chapter is to explain one way in which such scepticism can indeed be fuelled by Gettier cases. I call this new way of arguing for (!) 'Gettieristic scepticism'.

I will not argue that Gettieristic scepticism is true, though. Nor will I claim that, by using Gettier cases, we can construct an unanswerable sceptical argument. In fact, I will not assign any determinate degree of plausibility to the Gettieristic sceptic's reasoning. I will claim only a *parallelism* between Gettieristic sceptical reasoning and the classic Cartesian dreaming argument, for example. Epistemologists, when asked to discuss scepticism (such as when teaching its ideas to a class), standaidly call on a favoured listing of paradigmatic kinds of scepticism – such as Cartesian scepticism (dreams, evil demons), Humean scepticism, rule scepticism, and Pyrrhonism. I contend that epistemologists should also include Gettieristic scepticism in this list. It is a new scepticism and, if it even *might* be true, it poses as pressing a sceptical problem as do some of the more standard forms of scepticism. Like them, it denies us knowledge which we all-but-automatically assume is ours. So, to ignore it would be to neglect an opportunity to perhaps correct a fundamentally false self-image. Gettieristic scepticism, like other scepticisms, is relevant to almost everyone's sense of self.

4.2 Gettier cases and Cartesian sceptics

One way in which someone might attempt to use Gettier cases sceptically is by arguing for their ubiquity. A Gettier case is a situation in which a person (for specificity, I will assume that it is you) has a justified true belief which fails to be knowledge. It is a situation which makes (*) true. By definition, therefore, to be Gettiered in a belief that p is to lack knowledge that p.[2] Hence, if all beliefs were Gettiered, none of them would be knowledge. Radical scepticism would be true: (!) would be true.

Applied to you and your beliefs (for any proposition p), such reasoning gives us this argument:

(A) 1. You know that p only if you are not being Gettiered in believing that p.
2. But you are always being Gettiered in believing that p.
3. So, you never know that p. [from 1 and 2]

Even sceptics, though, are unlikely to embrace (A) – specifically, its premise A2. (A1 is definitionally true.) After all, who would be willing to argue that you really are always being Gettiered? What would be the evidence for such an accusation? I take it that there is none (and that this is why no epistemologists have argued for A2).

By analogy, recall that Cartesian sceptics, for instance, never argue that we are dreaming whenever we form beliefs that are ostensibly about the external world. That is, they never use the following analogue of (A) (for any external world proposition p).

(B) 1. You know that p only if you are not dreaming that p.
2. But you are always dreaming that p.
3. So, you never know that p. [from 1 and 2]

As with A2, what would be the evidence for premise B2? There is none. There is evidence for sometimes having been dreaming, just as there is for sometimes having been Gettiered. But A2 and B2 claim that you are forever dreaming or being Gettiered.

So, Cartesian sceptics generally offer an argument that differs slightly from (B). Instead of building an argument around the claim that you are always dreaming, they turn to the claim that you never know that you are not dreaming. And Gettieristic sceptics can do likewise, as we will see. No matter whether or not what results is an argument that strikes epistemologists in general as plausible, it should satisfy sceptical epistemologists – as being true to the spirit of their currently standard arguments. In any event, the immediately pertinent point is that argument (A) is not the Gettieristic sceptical argument I am presenting in this chapter. Not even sceptical epistemologists would be tempted by it. It would appeal to them no more than (B) would.

4.3 Gettier cases and Cartesian sceptics, Redux

Here, then, is a more standard way to present the Cartesian dreaming argument (where p is any external world proposition).

(D) 1. You know that *p* only if you know that you are not dreaming that *p*.
     2. But you never know that you are not dreaming that *p*.
     3. So, you never know that *p*. [from 1 and 2]

A Cartesian sceptic asks you, via premise D1, to know that you are not dreaming – and claims in D2 that you cannot do so.

Not all epistemologists accept (D), of course. But Cartesian sceptics do, and I say that their way of thinking (which takes the phenomenon of dreaming and turns it into a sceptical worry) should find no less to work with in the phenomenon of being Gettiered. Just as the Cartesian sceptic asks you to know that you are not dreaming, a Gettieristic sceptic would ask you to know that you are not being *Gettiered*. Prior to encountering the Cartesian argument, most of us would have thought that it was good enough to not *be* dreaming, and that *knowing* that one is not dreaming would be a superfluous requirement. Well, whether or not it is superfluous, what matters right now is that Cartesian sceptics do not think that it is. And I am suggesting that a similar requirement – with similar plausibility – can be grounded in a consideration of Gettier cases. To whatever extent your knowing that you are not dreaming is essential to your knowing that *p* (for external world *p*), your knowing that you are not being Gettiered is essential to your knowing that *p* (for any *p*).

Once he notes this, of course, a non-sceptic might dismiss both requirements as equally implausible. No matter; sceptics, at any rate, find the former one appealing, and hence they should be equally interested in the latter one. They would use it in the following way (where *p* is any proposition at all).

(G) 1. You know that *p* only if you know that you are not being Gettiered in believing that *p*.
     2. But you never know that you are not being Gettiered in believing that *p*.
     3. So, you never know that *p*. [from 1 and 2]

I think that (G) – the Gettieristic sceptical argument – is neither more nor less plausible than (D). And how plausible is that? Again, I take no stand on this. Regardless of whether you find (D) plausible, my point is that you should view (D) and (G) analogously. Regardless of whether you accept (D), it is the usual way to encapsulate the Cartesian reasoning; I will argue that Gettier cases can be used analogously to give us (G). In what follows, then, I explain how a Cartesian sceptic can apply his thinking, *mutatis mutandis*, to Gettier cases. The result will be a fresh form of scepticism. And I do not say that you should accept it. I say only that sceptics should embrace it. They should add it to their existing 'kit bag'.

Let us begin by seeing how a Gettieristic sceptic can try to motivate (G)'s first premise, G1, perfectly analogously to how the Cartesian sceptic would generally try to motivate D1. In arguing for DI, a Cartesian sceptic reasons in the following way.

If you were dreaming *p*'s being the case (for any external world *p*), you would not know that *p*. So, until you know that you are not dreaming that *p*, your dreaming that *p* (and hence your not knowing that *p*) is compatible with all of your justification for believing *p*. For all that you would know to the contrary, therefore, you would be dreaming that *p* – and hence you would not know that *p*. What knowledge (if any) you do have thus fails to rule out your not knowing that *p*. So, D1 is true: your knowing that *p* depends on your knowing that you are not dreaming that *p*.

And a Gettieristic sceptic can reason analogously, as follows, for G1.

If you were Gettiered in your belief that *p* (for any *p*), you would not know that *p*. So, until you know that you are not being Gettiered in your belief that *p*, your being Gettiered in believing that *p* (and hence your not knowing that *p*) is compatible with all of your justification for *p*. For all that you would be justified in believing to the contrary, therefore, you would be Gettiered – and hence you would not know that *p*. What knowledge (if any) you do have thus fails to rule out your not knowing that *p*. So, G1 is true: your knowing that *p* depends on your knowing that you are not being Gettiered in believing that *p*.

Once again, I am not arguing that these pieces of reasoning should be accepted. All I am saying is that if one of them clearly can have a sceptical role, both can. And sceptics do routinely present the dreaming argument as one of their own. By analogy, therefore, since D1 is part of a clearly sceptical argument, G1 can be part of an equally sceptical argument. So far, there is reason to think that Gettier cases can be used sceptically.

Naturally, I am aware that epistemologists never do argue for G1. But this reflects nothing more than their not having realised that Gettier cases can be used by epistemologists of a sceptical bent. (They have not argued against G1, either.) I aim to correct that general oversight.[3]

4.4 Being unknowingly Gettiered

Next, we will find that a Gettieristic sceptic could motivate (G)'s second premise, G2, in a way that is perfectly analogous to how a Cartesian sceptic thinks. Specifically, a Gettieristic sceptic can motivate G2 in a way that is, *mutatis mutandis*, just like the way in which a Cartesian sceptic motivates the more standard D2.

In arguing for D2, the Cartesian sceptic reasons along the following lines.

Let *e* be any evidence which supposedly contributes to your knowing that you are not dreaming that *p* (for any external world proposition *p*). This evidence is either (i) evidence for the proposition that you are not dreaming that *p*, or (ii) fresh evidence for *p* itself. In either event, *e* is meant to strengthen your case for *p*. But *e* is an external world proposition itself. Hence, *your belief in e is as susceptible to a dreaming worry as was your belief in p*. Hence, until you dispose of the dreaming worry in some other way, it remains a worry. That is, no external world evidence *e* can eliminate the worry – and external world evidence is the only relevant kind in this case. (For all that *e* can prove to the contrary, you are dreaming that *p*. You could even be dreaming that *e*.) Thus, D2 is true: because the dreaming worry is ineliminable by any evidence *e*, you never know that you are not dreaming. (No amount of justification can overcome the dreaming worry. The justification could be being dreamt!)

And a Gettieristic sceptic can reason analogously for G2, as follows.

> Let *e* be any evidence which supposedly contributes to your knowing that you are not being Gettiered in believing that *p* (for any proposition *p*). This evidence is either (i) evidence for the proposition that you are not being Gettiered in believing that *p*, or (ii) fresh evidence for *p* itself. In either event, *e* is meant to strengthen your case for *p*. But your belief in *e* is as susceptible to a Gettier worry as was your belief in *p*. So, until you dispose of the Gettier worry in some other way, it remains a worry. That is, no evidence, *e*, can eliminate the worry. (For all that *e* can prove to the contrary, you are being Gettiered in believing that *p*. You could even be Gettiered in your believing that *e*. After all, won't *e* be putative knowledge itself? Yet the Gettier issue is being supposed to be a worry for any putative knowledge. So, the worry also applies to *e*.) Thus, G2 is true: because the Gettier worry is ineliminable by any evidence *e*, you never know that you are not being Gettiered. (No amount of justification can overcome the Gettier worry. The justification could be being Gettiered!)

What generates D2 is the idea that any relevant evidence, *e*, for an external world proposition, *p*, is external world evidence itself (e.g. for your not dreaming – perhaps because you are not asleep) – but that any apparent sensing of the external world could be part of a Cartesian dream itself. Cartesian sceptics posit one simple, distinctive, mechanism (dreaming) – applying to one kind of belief (external world belief).

Things are not quite so simple for the Gettieristic sceptic. Being Gettiered is seemingly a more complicated phenomenon than is dreaming. Correlatively, there is no one kind of belief that is supposedly susceptible to the Gettier worry. Does this apparent disanalogy with D2 weaken the argument for G2?

Not at all; if anything, it strengthens that argument. The objection concedes that Gettier cases can arise for any kind of belief. Not only justified and true empirical beliefs can be Gettiered; justified and true *a priori* ones can be Gettiered, too. Maybe we cannot specify (in any generally agreed-on detail) one simple form which each Gettier case will take. But this limitation need not deter a Gettieristic sceptic. For he need only call on the vast range of Gettier cases that have already appeared in post-Gettier epistemology – different cases applying to different approaches to knowledge. There is no obvious reason to assume that the supply will suddenly end – and that there are cases in which evidence is used that could not be Gettiered itself. Isn't it always possible to imagine a given belief being Gettiered?

Our calling on that wide range of different Gettier situations might seem, though, to make the Gettier worry more cumbersome and less elegant than the dreaming worry. The Gettier worry directs us to a large, comparatively heterogeneous, body of problem cases; the dreaming worry keeps on using one simple kind of worry. But is that a *failing* of Gettieristic scepticism, as against Cartesian scepticism? (Is a sceptical claim more likely to be true if it is simple?) Can't we look at this issue in another light? Can't we say, instead, that Gettieristic scepticism's calling on such a wide range of cases might make G2 *more* worrying than D2? For it suggests that G2, unlike D2, can be true in many different ways. D2 is true (when it is) because of your inability to know that you are not dreaming – whereas in principle there is no end to the number of ways in which you might be Gettiered. (Analysis after analysis of what is problematic in the structure of various Gettier cases has run afoul of new Gettier cases with new structures, each one designed to undermine the new analysis in particular.) Isn't such a foe harder to guard against than one who always employs the same tactic?

In another form, then, here are the arguments for D2 and G2.

For D2. Do you know that you are not dreaming that p (for any external world proposition p)? No, you do not. For you could know it only by way, in part, of some external world evidence (more generally, some external world justification) – call it e. But e could be being dreamt. Until you know that you are not dreaming that e, you do not know that e – and hence you do not know that p. But you know that e, only by way (in part) of some further external world evidence – call it e^*. And e^* could be being dreamt. Until you know that you are not dreaming that e^*, you do not know that e^* – and hence you do not know that e (in which case, you do not know that p). But you know that e^*, only by way of … and so on. Our dreaming worry was initially applied to p in particular, but p was meant to be representative of all external world beliefs: the dreaming worry was applying, via the example of p, to any external world belief. Yet e, e^*, etc. – external world beliefs or claims themselves – are being asked to save p from the worry. And, given the worry's stated scope, this is something they cannot do. For the worry applies to them even *when* they are purporting to remove it from p. They therefore fail to render the (external world) belief that p a case of (external world) knowledge that p.

For G2. Do you know that you are not being Gettiered in your belief that p (for any proposition p)? No, you do not. For you could know it only by way, in part, of some evidence (more generally, some justification) – call it e. But e could be being Gettiered. Until you know that you are not being Gettiered in believing that e, you do not know that e – and hence you do not know that p. But you know that e, only by way (in part) of some further evidence – call it e^*. And e^* could be being Gettiered. Until you know that you are not being Gettiered in believing that e^*, you do not know that e^* – and hence you do not know that e (in which case, you do not know that p). But you know that e^*, only by way of … and so on. Our Gettier worry was initially applied to p in particular, but p was meant to be representative of all beliefs: the Gettier worry was applying, via the example of p, to any belief. Yet e, e^*, etc. – beliefs or claims themselves – are being asked to save p from the worry. And, given the worry's stated scope, this is something they cannot do. For the worry applies to them even *when* they are purporting to remove it from p. They therefore fail to render the belief that p a case of knowledge that p.

I conclude that if D2 is part of a sceptical argument, G2 is part of an equally sceptical argument. We have even more reason than before to think that Gettier cases can be put to sceptical use. D2, whether plausible or not, plays a key role in standard Cartesian sceptical reasoning. It is now apparent that an analogous claim is true of G2. Whether plausible or not, it plays a role in Gettieristic sceptical reasoning. (As ever, the fact that at present, so far as I am aware, there are no admitted Gettieristic sceptics is irrelevant to this point. The dearth of such sceptics is due only to epistemologists having overlooked the sceptical potential of Gettier cases. After all, it is not as if epistemologists discuss and reject Gettieristic scepticism, either. They have simply been unaware of the possible sceptical uses for Gettier cases.)[4]

4.5 Cartesian dreams and being unknowingly Gettiered

There is another way, too, in which we might argue for a parallelism between premises D2 and G2. For (as I will explain) being Gettiered shares with Cartesian dreaming a special way of being self-insulating.

To see this, we should first notice that you can never have evidence *for* being in a Cartesian slumber, dreaming wholly lifelike dreams. Evidence for dreaming (in any standard sense of 'dreaming') is never evidence for *Cartesian* dreaming. Your having evidence that you are dreaming is your having evidence that you are not really in the kind of sensory contact with the external world that you seem to be enjoying. Yet in a Cartesian dream – a dream of the kind considered by Descartes – you have no idea at all that you are not really sensing the world, and that your state is really one of dreaming. A Cartesian dream fools you good and proper as to its presence (at least at the time).

Being Gettiered fools you like that, too. Consider this representative Gettier case, from Chisholm (1989: 93). You are standing outside a field, and the animal inside the fence looks exactly like a sheep. So, you justifiedly believe that it is a sheep. From that belief, you validly infer another belief – that there is a sheep in the field. (Call this your *target* belief.) And there is a sheep in the field – but it is not the animal in front of you. The latter animal is a dog. Not all is lost, though: since there is a sheep in the field (elsewhere, out of sight), your target belief is true. Apparently, too, it is justified (via your original use of your senses to justify your belief that the animal in front of you in the field is a sheep, plus your deducing the target belief from that one). But is your target belief knowledge? Surely not: you do not know that there is a sheep in the field. Something has gone wrong: you are Gettiered.

And – crucially, in the view of the Gettieristic sceptic – you do not know this at the time. For you do not believe at the time that you are being Gettiered, and you have no evidence at the time for your being Gettiered. Nor is it clear how you could have any such evidence. What form would such evidence take? Presumably, at the very least, it would be your believing that the animal in front of you is not a sheep. By hypothesis, though, your senses are misleading you about this, giving you no hint that the animal is not a sheep. Indeed, this deception is crucial to your being Gettiered – to your ultimately not knowing that there is a sheep in the field. So, it seems, if you have *evidence* for being Gettiered (in a given way), you thereby fail to *be* Gettiered (in that way). Why is that? It is because for you to be given a sign that the animal in front of you is not a sheep is for you to lose the justification you formerly had (for the animal's being a sheep). (Your justification would be defeated by that sign: your sensory evidence for the animal's being a sheep is now compromised by this sign – whatever it is – that the animal is not really a sheep.) And, in that event, your target belief would no longer be justified as it was before – in the way which made it Gettiered. In short, you would no longer be Gettiered (in the way in which, supposedly, you were being Gettiered).

Interestingly, however, this implies that any evidence you might ever have for your being Gettiered (in a given way) is misleading. For it entails that, by your having such evidence, your circumstances change in such a way that no longer would you *be* Gettiered (in that way). To have evidence for being Gettiered by a given aspect of your circumstances, then, is to *not* be misled by that aspect – in which case, you are not being Gettiered by it. Thus, it seems your having evidence for being Gettiered is never part of your knowing that you are being Gettiered. For (as I have just explained) if you have *evidence* for being Gettiered (in a given way), it is not *true* that you are being Gettiered (in that way). The truth condition on your knowing that you are being Gettiered, and the justification condition on such knowledge, can never be jointly satisfied. You never know that you are being Gettiered.[5]

But what (you might ask) is worrying about not being able to know that you *are* in a Cartesian dream, or that you *are* being Gettiered? After all, might not these lacks of knowledge be due to your always knowing that you are *not* dreaming, or that you are *not* being Gettiered? Might not those lacks of knowledge just show (even by the sceptic's own standards) that D2 and G2 are not true? I think the Gettieristic sceptic would reply to that question in the following way.

Your inability to know that you are being Gettiered *is* a problem. For (whether or not there are times when you think that you have been dreaming in a Cartesian way) presumably there are times when people think that they have been Gettiered (or would think this, were they aware of the concept of being Gettiered). I, for one, have had a few such experiences. I believe, therefore, that there have been times when I did not know that I was not being Gettiered. (Because knowledge entails truth, at no time can I know that I am not being Gettiered, if I am being Gettiered at that time.) And now the sceptical worry gathers strength. If people are sometimes Gettiered, they do not always know that they are not being Gettiered. At best, they sometimes know it. But wouldn't such knowledge involve having evidence for one's not being Gettiered? Yet if (as I have just argued) no one can have evidence for being Gettiered (when they are being Gettiered), how good can a person's evidence be for her not being Gettiered? Naturally, it always seems to her, at the time, that she is not being Gettiered. Yet this appearance can be misleading: people are sometimes Gettiered (and, I have argued, they are never simultaneously aware of it). Hence, the appearance of not being Gettiered is no more to be relied on than is the appearance of not being stuck in a Cartesian dream. Of course it never seems to you, at the time, that you are merely dreaming (in a Cartesian way) or that you are being Gettiered. (Dreaming in a Cartesian way and being Gettiered are states of affairs that are epistemically *hidden* from you at the time.) To rely on how things seem to you is, therefore, to rely on inadequate evidence – inadequate against such self-insulating possibilities as Descartes's and Gettier's.

On this issue, appearances are inherently one-sided evidence. How, then, can its seeming to you that you are not being Gettiered be good evidence for your not being Gettiered? The justification provided by (1) for (2) is no better, and no worse, than that which (3) provides for (4):

(1) It seems to me that I am not dreaming (in a Cartesian way).
(2) I am not dreaming (in a Cartesian way).
(3) It seems to me that I am not being Gettiered.
(4) I am not being Gettiered.

I conclude, as before, that if D2 is part of the dreaming argument then G2 is part of an equally sceptical argument.

4.6 Disanalogies between Cartesian sceptics and Getteristic arguments?

The previous sections stressed analogies between the Cartesian dreaming argument, (D), and the Getteristic argument, (G). G1 and G2 parallel D1 and D2, respectively. And G3 is, if anything, even more sceptical than D3: it denies us all knowledge, not only external world knowledge. Are there any important disanalogies between (G) and (D), though? In this section, I consider four possible ones.[6]

(1) When a Cartesian sceptic asks whether you know that you are not dreaming, don't we have an intuitive sense of the kind of phenomenon (namely, dreaming) which he is describing? Cartesian dreaming can be thought of as a way of 'summing up' (and perhaps idealising) the many ways in which a person can be deceived about the external world (that is, via standard perceptual error, standard illusion, standard dreaming, hallucination). Can we say something similar about the phenomenon of being Gettiered? Seemingly, we cannot. There is no agreement among epistemologists as to the existence of a simple phenomenon underlying all cases in which a person is Gettiered. No one has reduced the idea of being Gettiered to a more intuitive notion; at any rate, epistemologists in general do not accept that anyone has yet done so.

Still, this might be a merely temporary disanalogy. There have been many attempts to understand why there is a lack of knowledge in Gettier cases; maybe the successful attempt is just around the corner! Can't sceptics watch these efforts with interest, happily awaiting a simple distillation of the underlying Gettier problem? If one does ever eventuate, sceptics will then be able to replace (G) with a more engaging and intuitive argument.

For instance, suppose that to be Gettiered is to have a justified true belief which is based on at least one importantly false piece of evidence. Then (G) is equivalent to (G*).

(G*) 1. You know that *p*, only if you know that your belief that *p* is not based on some importantly false piece of evidence.
2. But you never know that your belief that *p* is not based on some importantly false piece of evidence.
3. So, you never know that *p*. [from 1 and 2]

(2) Whatever else it is, a Gettiered belief is justified. (Although true and justified, it fails to be knowledge.) Can that much be said for an external world belief which is present because you are dreaming its being true? Or is any such belief not even justified, let alone knowledge? If a dreamt (external world) belief fails to even be justified, though, how can being Gettiered be as sceptical a phenomenon as Cartesian dreaming? Isn't there a significant disanalogy between how epistemically threatening the two phenomena are?

But this difference (if it exists) is irrelevant to whether (D) and (G) are equally sceptical as regards *knowledge*. It shows, at most, that they do not argue in the same *way* for their respective knowledge-denials. They do not both deny you knowledge by denying you justification. One does; the other does not. Yet each denies you knowledge.

In any event, I do not think that it is so clear that in Gettier cases there is, while in Cartesian dreaming cases there is not, justification present. It is true that in Gettier cases there is justification present. But it is not clear that the amount which is present is much (if any) more than is present in a Cartesian dreaming case.

Thus, it is quite common for epistemologists to claim that a Gettiered belief, although justified, is not justified enough – not justified enough to be knowledge. Defeasability theorists, for example, say that a Gettiered belief is only defeasibly justified. And infallibilists think that Gettier cases arise only when we allow knowledge to be a less than conclusively justified true belief.

It is possible to interpret the dreaming case similarly. We could say that even if you are in a Cartesian sleep, the external world beliefs which you are having in your (Cartesian) dreams are justified. In spite of not being justified enough to be knowledge, they might be justified in a weaker sense. For instance, we could follow Alvin Goldman (1988) on evil demon scepticism. We might say that if you are dreaming in the way Descartes describes, your beliefs are justified in a weak sense, but not in a strong sense. The strong sense is that which is appropriate to having knowledge; the weak sense is a kind of justification that you have for a given belief when you at least think that you have justification in the strong sense. By lacking strong justification but possessing weak justification, you would lack knowledge – but not all (kinds of) justification.

(3) Whatever else it is, a Gettiered belief is true. Can that much be said for an external world belief which is present because you are dreaming its being true? Or is no such belief true, let alone knowledge? If a dreamt belief fails to be true, though, how can being Gettiered be as sceptical a phenomenon as Cartesian dreaming? The Cartesian sceptical worry is a way of doubting that, for all you know to the contrary, your belief that *p* is *true* – and the Gettieristic sceptical worry is not like that, since any Gettiered belief is true, not false.

But this difference (if it exists) is irrelevant to whether (D) and (G) are equally sceptical as regards *knowledge*. It shows, at most, that they do not argue in the same *way* for their respective knowledge-denials. They do not both deny you knowledge by denying you truth. One does; the other does not. Yet each denies you knowledge.

Still (as I will now explain), I am not sure that there *is* even that difference between the cases.

(i) Although it is true that any Gettiered belief is true, dreamt beliefs, too, can be true. You can be dreaming that you are lying on a lawn, and you can be right about this: dreams can be veridical. Nevertheless, even when your dream is veridical it does not give you knowledge of lying on a lawn. The Cartesian argument is not necessarily contemplating your dreaming that *p*, for a *false p*. Its point is that, even if you have what you think is good sensory evidence for *p*, you lack knowledge that *p* – whether *or* not *p* is true.[7] (It would therefore be misleading to present (D) in terms of *merely* dreaming, rather than dreaming. To merely dream that *p* is to dream that *p*, where *p* is false. To ask you to know that you are not merely dreaming is to ask more than the Cartesian sceptic asks.)[8]

(ii) But does a disanalogy remain because *all* Gettiered beliefs are true, whereas not all dreamt beliefs are true (even if some are)? A Gettieristic sceptic tells us of a situation in which you gain a true belief; a Cartesian sceptic tells us of one in which you might, or might not, have a true belief. Does *this* make the Cartesian argument more sceptical than the Gettieristic argument? It does not – for two reasons.

(a) If your life was to be one Gettiered belief after another, it would be a sequence of true beliefs. Yet you would be no closer to ever having knowledge than you would be if your life was to be a procession of dreamt external world beliefs.

(b) Neither sceptic describes a given possibility (dreaming, or being Gettiered) merely in order to then point out that, if it were actual, you would lack knowledge. Rather, each relies on claiming that you do not *know* that the possibility is not actual. *This* – rather than the possibility as such – is the sceptical worry. But in that case it is not true (as suggested by the objection) that the Gettieristic worry does, while the Cartesian one does not, concede you a true belief. For your not knowing that you are not Gettiered does *not* entail your belief's being true.

Here is why that is so. A Gettiered belief is true; it is also justified; and it is whatever else, if anything, is required of a Gettiered belief. For short: it is true and justified and *X* (where *X* is whatever else – beyond truth and justification – makes a belief Gettiered). Therefore, your knowing that your belief is not Gettiered – your having the knowledge demanded of you by the Gettieristic sceptic's G1 – is your knowing that your belief is not (i) true and (ii) justified and (iii) *X*. Now, the Gettieristic sceptical worry – in G2 – is that you lack such knowledge. But that worry does *not* concede your belief's truth. In denying you knowledge that your belief is not true-and-justified-and-*X*, it denies you knowledge that your belief is not true *or* not justified *or* not *X*. This lack of knowledge, though, does not entail – and hence need not be due to – your knowing that your belief *is* true.[9] On the contrary: your belief could be false (hence not Gettiered at all) – yet, even so, you might not know that you are not Gettiered. Neither G1 nor G2, therefore, concedes you a true belief.[10]

So, Gettieristic scepticism is *like* Cartesian scepticism in that respect. Each can be seen as a way of doubting that, for all you know to the contrary, a given belief of yours is true. For, as we now see, your not knowing that your belief is not Gettiered – like your not knowing that you are not dreaming your belief – is consistent with the belief's being false. Hence, the suggested disanalogy is nonexistent.

(4) Interestingly, the parenthetical point made at the end of (3)(i) is sufficient to undermine recent attempts – by, for instance, Dretske (1970) and Nozick (1981: 204–8) – to criticise scepticism on the basis of its supposed reliance on a principle of closure under known entailment. Closure is false (they argue); yet sceptics rely on it (they also argue); hence, sceptical arguments are unsound (they conclude). That is what Dretske and Nozick say, at any rate. But I will argue that they are wrong – and, in so doing, I will dispel any worry that, because the Gettieristic argument does not rely on a closure principle (and the Cartesian argument does), there is an important disanalogy between the underlying structures of, and motivations for, Gettieristic scepticism and Cartesian scepticism.

Consider these propositions (as used by you):

p I am lying on a lawn.
d I am dreaming that I am lying on a lawn.
d^* I am merely dreaming that I am lying on a lawn. (That is, I am dreaming lying on a lawn, but my dream is false. For short: d-and-not-p.)
g I am Gettiered in believing that I am lying on a lawn.

On what grounds might someone say that closure is being presumed by a Cartesian sceptic? The sceptic asks whether you know that p. And, he speedily notices, p entails not-d^*. (After all, if you are lying on a lawn, it is false that you are dreaming of doing so, yet not doing so. Since d^* is d-and-not-p, p entails not-d^*.) So, if a Cartesian sceptic claims that knowledge-that-p entails knowledge-that-not-d^*, he calls on a closure principle. He assumes that you know of p's entailing not-d^*; and he infers, from this, that you know that p only if you know that not-d^*.

The Gettieristic argument (G) makes no analogous use of a closure principle. First, you cannot know that p entails not-g. This is because p does not entail not-g – as the following reasoning shows. (i) By contraposition, if p entails not-g, then g entails not-p. (ii) But, since any Gettiered belief is true, g entails p. (If you are Gettiered in thinking that you are lying on a lawn, it is true that you are lying on a lawn.) Hence, g does not entail not-p. (iii) By *modus tollens* from (i) and (ii), therefore, p does not entail not-g. Consequently, you cannot know that p *does* entail not-g. No Gettieristic sceptic, then, can motivate G1 – your needing to know that not-g, if you are to know that p – on the basis of your knowing that p entails not-g. You cannot have the latter knowledge, because p does not entail not-g. But the closure principle is applicable only if you do know that p entails not-g. Hence, the Gettieristic sceptic cannot be using a closure principle in motivating his sceptical argument, (G).

So, if the Cartesian premise D1 is motivated by a principle of closure under known entailment, the Gettieristic premise, G1, is either motivated differently to D1, or not motivated at all. Either way, (G) and (D) drift apart.

That is the argument, at any rate. If it succeeds, it might weaken my case for treating Gettieristic scepticism analogously to Cartesian scepticism.

But the argument does not succeed. It is unsound: it employs a false premise. As was explained in (3)(i), the Cartesian argument (D) turns on d, not d^*: D1 asks you to know that not-d, rather than not-d^*. And, as we also saw in (3)(i), p does not entail not-d. So, D1 asks you to know that not-d, in order to know that p – even though p does not entail not-d. D1 does not ask you to know that not-d^*, even though not-d^* is entailed by p. Hence, (D) does not covertly rely on a closure principle. There is no fact of p's entailing not-d for you to know – where that knowledge, in turn, would motivate the dependence of your knowing-that-p on your knowing-that-not-d.

(D) is thus *like* the Gettieristic argument (G). In each argument, your knowledge-that-p is said to depend on your knowing that some given proposition is false: D1 asks you to know that not-d, whereas G1 asks you to know that not-g. But in neither case is this requirement motivated by a recognition that p entails the given proposition (respectively, not-d or not-g) – let alone that you know of the entailment. For, just as p does not entail not-g, p does not entail not-d. Hence, neither argument springs from the idea that your knowing-that-p entails the absence of the respective sceptical worry – since in neither case *does p* entail that absence. Considerations of closure do not reveal a disanalogy between (G) and (D).

4.7 Concluding remarks

I have found no definite and significant disanalogies between the dreaming argument and the sceptical use of Gettier cases. I conclude that Gettieristic scepticism is every bit as legitimate a form of scepticism as Cartesian scepticism. This is not to say that I accept either of them, or that non-sceptical epistemologists who have not been swayed by Cartesian reasoning should embrace our newly identified kind of sceptical argument. I claim only that sceptics should welcome the Gettieristic argument, (G), at least as much as many of them have welcomed the Cartesian argument, (D).[11]

Notes

1   Elsewhere, I use Gettier cases to support a kind of scepticism – a higher-level scepticism about knowledge of what knowledge is – other than the one I discuss in this chapter (Hetherington 1992).
2   To be Gettiered is to be the hapless protagonist in a Gettier case. It is to have a justified true belief which is nevertheless not knowledge. It is to instantiate (*). (I presume a familiarity, on the part of readers, with Gettier cases.)
3   Consequently, it is beside the point to object (as has occurred) to my reasoning in any of the following three ways. 1. Since sceptical arguments are implausible, so is (G). Hence, we should ignore it. 2. Since we can defuse sceptical arguments easily enough, (G) poses no deep problem. Hence, we should ignore it. 3. Your knowing that p requires your not being Gettiered in believing that p, rather than your knowing that you are not being Gettiered in believing that p. Almost all epistemologists would accept the former requirement and reject the latter one. But G1 captures the latter requirement. Hence, it is either irrelevant or unacceptable.

These objections fail, for the following reasons. Objections 1 and 2 actually concede my main claim, which is that (regardless of what use non-sceptical epistemologists make of Gettier cases) sceptics can use Gettier cases quite happily. These objections concede this because they reject (G) in virtue of its being sceptical. And objection 3 concedes the significance of my main claim. For it reflects nothing deeper than the fact that epistemologists have not seen that Gettier cases admit of this non-standard use. Of course, most epistemologists would not see G1 as capturing any use which they have yet made of Gettier cases. But this is their failing, not G1's. Until now, epistemologists have noticed only the Al way of using such cases. They have overlooked the possibility of the G1 way of using the cases. (And even if G1 still seems implausible to non-sceptical epistemologists, what of it? Sceptical epistemologists should welcome G1 with open arms – and, in effect, this chapter is addressed only to sceptical epistemologists.)

4   I say 'uses', rather than 'use'. For Gettier cases can be used in at least two sceptical ways. They can be used in the way described so far, and in a way identified elsewhere (Hetherington 1992).

5   In any Gettier case concerning you, for example, there is *some* crucial fact, f, which, somehow or other, makes you Gettiered in your belief that p. (As a heuristic, we can think of f as being the most complete, or inclusive, fact which an ideal epistemologist, looking on at you and deciding that you are being Gettiered, would cite as making you Gettiered.) And at least part of how f makes you Gettiered is by your not being *aware* of f (and hence not including it in your evidence). If you were to be aware of f (and to include it in the evidence which you use in the situation), you would no longer have sufficient justification for your belief that p. At any rate, you would no longer be in the Gettier situation you were in. (But could there be more than one fact, each of which suffices to make you Gettiered – such that, even if you become aware of one of them, the remaining one or more still Gettiers you? Could there be an oversupply of Gettier facts? For my purposes, this possibility is irrelevant – which is why I am allowing f to be as complex (as complete and inclusive) as a full epistemological account of the given epistemic situation would require. What Gettiers you, for instance, is not just the animal's not being a sheep, but also the existence of the sheep elsewhere. For the former fact does not make your final belief true – and your final belief's being true is part of that belief's being Gettiered. So, in that case, let f be the conjunction of the animal's not being a sheep and the existence of the real sheep elsewhere in the field.

6   The first is a variant of a question raised in the previous section.

7   As Barry Stroud explains, dreaming that p – even when p is true – is enough to fuel the Cartesian worry (1984: 25–9). To dream that you are lying on a lawn is not to know that you are there – even if you are there!

8   Your *merely* dreaming that p is (i) your dreaming that p, plus (ii) p's being false. So, a sceptic who (in a revised version of D1) asks you to know that you are *not* merely dreaming that p is asking you to know (a) that you are not dreaming that p, or (b) that p is true. Now, it is trivially true that if you have knowledge of the second disjunct, (b), you have knowledge that p: if you know that p is true, you know that p. But, unlike knowledge of (a), knowledge of (b) is not *extra* knowledge which you need in order to know that p. It is therefore not part of the sceptic's demand. For he purports to specify some knowledge which you need *before* you can know that p. Obviously, it is pointless to require you to have knowledge that p before you have knowledge that p! No self-respecting sceptic makes that demand.

9   The general form of that non-entailment is as follows: not knowing that [not-p or not-q or not-r] does not entail knowing that p. Thus, in this specific case, your not knowing that your belief is [not true or not justified or not X] does not entail your knowing that the belief is true. (Perhaps it entails your not knowing that the belief is not true. But this does not entail your knowing that the belief is true.)

10 G2 will seem to do so, if we treat your not knowing that your belief is not Gettiered as equivalent to (i) your knowing that your belief is true and justified, plus (ii) your not knowing that your belief is not X (i.e. your not knowing that it lacks whatever further property, if any, is required of a Gettiered belief). But, given (i), that putative equivalence *concedes* that your belief is knowledge. (For it concedes that you know that your belief is true.) And, since this is clearly not what the Gettieristic sceptic aims to do, he will – quite consistently – deny that equivalence.

11 What I have called the Gettieristic sceptical reaction to Gettier cases is embodied in (G). But part of (G) – namely, G1 – is itself a supposedly necessary condition on knowledge. It makes knowing that one is not Gettiered necessary to knowing. Can a Gettieristic sceptic therefore claim that this condition on knowledge is (his candidate for) the elusive fourth condition on knowledge? If we add it to the standard three conditions (as follows), do we have a full account of knowledge?

> K You know that p if and only if (1) you believe that p, (2) your belief is true, (3) your belief is justified, and (4) you know that your belief is not Gettiered.

Of course, to any non-sceptical epistemologist, $K(4)$ will sound like a quite implausible requirement on knowing. But that is no reason for a sceptic to baulk at it. After all, since he does accept G1, part of the moral of Gettier cases (he will say) is that anything less than $K(4)$ leaves us with a false account of knowledge – one which allows that there *is* some knowledge. In the sceptic's view, I take it, a true account of knowledge might well be one that makes sceptical claims look tempting. And $K(4)$ does exactly that, since it renders epistemic regress imminent. It does this because, according to it, a given piece of knowledge is present only if a special further piece of knowledge is present. Keep applying that condition, and a regress will result, as I explained in the previous sections. (Notice that K is not a *reductive* definition or analysis of knowledge, since $K(4)$ mentions knowledge. But this does not entail that K is not extensionally adequate, or that K does not accurately capture what it is to know a *given p*. Perhaps it does entail, though, that there can be no reductive understanding of knowledge: if K is correct, and it is the best we can do as regards understanding knowledge, we cannot have a reductive understanding of knowledge. Well, the sceptic, at least, might not resist such an interpretation of his suggestions. And who knows? Maybe a sceptical interpretation of Gettier cases – such as is sketched in this chapter – is even the correct interpretation of them. Could that be why there has not yet been a clear-cut *non*-sceptical solution of them? Maybe epistemologists went wrong from the start, in reacting to Gettier cases non-sceptically!)

References

Chisholm, R.M. (1989), *Theory of Knowledge*, 3rd edn, Englewood Cliffs, NJ: Prentice-Hall.

Dretske, F.I. (1970), 'Epistemic Operators', *The Journal of Philosophy*, 67: 1007–23.

Gettier, E.L. (1963), 'Is Justified True Belief Knowledge?' *Analysis*, 23: 121–3.
Goldman, A.I. (1988), 'Strong and Weak Justification', *Philosophical Perspectives*, 2: 51–69.
Hetherington, S. (1992), 'Gettier and Scepticism', *Australasian Journal of Philosophy*, 70: 277–85.
Nozick, R. (1981), *Philosophical Explanations*, Cambridge, MA: Harvard University Press.
Stroud, B. (1984), *The Significance of Philosophical Scepticism*, Oxford: Clarendon Press.

5

Epistemic disaster averted

(1) Peter Klein and Ted Warfield (1994; 1996) have argued that epistemic coherence *per se* is not truth-conducive. Charles Cross (1999) agrees with them about that – while nevertheless showing why Laurence BonJour's (1985) coherentism evades their clutches. I will generalize that dimension of the debate, from coherentist justification in particular to all epistemic justification. Justification is nothing if not truth-conducive. And I will show that Cross's kind of reasoning undermines an extension of Klein and Warfield's argument, an extension which aims to establish that justification as such is not truth-conducive.

(2) Consider belief set B:[1]

{Dunnit had a motive for the murder, Witnesses claim to have seen Dunnit do it, A credible witness claims to have seen Dunnit two hundred miles from the scene of the crime at the time of the murder, Dunnit committed the murder}

Let B^* be this belief set:

$B \cup$ {Dunnit has an identical twin who was seen by the credible witness two hundred miles from the scene of the crime during the murder}

B^* is more coherent than B; yet $\text{Prob}(B^*) < \text{Prob}(B)$.[2] Hence, although one's replacing B with B^* increases the coherence of one's beliefs about the murder, this does not give one a set of beliefs whose conjunction is more likely to be true. Far from it: one would gain a set of beliefs whose conjunction is less likely to be true. Accordingly, increased coherence does not entail a greater likelihood of truth. Thus, coherence as such is not truth-conducive.

That is Klein and Warfield's argument. And Cross shows why it leaves BonJour's coherentism unscathed. For BonJour, the justifiedness of a set of beliefs is relativized to the coherence of the set and to the extent to which there is stability in the beliefs' joint portrayal of the world and to the existence of an agent who has had those beliefs and to how long she has had them. Some of these conditions are satisfiable to a greater or lesser degree; and (roughly) the more a belief set satisfies them, the more justified it is, on BonJour's theory. For any belief set E, let '$O(E, d)$' say that E satisfies BonJour's conditions to degree d. Then Klein and Warfield's argument succeeds against BonJour if, and only if, $\text{Prob}(B^* \mid O(B, d^*)) < \text{Prob}(B \mid O(B, d))$. For then, even if – in BonJour's sense of justification – B^* is more justified than B (i.e. even if $d^* > d$), to replace B with B^* is not to gain a set of beliefs whose conjunction is more likely to be true. Far from it: one would gain a set of beliefs whose conjunction is less likely to be true. Accordingly, increased justification – in BonJour's sense of justification – would not entail a greater likelihood of truth. BonJour-coherence would not be truth-conducive.

But we are not entitled to assume that $\text{Prob}(B^* \mid O(B^*, d^*)) < \text{Prob}(B \mid O(B, d))$. As Cross points out, the conditional probabilities of B^* and of B are being relativized by BonJour to potentially quite different backgrounds. Perhaps B^* has a more stable view than B does of the world, maybe B^* would survive longer than B as a belief set for the particular epistemic agent; and so on. So, it is possible that $\text{Prob}(B^* \mid O(B^*, d^*)) > \text{Prob}(B \mid O(B, d))$. Although $\text{Prob}(B^*) < \text{Prob}(B)$, this is not enough to entail that B^* is less likely to be true than B when truth-likelihood is assessed in relation to how well B^* and B (respectively) satisfy BonJour's coherentist conditions for justification. Hence, Klein and Warfield's argument is not sufficient to show that BonJour's kind of coherentist justification is not truth-conducive.

Of course, if truths of the form '$O(E, d)$' were necessarily true, Klein and Warfield's argument would be forceful against BonJour. For then it would be the case that $\text{Prob}(O(B^*, d^*)) = \text{Prob}(O(B, d)) = 1$. And if that was so, we would have this result: $\text{Prob}(B^*) = \text{Prob}(B^* \mid O(B^*, d^*)) < \text{Prob}(B) = \text{Prob}(O(B, d))$. But BonJour avoids that fate (as Cross explains), because instances of '$O(E, d)$' are contingent – in which case, instances of '$\text{Prob}(O(E, d))$' do not equal 1. Instances of '$O(E, d)$' are contingent because the existence of an actual epistemic agent who has the beliefs in the designated belief set is contingent (as is, *a fortiori*, the existence of an actual agent who has had those beliefs for some particular length of time and in some more or less stable way).

(3) Cross's defence of BonJour is even more instructive than he claims it to be. That is because Klein and Warfield's way of reasoning, if not defused, is even more widely applicable – and worrying – than they claim it to be. (This section generalizes their reasoning. Section (4) will extend Cross's argument, so as to defuse this section's generalisation of their reasoning.)

There are two cases to consider if we are to generalize Klein and Warfield's reasoning as I am suggesting can be done.

Case 1. Internalist justification. Consider belief set L:

{Mary claimed to see Mark's death occur, Sue saw a deed which she believed caused Mark's death}

Let L^* be this belief set:

$L \cup$ {Mary and Sue are reliable perceivers and reporters}

L provides good evidence for the belief, M, that Mark has died – and L^* provides even better evidence for M than L does. In other words, L provides good internalist justification for M – and L^* provides even better internalist justification for M than L does.[3] Even so, $\text{Prob}(L^*) < \text{Prob}(L)$. So, the better evidence is less likely to be true. Is it therefore *not* better evidence (i.e. not better internalist justification)? To infer that it is therefore not better evidence would be to overreact. We have no reason – other than why we assigned these probabilities – for thinking of L^* as being poorer evidence for M than L is. And this by itself does not seem to be a good reason for thinking of L^* as being poorer evidence for M than L is. On Klein and Warfield's way of reasoning, then, improving even good evidence – good internalist justification – does not make for a greater likelihood of truth in the evidence. Nor, therefore, does it make for a greater likelihood of truth once one adds the belief for which the evidence is evidence to the evidence: Prob(L^* & M) < Prob(L & M); that is, Prob($L^* \cup M$) < Prob($L \cup M$).[4] So, Klein and Warfield's view of coherence as not being truth-conducive seems to be readily generalizable to the conclusion that internalist justification as such is not truth-conducive.

Case 2. Externalist justification. We were able (in Case 1) to discuss internalist justification by talking about belief sets, because internalist justification is justification which is mentally accessed by (or is easily accessible to) the epistemic agent. But externalist justification includes some (one or more) features of the epistemic agent and her circumstances which are not so readily accessible to her. That is what distinguishes externalist from internalist justification (see fn. 3). Let $L+$, then, be a set that contains belief contents and at least one (externalist) fact. The fact in question will be that Mary and Sue are reliable perceivers and reporters – a fact whose content is the same as the belief content which was the difference between L^* and L. Accordingly, $L+$ is L^* – except that one specific belief content in L^* is a fact (not functioning as the content of a belief) in $L+$.[5] With that difference between L^* and $L+$ understood, though, it is clear that the rest of Case 1's reasoning about L^* is repeatable, *mutatis mutandis*, for $L+$. Thus, although L provides good justification for M, $L+$ provides even better justification for M than L does. It improves the justification in an externalist way, with an extra fact – external to the epistemic agent's perspective – contributing to her justification. Even so, Prob($L+$) < Prob(L). So, the better justification is less likely to be true. Is it therefore *not* better justification? To infer that it is therefore not better justification would be to overreact. We have no reason – other than why we assigned these probabilities – for thinking of $L+$ as being poorer justification for M than L is. And this by itself does not seem to be a good reason for thinking of $L+$ as being poorer justification for M than L is. On Klein and Warfield's way of reasoning, then, an externalist improvement in one's justification does not make for a greater likelihood of truth in the justification. Nor, therefore, does it make for a greater likelihood of truth once one adds the belief for which the justification is justification to the justification: Prob($L+$ & M) < Prob(L & M); that is, Prob($L+ \cup M$) < Prob($L \cup M$) (see fn. 4). So, Klein and Warfield's view of coherence as not being truth-conducive seems to be readily generalizable to the conclusion that externalist justification as such is not truth-conducive.[6]

But the conjunction of Cases 1 and 2 threatens us with epistemic disaster. If neither internalist justification nor externalist justification is truth-conducive, then justification as such is not truth-conducive. (All justification is either internalist or externalist.) And if justification as such is not truth-conducive, then radical sceptics are correct. The heart would have been plucked from the concept of epistemic justification. Yet each of Cases 1 and 2 flows from Klein and Warfield's way of reasoning about coherentism. Has that reasoning therefore sown the seeds of a fundamental epistemological challenge to perhaps the most central of all epistemic concepts?

(4) When generalized correlatively, Cross's defence of BonJour shows why Klein and Warfield's way of reasoning has not shown any such seeds.

First, let E be any belief set, or any set that contains beliefs (their contents) and at least one (externalist) fact; and let '$J(E, p, d)$' denote E's justifying a belief that p to degree d.[7] (For short: E d-justifies p.) We may leave the kind of justification unspecified.[8] More carefully: we may leave it unspecified except for requiring that the beliefs within E be an actual agent's beliefs. So, '$J(E, p, d)$' would say that there is an actual agent with the beliefs in E and that those beliefs – along with whatever else is in E – d-justify p. Accordingly, instances of '$J(E, p, d)$' are contingent.

This entails that Prob($J(L^*, M, d^*)$) ≠ 1 and that Prob($J(L, M, d)$) ≠ 1. And then, even though Prob($J(L^*$ & $M)$ < Prob(L & M), this does not entail that Prob(L^* & M | $J(L^*, M, d^*)$) < Prob(L & M | $J(L, M, d)$). Consequently, even though neither improved evidence in the abstract, nor the hypothetical adoption of that evidence along with the belief for which it is evidence, is truth-conducive, the actual adoption of that evidence and that belief – their adoption by an actual epistemic agent – does not thereby fail to be truth-conducive.

That is how Cross's kind of thinking applies to Case 1, the challenge to internalist justification. It undermines Case 2 similarly. Because '$J(L+, M, d+)$' is contingent, Prob($J(L+, M, d+)$) ≠ 1. So, even though Prob($L+$ & M) < Prob(L & M), this does not entail that Prob($L+$ & M | $J(L+, M, d+)$) < Prob(L & M | $J(L, M, d)$). Consequently, even though neither improved externalist justification as such, nor the hypothetical use of that justification to adopt the belief for which it is justification, is truth-conducive, the actual use of that justification, and the associated adoption of that belief, by an actual epistemic agent does not thereby fail to be truth-conducive.

What is common to these responses to Cases 1 and 2 is what grounded Cross's defence of BonJour. We need only conceive of justification as being truth-conducive in a way that is conditional on the *contingent* existence of those features of the epistemic agent and/or her beliefs and/or the world that are being claimed to make her belief justified. Doing so protects the generic concept of epistemic justification from the generalisation of Klein and Warfield's way of reasoning about coherence – from the accusation that it is not truth-conducive.

(5) That result entails this minimal moral about epistemic justification:

> Justification is truth-conducive only if being justified is not a necessary feature of whatever is justified. That is, only contingently present justification is truth-conducive. Hence, no conception of justification is adequate unless to satisfy it is to do so contingently – because only then is the conception of something that is truth-conducive.

This moral, although minimal, is substantive. Cross himself showed that Naive Coherence Theory fails this condition: It is because Naive Coherence Theory characterizes coherentist justification in purely logical terms that Klein and Warfield's original argument reveals it as not being truth-conducive. The moral also reinforces

Hilary Kornblith's (1980) well-known criticism of what he called the *arguments-on-paper* thesis about epistemic justification – a thesis that construes inferential justification *per se* as being simply a logical relation between premiss(es) and conclusion. That thesis fails our moral. Insofar as inferential justification is just a logical relationship, all instances of '$J(E, p, d)$' are necessarily true when true, and hence $\text{Prob}(L^* \,\&\, M \mid J(L^*, M, d^*)) = \text{Prob}(L^* \,\&\, M) < \text{Prob}(L \,\&\, M) = \text{Prob}(L \,\&\, M \mid J(L, M, d))$, just as $\text{Prob}(L+ \,\&\, M \mid J(L+, M, d+)) = \text{Prob}(L+ \,\&\, M) < \text{Prob}(L \,\&\, M) = \text{Prob}(L \,\&\, M \mid J(L, M, d))$ – in which case, once again, the generalisation of Klein and Warfield's argument shows that justification is not truth-conducive. And if justification is not truth-conducive, then it is not what we want it to be. Being contingently justified is thus a necessary condition of being justified in a truth-conducive way – and hence, we might plausibly say, of being justified at all.

A final thought: the moral might be even more substantive still, by revealing a fundamental flaw in all infallibilist conceptions of justification. Call a conception of justification *shallowly* infallibilist if it equates infallible justification with deductive justification:[9] the above demise of the arguments-on-paper thesis entails the demise, too, of the shallowly infallibilist conception of justification. Call a conception of justification *deeply* infallibilist if it equates infallible justification with deductive justification by necessary truths – justification whose existence is incompatible with the falsity of that which it justifies. If a belief is deeply infallibly justified, this is a necessary truth about it. Consequently, that justification for it is not truth-conducive. Ironically, therefore, no infallibilist justification is truth-conducive. The irony is due to the fact that at least part of whatever motivation there is for infallibilism is undoubtedly the aim to maximize truth-conduciveness. Yet, because justification is nothing if not truth-conducive, infallibilist justification is not really justification at all. Only fallibilist justification can be truth-conducive.[10]

Notes

1. Like Cross, I will use Merricks's (1995: 308) formulation of Klein and Warfield's example.
2. For any belief set E, $\text{Prob}(E)$ is the probability of the joint truth of E's members. Here, and elsewhere, I refer, with systematic ambiguity, to a belief set and to the conjunction of the contents of its members. (I will do likewise, too, when we encounter sets that contain beliefs and other facts.)
3. There are different formulations of the internalism/externalism distinction for epistemic justification. I will conform to those by BonJour (1992), Kim (1993), and Hetherington (1996: chs 14–15). If you like, think of my talk of externalist justification as being talk of justification which is not purely internalist – so that it has at least one component of which the epistemic subject is not, and could not easily be, aware.
4. If one has good evidence for a belief, and this is why one then adopts the belief, one should adopt the belief in that way only by retaining that evidence.
5. Hence, within L^* that content is playing an epistemically internalist role, whereas within $L+$ its role is epistemically externalist.

6   Case 2 could also be developed by letting L contain, not two belief contents (as it does at present within the case), but one belief content and one fact. ($L+$ would still stand to this version of L – by adding the further fact about Mary and Sue to L's contents – as it does to L within the case as at present.) Then the improvement within the case would be by externalist justification to externalist justification, instead of just by externalist justification (as at present).

7   For simplicity, I assume that all justifiers are representable propositionally. That is an acceptable assumption in this setting, because I am responding to reasoning – Section (3)'s generalisation of Klein and Warfield's – which itself uses that assumption.

8   Coherentist justification would be just one instance. It would be a special instance, too – in which p is the belief whose content is the conjunction of all of E's members. This is because, in coherentist justification, the belief set's members, taken as a group, justify themselves.

9   This is probably the usual form taken by infallibilism: see, for example, Feldman (1981: 266) and Cohen (1988: 91).

10 I am grateful to Chuck Cross for some clarificatory and constructive and corrective correspondence about both his paper and mine.

References

BonJour, L. (1985), *The Structure of Empirical Knowledge*, Cambridge, MA: Harvard University Press.

BonJour, L. (1992), 'Externalism/Internalism', in J. Dancy and E. Sosa (eds), *A Companion to Epistemology*, Oxford: Blackwell.

Cohen, S. (1988), 'How to Be a Fallibilist', in J. Tomberlin (ed.), *Philosophical Perspectives*, 2: 91–123, Atascadero, CA: Ridgeview Publishing Company.

Cross, C.B. (1999), 'Coherence and Truth Conducive Justification', *Analysis*, 59: 186–93.

Feldman, R. (1981), 'Fallibilism and Knowing that One Knows', *The Philosophical Review*, 90: 266–82.

Hetherington, S. (1996), *Knowledge Puzzles*, Boulder, CO: Westview Press.

Kim, K. (1993), 'Internalism and Externalism in Epistemology', *American Philosophical Quarterly*, 30: 303–16.

Klein, P. and Warfield, T.A. (1994), 'What Price Coherence?' *Analysis*, 54: 129–32.

Klein, P. and Warfield, T.A. (1996), 'No Help for the Coherentist', *Analysis*, 56: 118–21.

Kornblith, H. (1980), 'Beyond Foundationalism and the Coherence Theory', *The Journal of Philosophy*, 77: 597–612.

Merricks, T. (1995), 'On Behalf of the Coherentist', *Analysis*, 55: 306–9.

6

Knowing failably and knowing imperfectly

6.1 Knowing failably

Almost all epistemologists are non-sceptics: they accept that people have knowledge. Almost all epistemologists say, too, that most – maybe all – human knowledge is fallible. But what is it for an instance of knowing to be fallible? The usual answer will be something like this:

> FalK. One's knowledge that p is fallible, if and only if (1) one knows that p but (2) one's justification for one's belief that p is compatible with one's being mistaken in believing that p.[1]

Yet this is not a wholly satisfactory characterisation. No belief in a necessary truth can be mistaken – because no necessary truth can be false. So, FalK entails that no such belief could be fallible knowledge; and that seems like a mistaken result itself. One's justification for a belief in a necessary truth could be less-than-perfect, and this should make the belief fallible knowledge at best – even though this justification is incompatible with the belief being mistaken. Should we therefore broaden FalK, so that a piece of knowledge that p can be fallible because of something *other* than p's possible falsity (in some pertinent sense of 'possible')?

In my experience, epistemologists will be reluctant to do that. Fallibility (they will say) is definitionally tied to a possibility of being mistaken. The problem with that reluctance to seek a broader analysis of fallible knowledge, however, is that it can prevent our noticing a more general kind of epistemic failing – in fact, the kind of failing that underlies the traditional concept of knowing fallibly. Were it not for that reluctance, I would be happy to extend the term 'fallible knowledge' to this more general kind of failing. Given that reluctance, however, I shall call this more general phenomenon *epistemic failability* – a way of knowing which generates what I call *failable knowledge*. And it will be the subject of this chapter.[2]

(A) The underlying motivation for the usual epistemological analysis of what it is to know fallibly is clear. The motivation is the fact that possible falsity is a possible lack of knowledge. Because knowledge is of only what is true, a given p's being false entails that no one knows that p. So, any belief that p (for that given p) could have *failed* to be knowledge – even when, in fact, it *is* knowledge.

With that observation, though, we are already on our way to a broader, hence more widely applicable, conception of knowing-in-a-less-than-ideal-way than is provided by the usual conception of failible knowing. Instead of restricting ourselves to an analysis of fallible knowing, we should focus on this more general idea:

FailK1. One's knowledge that p is failable, if and only if (1) one knows that p but (2) one might have failed to do so.

Knowing *failably* thus entails possibly not knowing. And knowing *fallibly* entails knowing failably: if one's belief that p is knowledge yet it could be mistaken, then it is knowledge which could fail to be knowledge, and hence it is knowledge which might not have been knowledge. I shall accept FailK1 as a minimal – formal, generic, schematic – condition to be satisfied by any more specific account of failable knowing.

(B) In order to find a more specific instantiation of FailK1, we need only describe the various routes to a possible lack of knowledge (the possible lack referred to by FailK1(2)). Possible falsity is one of them, but there are also other ways possibly to lack a piece of knowledge. Let us assume that knowing involves having at least a well-justified true belief that p. That being so, one lacks knowledge that p if p is false, or if one does not believe that p, or if one lacks good justification for the belief that p. Consequently, there are at least the following three examples of ways in which one might not have known that p.

(i) It could be the case that one's evidence for p is good, but not so good as to be incompatible with p's being false. In that event, p might not have been true, even if it is true and even if the evidence for its truth is itself true. This is a way for knowing to be failable due to one's relying on non-deductive justification – that is, due to the knowing's being fallible.
(ii) It could be the case that one believes that p, but not so confidently or firmly that one might not have decided not to have that belief, even though the belief is true and even if in fact the belief is produced in response to one's good evidence for its truth. This is a way for knowing to be failable due to one's belief being present in too fragile a way, let us say.
(iii) It could be the case that even though one has good evidence for one's true belief that p and even though one does base one's belief that p upon that evidence, one might have had that true belief anyway, even without that evidence for it. This is a way for knowing to be failable due to one's belief being present in too dogmatic a way, let us say.

Each of (i)–(iii) describes a *minimal* possible way to fail to know that p. Each is minimal because each describes one's lacking just one of the three features described so far as being required for knowing. In (i), truth is absent (p is false), while the belief that p and good justification for that belief are present. In (ii), the belief that p is absent, while p is true and one has good justification for that belief. And in (iii), one lacks good justification for the belief that p, while having a true belief that p.

Of course, one's knowing on a given occasion would also be absent if one lacked even more than just one of those three features (and of any other features that knowledge requires, if there are any); sub-section (D) will discuss that kind of situation. But our first need here is for a *core* conception of knowing failably. That is why I have outlined some minimal possible ways to fail to know that *p*. What will soon prove to be a useful heuristic with which to sum up the core analysis I am about to present, then, is this: to know failably that *p* is to know that *p* even while coming at least a little close to not knowing that *p*. More formally:

FailK2. A person *x* knows failably that *p*, if and only if (1) *x* knows that *p*, and (2) there is an accessible possible world where (i) *p* is false (but *x* believes that *p*, with the same good evidence for *p* as he has here), or (ii) *x* fails to believe that *p* (even though *p* is true and he has the same good evidence for *p* as he has here), or (iii) *x* fails to have the same good evidence for *p* as he has here (but he still believes that *p*, and *p* is true).[3] (And an accessible possible world, as regards *x*'s knowing that *p* in this world, is a world which contains at least two members of this set: {*p*'s being true, *x*'s believing that *p*, *x*'s having the same good evidence for *p* as he has in this world}.)[4]

FailK2 entails that for *x* to know infailably that *p* is for there to be not even a *possibility* of *x*'s lacking that knowledge. And FailK2 describes three minimal ways to instantiate that possibility. I shall refer to worlds containing those instantiations as being *epistemic-failure* worlds for *x* in relation to *p*.[5] Failable knowledge is knowledge for which there is a possible epistemic-failure world.

(C) Is my account of infailably knowing really an account of necessarily knowing? After all, the account begins with FailK1, which says that infailable knowing is knowing which is not such that it might not have existed. That is (it seems), one's infailably knowing that *p* is one's necessarily knowing that *p* – where one's necessarily knowing that *p* is either (i) in every possible world, one's knowing that *p*, or (ii) in every possible world where one exists, one's knowing that *p*.

In fact, FailK1 does not have that commitment. FailK1 has led to FailK2 – an account which describes infailable knowledge's infailability component in this way:

In each world where one exists and where one has two of the elements of knowing that *p*, one also has the third element.[6]

Necessarily, to be that close to knowing that *p* is to know that *p*; at least it is, when the knowing is infailable. That is what FailK2 implies – clearly, a weaker commitment than is involved in necessarily knowing.[7]

The usual analysis – FalK – of fallible knowledge that *p* describes it as being knowledge that *p* which could be absent via the truth that *p* being absent, even when the belief that p and the good justification for that belief are present. In my terms: it describes fallible knowledge that *p* as knowledge that *p* which is compatible with (i) being that close to knowing that *p*, yet (ii) still not knowing that *p*. I am generalizing that conception of fallible knowledge to obtain the concept of failable knowledge –

so that failable knowledge that p is knowledge that p which could be absent via any one of the truth that p, the belief that p, and the good justification for that belief being absent, even when the other two are present. Can a person be that close, in any of those respects, to knowing that p – yet without knowing that p? The distinctive feature of one's infailably knowing that is its being impossible for one not to know that p once one is so close to having the knowledge that p.

(D) Although infallibility is absolute, fallibility is not. It can be more or less. We talk of a person's being more, or his being less, failable, at any rate: he is more, or he is less, likely to be mistaken, even given his evidence. The same way of talking is appropriate for epistemic failability. A person can be more, or he can be less, epistemically failable: he is more, or he is less, likely to fail to know various facts. And can that qualitative or comparative dimension of epistemic failability be applied to a particular instance of knowing? Can one person know that p *more* failably than another person does? Can one know that p more failably today than yesterday?

That certainly can occur, at least in principle. If (as FailK2 tells us) x's knowing that p being infailable involves there being no epistemic-failure worlds for x in relation to p, then x's knowing that p being more, or its being less, failable involves (respectively) there being more, or there being fewer, and there being closer, or there being more distant, epistemic-failure worlds for x in relation to p. More fully:

> FailK3. A person x knows more, or x knows less, failably that p if and only if (1) x knows that p, and, respectively, (2) there are more, or there are fewer, and there are closer, or there are more distant, possible worlds where (i) p is false (but x believes that p, with the same good evidence for p as he has here), or (ii) x fails to believe that p (even though p is true and he has the same good evidence for p as he has here), or (iii) x fails to have the same good evidence for p as he has here (but he still believes that p, and p is true).

Exactly (or even approximately) how failable a particular piece of knowledge is will be a function of the pertinent epistemic-failure worlds, the worlds that satisfy clause (2) of FailK3. Correlatively, whether one piece of knowledge is more failable than another is also a function of those worlds. If x knows that p and knows that q, but there are more close epistemic-failure worlds for x in relation to p than in relation to q, then – other things being equal – x's knowledge that p is more failable than his knowledge that q.[8]

For example, right now I know failably that I am typing. I also know failably that 13 x 14 = 182. As far as I can tell, though, the former piece of knowledge is more failable than the latter one. In rather rough outline, here is why that is so.

(a) There are possible worlds where I am not typing even though I believe that I am and even though I have the same sensory evidence as I have here for my typing. (In those worlds, I am hallucinating, say.) There are worlds where I am typing and where I believe that I am, but where my evidence is not as it is here. (In those worlds, I am sensorily deprived, yet I remember intending to be typing now, say.) There are worlds where I am typing and where I have the same sensory evidence as here, but where I fail to believe that I am typing. (In those worlds, I distrust that evidence, say.) These are thus three kinds of epistemic-failure world for me in relation to the fact of my typing.

(b) There are possible worlds where I have the same mathematical evidence as here for the fact that 13 x 14 = 182, but where I fail to believe that 13 x 14 = 182. (In those worlds, my caution about such calculations prevents me from having that belief, say.) There are worlds where I have the belief without that evidence. (In those worlds, I remember being told that 13 x 14 = 182, say.) But there are no worlds where 13 x 14 ≠ 182.

All else being equal, then, there are more epistemic-failure worlds for me in relation to the fact of my typing than for me in relation to the fact that 13 x 14 = 182. I have distinguished between three kinds of epistemic-failure world. We could call them (in turn) *truth*-failure worlds, *belief*-failure worlds, and *justification*-failure worlds. For me in relation to the fact of my typing, there are truth-failure worlds, belief-failure worlds, and justification-failure worlds. For me in relation to the fact that 13 x 14 = 182, there are only belief-failure worlds and justification-failure worlds – no truth-failure worlds. Therefore, all else being equal, my knowledge of my typing is more failable than my knowledge that 13 x 14 = 182.[9]

6.2 Knowing failably and sceptical possibilities

Armed with Section 6.1's concept of knowing failably, let us now see how your not knowing that you are not dreaming can contribute to the failability of your knowing that you are seeing zebras – and hence is compatible with your having the latter knowledge. I will describe two ways in which this might occur.

(1) Suppose that you fail to know, in this world, that you are not dreaming; suppose that this is because, relying as you do on 'normal' evidence in support of your belief that you are seeing zebras, the thoughts that you might be, or that you might not be, dreaming never enter your mind. Still, we may also suppose, you are not so arrogant that, if the possibility of your dreaming were to be mentioned, you would never take it seriously. Accordingly, there are possible worlds where you do take it seriously, sufficiently so to include it in your evidence for and against – thus, your total evidence bearing on the truth-value of – your belief that you are seeing zebras. In some of those worlds, therefore, this state of affairs obtains:

> You are seeing zebras. And you believe that you are doing so, even though your evidence now includes the possibility that you are dreaming.

Such worlds are epistemic-failure worlds for you in relation to your seeing zebras. In each, you have a true belief that you are seeing zebras, but you do not have the same evidence as in this world. So, if in this world you know that you are seeing zebras, this is in part because of *how* you do not know that you are not dreaming. Nevertheless, by the same token, the way in which you do not know that you are not dreaming is part of how (as those epistemic-failure worlds signify) you might easily have had different evidence to that which you have; and if that had occurred, you would not have had the knowledge (of your seeing zebras) which in fact you have. The latter knowledge is thereby vulnerable to not having been present: if you know that you are seeing zebras, you do so only failably – in part because of how you lack the knowledge that you are not dreaming.

(2) Imagine this time that, although you have thought of the possibility that you are not dreaming, you dismiss it as unworthy of your attention. You concentrate on your 'normal' evidence instead, the result being your knowing that you are seeing zebras – along with your not knowing that you are not dreaming, if only because you refuse to think about whether you are dreaming. But there are worlds where you do not dismiss the dreaming possibility so peremptorily, and in some of them the following scenario is realized:

> You are seeing zebras, and you have the same evidence as in this world (including your being aware of the possibility that you are dreaming). Even so, you take the dreaming possibility seriously enough to suspend your belief that you are seeing zebras.

Such worlds are epistemic-failure worlds for you in relation to your seeing zebras. In each, you fail to believe that you are seeing zebras (although you are indeed seeing them and you have the same evidence as in this world). So, in this world you know only failably that you are seeing zebras – and this is *due* in part to your failing to know that you are not dreaming. Given what occurs in those epistemic-failure worlds,[10] if you had engaged with the dreaming possibility, you might well have lacked the knowledge that you are seeing zebras. So, if you know that you are seeing zebras, this is in part because of *how* you do not know that you are not dreaming. Nevertheless, by the same token, the way in which you do not know that you are not dreaming is part of how (as those epistemic-failure worlds signify) you might easily have failed to know that you are seeing zebras. The latter knowledge is thus vulnerable to not having been present: if you know that you are seeing zebras, you do so only failably – in part because of how you lack the knowledge that you are not dreaming.

Each of (1) and (2) reveals part of what we could call the modal texture – the modal aura – of your knowing that you are seeing zebras. If you lack the knowledge that you are not dreaming, this is compatible with your knowing that you are seeing zebras – because it need only contribute to the *failability* of the latter knowledge. And a piece of knowledge's being failable because of your not knowing that you are not dreaming is not its failing to be, *simpliciter*.

There is a further pertinent significance in that result. Insofar as your lacking the knowledge that you are not dreaming contributes to the failability of your knowledge that you are seeing zebras, it also contributes to the *epistemic quality* of the latter knowledge. Other things being equal, your knowledge that you are seeing zebras is *less good* – purely *qua* knowledge of seeing zebras – if you do not know that you are not dreaming, than it is if you do know that you are not dreaming.

There is thus an inverse correlation, all else being equal, between a piece of knowledge's epistemic quality and its failability. For instance (and all else still being equal), your knowledge that you are seeing zebras is less good *qua* knowledge of that fact, insofar as it is failable knowledge. If (with all else remaining equal) you were to know of your not dreaming, your knowledge that you are seeing zebras would be better in these two ways: your evidence for your seeing zebras would be that much more thorough; and your belief that you are seeing zebras would be that much less likely to waver, to fade away. These are modal facts about your knowledge within the particular situation. They are modal facts about key constituents of your knowing that you are seeing zebras. They contribute to the modal fact constituted by your knowledge's being failable – its being failable in whatever specific way(s) it is failable. And your not knowing that the sceptic's possibility in particular is not being actualized is part of that failability. Rather than entailing your not knowing that you are seeing zebras, therefore, your not knowing that the sceptic's possibility is not being actualized need be nothing more than part of *how* you know that you are seeing zebras. Admittedly, it becomes part of what makes that knowledge more vulnerable to not having been present. It contributes to your knowledge's potential for not having been present. But that vulnerability – that potential – is a modal aspect of the knowledge. So, even if we concede that you fail to know that you are not dreaming, we may still coherently claim that your knowledge that you are seeing zebras is being characterized, rather than destroyed, by your not knowing that you are not dreaming. Your knowledge of your seeing zebras is being characterized modally.

The point is that, in response to the sceptic's denying you the knowledge that you are seeing zebras, we may reply that, even if you do not know that the sceptic's possibility – your dreaming in the way Descartes discussed – is not being actualized, this need not be regarded as entailing anything more than that your knowledge of seeing zebras is failable if present. Your not knowing that you are not dreaming does not therefore entail that your knowledge of seeing zebras is not present – *a fortiori*, that it is not present because it would be failable if present. There is thus a logical gap in the sceptic's reasoning, one that may be filled by this conceptual possibility: specifically, we may interpret the sceptic's argument as reminding us of what can be a *feature of* our knowing, rather than as showing that there cannot *be* any knowledge on our part. So, even if we concede that you do not know that you are not dreaming, we may interpret this lack of knowledge just as helping to constitute the modal aura of your knowing that you are seeing zebras. There is logical space for this interpretation.

6.3 Imperfect knowledge

Section 6.2 tells us that various standard sceptical arguments are unsound. For example, D includes the false premise D1:

D
1. You know that you are seeing zebras, only if you know that you are not dreaming seeing zebras.
2. You do not know that you are not dreaming seeing zebras.
3. So, you do not know that you are seeing zebras.

In D1, a piece of comparatively everyday knowledge is said to depend on a further piece of knowledge. My basic objection to this is that the latter piece of knowledge is a necessary condition only of the former piece of knowledge's being *better* knowledge than it is – the knowledge's being improved as knowledge of the fact of which it is knowledge. Consequently, having the former piece of knowledge does not entail having the latter piece. The former piece of knowledge could be possessed less well than it would have been if the latter piece of knowledge had also been present. So, if there can be better or worse knowledge that *p*, we can have knowledge in spite of the sceptic's efforts.

Nevertheless (it might be replied), what if the other premise is true? What if D2 is true? Would it follow, from your not knowing that you are not dreaming seeing zebras, for instance, that you lack *very good* knowledge that you are seeing zebras? If it would, then we should reformulate the purported sceptic's reasoning to make explicit how he could argue soundly for *that* sort of limitation on our knowledge. He tried to argue for your lacking the knowledge *simpliciter*, and we have begun to see that his reasoning falls short of establishing soundly such a dire result. Still, can he show that, even if you have knowledge, it is never very good knowledge? Should the sceptic – insofar as he wishes to be reasoning soundly – replace his argument D with something like D^+?

D^+
1. You have very good knowledge that you are seeing zebras, only if you know that you are not dreaming seeing zebras.
2. You do not know that you are not dreaming seeing zebras.
3. So, you do not have very good knowledge that you are seeing zebras.

No, even D^+ is an unsound argument. Suppose that you have eliminated all alternatives to your seeing zebras – except for the possibility that you are dreaming seeing them. In such a case, it is fair to say, your knowledge that you are seeing zebras is actually very good. Certainly it is much better than what would standardly pass for very good such knowledge: in standard settings, you might manage to eliminate many alternatives – but you are unlikely to eliminate every alternative other than your dreaming looking at zebras. Accordingly, even the truth of D^+2 is compatible with your knowing very well that you are seeing zebras – hence with the falsity of D^+3. Even if we concede your not knowing that you are not dreaming seeing zebras, we are not committed to concluding that you lack very good knowledge of seeing zebras. Probably, if D^+2 is true, then D^+3 is true; even so, it might not be; so, D^+1 is false. D^+ is not a sound argument.

What does follow from D^+2, then? D^+1 is too restrictive: even very good knowledge that *p* is rarely tied to having some other specific piece of knowledge. Your lacking the specific knowledge that you are not dreaming seeing zebras is probably a sign that your knowledge of seeing zebras is not very good. But, as we have seen just now, the sceptic cannot be sure of your having the latter failing (given your having the former one). What he can be sure of is that if D^+2 is true, then your knowledge that you are seeing zebras is not as good as is (conceptually) *possible*. Perhaps it is good knowledge; definitely it is imperfect knowledge. That is the only limitation on your knowledge that the sceptic will definitely have revealed if he could establish D⁺2. Maybe he wanted and intended to establish something more remarkable; but he cannot do so via sound reasoning.

Consequently, the putative sceptic should replace D+ with D˙

D˙
1. Your knowledge that you are seeing zebras would be improved by, or be better for, your knowing that you are not dreaming seeing zebras.
2. You do not know that you are not dreaming seeing zebras.
3. So, even if you know that you are seeing zebras, this knowledge is not the best possible knowledge of seeing those zebras. At best, it is imperfect knowledge of that fact.

This chapter has suggested that D˙1 is true; and for argument's sake let us suppose D˙2 to be true. Then D˙3 will follow, because D˙1 and D˙2 jointly entail that in principle your knowledge that you are seeing zebras could be improved – and because the best possible knowledge of one's seeing zebras could not be improved, even in principle. At most, therefore, sceptical considerations soundly establish the *imperfection* of our knowledge.[11]

This is not to say that sceptics *seek* nothing stronger than that result. I have not assumed that their arguments begin by requiring certainty in knowing, for example (or, therefore, that they conclude only with a denial that anyone ever attains such certainty). D˙ characterizes sceptics only as being *able* to show – via sound reasoning – nothing more than that our knowledge is imperfect. D˙ did not begin by characterizing sceptics as consciously setting out to challenge at most the claim that we have perfect knowledge.

Of course, D˙ begins – in D˙1 – with a non-absolutist claim about knowledge; and we might object that no sceptic will accept D˙1 as a starting-point for her sceptical reasoning. Even if sceptics do not profess to be denying us only an infallibilist kind of knowledge, they do claim to be denying us an absolutist kind of knowledge. That is what people in general assume knowledge to be like (the sceptic will say); they are correct to do so (the sceptic will continue); and they are unable to have any such knowledge in the face of sceptical challenges (the sceptic will conclude).

But standard sceptical challenges to our knowing that *p* amount to demands that we improve our epistemic relationship to *p*; and these, I have argued, should be viewed as being demands – usually unreasonable ones – that we improve our knowledge that *p*. Upon analysis, therefore, we find that sceptical challenges rely upon a fundamental equivocation: They purport to threaten an epistemically absolutist conception of knowledge; yet they do so in a way that is ultimately appropriate only for an epistemically non-absolutist conception of knowledge.

So, scepticism should not seem so threatening to so many. Still, perhaps the fault belongs as much to non-sceptics as to sceptics: non-sceptics should not agree with sceptics that knowledge has to be absolute. In any event, the equivocation can be removed by discarding epistemic absolutism. And then – as D˙ shows, by revealing what the sceptic can derive soundly from a non-absolutist starting-point – the sceptical threat is removed. To discard epistemic absolutism is to discard an essential part of what makes sceptical challenges threatening. It also allows us to see that if sceptics nevertheless wish to return to the dialectical fray by accepting and working within an epistemically non-absolutist framework, and if they wish to do so via sound sceptical reasoning, then they will end up denying us only a perfectionist kind of knowledge (even if they retain a desire to end up with a stronger denial than that). They will end up with D˙3, not with D3. Being restricted in that way to D˙, the sceptic will show only that our knowledge is imperfect if present, rather than (as he was originally aiming to show) that our knowledge is not present.

Thus, there is a disparity between what sceptics strive to establish and what they can establish by way of sound reasoning. Consider those sceptics who reason in the way described by Thomas Nagel (1986). They deny that any of our 'ordinary or scientific beliefs about the world' can rationally be retained, and hence that any such beliefs constitute objective knowledge (1986: 68). That is, not even one of those beliefs is part of a body of knowledge of how the world is – where that body of knowledge includes the knowledge of how we are part of the world when having knowledge of how it is (1986: 70). This sceptical denial is said to be grounded in the following beguiling thinking, which arises as we seek an objective view of the world (1986: 68):

> However often we may try to step outside of ourselves, something will have to stay behind the lens, something in us will determine the resulting picture, and this will give grounds for doubt that we are really getting any closer to reality [...] The aim is to form a conception of reality which includes ourselves and our view of things among its objects, but it seems that whatever forms the conception will not be included by it. It seems to follow that the most objective view we can achieve will have to rest on an unexamined subjective base, and that since we can never abandon our own point of view, but can only alter it, the idea that we are coming closer to the reality outside it with each successive step has no foundation.

Although sceptics take comfort from such reasoning, they should not do so. In particular, they should not regard such reasoning as soundly grounding a denial of there being any objective knowledge. That would be an overreaction, symptomatic indeed of the epistemic absolutism underlying – and misshaping – the usual debates about this sort of case. Clearly there are different grades of the kind of objectivity Nagel has in mind: There can be 'advances in objectivity', as we 'subsume our former understanding under a new account of our mental relation to the world' (1986: 75). Accordingly, there can be better, or there can be worse, understanding, depending partly on whether one's understanding is more, or whether it is less, objective. And so an epistemic non-absolutist can embrace Nagel's picture of inquirers seeking greater objectivity in their view of the world and of themselves: one can improve one's objectivity, and thereby one's objective knowledge. But an epistemic absolutist has to view the perennially present possibility of improving one's understanding of various facts as entailing that, at any time, what seems to be objective understanding is not objective understanding; and scepticism flows swiftly from that interpretation. However, that bespeaks the falsity of the interpretation, rather than the inescapability of scepticism. Specifically, it reveals that we should not accept epistemic absolutism. After all, there are alternative – and plausible – interpretations available. Here is an anti-sceptical (and epistemically non-absolutist) moral that we may infer from Nagel's picture of inquirers seeking ever greater objectivity:

> At most, the sceptic's reasoning shows that our objective knowledge of the world will never be perfect. One manifestation of this lack of epistemic perfection is the fact that we will never attain a perspective giving us wholly objective knowledge. Even so, this does not entail that we never gain knowledge. It entails at most that we will be gaining knowledge that is less than wholly objective. It is therefore compatible with our gaining some knowledge which, although less than wholly objective, is nevertheless very objective.

Other things being equal, if one's knowledge that p is more, rather than less, objective, it is better knowledge that p. Nagel's view of the quest for objectivity highlights one more way in which no knowledge we will ever gain is perfect. We should not be led by our natural desire to gain objective knowledge into frustratedly inferring, from our inability ever to attain perfect objectivity, that we are unable to have any objective knowledge. Epistemic non-absolutism allows that objective knowledge can be better, or it can be worse, objective knowledge – partly because it can be more, or it can be less, objective.

Notes

1   See, for example, Cohen (1988: 91).
2   Philosophers use the term 'fallibilism' in two ways – to denote fallible knowledge, or to refer to human cognitive fallibility in general; see, for instance, Haack (1979) and Carrier (1993). I shall eschew the term 'fallibilism' and its cognates, as used in the second of these two ways. Instead, I shall be generalizing the *first* of those two ways.
3   Should clause (iii) be the following more sweeping condition instead?

> x fails to have good evidence for p (but he still believes that p, and that p is true).

I do not believe that it should be. I am discussing whether a particular piece of knowledge that p is failable. From FailK1, it is failable if it could be absent (while the person is still present); and a minimal way for it to be absent is for there to be an accessible possible world where the person's true belief that p is supported by different good evidence. For that is a world where at best the person has a different case of knowing that p. From FailK1, to know *in*failably on a given occasion is for that knowing – characterized by whatever features make it the instance of knowing it is – to be infailable. And the features that make it the instance of knowing it is include at least the particular belief it is, and that belief's being true, along with the particular good evidence for it. Hence, if there is to be identity of knowing across worlds, then at least the same belief and truth and good evidence are required in each such world. (But if you reject the transworld identity of knowing, you might replace clause (iii) with this note's suggested alternative. That would affect some subsequent parts of this chapter in detail but not principle.)

4   Any epistemic-failure world for x in relation to p is thus an accessible world as regards x's knowing that p. (Hence, when I talk below of epistemic-failure worlds, I shall not need to make explicit that they are accessible worlds. And because any world that satisfies one of (i)–(iii) in FailK2(2) is an epistemic-failure world for x in relation to p, it is also an accessible world, as regards x's knowing that p. (So, strictly, there was no need to say, as FailK2(2) does, that it is referring to accessible worlds.) But the converse implication fails because if x knows *infailably* that p then any world containing at least two members of the set {p's being true, x's believing that p, x's having the same good evidence for p as he has here} also contains the third member of the set. That is, if x knows infailably that p, then none of the pertinent accessible worlds is an epistemic-*failure* world for x in relation to p.

5   Implicit in this, too, is a relativisation to a particular time – a world being an epistemic-failure world for x in relation to p *at time t*. But, for simplicity and because no unclarity will result, I ignore this extra relativisation in what follows.

6   'Does knowing not have more than three elements – truth, belief, good justification, and something else? Did Gettier not teach us that?' Maybe not. See Chapters 12–14 for critical engagement with that question.

7   Haack presents dogmatism – the contradictory of what she calls fallibilism – as saying that 'there are some propositions which we can't fail to believe *and which* are such that it follows from our believing them that they are true' (1979: 52). Adapting that to our present concerns gives us this:

> x's knowing infallibly that p includes (i) x's believing that p in every world where x exists, and (ii) p's being true in every world where x believes that p.

That is, in every world where one exists, one has a true belief that p – this being so, for any p which one infallibly knows. My account of infailable knowing is less demanding than that account of infallibly knowing. I require that, if one is infailably to know that p, then each world where one exists *and* which includes at least two members of this set – {p's being true, one's believing that p, one's having good evidence for that belief} – also includes the third member.

8   Could x also know that p more failably on one occasion than on another? If so, would his more failable knowledge that p be less good, purely *qua* knowledge that p, than his less failable knowledge that p? The idea that propositional knowledge can admit of such qualitative gradations is rarely countenanced by epistemologists. I have accepted it elsewhere (Hetherington 1998); and I will expand on the idea soon, in the rest of this chapter. David Lewis (1996: 562–3) has also endorsed that idea.

9   And *is* all else equal? It seems to me that I am more likely not to be typing, even when I think that I am doing so, than I am to suspend my simple mathematical beliefs when I engage in apparently normal calculations. In other words, the truth-failure worlds for me in relation to the fact of my typings are closer possible worlds than are the belief-failure worlds for me in relation to the fact that 13 x 14 = 182. If so, then on this score, *too*, my knowledge of my typing is more failable than my knowledge that 13 x 14 = 182.

10 How close are those epistemic-failure worlds to this world? Lewis (1996), it seems, would regard them as being very close to it, given how readily he thinks one's paying even some attention to sceptical possibilities destroys one's knowledge. But surely it depends on the individual case. Some people are more suggestible than others, more likely to allow the mention of a sceptical possibility to affect their evidence and their

beliefs. Relative to them, these epistemic-failure worlds are close. Relative to someone less suggestible to sceptical possibilities, they are not so close.

11 We might usefully compare knowing a person and knowing a fact. Meeting a sceptic's standard for knowing a fact would be analogous to knowing a person *very well*. Now we see that your meeting the only standard which is such that the sceptic can argue soundly for your failing it would make your knowing a fact more like your knowing a person *perfectly*. And, just as perfect knowledge of a person is not required if you are to know him (even quite well), you need not satisfy a standard of epistemic perfection in relation to p if you are to know the fact that p (even quite well). If knowing a fact is like being friends with the fact, this section reveals why the sceptic can show, at least via sound reasoning, nothing more than that – like personal friendships, even good ones – no friendship with a fact is perfect.

References

Carrier, L.S. (1993), 'How to Define a Nonskeptical Fallibilism', *Philosophia*, 23: 361–72.
Chisholm, R.M. (1989), *Theory of Knowledge*, 3rd edn, Englewood Cliffs, NJ: Prentice-Hall.
Cohen, S. (1988), 'How to Be a Fallibilist', in J.E. Tomberlin (ed.), *Philosophical Perspectives*, 2: 91–123, Atascadero, CA: Ridgeview Publishing Company.
Gettier, E. (1963), 'Is Justified True Belief Knowledge?' *Analysis*, 23: 121–3.
Goldman, A.I. (1976), 'Discrimination and Perceptual Knowledge', *The Journal of Philosophy*, 73: 771–91.
Haack, S. (1979), 'Fallibilism and Necessity', *Synthese*, 41: 37–63.
Harman, G. (1973), *Thought*, Princeton: Princeton University Press.
Hetherington, S. (1996), 'Gettieristic Scepticism', *Australasian Journal of Philosophy*, 74: 83–97.
Hetherington, S. (1998), 'The Sceptic Is Absolutely Mistaken (As Is Dretske)', *Philosophical Papers*, 27: 29–43.
Hetherington, S. (2001), *Good Knowledge, Bad Knowledge: On Two Dogmas of Epistemology*, Oxford: Clarendon Press.
Lewis, D. (1996), 'Elusive Knowledge', *Australasian Journal of Philosophy*, 74: 549–67.
Nagel, T. (1986). *The View from Nowhere*, New York: Oxford University Press.
Sartwell, C. (1991), 'Knowledge Is Merely True Belief', *American Philosophical Quarterly*, 28: 157–65.
Sartwell, C. (1992), 'Why Knowledge Is Merely True Belief', *The Journal of Philosophy*, 89: 167–80.

7

Sceptical possibilities? No worries

I doubt that sceptical doubts – certainly those fashioned around putatively challenging possibilities – should be thought to deprive us of knowledge. In this chapter, I explain why this is so. My conclusion will not be that sceptical claims are false; truth or falsity will not be my direct concern. Rather, aspects of the *inferential power* of any would-be sceptical challenge will be my focus. I will describe a way in which would-be sceptical challenges are dialectically self-defeating.

7.1 Sceptical possibilities

Purely for illustrative purposes, I will focus upon paradigmatic sceptical denials of *external world* knowledge. These concede that we have experiences which strike us as being of a world beyond those experiences, while nonetheless denying us any correlative knowledge of the existence or nature of such a world. The physical world appears to you to be thus-and-so; do you know that it is really thus-and-so? After all, might not a particular appearance be *merely* an appearance – in short, misleading? This is a possibility. And sceptical reasoning could well insist that we need to know that it does not obtain. What price would we pay for lacking this knowledge? A drastic one: we could not use our knowledge of how, it seems to us, reality is, in order to know how, in reality, it is (in any respect other than its including our having experiences, seemingly of how it is).

Thus, recall Descartes's justly famous description of a particular way of possibly being mistaken:

> How often has it happened to me that in the night I dreamt that I found myself in this particular place, that I was dressed and seated near the fire, *whilst in reality* I was lying undressed in bed! [...] But in thinking over this I remind myself that on many occasions I have in sleep been *deceived by similar illusions* [...].
> (Descartes 1911: 145–6; my emphases)

That is Descartes's sceptical dreaming possibility; and we should parse it as describing a possible situation in which a person is *merely* dreaming that *p* – that is, dreaming that *p*, while it is nevertheless not true that *p*.

But we must be careful not to mistake his possibility of merely dreaming for what is merely a possibility of dreaming. This potential confusion could be encouraged by Stroud's (1984: ch. 1) discussion, ostensibly of the Cartesian sceptical argument but ultimately of a more generic form of sceptical reasoning. As Sosa (1988: 153–5) notes, Stroud presents the Cartesian dreaming argument more generally – as being about the comparatively generic possibility of *dreaming*, not the more specific possibility of *merely dreaming*. Stroud (1984: 25) allows, on the supposedly Cartesian sceptic's behalf, that a person could, in the relevant sense, be dreaming that p (for an external world p), even while p is true.

Still, there is an important link between these two ways of conceiving sceptically of a dreaming possibility. Roughly and presumably, the link is that an instance of (generic) dreaming is *likely* to be an instance of merely dreaming – of one's being deceived. Stroudian dreaming is likely – or so we typically think – to be manifested as Cartesian dreaming.

Let us generalize that distinction and that link. We may distinguish between *direct* sceptical possibilities and *indirect* ones. The strictly Cartesian possibility, of merely dreaming, is a direct sceptical possibility. Stroud's putative extension of that strict Cartesian possibility – talking merely of dreaming (rather than of merely dreaming) – describes an indirect sceptical possibility.[1] Thus, the possibility of your merely dreaming that p is directly sceptical because *if* it were to obtain then p would be false. By definition, part of your merely dreaming that p is its not being true that p. In this way, the non-modal content[2] of a direct sceptical possibility is incompatible with the truth of the belief in relation to which the possibility is supposedly sceptical at all.

In contrast, the possibility merely of your dreaming (where this does not entail your merely dreaming) does *not* have a non-modal content incompatible with the truth of the belief in question.

It is clear why actualising a direct sceptical possibility for an epistemic agent – a possibility pertaining to p – would eliminate her knowing that p: the knowledge that p would be absent because the agent's belief that p would be false.

But actualising an indirect sceptical possibility pertaining to p would lack that immediate impact. What is the supposed source of *its* epistemic threat? The sceptic will claim that one's knowledge that p would be absent because one would lack sufficient *justification* for the belief that p – if, that is, one *were* actually in the situation non-modally described by the indirect sceptical possibility. Suppose that you are dreaming there being a table in front of you. Then although your being in this state is compatible with the dream's accuracy (its truth), you are not really justified in believing there to be a table present. Or so the sceptical reasoning will aver. On what grounds? There are a few possibilities, reflecting competing conceptions of epistemic justification. For example, one reason that may be offered is that once you are dreaming at all, there is a significant susceptibility to mistake. Being mistaken would be unreasonably *likely*. This likelihood would be conditional, relative to the non-modal content ('you are dreaming') of this dreaming possibility, the possibility as such that you are dreaming. Any form of justification (such as a reliabilist form of justification) which requires mistake *not* to be so likely would thereby be absent.[3]

7.2 Explanation and underdetermination

Not all sceptical arguments rely so overtly upon describing what they regard as dangerous possibilities. Sometimes, the reliance is covert. I will mention two such contenders.

Explanation. A sceptical argument might be framed in terms of competing explanations. For instance, Pryor says that

> this dreaming hypothesis [namely, Stroud's] does [...] introduce a non-standard explanation of your experiences. And this explanation would *undermine* the support your experiences give you for your perceptual beliefs.
>
> (2000: 527)

Why do you have the experience as of there being a table in front of you? Is it because there is indeed a table there, which you are sensing normally? Or is there an alternative explanation, such as your dreaming these experiences? Can we choose, knowledgeably, between these two candidate explanations (and others)?

That question directs us to consider possibilities. The alternative explanations are intended to be alternative *possible* explanations, each describing a way the world might be. Underlying the accompanying question, too (asking us to choose, knowledgeably, between these possibilities), is the distinction between direct sceptical possibilities and indirect ones. Consider the content of any alternative possible explanation, with content E, that may be proffered by a sceptic, regarding your believing that *p*. Either E entails not-*p*, or it does not: either the-world's-including-your-dreaming entails not-*p*, or it does not. In the former case, the possible truth of the alternative putative explanation constitutes a *direct* sceptical possibility: 'Do you know that the world is not really such that the explanation of its-seeming-to-you-that-*p* includes your being mistaken as to *p*?' In the latter case (where the alternative possible explanatory content does not entail not-*p*), what is proffered is instead an *indirect* sceptical possibility: 'Do you know that the world is not really such that the explanation of its-seeming-to-you-that-*p might well* include your being mistaken as to *p*?'

Underdetermination. A.J. Ayer's elegant distillation of sceptical reasoning challenges us to surmount a sceptical problem of evidential underdetermination. The underdetermination would arise for at least some notable forms of belief, such as ones putatively concerning the external world: no matter what experiences we have had, our conclusions about the external world remain evidentially underdetermined by those experiences. The inferential use of evidence (even if the inference is unwitting) is the model here; justificatory advance is the aim of such inference. 'The problem [...] is that of establishing our right to make what appears to be a special sort of advance beyond our data' (Ayer 1956: 84).

And at first glance, in developing that analysis on behalf of such sceptics, Ayer cites no awkward possibilities. He does not direct our attention to any perturbing and unusual states of affairs afflicting one's believing that *p* – such as one's dreaming that *p* in a seemingly life-like and belief-forming way. Rather, Ayer's method is to describe only what the sceptic takes to be logico-epistemic gaps inherent to any putative justification that might be adduced in support of the belief that *p*. Does this mode of sceptical thinking thereby eschew reliance upon sceptical possibilities as such?

No, because (even if covertly) Ayer *is* advertising to what many people would regard as being a sceptical possibility. It is an indirect one. By mentioning the non-deductive nature of the evidence-conclusion relation, for instance, Ayer is recognizing that the evidence allows for the falsity of *p*. In other words, the *possibility* of not-*p* is being highlighted.

This is done in a generic way. Ayer specifies none of the oh-so-many specific ways in which, even given the truth of the evidence (such as if one's evidence was actually part of a dreaming experience), not-*p* could be realized. But that kind of specificity is not required within a sceptical possibility. The point of an indirect sceptical possibility is to highlight, either specifically (as in Stroud's dreaming story) *or* generically (as in Ayer's analysis), how *p* need not be true. This 'need not' admits of different strengths or degrees, of course. The indirect possibility's non-modal content might include not-*p*'s being very likely to be true. Or it could be weaker in its embrace of not-*p*, raising only a less-likely possibility. In either event, it can be sceptical even while remaining indirect in its assault upon *p*'s truth as such.

7.3 The sceptical-independence presumption

Whether covertly or not, then, sceptical reasoning relies routinely upon expecting would-be knowers to eliminate, either covertly or not, various sceptical possibilities. And, whether directly or not, some link with falsehood is at the heart of any such sceptical possibility.

It is unsurprising that the traditional sceptical gambit is to require people, if they are to know that *p*, to eliminate those possibilities by *knowing* of those possibilities not obtaining. Anything less than knowledge leaves some correlative room for doubt; and any such doubt would undermine the quest for the knowledge that *p*, too. So says the sceptical thinking.

It is also traditional to notice that such thinking relies upon a claim of there being a kind of metaphysical *priority* between the knowledge that *p* and the associated knowledge required by the sceptic (namely, the knowledge of the sceptical possibility's not obtaining): the one cannot exist until the other does.[4] This claim may be articulated simply. Consider a sceptic who adduces a dreaming possibility (in either its strict Cartesian form or its looser Stroudian shape). His core claim of priority says this:

> You have no knowledge that *p* (for any external world *p*) *until* you know, independently, that you are not dreaming that *p*.

It is not good enough to reply to the sceptic, for example, that once you know that *p* you can *thereby* know that you are not dreaming that *p*. Non-sceptical epistemologists should be well aware that sceptics will view this reply askance, as begging the question at issue. How so? Simple: the careful sceptic will not allow your evidence as to *p* to be part of your knowing that *p*, *until* you know that you are not dreaming that *p*. Then, and only then, your evidence as of *p* can help to constitute your knowing that *p*. On the sceptic's way of thinking, *two* epistemic tasks await you. First you need to complete the one, by knowing that you are not dreaming that *p*; only then are you in a position to complete (indeed, even to begin) the other, thereby knowing that *p*.[5]

The sceptic's demand is thus that you complete, or at least be able to complete, an *independent* epistemic task before you will be able to complete the epistemic task of knowing that *p*. In that sense, the knowledge that you are not dreaming, for example, must already be attainable 'in its own right'.[6] The sceptic will not allow that you can argue non-question-beggingly for your satisfying his demand, if you try to do so by arguing first for your having knowledge that *p* – and only then inferring that, as part of your having such knowledge, you thereby have knowledge of your not dreaming that *p*. The sceptic will say that the latter knowledge can be present in a way that satisfies his demand, only if it was at least able to be present already, 'in its own right'.

We may say, therefore, that the sceptic is requiring there to be a *metaphysically constitutive* priority on the part of the extra knowledge he is asking you to have (if you are to know that *p*).[7] Sceptics describe what, in their view, is in itself a metaphysical possibility, such as that you are dreaming that *p*. Then they demand that, independently, it be known not to obtain – independently of your knowing that *p*. This knowledge of the sceptical possibility's not obtaining must be constituted in its own right. (And if you are seeking to *show* that it is not to obtain, you must not *call upon* your knowing that *p*, citing it as part of how you know that the sceptical possibility does not obtain.) Otherwise (we are told by the sceptic), knowledge that *p* is not constituted; a necessary condition of its being constituted would not have been satisfied.

Two clarificatory points are now needed. First, I am not making a point about certainty, infallibility, or some cognate high epistemic standard being set by the sceptic. My point is merely locational. It concerns just *where*, in the associated process or structuring of justification (or whatever else contributes to the epistemizing of the belief that *p*), the epistemic subject's eliminating of the distinctively sceptical possibilities would need to be located.

Second, recall that the sceptic is not allowing that if you could come to know later that you are not dreaming that *p*, you would *thereby* satisfy his proposed necessary condition on knowing that *p*. That is, if you are to avoid begging the question in reply to the sceptic's attempt to challenge your knowing that *p*, you may not purport to satisfy his challenge by gaining the required knowledge (of your not dreaming) as an *extension*, attained later, of already-attainable knowledge that *p*.

Consequently, what is at stake here will not be an epistemic *closure* principle – one according to which, for example, the conjunction of (i) one's knowing that *p*, with (ii) one's knowing that *p* entails *q*, entails one's knowing that *q* (all of this at the same time or at relevantly close times). For short:

© $[k(p) \, \& \, k(p \to q)] \to k(q)$.

The reason why © is *not* what I will be discussing is that such a principle could be satisfied by someone's having an instance of knowledge that *p* which leads only *subsequently* to her having the further knowledge that q (where q is known by her to be entailed by p). And that situation is anathema to the sceptic. It is *not* an instance of what he is challenging you to have. It would be an instance of the ability to know that you are not dreaming that p, *once* you know that p – whereas the sceptic is challenging you to know that you are not dreaming that p, if you are *then* to know that p.

Nevertheless, in recent years it has become common for epistemologists to treat closure principles as being at the heart of sceptical efforts.[8] According to these epistemologists, sceptics rely on a closure principle by arguing that because the further knowledge – such as the knowledge that one is not dreaming (where the epistemic agent knows her not dreaming that p to be entailed by p) – is forever unavailable, so too is the knowledge that p. Hence, given how many contemporary epistemologists, it seems, assume that epistemic closure principles are pivotal to sceptical arguments, assessments of the truth or falsity of such principles are being assumed to be needed whenever scepticism is discussed. But if I am right, that focus upon closure principles is unfortunate because it obscures the proper view of how the sceptic is proceeding: he is relying on something *other* than a closure principle. (And *am* I right about this? We will see, as we progress. In Section 7.10, I will close the chapter by returning to this issue.)

In characterizing these in-principle commitments of sceptical reasoning, therefore, we may talk of the *sceptical-independence* presumption.[9] Part of the *prima facie* power of these sceptical arguments is traceable to this presumption. *Prima facie* powerful sceptical reasoning describes what seems, certainly at first glance, to be a possibility which needs, in some constitutively prior way, to be known not to obtain, if there is to be knowledge that p. Implicit in this, of course, is the sceptic's presuming that the sceptical possibility *could* already be known – if it could ever be known at all – not to obtain.

7.4 The sceptical-independence problem: Direct sceptical possibilities

Unfortunately for would-be sceptics, however, their reliance upon the sceptical-independence presumption is self-defeating. This section and the next will show why that is so. In each section, the question will be that of whether a sceptic can satisfy her independence presumption when using a sceptical possibility in order to challenge a person's having some knowledge that p. (This section discusses direct sceptical possibilities; indirect ones will be Section 7.5's focus.) The conclusion will be that when a sceptic is engaged in trying to *challenge* a person to show that she has knowledge that p, the sceptic fails to satisfy his own sceptical-independence presumption. When confronted by such a would-be sceptical challenge, therefore, no one needs to *engage* with it. The sceptic might continue to claim truth for her premises, of course. But she cannot convert this claim into a substantive *inference* to a sceptical conclusion. Let us begin to see why this is so.

Consider, again, the direct sceptical possibility of *merely* dreaming that p. When this possibility is used as the centrepiece of a supposed sceptical challenge to your knowing that p (for some external world p), the sceptical reasoning is asking that, in order to know at time t that p, you satisfy the following condition:

1. Independently (either at t or earlier), you know that not-[you are merely dreaming that p].[10]

Now, 1 amounts, within this dialectical setting of sceptical putative challenge, to 2:

2. Independently (either at t or earlier), you know that not-[(you seem, to yourself, to be experiencing p as true) & (you are dreaming that p) & not-p].

But 2 includes a redundant clause, insofar as 2 is intended by the sceptic to describe a condition you need to satisfy, as part of meeting a sceptical *challenge* to your knowing at t that p. The possibility of your dreaming that p is relevant to the sceptical challenge only insofar as it is at least a *prima facie* threat to your knowing that p. And, as we are analysing it in this section (taking our cue from Descartes's words, as these were explained in Section 7.1) this *prima facie* threat would obtain only insofar as (i) your dreaming that p includes your seeming, to yourself, to be experiencing p as true, even while (ii) p is false (with your therefore being mistaken in thinking that p is true). So (on the strictly Cartesian interpretation of the dreaming possibility), the dreaming as such is even a *prima facie* threat only because of those two *other* conjuncts embedded in 2, the ones that would be true *because* of your dreaming in the way envisaged by Descartes. Once we make their respective roles explicit, then, we have no further need to mention the dreaming as such.[11] Accordingly, 2 gives way to 3 (with 3 capturing whatever it is that performs any *prima facie* sceptically challenging work in 2):

3. Independently (either at t or earlier), you know that not-[(you seem, to yourself, to be experiencing p as true) & not-p].[12]

And 3 is equivalent to 4 (by standard logic):[13]

4. Independently (either at t or earlier), you know that [not-(you seem, to yourself, to be experiencing p as true) or p].

Then 4 can be simplified. Your seeming, to yourself, to be experiencing p as true is your having whatever apparently observational evidence it is that, by hypothesis, you have for p. And the Cartesian sceptic about external world knowledge that p is not disputing your knowing what your subjectively experienced evidence is. He is certainly not asking you to know that you do *not* have that apparently observational evidence. Instead, he is challenging whether, *given* your knowing that you seem, to yourself, to be experiencing p as true, you know that p. We may therefore eliminate the first disjunct within the scope of 'You know that' in 4 because that disjunct is not describing something which our Cartesian sceptic is challenging you to know. Yet once we do eliminate that disjunct, this is all that remains of the supposedly sceptical challenge that began by asking you to satisfy 1:

5. Independently (either at *t* or earlier), you know that *p*.

And assuredly there is no challenge in *that* to your knowing that *p*. It is what remains, upon analysis, of what the sceptic was regarding, via 1, as an epistemic task needing to be accomplished (or at least needing to be able to be accomplished) *before* you can accomplish the independent epistemic task of knowing that *p*. Thus, we see that the sceptic's putative challenge amounts to this (now that we have put to one side the 'psychological colouring' in 1, along with the elements of it, uncovered by analysis, that could not be real challenges here):

6. If at *t* you know that *p*, then independently (either at *t* or earlier) you know that *p*. (That is, if at *t* you know that *p*, then 5 obtains.)

And it is impossible, of course, for one's knowledge at *t* that *p* to be present independently of one's knowledge at *t* that *p*. No instance of that sort of constitutive priority could sensibly be demanded. So, there is no sense in a would-be sceptic's challenging you in a way that would amount, upon analysis, just *to* your knowing that *p* independently of your knowing that *p* – so that (with all else being equal) the latter knowledge that *p* may *then* come to exist. First, it is incoherent to expect you to know that *p before* you know that *p*, as part of a challenge to your knowing that *p* at all. Second, if you are being asked to know that *p simultaneously* with having knowledge that *p*, this is incoherent if the intention is to ask you also to have knowledge that *p*, at that time, *apart* from having knowledge that *p* at that same time. (You cannot have two instances of knowledge that *p* at a single time. You cannot have one as an independent condition of coming to have the other.)

Thus, the Cartesian sceptic, it transpires, is failing to alert us to an *independent* piece of knowledge which you need if you are to know that *p* – or, equivalently, a piece of knowledge which you need to have prior to knowing that p.[14] And that implication renders the would-be sceptical challenge futile. We may call this the sceptical-independence *problem*. This section has shown how it arises for *direct* sceptical possibilities.[15]

7.5 The sceptical-independence problem: Indirect sceptical possibilities

Now let us see how the sceptical-independence problem also arises for *in*direct sceptical possibilities. This will strike many epistemologists as the more pressing kind of sceptical possibility, given that indirect sceptical possibilities reflect directly upon justification (by somehow indirectly reflecting upon truth).

Thus, let *p* be, as before, an external world proposition. Then recall (from Section 7.1) that an indirect sceptical possibility, as regards *p*, is one whose non-modal content is compatible with *p* but incompatible – or so we are told – with the epistemic agent's being justified in believing that *p*.[16] For instance, the associated sceptical reasoning will say, 'You are not *justified* in believing that *p* if you do not know independently that your seemingly sensory evidence as of p is not actually a dreaming experience. And if your belief that p is not justified, it is not knowledge'. By the same token (the sceptical reasoning might allow), if you *were* to know independently that you are not dreaming that p, this could constitute your having (independently specifiable) justification for your belief that p.[17]

Does this indirect sort of sceptical possibility – of dreaming, not of merely dreaming – evade Section 7.4's sceptical-independence problem? Does the latter problem afflict only *direct* sceptical possibilities?

No, it does not. Indirect sceptical possibilities, too, when used in sceptical inferences, are supposed to undermine the epistemic agent's tether to the truth of his belief that p. Yet, by definition, even such a possibility's being actualised remains compatible with the belief's being true. How, then, is there supposed to be a truth-directed threat at all? Well, if the requisite justificatory tether is absent, then a given context of belief *could* (for all that the agent can know to the contrary) be one where the sceptical possibility that is not being eliminated is a direct one. The possibility thereby remains open of a direct sceptical possibility's being actualised. Thus, given the former possibility of the latter possibility (a direct sceptical one), mistake is possibly possible. Will this be *enough* of a possibility of mistake for sceptical purposes? A sceptic will no doubt believe so. Seemingly, he should infer that an indirect sceptical possibility could be part of an effective sceptical challenge, only insofar as the epistemic agent cannot distinguish being 'in' it from being 'in' a direct sceptical possibility.[18] Dreaming – the Stroudian generic possibility – will *feel* indistinguishable from merely dreaming – the Cartesian strict possibility. You cannot know which, if either, of these states you are in. To raise the former possibility, the generic one, is thereby to raise the significant possibility of the latter possibility, the strict one. You could not know which, if either, of these states you are in.

So, your being told merely that you could be dreaming, say, is an effective sceptical possibility, only if you cannot know that you can know that you are not *merely* dreaming. The former, indirect, sceptical possibility – merely of dreaming – thereby indirectly depends, for any putative sceptical impact it might possess, upon the sceptical impact of the latter, direct, sceptical possibility – of merely dreaming. There is a substantive sceptical challenge associated with a given indirect sceptical possibility, only if there is a substantive sceptical challenge associated with some *direct* and conceptually related sceptical possibility.

We might formulate that analysis in the following terms. A sceptic could challenge you only via either a 'base clause' challenge or an 'inductive clause' challenge. The former would involve some direct sceptical possibility. Indirect sceptical possibilities will feature only in 'inductive clause' challenges. Hence, if the 'base clause' challenges fail, so do the 'inductive clause' ones.

Or the point might be made via this 'sceptical-reach' principle:

A given *indirect* sceptical possibility needs to be known not to obtain (as an independent and prior condition of knowing that p), only if there is some associated *direct* sceptical possibility that needs to be known not to obtain (also as an independent and prior condition of knowing that p).

For example, the possibility merely of your dreaming can be part of a substantive sceptical challenge to your knowing that *p*, only if the possibility of your merely dreaming can be.[19]

But, we saw (in Section 7.4), no direct sceptical possibility *can* have that sort of impact. Hence, given the sceptical-reach principle, we may now infer that no real inferential challenge emanates from any indirect sceptical possibility, either. Merely dreaming is the most 'extreme' form, epistemologically speaking, that dreaming can take; and if even *it* cannot be used to generate a substantive sceptical worry, then the (indirect, generic) possibility of dreaming fares no better.

Accordingly, we should be unperturbed when encountering such sceptical arguments as Stroud's not-strictly-Cartesian version of Descartes's dreaming argument. Because there can be no successful challenge centred upon the direct-and-strictly-Cartesian possibility of merely dreaming, none springs forth from the indirect-and-Stroudian possibility merely of dreaming. Neither sort of possibility, when used as sceptics seek to use them, can deprive us of external world knowledge.

And the point may be generalized. For example, the same is true, *mutatis mutandis*, of Greco's (2000) presentation of Hume's version (1902: sec. XII) of external world scepticism. Greco's Hume requires us to know (non-circularly) of the *reliability* of the apparently sensory appearances we experience (Greco 2000: 25–34). Your senses could be unreliable in the appearances with which they are presenting you; and you need to know that they are not being unreliable in that way. Otherwise, even when sceptical reasoning is not raising the possibility of your being misled by a *specific* deceptive or misleading appearance, you are vulnerable to his raising the possibility of your relying on a *generally* unreliable, untrustworthy, way of forming beliefs about the external world. (The former possibility would be a direct sceptical one; the latter would be indirect.) But the sceptical-reach principle implies that being confronted with the possibility of a belief's being formed unreliably – a possibility of a significant possibility of mistake – has sceptical impact only if being confronted with the possibility of the belief's actually being mistaken does so. Yet the latter possibility, we have seen, *cannot* function to that effect within sceptical reasoning. Because (as Section 7.4 showed) the sceptical-independence problem undermines inferential attempts via *direct* sceptical possibilities to challenge anyone's ever knowing that *p*, inferential attempts to use *in*direct sceptical possibilities towards that same end also fail (as this section has established).

7.6 Sceptical doubts as such

My focus has been on sceptical *possibilities* as such. Noting this is important to understanding what makes a doubt sceptical. It is also important for countering an otherwise tempting objection to my argument.

The objection is that my argument for the sceptical-independence problem is too strong. The objection is that I am rendering unchallenging, and thereby insubstantial, *any* doubt that reflects (either directly or indirectly) upon the truth of a particular belief, including therefore some sensible 'everyday' doubts. Suppose you believe that you are seeing an elephant in front of you; but you also reflect, perhaps at someone's prompting, that you are rather tired, and that if you were not so tired you would be unlikely to have that belief about there being an elephant in your presence. It occurs to you that in the past this sort of belief has arisen only when you have been quite tired – and that, on each occasion, it was subsequently found to have been false. You ask yourself, 'Could my belief therefore be mistaken this time?'; to which, you answer that, yes, it could be. You are thereby contemplating a possibility which directly targets your justification for your belief, targeting indirectly the belief's truth. And you are doubting yourself quite sensibly, it seems. Yet – claims the objection – my anti-sceptical argument would permit even your sensible doubt to be set aside, dismissing it as presenting no real challenge to your elephant-belief (as we may term it). In which case, my anti-sceptical argument is too strong: it is implying an unreasonable assessment of what, in this example, is a perfectly normal and reasonable doubt. Moreover, your particular doubt (reflecting upon your history of being mistaken when having this sort of elephant-belief) does not even seem to be *sceptical* in nature. It is an instance of a kind of careful doubt that would arise within everyday, standardly non-sceptical, inquiries.[20]

In order to defuse that objection, therefore, I must distinguish between sceptical doubts, to which the sceptical-independence problem properly applies, and non-sceptical doubts, which should be left untouched by that problem. How may this be done?

We need only notice two distinct features of sceptical doubts. Here is the first.

Feature 1. Any sceptical doubt raises *only* a possibility as such, whereas (good) non-sceptical doubts do more than that.

The doubt you raised about your elephant-belief adduces evidence of past actual mistakes – of *false* beliefs with a content like your present one – having arisen in the same sort of circumstance. This evidence is accepted by you; and, crucially, the doubt it grounds is used by you in the following way. You are asking yourself, *not merely to eliminate a possibility, but instead to weigh or balance competing pieces of standard evidence.* ('It looks to me as though there is an elephant here. On the other hand, I must remember my non-trivial record of similar *yet false* beliefs. Given that history, there is a real likelihood of my being mistaken this time, too – not merely a possibility, but a probability, as it were. I wonder: which of these possibilities is *more* probably true?')[21] Evaluating the competing claims of these pieces of evidence – the sensory appearance vs the history of mistakes – will involve its own difficulties. Nonetheless, the doubt being engaged with remains non-sceptical because *not merely* a possibility of mistake is being contemplated.[22] Consequently, is this a sufficient basis on which to infer that my anti-sceptical argument – the sceptical-independence problem – leaves untouched this reasonable doubt about your elephant-belief?

Not quite. That is because, in Section 7.4's unravelling of the supposedly direct sceptical challenge, the progression of my anti-sceptical argument, from thesis 1 through to thesis 6, never overtly depended upon those theses describing (on the sceptic's behalf) only possibilities as such. (The progression focussed just upon the respective contents of those conditions, not on any associated modalities.) Nonetheless, the fact that sceptical doubts raise only possibilities is what leads to the second distinctive feature of sceptical doubts, as follows.

> *Feature 2.* A sceptical possibility as such is taken to be a genuine challenge to the presence of knowledge[23] in spite of being only a possibility. How could this be so? That possibility is thought (by the would-be sceptic) to accomplish this through the *sceptical-independence* presumption.

Consider again, by way of contrast, the non-sceptical case of your elephant-belief. The doubt you raise within that case is *not* taken to be epistemically prior to the evidence supporting your elephant-belief (so that the doubt needs to be known not to obtain, *before* your evidence can even have a chance of making your elephant-belief knowledge). Rather, the doubt raises *just more evidence*. You are not expecting yourself to assess the doubt independently, to know whether or not it is true – in principle, *prior* to resuming any reliance upon the evidence you already had in support of your elephant-belief. You accept that the doubt *is* true; your question is only that of how to *balance* this truth against your sensory experience (as of an elephant's presence).

So, even if you do choose to reflect independently upon the doubt, the fact of its not being used sceptically prevents it from having the following dramatic disjunctive characteristic – being such that *either* (i) it triumphs wholly, *or* (ii) it can be dismissed entirely, such as by being known to be false. That is, a sceptical possibility is intended to be such that it *triumphs* wholly (depriving you of the knowledge in question) unless you can effect a complete *counter*-triumph (most clearly, by knowing it to be false). Again, though, in this case you concede that your doubt – the belief in your history of mistaken elephant-beliefs – is true: you *do* have that relevant history of mistakes. The non-sceptical question you then face is that of what effect this history of mistakes has on the *rest* of your evidence. The non-sceptical question is that of how you should *absorb* this further evidence – this (non-sceptical) doubt – into your evidence as a whole, all of your evidence bearing upon the truth or otherwise of your elephant-belief. In contrast, a sceptical possibility *demands epistemically independent and prior attention*. In principle, you are expected by the sceptic to 'take time out' to eliminate the sceptical possibility; otherwise (according to the sceptic) any justificatory move you might make is of no relevant epistemic consequence. You are expected to dispose of the sceptical possibility before your other evidence can, in effect, even function *as* evidence at all. The other evidence's functioning as evidence thus presupposes your at least being able to dispose of the sceptical possibility.[24]

A non-sceptical doubt introduces counter-justification, *complicating* the justificatory situation, perhaps weakening greatly the force of the original justification. But a sceptical doubt serves to deny that, in effect, there is any real justification present in the first place. A non-sceptical doubt could adduce past mistakes that make one's belief that *p* likely to be false, for example. And this (with all else being equal) would be a manifest feature *within* the justificatory situation. That is, it would be a *weakness within* the justification that could, at least in principle, be corrected by new justification. This could occur even if a possibility of mistake (and hence of not knowing) would remain uneliminated. However, the sceptic would not accept the possibility of that outcome. The sceptic intends a sceptical possibility to show that if it is not eliminated, then there is no point to seeking extra, prior and independent, justification.

7.7 Scepticism and justification

Section 7.5 has shown how, once again,[25] this chapter's argument applies not only to knowledge, but also to justification. A 'justification-sceptic' argues that there is never any 'real' justification for a belief that p – no justification that can assure us, for example, of the truth of that belief. Such a sceptic, too, is relying upon using some supposedly significant possibility, one which the would-be knower is expected to eliminate already and independently – regardless of whether the price to be paid for failure in this respect is anticipated as being a lack or knowledge or a lack only of justification. Yet, again (as Section 7.6 has emphasized), such a sceptic is still doing this in a way that purports to undermine at least – even before any other evidence has the opportunity to provide any real justification – the claims of some particular belief to be justified.

This is so, even (as Section 7.2 acknowledged) when the possibility in question is of the truth of a competing explanation, say, of the truth of one's evidence for a belief that p. What makes the use of that possibility sceptical is the alternative possible explanation's supposedly needing to be eliminated independently of any other evidence's being able to justify one's belief that p. However, this sceptical methodology returns the sceptical-independence presumption, *mutatis mutandis*, to centre stage. At which point, even if the sceptic deems this possibility to be undermining a belief's claim to be justified (rather than to be knowledge), the sceptical-independence problem persists, *mutatis mutandis*.

We may appreciate this simply by substituting 'You are justified in believing' for 'You know' throughout my argument in Section 7.4, specifically in each of 1 through 6. Here is the new sequence (which we may assume to be accompanied by the same explanatory commentary as before, *mutatis mutandis*), all of this meant by the sceptic to bear upon your being justified in believing at t that p:

1_J Independently (either at t or earlier), you are justified in believing that not-[you are merely dreaming that p].
2_J Independently (either at t or earlier), you are justified in believing that not-[(you seem, to yourself, to be experiencing p as true) & (you are dreaming that p) & not-p].
3_J Independently (either at t or earlier), you are justified in believing that not-[(you seem, to yourself, to be experiencing p as true) & not-p].
4_J Independently (either at t or earlier), you are justified in believing that [not-(you seem, to yourself, to be experiencing p as true) or p].
5_J Independently (either at t or earlier), you are justified in believing that p.

But what was initially at stake was your having justification for your belief that p. So, 5_J will become part of 6_J (as 5 became part of 6):

6₁ If at *t* you are justified in your belief that *p*, then independently (either at *t* or earlier) you are justified in a belief that *p*. (That is, if at *t* you are justified in your belief that *p*, then 5₁ obtains.)

And 6₁ is as clearly false as was 6, the corresponding thesis about knowledge.

Even the (truth-directed) *justification*-sceptic, then, fails when relying upon a direct would-be challenge, trying to confront you with a direct sceptical possibility. The fact that justification, not knowledge, is her professed target does not alleviate her plight.[26]

7.8 Beyond Sosa and Pryor[27]

The power of the sceptical-independence problem may be more fully appreciated by comparing it with its most similar predecessor. Both Sosa (1988: 158–9) and Pryor (2000: 529–30) present versions of that predecessor. Neither reaches as anti-sceptical a conclusion as the sceptical-independence problem does.

In order to understand why that is so, let us return to this standard condition at the heart of many an external world scepticism (for any external world proposition *p*):

7 You know that *p* → You know that you are not dreaming.

According to the sceptical thinking, 7 could never be satisfied. As Stroud (1984: 21–3) illuminatingly explains upon the sceptic's behalf, 7's consequent can be satisfied only by your knowing that you satisfy some appropriate *test*, say, of whether you are dreaming. But this knowledge would itself be external world knowledge. So, by 7, you could have this knowledge, too, only if you know that you are not dreaming. Hence, (by the transitivity of '→'), there is circularity, and thus a failure, in your attempt to know that you are not dreaming. By 7, you therefore fail to know that *p*.

However, as Sosa and Pryor observe, that reasoning is invalid. All that follows from that circularity is either *S* (in Sosa's argument) or *P* (in Pryor's), depending upon what is being emphasized in a given analysis of the sceptic's reasoning:

S You know that you are not dreaming → You know that you are not dreaming.[28]

P You know that you are not dreaming ←→ You have some external world knowledge.[29]

S is true – but trivially so, providing no basis for a substantive sceptical challenge. In particular, it does not entail that you do not know that you are not dreaming. And *P*, regardless of whether it is true, does not entail that its right-hand-side is never satisfied. So, *P* also presents no real sceptical challenge.

Is the sceptic therefore defeated? Not quite; Sosa and Pryor realize that the sceptic has a choice in how to interpret '→' (either on its own or as part of the correlative '←→'). In order to resuscitate his argument, the sceptic must interpret the '→' not simply as a conditional or as indicating a necessary condition. Instead, he needs to view it as reporting an asymmetric relation of epistemic *priority*. For instance, the sceptic might well rewrite 7 as 8 (still applying to any external world proposition *p*):

8   For any time t_i: [At t_1, you know that p → At some minimally earlier time t_2, you know that you are not dreaming].³⁰

Then the sceptic's reasoning could derive this replacement for *S* and for *P*:

S/P   You know that you are not dreaming → At some earlier time, you know that you are not dreaming.³¹

And *S/P* becomes a threat because, in effect, the sceptic applies it to the question of how you could ever know, for the *first* time, that you are not dreaming. In that context, *S/P* is unsatisfiable. You cannot ever have your first piece of knowledge that you are not dreaming, if you need to know *already* that you are not dreaming. So, if 8 is true, you cannot ever know that *p*. There is a further piece of knowledge, specifically the knowledge that you are not dreaming, which you need prior to having the knowledge that *p*; and, as we see, the conditions for having that further piece of knowledge are unsatisfiable.

Accordingly, neither Sosa nor Pryor claims to have wholly undermined the sceptic. Pryor, for example, pursues what he calls the *modest* anti-sceptical project (2000: 517–18). He does not seek to disprove scepticism by using premises that the sceptic must accept; he doubts that this can be done. His goal is to explain to *non*-sceptics how best to be non-sceptical. And, having followed Sosa in identifying the sceptic's covert reliance upon a challenge framed in terms of epistemic priority, Pryor sets out to formulate a coherent concept of *immediate* justification or knowledge – a kind of justification or knowledge which does not depend upon having *any* epistemically prior or antecedent justificatory support (let alone any of the specific epistemically prior justification or knowledge insisted on by a sceptic).

Yet our noticing the sceptical-independence problem allows us to take a decisive step *beyond* the modest anti-sceptical project, towards what Pryor calls the ambitious anti-sceptical project. He describes the latter's prospects as being 'somewhat dim' (2000: 517). But that pessimism is mistaken. We *can* undermine scepticism by using only reasoning which a sceptic should accept. This chapter's approach has shown, using some simple analysis incorporating no anti-sceptical theses, that a sceptic's core condition grounds no real challenge. Focusing upon how to interpret '→' (as Sosa and Pryor do) will not reveal a sceptic's most fundamental failing in his endeavour to develop a real challenge. By applying the lesson of the sceptical-independence problem, we may infer that a sceptic is more seriously undermined by his reliance upon the false assumption that what flanks the '→' in his apparent challenge are two *different* items of knowledge. Appropriately, Sosa (1988: 159) saw that there is a *need* for them to be different items of knowledge. However, in Sections 7.4 and 7.5 we have found that, at least as a sceptic would use them in formulating his challenge, they *cannot* be different. Apparently or initially, they are different: 'you know that you are not dreaming that *p*' sounds quite different to 'you know that *p*'. Upon analysis, though, this apparent difference melts away, at any rate *within* the context of a would-be sceptical challenge.³²

7.9 On apparent sceptical doubts

Let us now reflect upon standard sceptical methodology, and upon why we should resist it.[33] In particular, we should regard the concept of *sceptical doubting* as being of dubious coherence. It is routine for sceptics to incorporate their apparent challenge – their expecting you to have some designated further piece of knowledge – within a process of doubt. Yet, I will argue, insofar as the sceptic lacks the rational right to frame his challenge in terms of the constitutive priority of the particular piece of knowledge he highlights, we should view the very idea of sceptical doubt as being correlatively impugned.

Consider again an external world sceptic who asks you to know that you are not merely dreaming that p (for some proposition p, ostensibly about the physical world). This sceptic has raised a doubt as to whether you know that p, a doubt reflecting the possibility of your merely dreaming that p. You are being expected to eliminate that possibility and to resolve that doubt, by knowing that you are not merely dreaming that p. And the doubt is taken by the sceptic to remain in effect, depriving you of the knowledge that p, *until* you gain the knowledge that you are not merely dreaming that p. Officially, therefore, the sceptic is doubting one piece of knowledge – the knowledge that p – while asking you to gain *another* piece of knowledge – the knowledge that you are not merely dreaming that p – in order to dispose rationally of that doubt. *Having* disposed of the doubt (or at least having the ability to have done so) is thus a presupposition of possessing the knowledge that p.

Yet something is amiss with that proposed process of inquiry. We have found that, within this context of sceptical challenge, the knowledge that you are not merely dreaming that p is already the knowledge that p, at least as the sceptic uses the former. It is not *further* knowledge at all, within this special context of inquiry. Consequently, the sceptic *merely* appears to have found an independent way of doubting your having the knowledge that p. That is, he *merely* appears to have found ground for doubt in your possibly lacking some extra piece of knowledge. Crucially, the sceptic purports to consider the respective epistemic statuses of some *distinct* pieces of knowledge (your knowing that p, and your knowing that you are not merely dreaming that p). But the sceptic does this by raising a doubt which, under analysis, does not really treat those pieces of knowledge as *being* distinct.

We might say, therefore, that the sceptic is relying covertly upon what is a kind and degree of *holism* about those respective epistemic statuses. He is covertly doubting *all* of those apparently distinct pieces of knowledge at once – even while apparently doubting only *one* of them (your knowing that p), and even while inviting you to remove that doubt by *first* finding some independently describable and seekable knowledge (such as the knowledge that you are not merely dreaming that p). Accordingly, in principle you cannot engage with, and *then* overcome, the sceptic's doubt as to your knowing that p, by gaining first the knowledge that you are not merely dreaming that p – for there is no such 'first'. Once you are trying to resolve the sceptic's doubt, *both* pieces of knowledge are lost (if even one of them is).

But this shows that the doubt is not well-formed from the beginning. It is not a well-formed instance of what it is meant to be – namely, a non-holistic doubt. More fully: It is not well-formed as a doubt of a *particular* piece of knowledge, a doubt rationally describing an *independent* piece of knowledge for you to gain, in order *then* (so long as all else is equal) to regain the first piece of knowledge. Instead, by doubting the presence of the first piece of knowledge (the knowledge that *p*), you have already *ipso facto* doubted the presence of the second piece of knowledge (the knowledge of not merely dreaming that *p*). Hence, you can never overcome that doubt by gaining the second piece of knowledge and *then* the first piece.

Again, though, this is not a problem on your part, because you would not be failing to overcome a reasonable doubt. The sceptic is really denying you, within a single doubt, both the knowledge that *p and* the knowledge that you are not merely dreaming that *p*. And he is doing so, even as his doubt *appears* to deny you just the former knowledge, and even as the doubt *appears* to ask you – perfectly sensibly – to gain the latter knowledge independently, as a constitutively prior condition of regaining the former knowledge. Thus, by entering into the doubt, you have already conceded your lacking both the knowledge which is your main goal *and* the knowledge which is supposedly a necessary step towards that goal. You can never engage with the sceptic's doubt by gaining first the knowledge that you are not merely dreaming that *p*, for instance, so as *subsequently* to gain the knowledge that *p*. The moral of all this is clear: There is no sensible doubt to overcome in the first place; you have no rational need even to try engaging with the sceptic's apparent doubt as such.[34]

7.10 Closure

As Section 7.3 presaged, contemporary epistemology's more technical and prominent anti-sceptical arguments have focused upon issues about epistemic *closure*. That is, they have asked whether some version of an epistemic closure thesis is true. In particular, many epistemologists have discussed (as being representative of possible epistemic closure theses) the principle that knowledge is closed under known logical entailment. This principle was mentioned in Section 7.3. It was formulated thus:

© $[k(p) \& k(p \to q)] \to k(q)$.[35]

Why has the truth or falsity of closure been taken to be pivotal to anti-sceptical arguments? It is because sceptics themselves have been thought to be assuming the truth of some such principle, in particular instances of this:

$©_S$ For any sceptical possibility q: $\{[k(p) \& k(p \to q)] \to k(\text{not-}q)\}$.

The claim that $©_S$ is present within sceptical thinking has become a standard conceptual observation about such thinking. Accordingly, it might seem that I should delve into more of that current anti-sceptical writing. However, there is a simple reason for not doing so (a reason which may further clarify this chapter's anti-sceptical strategy).

The problem with © is that it is *not* quite the form of principle upon which a would-be sceptical challenge should be relying. It pays no heed to the sceptical-*independence* presumption's role within that challenge. As was also mentioned in Section 7.3, the main failing with using © to articulate the sceptic's thinking is that, once we see © as driving the sceptical reasoning, we are saying that the sceptic's challenge to your knowing that *p* is one that, at least in principle, could be satisfied by your *subsequently* knowing that you are not dreaming that *p*. Yet (still from Section 7.3) the sceptic is not open to this possibility, even in principle. Rather, a constitutive *priority* is being required of your knowing that the sceptic's possibility does not obtain (with the sceptic not allowing any of your other evidence for *p* to have any epistemic force at all until you have that knowledge of his awkward possibility's not obtaining). And clearly such priority is not compatible with the possibility of only *subsequently* coming to have that knowledge. Hence, it is not the closure principle $©_s$ – it is the independence principle I_s – upon which the sceptic is relying:

I_s Where *q* describes a sceptical possibility: {[At *t*, k(*p*) & At *t*, k(*p* → not-*q*)] → Independently (either at *t* or earlier), k(not-*q*)}.

And I_s, we discovered, is not satisfiable. Accordingly, no substantive sceptical challenge may be grounded upon it. Analysis has revealed to us how, when a sceptic asks you to satisfy I_s's consequent (as an achievement necessary to your knowing that *p*), he is asking you to *know that p independently of knowing that p*. Of course, this cannot be done. Nor should it be asked of you in the first place. The sceptic has defeated his own aim of describing an independent epistemic task or goal for you to perform or satisfy, prior to your being able to know that *p*. The sceptic has thus failed his own dialectical standard, of sensibly subjecting you to a challenge that reflects what he takes to be the inferential fairness and power of the sceptical-independence presumption.

Accordingly, may this chapter end with the prospect of a pleasing compatibilism? Many non-sceptical epistemologists will still wish to retain the truth of epistemic closure ©, principally as a way of helping to explain how one's having a given piece of knowledge generates one's having further knowledge. May they do so with impunity, all else being equal, by retaining ©? I am not sure that © is true.[36] Still, even *if* it is, this need not have *sceptical* repercussions. Such repercussions descend upon us only through would-be sceptical *challenges*, with a sceptic arguing from your not knowing that you are not dreaming that *p* to your not knowing that *p*. But that style of argument is what we have considered in this chapter. We have seen that these would-be challenges, properly understood, involve at most independence principles such as I_s, not closure principles such as ©. And this chapter has shown how we are safe from I_s when it functions as part of a would-be sceptical challenge. No real sceptical challenge eventuates. I have not shown that there *is* knowledge, or that a sceptic speaks *falsely* when saying that there is no knowledge. What has been shown is that no sceptic can sensibly *argue*, by pointing to a sceptical possibility, for there being no knowledge.[37]

Notes

1. Barry Taylor suggested to me that Descartes himself might have been contemplating only an indirect possibility, not the direct one I have taken to be his concern. On that suggestion, Descartes was thinking as follows: 'Because I have been dreaming in the past (even sometimes when I thought I was awake), I could be dreaming now'. Still, irrespective of Descartes's intentions here, his description makes clear that such possibly-present dreaming was an epistemic worry, in his view, only because he would be *mistaken* if he was in such a dreaming state. So, his own possibility, even if indirect, would be challenging only because of the direct one that I have been assuming is his. (And, as I will explain in Section 7.5, at the core of any *prima facie* threatening indirect sceptical possibility is a direct one.)
2. I say 'non-modal' simply to distinguish the content of the possibility as such from the possibility as such of that content. 'I am dreaming' would be the non-modal content of the possibility, as such, that I am dreaming.
3. This does not entail that all conceivable kinds of justification would be absent. The sceptical reasoning could accord you responsibilist justification, for instance. But because *some* genuine aspersion is meant to be cast by the sceptic upon the truth of your belief, a correlative form of justification should be assumed to be at stake. The possibility I mentioned (in the sentence to which this note is attached) articulates the putative sceptical aspersion in terms of a supposed lack of some degree and kind of truth-aimed justification. And reliabilism (as I also mentioned) offers a natural way of parsing that link. But it is not the only possible way. For example, we may deem a dream-induced belief (be it reliably truth-indicative or be it not) to have too inappropriate a *causal* link to the world if the belief is to be justified. Nonetheless, this would remain a lack of an appropriately truth-aimed link (no matter how it is further understood). Note also that, as many epistemologists do, we may well regard sceptical reasoning as being directed more against *justification* than against truth. Any such sceptical impact, though, even upon the presence of justification, will ultimately be understood in terms of an actual or possible impact upon truth. This is why I will discuss both what I call direct sceptical possibilities (such as merely dreaming) and what I call indirect ones (such as dreaming *simpliciter*). I will be considering not only sceptical possibilities that directly question truth, but ones that question truth only indirectly (by directly questioning truth-aimed forms of justification).
4. This priority is often articulated in terms of *kinds* of proposition. For example, any members from the *category* of knowledge of physical objects would be deemed unavailable unless and until the *category* of knowledge of sensory appearances either is, or is able to be, instantiated. Then this generalisation about the categories would be applied to any case of knowledge of a specific physical object. The prior existence of knowledge of some specific sensory appearances would be said to be required. (And what does 'prior' mean here? I am about to explain that.)
5. The first task need not be done consciously, of course, such as by deliberately setting out to show that you know that you are not dreaming that *p*. The sceptic would require it to be true, nonetheless, that you have the 'before' knowledge at least implicitly – that you are epistemically *able* to have it, in the sense of there being no epistemic impediment to your having it (even if, for some other reason, you do not yet happen to possess it).

6   This is compatible with its being true, in a particular case of having knowledge that p, that the associated instance of knowing that one is not dreaming comes into existence only as part – literally part – of that instance of knowledge that p.
7   Epistemologists more commonly describe the sceptic as claiming the existence of a *conceptual* priority. Does this render my formulation inapt? Not at all; mine is simply an object-level version of that more usual meta-level description. I will explain how this is so, in three steps. (i) The claimed conceptual priority amounts to the following: To apply or understand the concept of having an instance of knowledge that p is already to apply or understand the concept of the extra knowledge (which is highlighted by the sceptic). So, according to the sceptic, the concept of the extra knowledge needs to be applicable or understandable as separable from – and thereby, at least in principle, satisfiable in advance of – the concept of the knowledge that p, if the latter concept is to be applicable or understandable itself. (ii) My description of the sceptic as claiming the existence of a metaphysical priority amounts to the following: The sceptic is saying that the extra knowledge needs already, at least in principle, to be able to be present, if the knowledge that p itself is to be able to be present. (iii) How is (ii)'s metaphysical priority an object-level version of (i)'s conceptual priority? To describe (i)'s conceptual requirement as satisfiable is to describe two possible states of affairs, with one of them being *understandable* as able to satisfy a specific epistemic concept ('knowledge that p') only if the other is already *understandable* as able to satisfy a specific epistemic concept (such as 'knowledge that one is not dreaming that p'). And the possible facts thereby understood – those possible states of affairs, able to stand to each other in that way – are what (ii) then describes.
8   This focus began with Dretske (1970) and Nozick (1981: 197–210). For an exemplification of its centrality to current debate, see Dretske (2005a, 2005b) and Hawthorne (2005).
9   For an understanding of it in terms of *regress* and *further* knowledge, see Hetherington (2004).
10 (i) We might have prefaced 1 with some epistemic modality operator, such as 'It is possible for the following to be so'. But that would be a needless complication. (ii) 1's use of the phrase 'Independently (either at t or earlier)' is to be understood in the way explained at the end of Section 7.3.
11 'No. Surely dreaming needs still to be mentioned, because the sceptical possibility is essentially an alternative possible *explanation* of your sensory experience. Your dreaming would be *why* the other conjuncts are present'. In the first instance, yes, we must mention dreaming; as 1 indeed does. Yet the move to 2 recognises part of what Section 7.2 explained, which was that a sceptic's alternative possible explanation is sceptical only insofar as it reflects upon the truth-directedness of the associated sensory experiences; and the other conjuncts capture how it does this. The rest – our caring about its being dreaming in particular, as against some other epistemically functional equivalent – is mere additional psychological colouring. And my aim here is only to capture the strictly or narrowly sceptical impact of 1. This is why the redundant conjunct within 2 is 'you are dreaming that p' rather than 'you seem, to yourself, to be experiencing p as true.' (We might have thought otherwise, because the challenge could have been framed in terms of dreaming that q, for some q distinct from p. Yet no challenge to the knowledge that p would be present unless this experience is still making it seem to you that p.)

12 This talk of 'experiencing p as true' should not be expanded now to something like 'experiencing, but in a justification-defeating way, p as true'. As I explained earlier, the possibility being discussed here is intended to be only (directly) *truth*-defeating. This is why 3 includes 'not-p' in the way it does. If you believe that the sceptic's concern is immediately with a putative *justification*-defeating possibility instead (this being what I am calling an indirect sceptical possibility), then Sections 7.5 and 7.7 are the ones you will regard as more pressing. (But, as will be clear in those sections, my argument against sceptical uses of 'justification-defeating possibilities' is parasitic *upon* the present argument against sceptical uses of 'truth-defeating possibilities'.)

13 3 is not equivalent to 4 by intuitionistic logic. (That is because the transition from 3 to 4 relies upon this rule: not-not-p ⊢ p (for any p). And that rule is invalid in intuitionistic logic (Makinson 1973: 67).) But we need not be restricted here by that observation. There is little reason, if any, not to interpret claims such as 3 via classical semantics. The sceptic would need to *earn* the right to interpret knowledge-attributions in a non-realist way; and, in order to do this, she will rely on reasoning such as we are discussing. She would thus be proceeding in an *ad hominem* way, accepting a classical semantics for knowledge-attributions, supposedly as a step towards showing that such attributions are not literally true. (And whether she *can* show this is what I am disputing right now.)

14 As I hope is clear, my present point is not that 'You know that you are not merely dreaming that p' is logically equivalent to 'You know that p'. Obviously, the two propositions as such are not logically equivalent. Nor do they mean the same in all contexts. Rather, I am considering 'You know that you are not merely dreaming that p' purely insofar as it is functioning within a strictly Cartesian would-be sceptical inferential *challenge* – with the sceptic presuming herself to be designating a further piece of knowledge you can sensibly be asked to have independently of having knowledge that p, with your being inferred to lack the knowledge that p if you lack the further knowledge.

15 For earlier applications of this section's core pattern of reasoning, see Hetherington (2001: 37–40, 2002: 95–7).

16 Recall, too (also from Section 7.1), that this denial of justification bears upon the presence only of truth-directed forms of justification. It is not necessarily a denial of deontological forms of justification being present, for example. In the rest of this chapter, I will take for granted this qualification (occasionally mentioning it in passing).

17 We might therefore interpret this section as reflecting upon how a sceptic would seek directly to deny us *justification* via a sceptical possibility – and only *in*directly to deny us knowledge via such a possibility. The previous section was about how a sceptic would seek *directly* to deny us knowledge via a sceptical possibility. As will become clear, then, I believe that this chapter's argument applies to any attempted uses of sceptical possibilities to deny us either knowledge or (truth-directed) justification, either directly or indirectly. In Section 7.7, I will return briefly to this case of the 'justification-sceptic'.

18 Note the parallel between this formulation and one traditional sceptical motivation (such as Descartes's own motivation, in Section 7.1) for *direct* sceptical possibilities. The latter sceptical reasoning might well claim to locate the power of a direct sceptical possibility within your not being able to distinguish (1) being in the situation it non-modally describes from (2) being in a normal, external world, situation. Now we find indirect sceptical possibilities standing analogously to direct

19 sceptical possibilities, with your not being able to distinguish (3) being 'in' the situation non-modally described by the indirect sceptical possibility from (1) being in the situation non-modally described by a direct sceptical possibility.

19 Frances (2005: 111–12) proposes a similar analysis. His general principle is as follows (2005: 112): If Q is fully consistent with P, but S needs to rule out Q in order to know P, then there is some R inconsistent with P such that (a) S needs to rule out R in order to know P and (b) S needs to rule out Q in order to rule out R.

20 Here is another example I have encountered. A badly injured soldier wonders whether she still has her hands. Although she thinks she feels them, she sees much blood around her, she remembers a grenade exploding in front of her, and she cannot move her body to check directly and immediately on whether her hands have remained in place. In order for her to know that she has hands, she first needs to rule out the possibility of her feeling (as of having them) being illusory. Yet does my anti-sceptical argument mistakenly deem this reasonable demand to be unreasonable? (No, as I will show in a moment. The doubt or demand in question is not sceptical. It is a sensible assessment of competing pieces of evidence as to actual states of affairs.)

21 Return to the example in the previous note. There, the soldier may think that it feels to her as though her hands are still present. But her doubt is based on her having looked around, her having noted circumstances that *do* obtain and that render *actually* unlikely her hands being where she wants them to be.

22 'What of *Pyrrhonist* scepticism? Doesn't it adduce genuinely incongruent pieces of evidence, not merely incongruent possibilities?' Only up to a point is that so. Sextus Empiricus (when presenting Pyrrhonism) did adduce competing pieces of evidence. But these would take him only so far, usually falling short of his sweeping sceptical conclusions. What else did he adduce, then, in order to reach his broad-ranging scepticism? He brought forth *possibilities*, such as the possible availability of competing evidence even when none had actually been cited.

23 A possibility of mistake, say, is not being used sceptically if it is serving merely to illustrate the fallibility, and not to question the existence, of the associated knowledge.

24 Remember how Descartes uses his possibility of merely dreaming. He concedes a history of being deceived by dreaming. However, his only use of this history, even though he presents it as factual evidence, is to infer a possibility – from which, given his inability at that moment to eliminate it entirely and independently, he infers his lack of external world knowledge.

25 As fn. 17 has already indicated.

26 The problem remains, too, if she claims to be reaching only for an *indirect* challenge. As before, the failure of any direct sceptical possibilities to mount a real inferential challenge entails the failure of any associated indirect sceptical possibilities to do so.

27 This section extends an earlier argument (Hetherington 2004: sec. 4).

28 S follows thus (where T reports your passing a test for not dreaming): $k(\sim d) \rightarrow k(T)$; but knowledge that T is external world knowledge; so, by 7, $k(T) \rightarrow k(\sim d)$; hence, by transitivity of '$\rightarrow$', $k(\sim d) \rightarrow k(\sim d)$. (This reasoning is adapting, not quoting, Sosa's.)

29 P follows thus: $k(\sim d) \rightarrow k(T)$ (where T remains as it was in the previous note); but knowledge that T is external world knowledge; so, by 7, $k(T) \rightarrow k(\sim d)$; hence, $k(\sim d) \leftrightarrow k(T)$; therefore, for some external world proposition q, $k(\sim d) \leftrightarrow k(q)$. (This reasoning is adapting, not quoting, Pryor's.)

30 Perhaps 8's contained consequent should be this: 'At some minimally earlier time t_2, you know that you are not dreaming *and* that you will not be dreaming at t_1.' But the

31 S/P follows thus (where t_3 is minimally earlier than t_2, which is minimally earlier than t_1; and where, for any i and p, t_i-k(p) is one's knowing at t_i that p): t_1-k($\sim d$) → t_2-k(T); but knowledge that T is external world knowledge; so, by 7, t_2-k(T) → t_3-k($\sim d$); hence (by transitivity of '→'), t_1-k($\sim d$) → t_3-k($\sim d$).
32 Sosa does notice the difference between dreaming and merely dreaming (1988: 153–4). Possibly, though, he does not notice the availability of the kind of analysis (of 'merely dreaming that p') that has introduced us to the sceptical-independence problem.
33 For further critical reflection on the methodology of analytic epistemology in general, see Hetherington (2006).
34 We thus derive what Macarthur (2003, 2004) calls a *quietism* about scepticism: 'The aim of quietism is not to refute the sceptic but to entitle oneself not to need to' (2004: 107).
35 Hawthorne (2004: 31–50) has defended both Single-Premise Closure and Multi-Premise Closure. The point I am about to make is no less applicable to these than to comparatively traditional renderings of closure.
36 Elsewhere, I have argued, on different grounds to any used in this chapter, for the *falsity* of closure, formulated here as © (Hetherington 2001: ch. 2 – for parts of which, see Chapter 6 above). Even when © is applied to non-sceptical values of 'q', it is false. My basic anti-closure idea in that earlier argument was that (i) when a person knows that (p → q), her knowing that q would (other things being equal) be a way for her to *improve* her knowing that p, but that (ii) in general, one can know that p *without* knowing even better still that p. On this analysis, then, closure is seen to be needlessly strong, due to its *entailing* that to have *any* particular piece of knowledge is to have even more knowledge. My alternative analysis offers a weaker possibility: one *can* gain new knowledge from old – gaining knowledge that q from knowledge that p, courtesy of knowing that (p → q) – even if one *need* not do so. For, again, one can know that p without knowing better that p. This amendment preserves the non-sceptical aim of modelling our ability to gain even further knowledge by gaining some new knowledge. In a commendably realistic way, however, the amendment denies that this expansion *need* always occur.
37 Versions of this chapter were presented at the University of Queensland and the University of Melbourne. I appreciated the careful comments by those audiences. Adam Morton's advice has also been invaluable.

References

Ayer, A.J. (1956), *The Problem of Knowledge*, London: Macmillan.
Descartes, R. (1911 [1641]), *The Philosophical Works of Descartes*, vol. 1, E.S. Haldane and G.R.T. Ross (eds and trans.), Cambridge: Cambridge University Press.
Dretske, F.I. (1970), 'Epistemic Operators', *The Journal of Philosophy*, 67: 1007–23.
Dretske, F.I. (2005a), 'The Case against Closure', in M. Steup and E. Sosa (eds), *Contemporary Debates in Epistemology*, 13–26, Malden, MA: Blackwell.
Dretske, F.I. (2005b), 'Reply to Hawthorne', in M. Steup and E. Sosa (eds), *Contemporary Debates in Epistemology*, 43–6, Malden, MA: Blackwell.

simpler condition will suffice for our purposes, given our understanding t_2 as being only minimally earlier than t_1.

Frances, B. (2005), *Scepticism Comes Alive*, Oxford: Clarendon Press.
Greco, J. (2000), *Putting Skeptics in Their Place*, Cambridge: Cambridge University Press.
Hawthorne, J. (2004), *Knowledge and Lotteries*, Oxford: Clarendon Press.
Hawthorne, J. (2005), 'The Case for Closure', in M. Steup and E. Sosa (eds), *Contemporary Debates in Epistemology*, 26–43, Malden, MA: Blackwell.
Hetherington, S. (2001), *Good Knowledge, Bad Knowledge: On Two Dogmas of Epistemology*, Oxford: Clarendon Press.
Hetherington, S. (2002), 'Fallibilism and Knowing that One Is Not Dreaming', *Canadian Journal of Philosophy*, 32: 83–102.
Hetherington, S. (2004), 'Shattering a Cartesian Sceptical Dream', *Principia*, 8: 103–17.
Hetherington, S. (2006), 'Knowledge That Works: A Tale of Two Conceptual Models', in S. Hetherington (ed.), *Aspects of Knowing: Epistemological Essays*, 219–40, Oxford: Elsevier.
Hume, D. (1902 [1748]), *An Enquiry Concerning Human Understanding*, 2nd edn, L.A. Selby-Bigge (ed.), Oxford: Clarendon Press.
Macarthur, D. (2003), 'McDowell, Scepticism, and the "Veil of Perception"', *Australasian Journal of Philosophy*, 81: 175–90.
Macarthur, D. (2004), 'Naturalism and Skepticism', in M. De Caro and D. Macarthur (eds), *Naturalism in Question*, 106–24, Cambridge, MA: Harvard University Press.
Makinson, D.C. (1973), *Topics in Modern Logic*, London: Methuen.
Nozick, R. (1981), *Philosophical Explanations*, Cambridge, MA: Harvard University Press.
Pryor, J. (2000), 'The Skeptic and the Dogmatist', *Noûs*, 24: 517–49.
Sosa, E. (1988), 'Beyond Scepticism, to the Best of Our Knowledge', *Mind*, 97: 153–88.
Stroud, B. (1984), *The Significance of Philosophical Scepticism*, Oxford: Clarendon Press.

8

Knowledge that works: A tale of two conceptual models

8.1 A methodological question

In this chapter, I describe two models of knowledge – two templates that might be used in fashioning a concept of knowledge, in assessing the presence or absence of knowledge. One of these models should be familiar, because it already guides much philosophical thinking about knowledge. But *should* it have that influence? It is epistemological orthodoxy; need it be? It amounts to a methodological choice, made at the beginning of many epistemological inquiries, as to how to approach thinking about knowledge in the first place. An implicit reliance upon this standard model is *why* epistemologists find so natural many of their claims as to when knowledge is, or is not, present. Yet, crucially, this usual methodological choice is not conceptually mandatory; an alternative model is available, as we will see. There is a real possibility of our having been thinking about knowledge in a way that is more conceptually restricted than we have realised. Moreover, it will transpire, that model springs from an historically explicable methodological choice, one we need never have made, and which we need not continue making.

8.2 Sceptical possibilities and the Not-Yet model

For reasons that will become apparent, I call the usual model the *Not-Yet model*. It reflects a way in which epistemologists habitually manifest a wariness when attributing knowledge. A wariness of what? A wariness of attributing knowledge when there is even a chance of being mistaken in one's attribution. We ask to be convinced that knowledge is present, before attributing it. Nowhere is this clearer than in some discussions of sceptical possibilities.

Consider this Cartesian sceptical doubt:

Although you seem, to yourself, to be sitting on a chair, it is possible for this inner experience to be part of your *dreaming* sitting on a chair.

In Stroud's (1984: ch. 1) reconstruction of Descartes's dreaming argument, you are required to know that no such possibility obtains. If you lack that knowledge, then (infers this sceptic), you fail to know that you are sitting on a chair.

That sceptical thinking directs us to this partial picture of how to conceive of knowledge:

1. Regardless of whatever else is involved in your knowing that *p*, this knowledge is not to be accepted as being present *unless and until* various sceptical possibilities are somehow removed.

It is a picture routinely accepted by non-sceptics, too. This is clear when we ask what 'removed' means in 1. The Cartesian possibility might be removed, for example, by your knowing that you are not dreaming: you would be *satisfying* this sceptic's demand. Or perhaps someone provides a philosophical *dismissal* of the sceptic's demand, showing its not needing to be satisfied. Sceptics challenge us either to satisfy or dismiss their demands; non-sceptics strive to meet that challenge. Both sceptics and these non-sceptics thus concur in not attributing knowledge that *p* unless and until sceptical possibilities are removed in some appropriate way – maybe by the epistemic subject, possibly by some 'onlooker'.

Now we may precisify the rest of 1 (where *XYZ* is a conjunction of conditions, which we may leave unspecified):

2. For any *XYZ*: your *XYZ*ing is to be accepted as your knowing that *p*, *only once* (i) various sceptical possibilities are somehow removed, and (ii) their-being-removed is included in *XYZ*.[1]

And 2 instantiates what I call the Not-Yet model of knowledge.[2] It is standard for an epistemologist to muse as follows: 'Is this *XYZ* knowledge? *Not yet may I say so.* Not unless and until these sceptical possibilities are removed may I say so. (Or so I must assume, if I am to avoid begging the question against sceptics.)' Thus, a sceptic's further condition – requiring the removal of a pertinent possibility – becomes accepted as an *enabling* or *constituting* condition of knowledge that *p*. Only then are other conditions accepted as being able, along with it, to constitute knowledge that *p*. In the meantime, the sceptic's condition's not being satisfied is claimed by sceptics (and often conceded, even if hypothetically, by non-sceptics) to prevent other conditions from constituting knowledge that *p*.[3]

8.3 Gettier circumstances and the Not-Yet model

The Not-Yet model has also guided epistemological reactions to *Gettier cases*. The concept of such a case arises with Edmund Gettier (1963).[4] Almost universally,[5] epistemologists say that each Gettier case is an actual or possible situation containing a belief which is true and well (although fallibly) justified – yet without being knowledge, due to some odd circumstance. That interpretation unhesitatingly assumes 3:

3   Knowledge that *p* is accepted to be absent from any pertinent Gettier situation *unless and until* some pertinent aspect of the situation is somehow removed.[6]

More precisely (with 4 standing to Gettier circumstances as 2 does to sceptical possibilities):

4   For any *XYZ*: your *XYZ*ing is to be accepted as your knowing that *p*, *only once* (i) any Gettier circumstance is removed (however this is to occur), and (ii) its-being-removed is included in *XYZ*.

The standard interpretation of Gettier cases thus perpetuates the Not-Yet model of knowledge. Epistemologists offer hypotheses as to what constitutes knowledge: they propose initial values of *XYZ*. Then they encounter Gettier cases, before debating how best, exactly, to eliminate the cases' odd circumstances.[7] Meanwhile, knowledge is deemed absent from the cases. Knowledge is to be attributed *only after* Gettier circumstances are removed. And by seeing how to achieve this removal, epistemologists discover knowledge to be a variation on the previously proposed *XYZ*.[8] So, the analytical investigation assumes that the epistemic significance of Gettier circumstances is constitutive: knowledge is absent if they are present; removing them would enable knowledge to be present.[9]

8.4 Some failings of the Not-Yet model

So far, the Not-Yet model is the conjunction of the easily recognisable 2 and 4. Nonetheless, familiar though it is, we should be dissatisfied with it. This section describes two respects in which that model is needlessly narrow in what it allows, from the outset, to be modelled about knowledge.

(1) The Not-Yet model does not do justice to the concept of some knowledge's *withstanding* a threat (such as from a sceptical possibility). We often talk of knowledge in that way. Yet how well can we understand it via the Not-Yet model? On that model, we find ourselves inquiring as if there is no knowledge that *p* – there is something epistemically lesser; we are asking whether it is knowledge – *until* the possible 'approach' of *p*'s being false, for example, has been independently evaded. But if no knowledge that *p* is allowed already to be 'in place', no such knowledge can be interpreted as having the opportunity, strictly speaking, to withstand that possible falsity. (What does not exist has no metaphysical chance to withstand threats to its existing.) Consequently, we need a way of inquiring that allows some knowledge to be present even when being assessed in relation to such threats.

The Not-Yet model has conceptual room only for the idea of knowledge being *recovered* – returned to us – in the face of the threats. It does not allow us to understand the knowledge as coexisting while the threats are being assessed. Prior to the knowledge's being recovered, the threats are to be removed. So, they are to be removed independently, without the knowledge's contributing. It is usual for epistemologists to try disposing of sceptical doubts independently, trusting that this will then allow the knowledge to be recovered.[10] (I think of this as a *Cartesian recovery program* for our knowledge. Conceptually, we relinquish the knowledge while independently disposing of threats; only then do we feel confident in reclaiming the knowledge – from where?)

(2) Use of the Not-Yet model also fails to do justice to what it is to know *fallibly* that *p*.[11] On that model, you are allowed to know that *p* only once sceptical possibilities, say, are somehow overcome or removed. In the meantime, you are deemed not to know that *p*. Hence, no instance of some *XYZ* can be regarded as knowledge which is *yet* to have overcome those threatening possibilities. In other words, any knowledge which the Not-Yet model allows to exist will have overcome all such distinctively philosophical knowledge-threats. But knowledge like that has a fair claim upon being classified as infallible. So, the Not-Yet model does not permit fallible knowledge to be understood as present.

8.5 Towards an alternative model

Section 8.4 reveals two *desiderata* for any alternative to the Not-Yet model. What unites these two is the idea of being able to assess a piece of knowledge *even as it is in place as knowledge*. *Desideratum* (1): Only knowledge already in place could *withstand* sceptical threats, say. *Desideratum* (2): Sometimes, knowledge needs to be able to be understood as *fallible* – in the sense of being in place, even if it has not yet overcome all sceptical possibilities, for example. We need a model that portrays – a way of conceiving of – knowledge as able to be present as knowledge, even while being tested, even in ways which might dispose of it. Maybe we must include its capacity for being tested within our conception of the knowledge's normal functions. How might we do this?

On the Not-Yet model, we consider a composite of conditions, *XYZ*, asking whether this is enough for knowledge, while assuming (so as to avoid begging various questions) that it is not. We ask whether specific further components are needed (such as knowledge of a sceptical possibility's not obtaining, or some Gettier circumstance's absence), if there is to *be* knowledge. (If these further components are needed, the previous specification of *XYZ* is to be revised accordingly.) In place of the Not-Yet model, we now see, a model of knowledge is needed which, at least for argument's sake, allows the putative components described in the analysis XYZ to *be* knowledge. Then we will be asking, not whether specific further components are needed if there is to be the knowledge, but what further features such knowledge could have, without *ceasing* to be knowledge. Within this altered methodological setting, new challenges to knowledge-attributions may well arise. Will traditional sceptical doubts and Gettier challenges retain the impact many epistemologists currently accord them? That is yet to be seen. (And if they do not, there could be a correlative change in the list of core epistemological challenges.) I will call the alternative model the *Working Knowledge* model.

8.6 An analogy

We may understand the basic idea behind my alternative model through an analogy between classifying something as knowledge and *hiring a new employee*. Ideally, the employer hires someone with all the skills, who knows all the details, to be required within the position. (Perhaps this person would have previously worked in a very similar position, needing either-no-or-minimal further training.) Alternatively, the employer could hire someone who shows enough signs of being *able* to learn the job's details efficiently. Obviously, this is the usual method. It results in someone's being hired who is yet to know everything which the employer will expect him to know. Maybe the employee is therefore hired on a tentative or probationary basis. Even so (other things being equal), he will be accorded full employment status, no matter that he does not yet possess every skill or piece of knowledge ultimately wanted within the job. He is accorded the title and status of a full-time employee anyway.

And, significantly, he is thereby more likely, other things being equal, to *become* as good an employee as is desired. With the opportunity, the new responsibility, and the trust being shown in him, he can 'grow into' the job – doing it more and more as, ideally, it should be done. Indeed, the onus is upon him to improve. This would occur as he learns the job while in the position. He would be using his potential, in building upon what was already enough to be doing the job. Promotions and salary increases, too, might ensue as this improvement occurs. All of this can happen within the scope of a single, continuing, job title and description.

Does this amount to guaranteeing the person a job 'for life'? No. Is it impossible for the person to lose the job? Of course not. Anyone could make bad mistakes in a job. And a person could do so before ever becoming the perfect employee (who could have been hired as someone needing no improvement or training). Nevertheless, it will be most evident whether the person is capable of doing the job, only once he is doing it. In general, the best test of his capacity to do the job is how he *does* do it. The best way to test him is to let him do the job.

This does not entail that just anyone should be hired, letting them be tested in that best way possible – namely, 'on the job'. Even without knowing for sure in advance when we are about to make a mistake in hiring, we apply discriminative criteria. Then we live with the results until we cannot do so any more: 'He has to go. He isn't up to the job'.

And all of that is analogous to our epistemic cases, with epistemological inquirers functioning analogously to the potential employers. Satisfying a *prima facie* apt description *XYZ* is like having at least the objective potential to be an excellent or even perfect employee:[12] one has done enough to be hired with that ideal in mind. But the Not-Yet model's way of assessing whether an instance of *XYZ* is knowledge is like a search for an already-perfect employee, who is not to be hired unless and until he is already a perfect employee. In contrast, the Working Knowledge model is like the initially-less-demanding employer. It is willing to treat being knowledge as like being an imperfect-but-trainable employee, who needs to develop within the job and who will be allowed to do so (even while risking failing to do so).

On the Not-Yet model's way of thinking, we would hire a person or accept an *XYZ* as being knowledge, only once no new development is needed in order for the person to do the job or for the *XYZ* to be knowledge. In other words, the knowledge is to be perfect, as that employee is to be perfect. On the Working Knowledge model's way of thinking, though, we may hire someone, or we may accept an *XYZ* as being knowledge, while accepting that assorted challenges of training or development (such as are posed by the distinctively philosophical knowledge-threats) still lie ahead, if the person is to do the job or if the *XYZ* is to be knowledge. The knowledge need not yet be what we ultimately want it to be as knowledge, just as that employee need not yet be what we ultimately want him to be as an employee. He will learn much of the job *in* the job. Even if he does not fully realise in advance that this will be so ('I'm qualified. I've got all the skills now!'), an experienced employer is likely to realise it. She should therefore not shy away from hiring the imperfectly experienced person. *And we may approach assessments of knowledge analogously.* By something's being *XYZ*, it has the objective potential for being knowledge; so we should accept it as knowledge, at least for now.

8.7 Fallibly working knowledge

Section 8.6's suggestion readily provides a way of conceiving of fallible knowledge. The simplest claim we could make towards that end is this: fallible knowledge is knowledge, with its fallibility just being part of it, one of its properties. Yet even that truism, as we saw in Section 8.4, is not obviously accommodated by the Not-Yet model. On this model (as Section 8.6 explained), knowledge is to be hired only as a perfect employee is to be hired: once knowledge *is* hired, therefore, it is not fallible; whatever potential there was for failure will already have been eliminated. But if knowledge is to be fallible, it must retain some chance of failure, even after it has been hired. In effect, its fallibility is now a capacity no longer to be knowledge. Its fallibility is thus its potential, even as something in place as knowledge, to *cease* being knowledge. Fallible knowledge, by being knowledge, is performing jobs that knowledge performs; however, it does so even while having the potential to be 'dismissed' from its role as knowledge. It is knowledge which performs its job *qua* knowledge as well as its fallibility permits. There is a correlative risk of its ceasing to perform that job. Hence, it is knowledge by satisfying some description *XYZ*, even if there are as-yet-unremoved threats to its continuing to be knowledge in that way. Schematically, this is how we should conceive of fallible knowledge.

Imagine being confronted with a putative instance of knowledge, satisfying some *prima facie* apt description *XYZ*.[13] Suppose we accept that if it is knowledge, it is most likely fallible. The Working Knowledge model tells us that we will best discover whether this instance of *XYZ* is fallible knowledge, by first hiring it as knowledge (hiring it as a cognitive employee), and by *then* looking for whatever fallibility it has. Only thus could we be finding its fallibility *qua* knowledge – that is, its *being* fallible knowledge. The Working Knowledge model is pragmatist. We accept and use the instance of *XYZ* as knowledge while accepting that, by being fallible, it could cease being knowledge. That moment could arrive suddenly. Like an unanticipated Humean alteration to the course of nature, what has been knowledge might no longer be knowledge. One day, its fallibility could be realised. Nonetheless, we need not – by acknowledging that the instance of *XYZ* could suddenly cease being regarded as knowledge – regard it already as not being knowledge.

Sceptics in particular would have us do so;[14] congruently, their Not-Yet model impels them towards that interpretation. By using that model, however, at the crucial interpretive moment they already treat the instance of *XYZ* as not being knowledge. So, it is not that sceptics hire – and then fire. They cannot even hire in the first place. Applications of the Not-Yet model begin by assuming that the knowledge in question within a given case is absent.

The Working Knowledge model reverses that methodological procedure. We assume that the knowledge is present (once an *XYZ* is present), in order to be testing this assumption (such as against distinctively philosophical knowledge-threats like sceptical possibilities). At least sometimes, the assumption could be what Jacquette (2004) calls a working hypothesis. This is an attempt to formulate an hypothesis so that it can be an 'official' hypothesis, to be tested as an hypothesis: 'There is less commitment to such a pre-formulation of an assumption even as an hypothesis' (2004: 185).

If this is the spirit in which an *XYZ* is being deemed knowledge, it would be correspondingly unfair for sceptics to complain that the question is being begged against them. All that is not being conceded is the *XYZ*'s not being knowledge – which is apt, because it is what the sceptics want us to *test*. The fact of our doing so by treating the *XYZ* as knowledge (at least for now) is not unfair. We will be asking whether such knowledge withstands particular sceptical possibilities, for instance. We will ask whether, given its presumed fallibility, it does so. And we will not follow the Not-Yet model in assuming that only once a given sceptical doubt is somehow removed is the knowledge wholly *constituted* – and hence to be deemed present. The Working Knowledge model portrays us as (1) testing independently (even if fallibly) constituted knowledge, rather than as (2) showing (even proving) that something is knowledge in the first place. The latter approach gives us the Not-Yet model, on which no instance of *XYZ* is accepted to be knowledge unless *and until* sceptical possibilities are overcome – with the overcoming of them being deemed to be a constitutive part of the knowledge (being added to, or modifying, the description *XYZ*). Alternatively, the former approach gives us the Working Knowledge model, one statement of which is this:

WK Any *prima facie* apt *XYZ* can be accepted as an instance of knowing that *p*, although various circumstances (including distinctively philosophical knowledge-threats, such as sceptical possibilities) could test *XYZ*'s capacity to remain as that knowledge that *p*.

In effect, knowing would be treated as something other than a '*final*' cognitive state, relative to *p*.[15] It would be accepted as something 'alive' – developing, ongoing, testable. It would be attributed as a *work in progress*. It need not be attributed with finality. All is testable, even something's being knowledge.

8.8 Gradualism and scepticism

We might wonder whether the Working Knowledge model really does allow the testing of whether instances of *XYZ* are cases of knowledge. Is it a dogmatic model, in the sense of attributing knowledge too easily?

Popperian destroyers. To assume that some instance of *XYZ* is knowledge is not to assume that it will survive all testing of whether it is knowledge.[16] Many people withdraw claims and lose beliefs when encountering sceptical thoughts or when deciding that they have been (and could still be) in a Gettier situation. In this sense, whatever is knowledge need not remain knowledge. Employees are tested even while they are employees. Sometimes they fail the tests, thereupon ceasing to be employees. They fail as employees, thereupon ceasing to be employees – just as some knowledge could fail as knowledge, thereupon ceasing to be knowledge. So, in principle sceptical doubts can destroy knowledge. This is how we should think of their potential to cause epistemic damage.[17] We are used to thinking of them as knowledge-*preventing* threats. But that is not mandatory. It reflects our being trained to think of knowledge in terms imposed by the Not-Yet model. Bypassing that model allows us to reconceptualise sceptical threats. (And if this seems to weaken their general epistemic impact, so be it.) We can think of them as akin to potential Popperian destroyers of knowledge which has been present so far (rather than as potential Cartesian preventers of there being knowledge in the first place). On the Working Knowledge model, attributions of knowledge can be discarded: what had previously been accepted as knowledge would *no longer* be regarded as knowledge (because now a sceptical possibility has not been overcome, say); and this could occur without entailing that knowledge never really *had* been present. The Working Knowledge model allows that there can be knowledge now, which fails to be knowledge later – by later ceasing to be knowledge, by later losing a battle with some threat. In effect, on the Not-Yet model, '*x* knows that *p*' means that, at least in theory, *x* can be proved to know that *p*; whereas on the Working Knowledge model, '*x* knows that *p*' means that *x* has not yet been proved not to know that *p*.[18]

Improved knowledge. Moreover, even if we decide that a sceptical threat is withstood by a piece of knowledge (some instance of *XYZ*), with the knowledge surviving that threat, we need not infer that the threat lacks all epistemic significance. For we might wonder whether the surviving of it has had a *qualitative* impact upon the piece of knowledge. The Working Knowledge model reveals how we may conceive of this as being so. The Not-Yet model allows us to regard sceptical possibilities only as having *absolutist* consequences: either we accept that they prevent some *XYZ*'s being knowledge; or (if they are overcome) it is allowed to be knowledge. But the Working Knowledge model permits us to accord such possibilities a further way, a non-absolutist way, of making an epistemic impact. We may think of such possibilities as akin to job-threatening challenges arising at work, threatening an employee with losing her position. Then we should call to mind this popular saying: Whatever does not kill a person makes her stronger. By applying what is true in that saying to the present case, we derive this moral: Whenever the employee survives one of these threats, she could well (all else being equal) be somewhat *better* as an employee for having engaged with, and bested, the threat. And the same is true, *mutatis mutandis*, whenever some knowledge survives a sceptical challenge. The Working Knowledge model permits us to interpret this survival as *strengthening* that knowledge (other things being equal). On the Not-Yet model, the knowledge is deemed *enabled* to be present if a sceptical threat is overcome; nothing else is thought to be achieved. (Notice how often epistemological focus is on whether there *can* be knowledge – in some sense supposedly established by undermining sceptical arguments.) On the Working Knowledge model, the knowledge can again be seen as enabled – *but it can also be deemed ennobled* – by overcoming a sceptical threat. Remember that, on the Not-Yet model, the knowledge itself cannot be conceived of as overcoming the threat, strictly speaking. *Independently*, the threat is to be overcome, thereby enabling the knowledge to exist. But on the Working Knowledge model we may say that the knowledge itself is what does battle with the threat. So, if it wins, *it* can be strengthened, ennobled, as the knowledge it continues to be. It can have 'grown' as that knowledge, a possibility not envisaged on the Not-Yet model.

That conceptual possibility of ennobling, rather than just enabling, a piece of knowledge flows naturally into a theory I have elsewhere labelled a *gradualism* about propositional knowledge (Hetherington 2001a). On that theory's central idea, any instance of knowledge that p (once constituted by satisfying some apt XYZ) is more or less qualitatively good as knowledge that p. This qualitative dimension is epistemic. Any case of knowledge that p can, equally well, be described as being of some epistemically lesser or greater degree or quality of knowledge that p. And this status need not be static or unchangeable. For instance, if you improve your evidence for p, then (other things being equal) you thereby improve your knowledge that p, insofar as the evidence's presence is part of the knowledge's presence. One instance of knowledge that p can be epistemically better than another, insofar as the former's epistemic core (such as some form of justification) is better than the latter's. (And it is epistemologically standard to accept that justification can be gradational.) One person's knowledge that p can be better than another's. A single person's knowledge that p can be better at one time than another.

There might be no limit to how much a case of knowledge that p could be improved in such ways. As sceptical possibilities mount, so do dangers to our knowledge – to knowledge we *have* (allows the Working Knowledge model). If that knowledge withstands those threats, it is correlatively stronger than it might have been. Even so, it never loses its fallibility. Accordingly, it is not only more or less fallible as knowledge; it is endlessly so. The Not-Yet model, we found, has a contrary implication: when it is applied to the evaluation of a sceptical possibility's impact, knowledge is treated as disappearing – at best, as going into hiding until danger passes. (So, as we also saw, on the Not-Yet model the knowledge itself cannot be interpreted as withstanding the sceptical possibility. Nor, therefore, can it rightly be thought to be fallible when doing so. It cannot be regarded as strengthened by that experience, either.) But the Working Knowledge model allows us to accept that any piece of knowledge, while ever it is being used, is open to being destroyed, even by philosophically distinctive knowledge-threats. Nonetheless, we may say, while ever the knowledge has not been destroyed, it continues surviving; and it can thereby be strengthened, improved, by the number and seriousness of the tests it has passed. In theory, too, there is no upper limit to how many tests it could undergo. In principle, therefore, it is endlessly fallible and endlessly improvable. More epistemic bounty can be gained from doing battle with scepticism than we might have anticipated gaining.[19]

Worsened knowledge. Still, there is no guarantee of such improvement. The Working Knowledge model allows a sceptical challenge also to be conceived of as lowering some knowledge's quality. At present, through the Not-Yet model, epistemologists generally treat sceptical challenges as being coherent and applicable in advance of – and hence as playing a part merely in conceptually constituting – whether a particular XYZ is knowledge. But this is like questioning whether a person should be hired, given only that there are pertinent tests which he cannot yet pass; *of course*, he cannot pass all of them before he is hired. Thus, the Working Knowledge model becomes significant. On it, coherent sceptical challenges to knowing arise only once there is a working presumption of knowing. They are like tests arising at work, subjecting an actual employee to actual pressure. We cease worrying so much about whether a *potential* employee would survive that kind of pressure.[20] And we should bear in mind that an employee who fails a test, even if she does not lose her job, might thereby be revealed to be less good at the job than had been assumed (by herself or others). The same is true, *mutatis mutandis*, of knowledge. Another gradualist moral appears among our conceptual options: Just as surviving a sceptical challenge might strengthen a piece of knowledge, failing the challenge might lower that knowledge's quality.

For example, suppose that you cannot eliminate the possibility of your dreaming. Do you thereby lack the knowledge that you are sitting in a chair? Sceptics say so, and the Not-Yet model abets that interpretation. But on the Working Knowledge model we are free to infer that you might pay only the price of knowing *less well* (all else being equal) that you are sitting in a chair, perhaps less well than you assumed you did.[21]

Thus, my proposal need not deny sceptics all possible conceptual victories. But it does conceive anew what forms their victories could take, hence what significance there could be in sceptical thinking. In general, the Working Knowledge model promotes a conception of knowledge which is ultimately less accepting of sceptical worries than is existing epistemological thinking, based upon the Not-Yet model. In effect, armed with the Not-Yet model, epistemologists treat knowledge that p as ultimate or unimprovable knowledge that p: only once the 'needed' improvements are completed is there accepted to be knowledge. (These improvements are made in one's overall epistemic situation, regarding p – such as if one gains knowledge of not dreaming that p. Only then is this summed up as ..., well, as one's knowing that p.) In contrast, with the Working Knowledge, epistemologists treat any instance of knowledge that p as potentially working *towards* being ultimate or unimprovable knowledge that p: in the meantime, however, almost all cases of knowledge that p are accepted as being improvable – non-ultimate. (Those improvements deemed by the Not-Yet model as being made only in one's overall epistemic situation regarding p are now able to be seen to be made in the knowledge that p itself, along the way.) By the same token, though, the Working Knowledge model allows epistemologists the conceptual option of seeing any case of knowledge that p as doubly fallible – able, alternately, to be lost *or* to be lesser. There could well be more to knowing that p than the Not-Yet model allows us to notice.

8.9 Working knowledge in Gettier cases

Does the Working Knowledge model offer us new conceptual freedom in interpreting Gettier cases? I believe so. The standard epistemological interpretation of these is that, within each, some justified true belief fails to be knowledge. And epistemologists say that this interpretation gives voice to their 'intuitions' about the cases. But we noted in Section 8.3 how the Not-Yet model, a substantive and theoretical model of knowledge, underlies those so-called intuitions: they are not *so* 'intuitive'. One indication of this is how differently we might wish to interpret Gettier cases once we adopt the Working Knowledge model. I will illustrate this briefly, via a representative case, adapted from Chisholm (1966: 23).

> *The sheep in the field.* You gaze into a field, seeing what looks like a sheep. So, you believe there is a sheep in that field. You are right, because there is one there – hidden from your sight, behind a hill. (What you are seeing is a disguised dog.) Hence, your belief is true. It is also justified, through a standard use of your senses, followed by a normally good inference. Is your justified true belief-that-there-is-a-sheep-in-the-field knowledge?

'Of course not', implies the Not-Yet model. But if we put that model to one side, we may interpret the case afresh. Thus, for a start, your belief within the case is fairly well qualified to be hired as knowledge. By being well justified and true, it satisfies a *prima facie* apt description *XYZ* of a sufficient condition of knowledge – in practise, of working knowledge. It is *fallibly* justified, though: even with its justification in place, the belief neither had to be true nor has to continue being true. (As soon as the unseen sheep wanders out of the field, the belief is false.) This implies that the belief neither had to be knowledge nor has to continue being knowledge. *Is* it therefore not knowledge, right now? The Working Knowledge model does not commit us to thinking so. Rather, we may regard this as an instance of knowledge which is *close* to not being knowledge. For it is close, and remains so, to *ceasing* to be a belief which is both justified and true. At present, it is like an employee who almost made a bad mistake but did not, and who remains close to making that mistake but is not making it, all the while somehow continuing to work professionally and reasonably. If the mistake *had* occurred, she would have been fired; it *could* easily have occurred, due to circumstances beyond her control; in the meantime, she is working well – even if more tenuously so than she realises.

To insist that there is a lack of knowledge in this case is like refusing to hire anyone in the first place unless and until no luck will ever be needed in her performing the job without mishap. That insistence is like saying, unrealistically, that a person is not fit to be employed initially in the job if she would ever (unwittingly) need to be somewhat lucky for a desired outcome within the job to occur (even when performing the job professionally and responsibly). Just as we hire people while accepting that at times luck might well (even in unseen ways) attend their good efforts, we may attribute knowledge, even quite fallible knowledge, in that same spirit. Just as we do not fire a person as soon as such luck arises, we should not deny knowledge as soon as the corresponding luck arises. In each case, we were allowing *for* some fallibility from the beginning; and fallibility, in turn, allows *for* some such luck. Once such luck does arise, then (given that no mistake or harm thereby occurs) it would be unfair to fire the employee. Similarly, it would be unfair to deny the presence of knowledge. (Remember that no mistake or harm occurs; the relevant belief within a Gettier case is true.)[22]

8.10 The Not-Yet model's reach

It might be objected that not all analytical epistemologists apply the Not-Yet model: 'We also discuss people whom we describe as *having* knowledge'. However, even then, contemporary epistemologists implicitly accept that there is such knowledge only so long as threats such as sceptical possibilities, and/or such actual or possible Gettier circumstances, have been overcome or removed (in the sense described in Section 8.2). In this way, the Not-Yet model remains at the core of contemporary analytic epistemology.

Accordingly, even when attributing knowledge, epistemologists do so within the shadows of a way of thinking that is overly concerned with possible ways of lacking knowledge. It is a way of thinking that is fundamentally reluctant to attribute knowledge when there are 'nearby' ways of lacking it (ways that involve luck, accidentality, fallibility, and so on). In particular, modern epistemologists worry deeply about possible ways of being mistaken. So, even when attributing knowledge, these theorists are attributing something that is meant to be understood in terms of the Not-Yet model – this way of *not* attributing that 'something', of *delaying* an attribution until any epistemic dangers are found to be overcome. Descartes is probably the paradigm exemplar of this way of thinking about knowledge, at least as it has influenced modern epistemology. But because I have presented an alternative to it,[23] I have shown how the Not-Yet model is conceptually optional.

8.11 A Platonic precedent and a Cartesian constriction

That model is also historically optional. Many epistemologists, I suspect, feel indebted to Descartes for his clear-minded use of what I am labelling the Not-Yet model. To them, it feels like a natural way of conceiving of knowledge, whenever they seek to reflect analytically and detachedly upon the nature and possibility of knowledge. Nonetheless, their reaction might reflect an historically implanted and reinforced conceptual limitation. After all, epistemology's history has not presented us with only that model. No less a philosophical predecessor than Plato used something like the Working Knowledge model. Why was it ever discarded?

Plato's endorsement of at least part of a Working Knowledge model of knowledge is attested to by Julia Annas. In her interpretation of the *Republic* (Book 10, 601b–602b), she presents this as his view:

Knowledge is not opposed to scepticism. The craftsman's beliefs are true, and fine as far as they go; Plato never suggests that they might be false, or that we should try doubting them. The user's state is better than the maker's, not because he is more sure of anything, but because he has understanding of the subject-matter and its point in a way that the maker lacks. [...] [T]he person with knowledge is contrasted not with the sceptic but with the person who, for practical purposes, takes over true beliefs in an unreflective and second-hand way.

(Annas 1981: 193)

To know is to understand, which is what a user of knowledge does (1981: 212). Moreover, such knowledge can involve improvement. This is improvement on true belief, an improvement in 'the knower's relation to the objects of his or her true belief' (1981: 212). And this 'kind of improvement [...] is not one familiar from the post-Cartesian tradition' (1981: 192), because '[i]t is not an increase in certainty, or a relief from doubt' (1981: 192–3). Thus, for Plato,

he has no reason to think that knowledge will be achieved by a negative, corrosive doubting of all our previous beliefs. Rather than undercutting the beliefs we have, we advance to understanding their significance and finding them intelligible. Of course, when we have knowledge, we may find that some of the beliefs we accepted are in fact false. But we do not *begin* by trying to doubt the truth of particular beliefs in a wholesale way, as Descartes recommends that we do.

(Annas 1981: 212)

Descartes's method of doubt applied a special case of the Not-Yet model. Hence, in conceptual terms it is far removed from this Platonic conception of knowledge. Annas tells us that, in Book V of the *Republic*, Plato

finds it natural to think of knowledge as coming in degrees which vary with the intelligibility of its object; and this is because he is not thinking of knowledge as the result of excluding sceptical doubt [...] [F]or him, the advance to knowledge is a progress to increased understanding, and this comes about not by focussing ever more sceptically on one's grounds for a particular belief, but by setting the belief in a wider context of one's other beliefs and their mutually explanatory relationships. It is because knowledge comes with an increase of explanation and of understanding that Plato finds it natural to think of it as a matter of degree, rather than as an all-or-nothing matter of sheer certainty.

(Annas 1981: 200)

Was it epistemological progress for Descartes to replace such a model of knowledge with his own – the Cartesian one, which has so markedly shaped the epistemological values and methods to which contemporary philosophers are introduced when reflecting upon knowledge? Not if this chapter is correct.

It is hardly the case that Descartes *showed* that there was a philosophical failing or inadequacy in instances, such as Plato's, of the Working Knowledge model of knowledge. What seems to have prompted Descartes's version of the Not-Yet model was more an *attitude* than a demonstration – specifically, an attitude of methodological caution. From where did this attitude come? When and where Descartes was writing, knowledge was a theologically charged prize. Certainly, knowledge as an object of Descartes's philosophical attention was like that, because he wished to prove that Christian knowledge could survive seventeenth-century scientific advances and Pyrrhonian sceptical worries.[24]

What would such Christian knowledge encompass? Part of it was to be knowledge of *essences* in the world – this being knowledge of how nature *has* to be in its details, given its necessarily existing and involved Creator. And this requirement upon the knowledge's content had a significant metaphysical implication regarding the knowledge's nature. It meant that the knowledge itself would have that same kind of metaphysical stability. In other words, instances of knowledge were to be essentially those instances of knowledge. That is, knowledge was conceived of (in advance, on doctrinally inspired grounds) as being such that any instance of it has to be the knowledge it is. Yet how could this be so, especially whenever there is knowledge of a contingent *p*? (If *p* had been false, the belief that *p* would not have been knowledge.) The answer is that nothing is to be knowledge if it has the potential within itself to cease being that knowledge. The Church would not have accepted that susceptibility, that kind of constitutive frailty, as ever being a feature of some knowledge. But one instance of that kind of susceptibility is what we now call epistemic fallibility, with fallible knowledge being so constituted that even with its other components being in place, its truth component need not have been. (Hence, even a belief's continuing to be justified as it presently is will not entail its remaining true.)[25] Fallibility would thus have been deemed to be incompatible with the kind of knowing which is needed if there is to be Church-approved religious knowledge. Such knowledge is knowledge essentially.[26]

It is not surprising, then, that from the outset Descartes applied a model of knowledge which reflected that expectation of what knowledge would need to be like. It was a methodologically cautious model, such caution being religiously appropriate – meaning that knowledge would be attributed only with complete confidence, having satisfied that model. Nothing was to be accepted in a tentative way as being knowledge, therefore, because no such mode of acceptance is appropriate unless the something in question is *essentially* knowledge. To use this chapter's description: No case of *XYZ* could be 'hired' as knowledge unless it was already seen to be fully or unimprovably formed and developed as knowledge. There could be no acceptance of the possibility of developing a piece of lesser knowledge that *p*, say, into what it was wanted to be – perfect or unimprovable knowledge that *p*. For there could never be an acceptance of the possibility of lesser or improvable knowledge that *p* in the first place. How could the existence of God, for example, be thought to be known of in that way? This would be unthinkable. Thus, an assumption of anti-gradualism – absolutism – about knowledge was spawned.

In that way, too, the Not-Yet model was adopted. And it was adopted prior to ascertaining whether any particular belief was knowledge. A Not-Yet *attitude*, as it may be called, was already in place. Descartes was being constricted from the start of his inquiry in his thinking about any putative instance of knowledge. He was being constricted, not only by the Pyrrhonian sceptical doubts being heatedly discussed at the time, but by the Church's demands upon people as knowers.

8.12 Modern epistemology and unwitting Cartesianism

That was then, though; this is now. And epistemologists no longer believe themselves to be beholden to the kind of doctrinally authoritarian power that, in effect, restricted how Descartes was allowed to conceive of knowledge. In general, philosophers do not seek to establish the presence or the absence of knowledge in accord with how some Church ordains knowledge to be. Moreover, although science's influence remains intellectually strong, its seventeenth-century emphasis upon finding natural essences does not. And, in keeping with that shift of focus, the fact of our fallibility has become generally accepted, even scientifically so. Most epistemologists believe that even when we know that p, we do this fallibly – with our evidence, say, not having guaranteed the truth of our belief that p. In such ways, I take it, most philosophers believe that epistemology has progressed since Descartes's time. Those antecedent doctrinal restrictions will be deemed to have been his, not ours, leaving us free to adopt a fallibilist conception of knowledge and to apply it when attributing or denying knowledge.[27]

Even so, we have seen why contemporary would-be fallibilists have not succeeded in moving as far from Cartesian epistemology as most probably believe has occurred. They have not fully cast off Descartes's impliedly infallibilist *methodological* shackles. They will believe themselves to have done so, with the Cartesian quest for certainty no longer being seen as central to epistemological thinking. Nevertheless, the underlying methodological key to Descartes's epistemology was not his search for certainty. As is widely accepted, a more fundamental element was his method of doubt. And we should now appreciate that his method of doubt depended in turn upon a prior receptivity to something more fundamental still – namely, the Not-Yet model of how to think about knowledge at all. Descartes was presuming that nothing could be determined only tentatively to be knowledge. Doubts would therefore need to be removed first of all. By thus applying the Not-Yet model, Descartes was methodologically bound to respect doubt and certainty. To expunge the strongest doubt would be to establish the strongest anti-doubt – certainty. Yet although contemporary epistemologists generally seek to be fallibilists in their conceptions of knowledge, and although they do not routinely and overtly embrace the method of doubt, we have seen how they do reach for the Not-Yet model of knowledge. This underlying aspect of Cartesian methodology has persisted. And Section 8.4 showed that anyone applying the Not-Yet model is committed (even if unwittingly) to an infallibilism about knowledge. Professed fallibilists still cleaving to the Not-Yet model are therefore confused, in a way of which the admitted infallibilist Descartes was innocent.

But there is no good reason for us to be relying upon the Not-Yet model. We have noted its conceptual limitations and conceptual optionality. Now we are noting its historical optionality. The surrounding social reasons that made it natural for Descartes to rely upon the Not-Yet model are no longer in place. For a start, contemporary epistemologists in general are not doctrinally answerable to any Church. Nor need they be methodologically constrained by any Church, having to regard knowledge with the exaggerated and pre-emptive caution that guided Descartes's assessments of knowledge's presence. So, in continuing to apply the Not-Yet model contemporary epistemologists seem mired in a philosophical *habit* of thought.

It is time to break that habit. A first step would be our recognising it *as* a habit. A second step involves remembering that habits can run deep, becoming 'intuitive' and reflexively attitudinal, without always *feeling* like habits. We have taken to evincing a Not-Yet attitude of caution towards attributing knowledge. And this can feel like something other than such a habit. (1) It can feel unlike an attitude of *caution*, as we reach confidently for 'intuitions' regarding particular cases. (2) It can also feel as though it is not *just* a habit, because it can feel like a process of reflecting, not reflexing – autonomous and free thinking, applied carefully and even surprisingly anew on different occasions of inquiry. Nonetheless, it can still be a methodologically cautious habit of thought – an eminently replaceable one, too. For what underlies it is our having adopted the correlative Not-Yet model of knowing; and this is not an inescapable model. Over time, its implicit use has come to feel natural, even unavoidable, for epistemologists. But some theses and issues about knowledge *arise* only because the Not-Yet model has been guiding inquiry; and given how second-nature that model has become for epistemologists, some of those implied theses and issues have come to feel unavoidable, even intuitive. What are actually doctrinal implications of adopting the Not-Yet model have been widely discussed without epistemologists *noticing* the presence and sustaining role of the substantive presupposition that is the Not-Yet model. Yet if this chapter is right, we are free to discard the Not-Yet model.[28]

And the heartening news is that once we do discard that model, we need not be left directionless, stranded nobody-knows-where on our epistemological journey. A replacement model, the Working Knowledge model, is ready to hand, even if schematically so. We may replace our professionally inculcated assumption of the Not-Yet model's inescapability, therefore, with a recognition of the Working Knowledge model's availability – all the while acknowledging the real possibility of some professionally trained ideas and expectations having been formed by our implicit acceptance of that replaceable Not-Yet model. Knowledge might well not look quite the same to us after we begin 'hiring' it in accord with the Working Knowledge model rather than the Not-Yet model.

Notes

1   Suppose that *XYZ* is the traditional justified-true-belief analysis. Cartesian external world sceptics, for instance, allow that your knowing that *p* (for an external world *p*) is your having a well justified true belief that *p*, *only once* you eliminate the independently specifiable possibility of your dreaming that *p*, and *only once* your eliminating this possibility is included in your justification for your true belief that *p*.

2   David Chalmers suggested this modification of 2:

>   2* For any *XYZ*: your believing that *p* is to be accepted as your knowing that *p*, in virtue of its being *XYZ*, *only once* (i) various sceptical possibilities are somehow removed, and (ii) their-being-removed is included in *XYZ*.

But I prefer 2's greater generality, to cover the possibility (mentioned more fully in fn. 15) that not all knowing is believing.

3   We might claim that only once *any* given condition within *XYZ* is satisfied are the remaining ones enabled, along with it, to constitute knowledge that *p*: if all are needed, each has this enabling power. But epistemologists generally proceed as though there is something methodologically special about the sceptic's condition. Sceptical arguments treat supposedly troublesome *further* possibilities as independently specifiable tests to be imposed upon any *XYZ* purporting to describe all there is to knowing that *p*.

4   For more on the concept and its history, see Shope (1983) and Hetherington (2005b).

5   Exceptions are Hetherington (1998, 1999, 2001a: ch. 3) and perhaps Weatherson (2003).

6   In what ways might this occur? One simple mode I have endorsed elsewhere involves becoming *aware* of the troublesome Gettier circumstance (Hetherington 2001b).

7   The 'best, exactly' elimination of Gettier circumstances would apply to all Gettier cases, while satisfying other theoretical *desiderata* (such as being simple, explaining further aspects of knowing, and so forth), yet hopefully without setting so high a standard for knowledge as to imply a scepticism about knowledge's ever being present.

8   For example, if *XYZ* is again the justified-true-belief analysis, and if a solution of the Gettier problem talks of there being no defeaters of one's justification, this no-defeaters condition would be added to any prior specification of *XYZ*.

9   Having noticed this, however, I will mostly discuss sceptical possibilities, not Gettier circumstances, in the rest of the chapter.

10 Non-sceptical epistemologists might not accept this description of the knowledge's being *recovered*. 'It is there all the time', they will say, 'although, in order to avoid begging the question, we must inquire as if it is absent. Only after besting the sceptic may we triumphantly display it again'. But when I say 'recovered', I mean something like 'included in our best epistemological analysis, which we hope to use when attributing or denying knowledge'.

11 Or, more generally, *failably* that *p*. This concept comes from Hetherington (1999, 2001a: ch. 2 – parts of each of which appear here as Chapter 6). In this chapter, I use the simpler, more standard, notion.

12 'Perfect' here (and in what follows) is to be understood as 'perfect, *for* the job in question', not as 'perfect, for *any* job'.

13 I have not commented on how the supposedly apt description *XYZ* is initially to be derived. Perhaps it takes into account many non-philosophical kinds of knowledge-threat. It might be scientific in nature; it could be more 'everyday'; maybe it has a conjectural aspect; and so on.

14 So too, I have urged (1998), do epistemologists in general when responding to Gettier cases. Instead (I argued), we may interpret those cases as situations where someone knows but *luckily* so, because he could easily have failed to possess the knowledge. See also Hetherington (1999, 2001a: ch. 3, 2005b: sec. 13).

15. Elsewhere, I argue for its not being a state at all. It is an ability, a kind of knowledge-how (Hetherington 2006). This chapter's point blends smoothly with that one.
16. Presumably, some of these tests will be subtle; any *prima facie* apt description XYZ should already have passed comparatively obvious tests. For instance, because one component in any *prima facie* apt description XYZ is a truth requirement, I am not saying just that something we think is knowledge might turn out to be false, hence not knowledge.
17. In this sense, they are worries especially for those who are thinking about them – a theme pursued by Lewis (1996) and other contextualists. It was also investigated by Hetherington (1992).
18. Andy Clark helped me with this formulation.
19. Was G.E. Moore's (1959) famous 'hand waving' reply to the sceptic applying the Working Knowledge model? Certainly it has been thought of as dogmatic. Certainly, too, it did not apply the Not-Yet model. Elsewhere, I provide a gradualist use of Moore's reasoning, one which could be regarded as applying the Working Knowledge model (Hetherington 2001a: 169–78).
20. It is not that we should never conduct this sort of pre-emptive imaginative test. Often, we must take a chance on hiring someone, recognising that although we can think of ever more demanding tests, these need not become initial tests, used when considering whether to hire the person in the first place. Sceptical challenges are indeed rarefied, appropriate only for a later stage in the cognitive employment process.
21. Elsewhere, I explain more fully how my gradualism defuses sceptical challenges (Hetherington 2001a: ch. 2, 2002). Does this beg the question against the sceptic? No, as I have also argued elsewhere (Hetherington 2001a: 38–40, 2002: 95–7, 2004.)
22. I hope it is clear that my case for the interpretive feasibility of thinking there is knowledge within Gettier cases is not stemming from an 'intuition' to that effect. The argument is more theoretical. If Section 8.3 is right, though, so are the putative intuitions with which epistemologists standardly deny knowledge to anyone featured within a Gettier case. That is, use of the Not-Yet model is a *theoretical* move.
23. Would-be fallibilists will say that they already have one. But we have seen that they are wrong about that until they discard the Not-Yet model. Simply claiming to be a fallibilist is not sufficient for being one.
24. On this motivation of Descartes's, see Popkin (1979: ch. IX).
25. I said that such fallibility is one instance of the constitutive frailty that the Church would not have accepted within a piece of knowledge. If we generalise that notion of fallibility, we derive the concept of failability (referred to in fn. 11): a piece of knowledge is failable insofar as *any* one of its components (not only its truth component) need not have been present, even given the presence of the other components. Accordingly, the concept of failability more accurately captures the deeper constitutive frailty that Descartes would not have accepted within knowledge. For simplicity, though, in this chapter I talk just of fallible knowledge, not of failable knowledge, as being anathema to Descartes's Church-formed investigative environment.
26. This is not to deny the role of faith in religious thinking. But it was the Pyrrhonist sceptics who were taken to be opening the door to faith (Popkin 1979: 52–3). In contrast, Descartes sought religious knowledge.
27. For more on the nature of fallibilism, see Hetherington (2005a).

28 There is some methodological similarity between this chapter and Williams's (1991) project of uncovering the substantive-and-therefore-not-purely-intuitive-and-unavoidable presuppositions of external world sceptical reasoning.

References

Annas, J. (1981), *An Introduction to Plato's Republic*, Oxford: Clarendon Press.
Chisholm, R.M. (1966), *Theory of Knowledge*, Englewood Cliffs, NJ: Prentice-Hall.
Gettier, E.L. (1963), 'Is Justified True Belief Knowledge?' *Analysis*, 23: 121–3.
Hetherington, S. (1992), *Epistemology's Paradox: Is a Theory of Knowledge Possible?* Savage, MD: Rowman & Littlefield.
Hetherington, S. (1998), 'Actually Knowing', *Philosophical Quarterly*, 48: 453–69.
Hetherington, S. (1999), 'Knowing Failably', *The Journal of Philosophy*, 96: 565–87.
Hetherington, S. (2001a), *Good Knowledge, Bad Knowledge: On Two Dogmas of Epistemology*, Oxford: Clarendon Press.
Hetherington, S. (2001b), 'A Fallibilist and Wholly Internalist Solution to the Gettier Problem', *Journal of Philosophical Research*, 26: 307–24.
Hetherington, S. (2002), 'Fallibilism and Knowing That One Is Not Dreaming', *Canadian Journal of Philosophy*, 32: 83–102.
Hetherington, S. (2004), 'Shattering a Cartesian Sceptical Dream', *Principia*, 8: 103–17.
Hetherington, S. (2005a), 'Fallibilism', *The Internet Encyclopedia of Philosophy*, URL: http://www.iep.utm.edu/f/fallibil.htm
Hetherington, S. (2005b), 'Gettier Problems', *The Internet Encyclopedia of Philosophy*, URL: http://www.iep.utm.edu/g/gettier.htm
Hetherington, S. (2006), 'How to Know (That Knowledge-That Is Knowledge-How)', in S. Hetherington (ed.), *Epistemology Futures*, 71–94, Oxford: Clarendon Press.
Jacquette, D. (2004), 'Editor's Page: Working Hypotheses', *American Philosophical Quarterly*, 41: 185–6.
Moore, G.E. (1959), 'Proof of an External World', in *Philosophical Papers*, 127–50, London: George Allen & Unwin.
Popkin, R.H. (1979), *The History of Scepticism from Erasmus to Spinoza*, Berkeley: University of California Press.
Shope, R.K. (1983), *The Analysis of Knowing: A Decade of Research*, Princeton: Princeton University Press.
Stroud, B. (1984), *The Significance of Philosophical Scepticism*, Oxford: Clarendon Press.
Weatherson, B. (2003), 'What Good Are Counterexamples?' *Philosophical Studies*, 115: 1–31.
Williams, M. (1991), *Unnatural Doubts: Epistemological Realism and the Basis of Scepticism*, Oxford: Blackwell.

9

Knowledge as potential for action

Can we conceive cogently of all knowledge – in particular, all knowledge of truths – as being knowledge-*how*? This chapter provides reasons for thinking not only that is this possible, but that it is conceptually advantageous and suggestive. Those reasons include adaptations of, and responses to, some classic philosophical arguments and ideas, from Descartes, Hume, Peirce, Mill, and Ryle. The chapter's position is thus a *practicalism* – a kind of pragmatism – about the nature of knowledge, arguing that all knowledge is knowledge-how to act – to do this, to do that. Such a conception can include, too, a distinctive view of the metaphysical relation between knowledge and belief. We see that, contrary to what most contemporary epistemologists say, knowledge need not be a form of belief. Instead, a belief that *p* can be a way simply of enriching or strengthening knowledge that *p*. It can do this in a practicalist way, by allowing one to do *more* with the knowledge.

9.1 A question

Western epistemology has long had a focus upon knowledge-that – knowledge of a truth or fact – when discussing knowledge at all. Within contemporary epistemology in particular, definitional analyses of knowledge-that have abounded, especially since Edmund Gettier's (1963) philosophical bee-sting. He set off a rash of epistemological agreement – allergy-like in its intensity and its speedy spread of the conviction that there is more to knowing than having a true and well justified belief; and putative stories about that 'more' have proliferated. In general, though, even those post-Gettier attempts to understand knowledge's nature[1] have not attempted to do so in terms of knowledge-*how*.

Perhaps the closest they have come to doing so[2] has been within some versions of a virtue epistemology. Ernest Sosa (2007, 2011, 2015, 2016) has emphasized the potential role of cognitive virtues within the production of an individual's knowledge. These may be regarded as cognitive skills on the part of the person – skills that could in turn be conceived of as instances of knowledge-how. Knowledge-how would thus be involved in at least a person's *gaining* some knowledge-that.

But should we contemplate an even stronger link than that causally productive one between knowledge-how and knowledge-that? Might the knowing-how be literally a *part* of the knowing-that, even *after* the knowledge-that has been produced through the agency that is inherent in activating and applying the pertinent knowledge-how? That *metaphysically* (not merely causally) constitutive possibility – about how knowledge-how might be a vital part even of the *nature* of knowledge-that – is this chapter's concern.

9.2 A traditional interpretation: Persisting belief

We can ease into that discussion by asking about knowledge and *belief*. And initially we can do this via an example. It describes a familiar sort of situation, involving an array of cognitively charged actions. What might it indicate about knowledge, about belief, and about any potentially constitutive relations between those two?

Imagine being asked whether you know that 58 + 68 = 126. You reflect for a moment, consciously performing a simple calculation, before replying that, yes, you do have that knowledge. Are you thereby committed to the view also that you believe that 58 + 68 = 126? You may well claim so. Yet what would be your evidence for those views of yourself?

At this moment, when you actively ponder those two questions – Do you know? Do you believe? – what you are most manifestly aware of are some *actions* on your part. You notice your engaging in some calculating. You monitor this activity. You might feel yourself accepting the result of that calculating. Then you give voice to – by asserting – that result: '126. That's the answer'. You hear yourself giving that answer, perhaps as anyone else hears your words, although maybe as only you could hear them.[3]

Yet where in all of this have you espied a belief – in the robust sense of a *persisting* or *continuing* belief? Presumably, no such belief is identical with any of those actions by you. Is the belief therefore something beyond or behind these actions, maybe underlying them? You have no direct awareness of interacting with a belief like that. Indeed, you cannot have such an awareness. For you cannot introspectively observe the persisting existence of the belief *beyond* its being interacted with by you. Even if somehow you experience a content within yourself, you experience it only in its capacity *as* a content present at that time of being experienced. Again, *where* within this experience is the persisting belief?

For that matter, where – within all of this – is your *knowledge* that 58 + 68 = 126? For instance, is it wherever the belief is (wherever that is), due to knowledge's always *being* a kind of belief? Many would say so, in tune with the epistemologically entrenched view – perhaps bequeathed to contemporary philosophy by Plato's *Meno* (97e–98a) – that any instance of knowledge is a kind of belief, an epistemically enriched belief. The belief (they will say, in explaining that view) is the metaphysically describable 'stuff' or substance that, once it is epistemically enriched, *is* the 'thing' that *is* the knowledge. The belief is the 'thing' in which the knowledge's further required properties – those that are enriching the belief epistemically, properties such as *being true* and *being epistemically justified* – 'inhere' or to which they 'attach.' Accordingly, is it possible, at least in principle, to describe your belief's presence in this situation *in advance* of ascertaining whether you also have the knowledge that 58 + 68 = 126?

Yet how would that happen (if indeed it can)? For example, could you find the belief indirectly, maybe by inference from some of your self-observations in this setting? Various of your actions, such as the calculating, could be said to be *generating* the belief's presence. Other actions, such as your accepting or your asserting, would probably be taken to be *reflecting* or *arising* from the belief's presence. The presence of any or all of these actions would supposedly either *explain* or be *explained* by the belief's own presence. In that spirit, should we say that the *best* explanation of these actions would mention the belief's presence?[4] Not only that; are such actions also best explained – in almost the same breath – as somehow generating and/or reflecting or arising from your *knowing* that 58 + 68 = 126? If knowledge is always a form of belief, then these actions reflect the belief that 58 + 68 = 126, for example, only if they also reflect – even if possibly not in quite the same way – the knowledge that 58 + 68 = 126.

Still, *is* knowledge always a form of belief? For a start, not all of philosophy's relevant history insists that it is. What, indeed, of the strongly contrary picture, on which knowledge and belief are metaphysically *disjoint*, so that to know that *p* is not, even in part, to believe that *p*? That contrary picture was also first painted for us by Plato, this time in the *Republic* (475b–480). On this picture, belief and knowledge are taken to be so deeply distinct in nature as to underlie the idiom, 'No, I don't believe it; I know it.' And *if* this disjointness thesis is correct, how should we interpret your actions, described in this section, as indications of your believing – or, distinctly, of your knowing – that 58 + 68 = 126?

Section 9.9 will discuss this issue more fully, by attending to a recent argument – from Blake Myers-Schulz and Eric Schwitzgebel (2013) – for the disjointness thesis. Until then, let us stay with the knowledge-as-a-kind-of-belief picture, given its being the most widely accepted view among contemporary epistemologists as to *what kind of thing* an instance of knowledge is.

9.3 An alternative interpretation: Inner actions

The line of questioning introduced in Section 9.2 might remind us of a famous argument by David Hume (1978 [1739–40]: Book I, Part IV, Sec. VI). I have in mind his objection to the thesis that within each person there exists an identifiable, distinct, and persisting personal *substance* – with its continuing existence being an essential explanatory element of a person's numerical identity over time. In presenting his argument, Hume conducted the same sort of self-search as I asked you to perform a moment ago.

So, look within – for your self (asks Hume) *or* for your belief (this is my request). Seek that privately persisting substance or that persisting belief. In neither case will you succeed: all that you will *clearly* meet are experiences occurring at that time of their being uncovered by your inner investigation. And whatever else, if anything, these are at a moment of being met by your inner explorations, you can meet such an experience only in its capacity *as* something itself active, something happening and alive.

An experience can have a content adverting to more than this moment. And often you may feel that you are meeting within you a persisting *attitude* to that content. But that feeling could be misleading. What you meet at that moment is an attitude present at least at that time; and you do not *thereby* meet something present at another time. Even if the attitude you meet has a content that you feel yourself to be accepting also *for* other times, you are not meeting it *while* it is functioning as an object of acceptance at other times. As Hume says,

> when I enter most intimately into what I call *myself*, I always stumble on some particular perception or other, of heat or cold, light or shade, love or hatred, pain or pleasure. I never can catch *myself* at any time without a perception, and never can observe any thing but the perception. When my perceptions are remov'd for any time, as by sound sleep; so long am I insensible of *myself*, and may truly be said not to exist.
>
> (1978: 252)

Is that merely a Humean eccentricity? Far from it; the similarity of this Humean reasoning to Descartes's *Cogito*, no less, is striking. In perhaps modern Western philosophy's *most* famous reasoning, Descartes reassured himself that, so long as he was thinking (even if only by doubting), he knew himself to exist – but only *as* that active thinking. He could not know himself within that setting – 'Meditation II' – as a persisting and independently existing substance, even when restricting his known features to mental ones. And with this assessment of what he can know and what he cannot know, Descartes claimed to answer his metaphysically foundational question, 'But what then am I?':

> I am, I exist – that is certain. But for how long? For as long as I am thinking. For it could be that were I totally to cease from thinking, I should totally cease to exist.
> [...] But what then am I? A thing that thinks. What is that? A thing that doubts, understands, affirms, denies, is willing, is unwilling, and also imagines and has sensory perceptions.
> [...] But what am I to say about this mind, or about myself? (So far, remember, I am not admitting that there is anything else in me except a mind.)
>
> (Descartes 1984 [1641]: 18–19; 22)

And so far I am saying something similar about your inner experienced self as a knower. You cannot ever know that you are finding within you (at least by introspection) a persisting and independently existing *epistemic* substance – such as a continuing state of belief – able to be the metaphysical 'stuff' of your knowing that $58 + 68 = 126$.[5] Only inner *actions* – cognitive ones – existing at the time of the introspective search will be knowingly encountered. Yet this should not be surprising. Only *by* acting could you know, as a result of effort at that time, something present within you at that same time. Such acting cannot know that it has found anything inner beyond something existing *as* an object of such acting. (Some acting is being known, we may suppose. And in order to know something inner and beyond that acting, one has to continue one's inner acting; with which effort, you continue meeting only what is thereby, at any such moment, not existing at any further moment.)

9.4 Knowledge-that as knowledge-how

Is that a worrying picture? Does it confront us with a reason never to regard ourselves *as* believers, or even as knowers? Not if we are prepared to make some correlative conceptual adjustments. Specifically, we can respond to that line of thought about knowledge somewhat as Hume responded to his own about persons. He proposed a reconception of the fundamental *nature* of personal identity. What *is* a person? Hume's answer was that each of us is a *republic* or *commonwealth* of experiences (1978: 261), a *bundle* of ideas and impressions (1978: 252). What persists as a person's persisting is the bundle as such – not necessarily its particular members, and not a further inner substance underlying and binding together those phenomena. Might an analogous picture illuminate the relationship between a person's persisting *knowledge*, such as her knowing that 58 + 68 = 126, and her related cognitive actions (such as calculating, accepting, and asserting)? This possibility merits attention.[6]

First, let me describe it a little less schematically. Let those cognitive actions – your calculating, your accepting, your asserting – be *expressions* or *manifestations*, in their different ways, of your knowledge that 58 + 68 = 126. But let them be expressing or manifesting this knowledge, precisely as actions can express or manifest knowledge-*how*.[7] For now, we may think of this as the actions expressing or manifesting associated *abilities* or *skills*.[8] (Thus, you would be calculating aptly *as* an expression of your knowing how to do so. The same would be true of the subsequent actions of your accepting, and your asserting, that 58 + 68 = 126.) Finally, we may also propose or hypothesize that this knowledge-how – this collection of skills – would *be* your knowledge that 58 + 68 = 126. To describe the knowledge-how would be to describe all that there is in having the knowledge-that.

Notice how the relationship being described as obtaining between your actions and your knowledge-how is *metaphysically constitutive*. Your cognitive actions, *in* being the actions they are, express or manifest those attendant abilities or skills, the accompanying knowledge-how. Their *nature* as those actions is to be such expressions or manifestations. They are not merely *caused* by your having the associated knowledge-how.

Notice also how a single case of knowledge-how can encompass several – maybe many – distinct kinds of action: knowing-how can be multi-twined in that way. It is a picture with a Peircean tenor. Think of C.S. Peirce's conception of evidential support:

> Philosophy ought to imitate the successful sciences in its methods, so far as to proceed only from tangible premises which can be subjected to careful scrutiny, and to trust rather to the multitude and variety of its arguments than to the conclusiveness of any one. Its reasoning should not form a chain which is no stronger than its weakest link, but a cable whose fibers may be ever so slender, provided they are sufficiently numerous and intimately connected.
> (Peirce 1931–58: Vol. V, par. 265)[9]

Your calculating, your accepting, your asserting: these are actions expressing or manifesting your knowing that 58 + 68 = 126. Equally, they are ways of expressing some or all of whatever skills are jointly constituting a *commonwealth* or *bundle* of your associated abilities. That commonwealth or bundle may then be regarded as some complex knowledge-how: you have some specific knowledge insofar as you have some pertinent abilities, each of which is such that an action expressing or manifesting it is *thereby* an expression or manifestation of knowing.

And so we have this explanatory hypothesis:

> Actions that seem to reflect knowledge-that are expressions of knowledge-how; and to note this is to explain all that would be explained in positing the knowledge-that. Hence, if we insist on knowledge-that's being present, we are free to regard the knowledge-that *as* the knowledge-how. In short, knowledge-that is knowledge-how and nothing else.

9.5 The order-of-explanation objection and intellectualism

But is that proposed order of explanation actually the *reverse* of what it should be? The objection generating this question would insist (as follows) that the knowledge-that's presence explains the knowledge-how's presence; and *not* vice versa.

> You know *how* to reach, accept, and assert '126' as an answer to our mathematical question (and hence, other things being equal, you *do* provide this answer) in a way that is recognizably knowledgeable – only in part because, independently and already, you know *that* 58 + 68 = 126. You can perform those actions – calculating accepting, asserting – as expressions or manifestations of the knowledge-how, only *because* you have the knowledge-that. Those skills – your abilities to calculate, accept, and assert in this circumstance – are means only of putting into effect your knowledge-that. The knowledge-how that enters this simple story amounts only to being your knowing how to manifest or give expression to what is already and independently your knowledge that 58 + 68 = 126.

This is the order-of-explanation objection. It bespeaks what is for many people a natural conception of how knowledge and action coalesce. The objection gives voice to what Gilbert Ryle (1949, 1971) called *intellectualism*. It was Ryle who brought to epistemology's attention the potential categorial difference between knowledge-that and knowledge-how – their being irreconcilably different *kinds* of knowledge. Whether there is that metaphysically deep difference between them depends upon whether intellectualism is true. Like Ryle, I say that intellectualism is false – demonstrably false.

Intellectualism concerns what Ryle called *intelligent* actions – what we have been referring to as exemplifications or manifestations of knowledge-how; what Jason Stanley (2011) calls skilful actions. How do these come to exist as actions with this epistemic character? According to intellectualism, they are guided into existence by some knowledge-that, perhaps regulative knowledge-that describing a method or technique. So, go ahead: climb aboard that bicycle. Then start riding. In doing so, you will be applying your knowledge that B – for some proposition B describing enough of what would suffice for successfully riding a bicycle. You will be putting into practice some practical knowledge – your knowledge how to ride a bicycle. But intellectualism claims that you can do this only in part through possessing, and being guided by, some already-present and independently constituted propositional or theoretical knowledge – in this case, your knowledge that B.

Nonetheless, here is one way in which, by taking our cue from Ryle, we might argue against any such intellectualist picture. The intellectualist hears of your riding the bicycle skilfully. She infers that you must have applied some knowledge-that, such as the knowledge that B. But your applying the knowledge that B is itself a further intelligent action. (Although it is perhaps not consciously applied, it is at least reliably directed. And it is relevantly different to digesting, which is also reliably directed yet which you never *learnt*, for example.) Somehow, you skilfully apply your knowledge that B. However, this will likewise attract the intellectualist's attention: she must posit a further piece of knowledge – this time, your knowledge that B_1 – as being applied by you. B_1 is knowledge of some means of applying your knowledge that B (your knowledge of a way of riding a bicycle). Can the intellectualist's analysis end there? Not if this further knowledge has also been applied skilfully. And surely it has; in which case, intellectualism requires you to have been applying yet another piece of knowledge – call it knowledge that B_2. As before, this new knowledge will be guiding into action the previously hypothesized knowledge – this time, the knowledge that B_1. And so on: in turn, you will be required to have known that B_3, to have known that B_4, etc. More and more knowledge is thus being expected from you, unendingly and impossibly, even to explain just a single intelligent action on your part. For Ryle, the reason for this unwelcome result was evident: namely, intellectualism is false.

In what follows, I will assume for argument's sake that Ryle was right about this – because he might well have been, and because I am asking what conceptual possibilities are realistic if he was right. *If* he was, then the following possibility is available as we try to understand how knowledge and action intermingle.

> There can be intelligent actions – ones manifesting or expressing knowledge-how – that need not have been guided into existence by knowledge-that.

This implies that it is possible for at least some knowledge-how not to include knowledge-that within itself. If in each case knowledge-that was to be part of the knowledge-how, then manifesting the knowledge-how would include manifesting the contained knowledge-that. But Ryle's form of reasoning implies that it is possible for an intelligent action to be performed – knowledge-how thereby being manifested – without any involvement by knowledge-that.

9.6 Knowing actions

I am hypothesizing that all knowledge-that is knowledge-how, not that all knowledge-how is knowledge-that. Accordingly, not all intelligent actions – even though they express or manifest knowledge-how – express or manifest knowledge-that. Still, we must face the question of whether all *knowing* actions (as I call them) do so.

Knowing actions encompass such actions as those that we imagined you performing in response to the question, 'What is 58 + 68?' – your calculating, your accepting, your asserting. Any knowing action has an *apparent* point of manifesting or expressing knowledge. We may parse this as the knowing action's point being that of *conveying* knowledge. Riding a bicycle, for example, is an intelligent action without being a knowing action. In contrast, answering the question 'What is 58 + 68?' with '126' does occur with the aim of conveying knowledge. Hence, it is a knowing action.[10]

Nonetheless, knowing actions remain a kind of intelligent action (in Ryle's sense of the latter). So, at this stage of our thinking, we have no reason not to apply Ryle's general anti-intellectualist argument to them. Courtesy of Ryle, therefore, we may infer this:

> Even when knowledge-how is being manifested by a *knowing* action, this need not be occurring because of some knowledge-that's guidance. (Yes, a knowing action typically has a point of conveying knowledge. Even this does not entail knowledge-that's also guiding the action.) In which case, equally, the knowing action need not be occurring under the guiding influence of some knowledge-that's presence. (For according to intellectualism, the pertinent point of the knowledge-that's presence would be precisely to provide such guidance. If – as is shown by Ryle's anti-intellectualism argument – guidance by knowledge-that is not needed, then neither is the presence of knowledge-that.)

Correlatively, too, we need not posit the existence of some knowledge-that as *accompanying* the knowing action. Doing so would be explanatorily idle. I am not saying that no knowledge-that could be present. But there need not be any, even given the occurrence of knowing actions. The latter actions can be *knowing* ones, given simply some accompanying knowledge-*how*.

9.7 Knowledge in action

Yet Section 9.6's picture of how we can act knowingly could well sound implausible, along the following lines:

> Maybe Ryle was right to deny that an intelligent action such as riding a bicycle must be accompanied, let alone guided, by some knowledge-that. Surely, however, when the intelligent action is also a *knowing* action in particular – such as your asserting an answer of '126' to the question, 'What is 58 + 68?' – knowledge-that does need to be present, playing some causal role in the knowing action's coming into existence.

Not only that (continues the objection); presumably some epistemologists will object that if no knowledge-that is present then the actions are knowing ones only in a distressingly weak way. These would be knowing actions only in the sense of being *intended* to convey knowledge.

But that objection begs the central question to which my proposal is offering an alternative answer. That answer begins by clarifying Ryle's result, as follows. What he showed (when his point is formulated more precisely) is that intelligent actions are not guided into existence by some *categorically distinct* knowledge-that. Nor, therefore (I infer), are knowing actions. And the significance of that added precision is its revealing how we have conceptual room for interpreting such actions (intelligent actions in general; knowing actions in particular) as able to exist as expressions or manifestations of knowledge-how – *and thereby of knowledge-that*. The knowledge-that would now *not* be categorically distinct from knowledge-how. So, we may say that, whenever a knowing action occurs, there *is* knowledge accompanying it. However, this knowledge is the knowledge-how that is being manifested or expressed by the knowing action.

And we can distinguish these cases of knowledge-how – the ones that are knowledge-that – from other cases of knowledge-how. We do this, not *categorically*, but by attending to the content of the respective intelligent actions that would be expressions or manifestations of the knowledge-how in question. Your knowledge that $58 + 68 = 126$ is a complex of abilities, each of which aims at conveying a truth. Your knowledge how to ride a bicycle is a complex of abilities, probably none of which aims at conveying a truth.

Knowing actions are thus instances of knowledge *in* action. Each such action is an instance of knowledge *activated* – knowledge *being* activated. In general, though, knowledge-how can exist even when it is not activated. After all, abilities need not be manifested – put into action – in order to exist.[11] And this is as it should be: much of your knowledge does not disappear when you sleep, even when all of your manifestations of that knowledge – the knowing actions distinctive of the knowledge in question – do so.[12] So knowledge is inactive or unactivated other than when knowing actions are expressing or manifesting it. Then it is activated, at least for a while. Your accepting the right answer; your uttering the right answer: each of these is your putting into action the knowledge-how that is your knowing that $58 + 68 = 126$. The knowledge as such, though, remains knowledge-how.[13]

9.8 Perceptual knowledge

We have focused upon a case of mathematical knowledge. How does my account apply to perceptual knowledge? Elegantly so. Imagine being outside a field, looking at what seems to be a barn; as indeed it is. So you think to yourself that it is a barn. You do not also consciously note its roof being red. Nevertheless, you can know that the barn's roof is red, by having pertinent abilities. Are you able to picture, if asked, the colour of the barn's roof? Are you able, if asked, to describe that colour? If you have one or both of those abilities, you have the knowledge – even if you are never asked those questions.

However, this knowledge could remain inactive if those questions are never posed. In that sense, the knowledge – by being knowledge-how – is a *potentiality* within you. It is your having a potential for many knowing actions, both inner ones and outer ones. It is a potential for answering questions and/or for forming questions and/or for consciously describing an aspect of the surroundings and/or for drawing that aspect and/or etc. If the knowledge was to be activated (such as if you were to be asked about the roof's colour), you might proceed to have a consciously held experience of believing about the roof's colour. Even so, this would not be your knowledge of the roof's colour. Your inner experience – even if it feels to you like it is the mere '*tip*' of an inner persisting belief – would instead be only a *manifestation* or *expression* of the perceptual knowledge, the perceptual knowledge-how.

9.9 Knowledge and belief

I have been outlining how we might begin to conceive of all knowledge as being knowledge-how. The idea has been that, in general, any instance of knowledge that p is a complex instance of knowledge-how – complex in the range and number of specific skills or abilities that are somehow bundled together within it, each of them bearing relevantly upon p. That idea should now be tested by our trying to answer the question – mentioned in Section 9.2 – of where *belief* fits into this picture of knowledge.

The question is pressing because many philosophers would say that the complex potentiality that, on my view, is the given instance of knowledge is present only because, in turn, knowledge is a kind of belief. More fully, the potentiality that, I have suggested, is part of an instance of knowing is actually part of the *belief* that is (by being suitably embellished) the instance of knowledge. And if so, there is no motivation to conceive of knowledge in practicalist terms. Rather (say those epistemologists), we could rest content with a traditional view simply of belief – as a required element within knowledge – as a *dispositional* state: that is, if confronted by a pertinent circumstance (such as one's being asked whether it is true that p), one would respond in a p-affirming or p-reflecting way.[14] Such an action could be an intelligent action, in Ryle's sense. It could also be a knowing action, in my sense. Is a dispositional conception of belief therefore already adequate for capturing the potentialities that I have described as constituting knowledge (and thus as motivating a move to a knowledge-practicalism)? If it is, then maybe knowledge could still be thought of in more traditional terms, as being a form of belief (albeit an epistemically blessed or augmented form). Consequently, we would *not* need to reach – in the less traditional way that I have been advocating – for a practicalism about knowledge's nature.

I grant that a belief-manifesting action, say, can also be a knowing action. Hence, I also grant, at least some of the dispositionality within believing could be at least part of the potentiality within a given instance of knowing. But this does not entail that the former dispositionality ever – let alone always – *exhausts* the latter potentiality. After all, there is an alternative explanation of this apparent overlap of potentialities – one that *preserves* a knowledge-practicalism. This alternative explanation also offers us a middle way between the *Republic*-Platonic disjointness thesis – whereby to believe that p is to not know that p, and to know that p is to not believe that p – and the *Meno*-Platonic tradition – whereby any instance of knowledge is at least a true opinion or true belief, bolstered by a *logos* (an account, an understanding).

Ryle is suggestive here:[15]

> 'Know' is a capacity verb, and a capacity verb of that special sort that is used for signifying that the person described can bring things off, or get things right. 'Believe', on the other hand, is a tendency verb and one which does not connote that anything is brought off or got right [...]
>
> Roughly, 'believe' is of the same family as motive words, where 'know' is of the same family as skill words; so we ask how a person knows this, but only why a person believes that [...] Skills have methods, where habits and inclinations have sources. Similarly, we ask what makes people believe or dread things but not what makes them know or achieve things.
>
> (Ryle 1949: 133–4)

Ryle thus emphasizes a standard sense in which knowledge *strengthens* belief. One has a success-relationship to a fact that p in knowing that p, a relationship that one need not have in believing that p: knowledge is always factive, while belief is not.

Nonetheless, Ryle overlooks a sense – a practicalist one – in which the *converse* strengthening relation can obtain: believing can strengthen knowing. Specifically, when one both knows and believes that p, the belief, even if dispositionally so, opens up some possible ways of *using* the knowledge. By having a belief that p, I suggest, one is able – indeed, one could be *well* able – to perform various actions that (i) can also be manifestations or expressions of the knowledge that p, (ii) do not exhaust the range of possible manifestations or expressions of the knowledge, and (iii) could be unavailable to one in the absence of the belief.

In support of that picture, we may consider the cases with which Myers-Schulz and Schwitzgebel have argued that there can be instances of knowledge *without* an accompanying belief. They offer five cases ('the unconfident examinee,' 'the absent-minded driver,' 'the prejudiced professor,' 'the freaked-out movie-watcher,' 'the self-deceived husband') – using these cases as experimental philosophers would (Myers-Schulz and Schwitzgebel 2013: 374–7). But we can also use the cases *a priori*, while engaging with this question: 'Is there *something missing from what the knowledge could be*, insofar as the knowledge is present yet the belief is not?'

The first case will suffice here. It is an adaptation of Colin Radford's (1966) oft-cited case. Myers-Schulz and Schwitzgebel imagine someone, Kate, being asked, in an exam, 'In what year did Queen Elizabeth I die?' Kate has studied for the exam; but this question arises for her only when the exam period has almost expired – as the teacher announces. Hearing the announcement, Kate panics, tries to recall the answer, fails – and writes, albeit with no confidence, the correct answer. Is that answer knowledge on Kate's part? Is she lacking belief (in the correctness of her answer) at that moment? A significant proportion of respondents surveyed by Myers-Schulz and Schwitzgebel attributed knowledge but not belief to Kate; as would I. For the sake of argument, therefore, I will accept that Kate has knowledge – not belief, though – as to Queen Elizabeth's dying in 1603.

And what does Kate – as that knower – lose by not having that belief? In particular, does she lose anything relevantly epistemic? Indeed she does. For example, deprived of the belief in the way described by Myers-Schulz and Schwitzgebel, she would lack the confidence *to express consciously* the knowledge, at least in many situations. Seemingly, she would qualify or weaken her answer of '1603' if that action was available to her. And, if not for being forced by the exam's strictures to provide an answer, she might well have opted not to do so. Clearly, there is a respect in which, by lacking the belief in this way, Kate lacks some meta-knowledge: she does not know that she knows the year of Queen Elizabeth's death, even though she does (I am assuming) have the latter knowledge, the knowledge directly about Queen Elizabeth. And the lack of that meta-knowledge, given its both reflecting and expressing itself for her in a conscious lack of confidence in her having the knowledge about Queen Elizabeth, will itself affect her ability to respond aptly in various circumstances where the latter knowledge is being investigated or sought. So, the lack of belief – as manifested in Kate's lack of conscious confidence – does weaken her epistemically in this setting. Even if it does not deprive her of the underlying knowledge, it could deprive her of at least some knowing *actions*, ones that would – by expressing the belief – express or manifest the knowledge. It thereby weakens the knowledge's *power* for her, at least in practise. Again, though, this is not to say that the knowledge is absent: there are still knowing actions that she will perform (such as providing, if forced, the correct answer in the exam). But there are others that she will not perform.

My practicalist suggestion, then, is that, insofar as knowledge that p is present without belief that p, a person can *do less* of what would count as manifesting or expressing the knowledge. In not believing that p, she loses the ability – the capacity – to perform, in at least some ways in at least some situations, actions that would be natural expressions or manifestations of the knowledge that p. Nonetheless, this remains consistent with her having enough other abilities that suffice for her having the knowledge. To believe is thus to have an ability, perhaps dispositional in nature, that can be present as part of having some knowledge – even if its being so is not *essential* for the knowledge's being present. Other things being equal, a given instance of knowledge's potential for producing knowing actions can be strengthened by including a belief among the sub-abilities that happen to jointly constitute it as being the complex potentiality that it is. Yet the knowledge that p's being stronger in this way than it might have been is not essential to its mere presence; what it is essential to is knowledge's having a specific epistemic strength *as* knowledge that p. It is not essential to the complex potentiality's being strong *enough* (however strong that is)[16] simply to be present as knowledge that p.

9.10 The state of knowing

Implicit in this chapter's practicalism is a metaphysics of knowing, one element of which is the following.

Insofar as all knowing is knowledge-how, we are free to maintain a view of knowing – and, for that matter, of believing – as a *state*.[17] That is a traditional picture, as far as it goes. But not everyone would accept it. Section 9.1 mentioned Ernest Sosa's recent attempts to develop a virtue-theoretic conception of knowledge. On that conception, both knowledge and belief are kinds of epistemic *performance*.[18] If such a conception succeeds, then epistemic *norms* – of behaviour, of action – are applicable; which is indeed what Sosa deems to be the case. Such a conception goes further in that direction than my practicalism does, in that it treats knowledge, say, *as* an action, whereas I treat knowledge only as *potential* for actions.

I take heart, then, from the linguistic data's being against Sosa in this respect. Matthew Chrisman explains:

> The basic result is that belief and knowledge attributions seem, by virtue of their meaning, to be about something nondynamic, whereas paradigmatic performance descriptions (for example, of arrow shootings [an example used often by Sosa]) seem to be about something dynamic and so nonstative. I think this shows that Sosa's suggestion that belief is a performance – which when successful (true) because skillful (justified) is apt and so a kind of knowledge – involves him in a sort of metaphysical category mistake in the way he uses these words.
> (Chrisman 2012: 601)

Again, on my picture believing and knowing are states. A belief that p, when present as part of some knowledge that p, brings with it various possibilities for action; and some of these (as we saw in Section 9.9) are possible actions that knowledge-without-belief would not ground. So, a belief-state can *enrich* a knowledge-state. It is not a *mere part* of a knowledge-state: to believe is to have *more* possible actions – specifically, further *knowing* actions – available to one, other things being equal.

Nevertheless, I am saying that, even when a person does both know that p and believe that p, the knowledge is *not itself the belief.* The contrary tradition – the *Meno*-Platonic one – tells us that knowledge *is* a belief, so long as the belief has various epistemically welcome features. Proponents of that tradition are using, in effect, a *substance-attribute* model of what knowledge is. They are treating the belief as needing to be present, and as amounting to some 'metaphysical unit' that is the knowledge, so long as it also has various epistemically pertinent features, such as being supported by good evidence. I am arguing, however, that this traditional metaphysical picture is optional at best. I am offering instead a *potentialities model* of knowledge. On this model, *all* that constitutes the knowing is the person's potential, however this is realised or grounded, for various suitably related actions.[19] I have explained that these actions may be conceived of as *knowing* actions: like other Rylean intelligent actions, they are manifestations or expressions of the knowledge, given its being knowledge-how; unlike some Rylean intelligent actions, though (such as riding a bicycle), these are ones whose point is at least to convey or express the knowledge.

These knowing actions can be useful, in turn, for further ends. But in all such circumstances this is *because* the actions express knowledge. C.I. Lewis's words are apposite here:

> The primary and pervasive significance of knowledge lies in its guidance of action: knowing is for the sake of doing. [...] [O]nly an active being could have knowledge [...] A creature which did not enter into the process of reality to alter in some part

the future content of it, could apprehend a world only in the sense of intuitive or esthetic contemplation; and such contemplation would not possess the significance of knowledge but only that of enjoying and suffering.

(Lewis 1946: 3)

I concur; and I extend Lewis's pragmatist point. His pragmatism is not as far-reaching as it could be, in that he retains the *Meno*-Platonic *structuring* – what contemporary epistemologists usually call the conceptual analysis – of knowledge. He tells us that knowledge is 'an assertive state of mind': that is, knowledge is at least a belief, of some or other form (1946: 9). Surrounding this, he holds in place the standard substance-attribute model that I described above. He says this: 'Knowledge is belief which not only is true but also is justified in its believing attitude' (1946: 9). In contrast, I say, knowledge is only a potential that *can* include whatever potential is inherent in believing; knowledge is not *automatically* in part an instance of believing.

9.11 Truth in action

If we are to conceive of knowledge-that as a kind of knowledge-how, it is imperative that we answer the following question.

> How *radical* a reconception of knowledge is being contemplated? Which of knowledge's constitutive properties (as these have formerly been envisaged by epistemologists) will stay? Which will depart?

I have already argued that *belief* – persisting belief – is not essential within knowledge. (I have *hypothesized* that knowledge is knowledge-how, having *argued* that knowledge need not include a persisting belief.) What now of *truth*? Where is it to be located within this alternative picture – what I have elsewhere called a *practicalism* about the nature of knowledge-that (Hetherington 2011a)?

Certainly we *expect* knowledge to incorporate truth. But this requirement must be formulated carefully. Suppose we say that part of your knowing that 58 + 68 = 126 is its being true that 58 + 68 = 126. Well, it remains true that 58 + 68 = 126, *regardless* of what it is to know this truth. So, that formulation was not quite correct. The question is one of how the specific truth is to be *part* of the knowledge – included in the knowledge – rather than of how the truth is to obtain regardless of the knowledge's nature. Traditional accounts of knowledge say that knowledge includes truth because knowledge includes a belief (or something similar) and because this belief's content is true. How will my practicalist analysis replace that supposed explanation? On my picture, *what* within the person is true (if not necessarily a belief?) I have not said that believing is never present within a case of knowledge. I have denied only that it always need be present: believing is just *one* of the possible ways of manifesting or expressing the knowledge in question.[20] When believing *is* present, it could be true – making the knowledge true – in the usual way. Nonetheless, that is not an adequate explanation, on my conception of knowledge. I need a more *general* account of truth's presence, covering also the *other* possible manifestations or expressions of the knowledge-how that is the knowledge-that.

Accordingly, I welcome Richard Campbell's discussion of the concept of truth. His key contention is that we need not restrict ourselves to what he calls the *linguistic* conception of truth (Campbell 2011: ch. 2); for that is not the most fundamental or general conception of truth. A traditionally motivated focus upon belief-contents as the only way in which truth can be part of knowledge would reflect only that more restrictive conception of truth. Campbell argues that we may think of truth first and foremost as a feature of *actions* (and only derivatively as a feature of believings, say) (2011: chs 4, 5). Reflect on how readily we *do* speak of an action's being true. Let us take such talk literally, by saying that an action is true when it is reliable or faithful. (For example, a kick can be true, as can a swimming stroke – in each case, pure and clean and effective and thus what it should ideally be, other things being equal.) We may then extend that insight. A true friend, for instance, is likewise reliable and faithful (2011: 104). She can be relied upon in her actions, or she will be faithful in her actions – all of this, given her character (2011: 110–11). We thus begin to understand how truth can be a property of actions and even of their agents. An action is true insofar as it treats – rather than represents – things as they are (2011: 123).

We may thereby speak similarly of your knowledge-how – including the particular knowledge-how that is your knowing that $58 + 68 = 126$ – being reliable and faithful. This will be part of *your* being reliable and faithful in relevant respects. *You* can be relied upon, and *you* will be faithful, in how you act when in relevant situations – all of this, when you are asked related questions, when you undertake to think about them, when you offer answers, etc. Such actions – including knowing actions – by you will thus be true. Hence, this knowledge-how of yours can *incorporate* truth. It would be true as a friend is true. It would be true in a 'larger' way. More technically: it would be true in a supervaluational way, by at least most[21] of its actual or possible manifestations – the knowing actions expressing it – being true. These would be true by *treating* the world aptly. And all of this is so, on any of the more specific ways in which the knowledge-how could be expressed or manifested by a knowing action.[22]

9.12 Conclusion

Arguments by Hume, Descartes, Ryle, and Peirce helped to motivate this chapter's reasoning. I will close with another pattern of welcome historical resonance. Berkeley's idealism about physical matter is surprisingly relevant. He faced the conceptual challenge of accounting for the nature of *un*observed physical matter. How does a tree in the quadrangle continue to exist once no one observes it? We are aware of Berkeley's answer: God observes the tree even when none of us does so.[23] We are also aware of John Stuart Mill's phenomenalist attempt to preserve Berkeley's idealist emphasis upon acts of perceiving, without relying on any Berkeleian talk of God. This was Mill's suggestion: 'Matter may be defined, a Permanent Possibility of Sensation' (1979 [1865]: 183). Matter thus has a modal dimension – this inescapable sort of permanent possibility. That dimension constitutes the physical object's persistence, when the object is not being perceived.

I regard knowledge in similar terms. I have been advocating an analogue of a Millian phenomenalism – mine is about knowledge-that as knowledge-how – built upon an analogue of a Humean bundling – mine is of manifestations or expressions of the knowledge-how that is the knowledge-that. That combination has generated the following picture.

Whenever you have a particular piece of knowledge-that, there are various actual and/or possible knowing actions standing to your knowledge much as various actual and/or possible perceptual experiences stand to an object's physicality. The knowledge is partly potential – a permanent possibility of being manifested or expressed. The knowledge is thus modal in its metaphysics, even if not its content; for it is knowledge-how; which is a more or less complex skill or ability; which will or can typically be manifested or expressed by various knowing actions; but which also might never be manifested or expressed. Still, when those actions do occur, they amount to the knowledge *in* action – that is, to activated knowledge. There need not be anything beyond those actions, uniting them, other *than* the particular knowledge-how to produce them – that particular potential for such performances. This is what knowledge is; or so I am proposing.[24]

Notes

1 For overviews of these attempts, see Shope (1983), Lycan (2006), and Hetherington (2016a).
2 Apart, that is, from Stanley and Williamson (2001) and those epistemologists responding to them. Stanley and Williamson's aim was to understand knowledge-how *as* knowledge-that. See also Stanley (2011). Section 9.8 will discuss this issue.
3 Here, I am thinking of Anscombe's account (1963) of one's knowledge of one's own intentional actions: perhaps only you know *qua* intentional action what you are asserting. (Of course, you might have uttered your words inwardly, too, perhaps rehearsing before giving them a public performance. That would be a distinct way in which only you would know of your words.)
4 And could one use that sort of explanation in a special way, in crediting *oneself* with having a continuing belief? I have two responses to that question. (1) Such a way of reaching an attribution of persisting belief to oneself is an onlooker's way, an external way. It bespeaks no pre-theoretical hint of privileged access. It could not be one's knowing of one's inner belief in a way that is possible only for oneself. (2) If we are restricted to such onlooker's knowledge of our persisting beliefs, we have a perspective from which the alternative account proposed in this chapter is even *better* supported. I will be talking of a person's ability to do this or that. Such an account (i) can accommodate the same data as would be explained by talking of a persisting belief, and (ii) fortunately has no pretension – unlike beliefs – to being able to be known introspectively.
5 I mention introspection here because it was what Hume and Descartes were using.
6 Here is a possibly significant aspect of it upon which I will not dwell (partly because it arises as a general question about Hume's picture): How could one know

introspectively that there is a bundle present at all, since one does not introspect the bundle's limits or boundaries? I have two tentative suggestions. You could observe (i) some bundl*ing*, if memory is available to you when you are introspecting, and/or (ii) a bundle as it is present so *far*, even if perhaps not thereby what might be the completed or final bundle.

7   Stanley (2011) talks at times of various actions as manifesting some knowledge-*that*. But actions more clearly manifest knowledge-how than knowledge-that, since knowledge-how *is* knowledge how to perform some sort of action. In any case, we will soon return to this issue, when we discuss what I call *knowing* actions.

8   On this way of conceiving of knowledge-how, see Hetherington (2008, 2011a, 2011b, 2015) and Glick (2012).

9   That advice is from Peirce's 1868 paper, 'Some Consequences of Four Incapacities'. An echo of it, apparently, drives Wittgenstein's concept of family resemblance: 'Why do we call something a "number"? Well, perhaps because it has a – direct – relationship with several things that have hitherto been called number; and this can be said to give it an indirect relationship to other things we call the same name. And we extend our concept of number as in spinning a thread we twist fibre on fibre. And the strength of the thread does not reside in the fact that some one fibre runs through its whole length, but in the overlapping of many fibres'. Importantly for this chapter's conception of knowledge, Wittgenstein continues thus: 'But if someone wished to say: "There is something common to all these constructions – namely the disjunction of all their common properties" – I should reply: Now you are only playing with words. One might as well say: "Something runs through the whole thread – namely the continuous overlapping of those fibres"' (Wittgenstein 1958: para. 67).

10 'But is your calculating intended to convey knowledge? Or is its aim instead to *reach* the knowledge?' The latter could be parsed as the action's aiming to convey the agent to the knowledge. I will not complicate my presentation with this detail.

11 'Yet how could one know that one has a persisting ability to perform such actions, if (as was argued earlier) one cannot know introspectively of one's having a persisting belief?' I have noted that abilities are in general not aspects of oneself that we would pre-theoretically expect to be known introspectively. In contrast, people do expect to be able to access purely by introspection at least many of their beliefs. (In my terms, though, that expectation misleads them. They self-attribute a persisting belief when what they experience is at most an *active manifestation* of what would be such a belief. Still, the expectation is present.) But an ability, by definition, is not like that. We expect in general that an ability's presence is known, if at all, not purely introspectively at a given time. This is so, even for cognitive abilities.

12 Elsewhere, I have argued for a distinction between knowledge and knowing (Hetherington 2011b). But in this chapter I am not relying upon the details of that distinction.

13 I am not sure that Ryle himself saw this. He does say that, when one knows that *p*, one acts in related ways (1949: 134). He also says that, for example, to say of someone 'who keeps to the edge, [that he does so] because he knows that the ice is thin, is to employ quite a different sense of "because" […] from that conveyed by saying that he keeps to the edge because he believes that the ice is thin' (1949: 135). Yet could this 'because' in the person's knowing be due to the actions being more an *expression* of the knowledge than, say, a *mere consequence* of it? Ryle does not say. Kremer (2017) portrays Ryle as offering a picture of knowledge-that and knowledge-how as interrelated. But the relations described by Ryle (and by Kremer on Ryle's behalf) are only

causal, not metaphysically constitutive. My focus *is* on the question of whether there are metaphysically constitutive relations here that reveal at least part of what it is to know even a particular truth.

14 For this traditional conception of belief, see Cohen (1992), for example.
15 For discussion of Ryle on this issue, see Scheffler (1968), Myers-Schulz and Schwitzgebel (2013), and Kremer (2017).
16 On the many respects in which traditional epistemology has side-stepped answering this implicit question, see Hetherington (2011a: ch. 1). On the general idea of some knowledge that *p*'s admitting of being better or worse – stronger or weaker – as knowledge that *p*, see Hetherington (2001).
17 Is that state only ever of a person – and of nothing else in addition? For the idea of some knowing being attributable not only to the person, but to the person *plus* some epistemically pertinent factors, see Hetherington (2012).
18 For statements of this approach, see Sosa (2011, 2015, 2016). Reed accommodates it in this way: 'even if knowledge is not itself an action, this is no bar to its being *action-like* in important ways' (2016: 108).
19 And because it *could* be a potential grounded in the person as such (I have said nothing to the contrary, at least), the potentialities model has the capacity to preserve what, for some, is an insight that belongs with virtue-theoretic accounts of knowledge – the idea that the virtues in question *are* whole-person rather than more narrowly cognitive. That idea is particularly prominent within character-based forms of virtue epistemology, such as Zagzebski's (1996). But it is also part of Sosa's reliabilist form of virtue epistemology: for an elegant explanation and expansion of its role within Sosa's approach, see Reed (2016).
20 'How does a belief – which is a state, not an event, let alone an action – express or manifest knowledge-*how*?' From Section 9.2's argument: what we find, when introspecting to ascertain what we believe, are *believings* – actions or occurrences to which we may choose to apply the term 'belief' but whose continued life past our interacting with them we are *not* experiencing. They are, in effect, themselves expressions or manifestations of belief.
21 An infallibilist would replace this 'at least most' with 'all.' My formulation is thus fallibilist. For more on the nature and viability of knowledge-fallibilism, see Hetherington (1999, 2001, 2002, 2005, 2013, 2016b).
22 There is a noteworthy overlap between this conception of the truth condition within knowledge, and Craig's (1990) influential view of our concept of knowledge. He regards that concept as reflecting our needs for *reliable informants* – people upon whom we can rely as we seek information. In Campbell's sense, Craig's approved informants are true, in that they are reliable and faithful in what they convey to us.
23 God is at least aware of the tree. Does He ever really observe it? Apart from our having to use a physical perceptual mechanism, we must await the tree's presence before we can observe it. Unlike God, we are partly dependent on contingent aspects of the tree, aspects beyond our making or our control. If that is perception, God does not perceive.
24 Brent Madison made very helpful comments on a draft of this chapter, as did audiences at Soochow University, Australian Catholic University, and Cambridge University.

References

Anscombe, G.E.M. (1963 [1957]), *Intention*, 2nd edn, Oxford: Blackwell.
Campbell, R.J. (2011), *The Concept of Truth*, Basingstoke: Palgrave Macmillan.
Chrisman, M. (2012), 'The Normative Evaluation of Belief and the Aspectual Classification of Belief and Knowledge Attributions', *The Journal of Philosophy*, 109: 588–612.
Cohen, L.J. (1992), *An Essay on Belief and Acceptance*, Oxford: Clarendon Press.
Craig, E.J. (1990), *Knowledge and the State of Nature*, Oxford: Clarendon Press.
Descartes, R. (1984 [1641]), 'Meditations on First Philosophy', in J. Cottingham, R. Stoothoff, and D. Murdoch (eds and trans.), *The Philosophical Writings of Descartes*, Vol. II, Cambridge: Cambridge University Press.
Gettier, E.L. (1963), 'Is Justified True Belief Knowledge?' *Analysis*, 23: 121–3.
Glick, E. (2012), 'Abilities and Know-How Attributions', in J. Brown and M. Gerken (eds), *Knowledge Ascriptions*, 120–39, Oxford: Oxford University Press.
Hetherington, S. (1999), 'Knowing Failably', *The Journal of Philosophy*, 96: 565–87.
Hetherington, S. (2001), *Good Knowledge, Bad Knowledge: On Two Dogmas of Epistemology*, Oxford: Clarendon Press.
Hetherington, S. (2002), 'Fallibilism and Knowing That One Is Not Dreaming', *Canadian Journal of Philosophy*, 32: 83–102.
Hetherington, S. (2005), 'Fallibilism', *The Internet Encyclopedia of Philosophy*, URL: http://www.iep.utm.edu/f/fallibil.htm
Hetherington, S. (2008), 'Knowing-That, Knowing-How, and Knowing Philosophically', *Grazer Philosophische Studien*, 77: 307–24.
Hetherington, S. (2011a), *How to Know: A Practicalist Conception of Knowledge*, Malden, MA: Wiley-Blackwell.
Hetherington, S. (2011b), 'Knowledge and Knowing: Ability and Manifestation', in S. Tolksdorf (ed.), *Conceptions of Knowledge*, 73–100, Berlin: De Gruyter.
Hetherington, S. (2012), 'The Extended Knower', *Philosophical Explorations*, 15: 207–18.
Hetherington, S. (2013), 'Concessive Knowledge-Attributions: Fallibilism and Gradualism', *Synthese*, 190: 2835–51.
Hetherington, S. (2015), 'Technological Knowledge-That as Knowledge-How: A Comment', *Philosophy & Technology*, 28: 567–72.
Hetherington, S. (2016a), *Knowledge and the Gettier Problem*, Cambridge: Cambridge University Press.
Hetherington, S. (2016b), 'Understanding Fallible Warrant and Fallible Knowledge: Three Proposals', *Pacific Philosophical Quarterly*, 97: 270–82.
Hume, D. (1978 [1739–40]), *A Treatise of Human Nature*, 2nd edn, P.H. Nidditch (ed.), Oxford: Clarendon Press.
Kremer, M. (2017), 'Capacity to Get Things Right: Gilbert Ryle on Knowledge', *European Journal of Philosophy*, 25: 25–46.
Lewis, C.I. (1946), *An Analysis of Knowledge and Valuation*, La Salle, IL: Open Court.
Lycan, W.G. (2006), 'On the Gettier Problem Problem', in S. Hetherington (ed.), *Epistemology Futures*, 148–68, Oxford: Clarendon Press.
Mill, J.S. (1979 [1865]), 'An Examination of Sir William Hamilton's Philosophy', in J.M. Brown (ed.), *Collected Works of John Stuart Mill*, Vol. IX, Toronto: University of Toronto Press.
Myers-Schulz, B. and Schwitzgebel, E. (2013), 'Knowing That p without Believing That p', *Noûs*, 47: 371–84.

Peirce, C.S. (1931–58), *Collected Papers of Charles Sanders Peirce*, Vols. I–VI, C. Hartshorne and P. Weiss (eds), Vols VII–VIII, A.W. Burks (ed.), Cambridge, MA: Harvard University Press.

Radford, C. (1966), 'Knowledge – by Examples', *Analysis*, 27: 1–11.

Reed, B.W. (2016), 'Who Knows?' in M.A. Fernandez Vargas (ed.), *Performance Epistemology: Foundations and Applications*, 106–23, Oxford: Oxford University Press.

Ryle, G. (1949), *The Concept of Mind*, London: Hutchinson.

Ryle, G. (1971 [1946]), 'Knowing How and Knowing That', in *Collected Papers*, Vol. II, 212–25, London: Hutchinson.

Scheffler, I. (1968), 'On Ryle's Theory of Propositional Knowledge', *The Journal of Philosophy*, 65: 725–32.

Shope, R.K. (1983), *The Analysis of Knowing: A Decade of Research*, Princeton: Princeton University Press.

Sosa, E. (2007), *A Virtue Epistemology: Apt Belief and Reflective Knowledge*, Vol. I, Oxford: Clarendon Press.

Sosa, E. (2011), *Knowing Full Well*, Princeton: Princeton University Press.

Sosa, E. (2015), *Judgment and Agency*, Oxford: Oxford University Press.

Sosa, E. (2016), 'Knowledge in Action', in A. Bahr and M. Seidel (eds), *Ernest Sosa: Targeting His Philosophy*, 1–13, Dordrecht: Springer.

Stanley, J. (2011), *Know How*, Oxford: Oxford University Press.

Stanley, J. and Williamson, T. (2001), 'Knowing How', *The Journal of Philosophy*, 98: 411–44.

Wittgenstein, L. (1958), *Philosophical Investigations*, 2nd edn, Oxford: Blackwell.

Zagzebski, L.T. (1996), *Virtues of the Mind: An Inquiry into the Nature of Virtue and the Ethical Foundations of Knowledge*, Cambridge: Cambridge University Press.

10

Sceptical challenges and knowing actions

First, we gain clarity about how a (Cartesian) sceptical challenge is intended to be challenging; then we find that it is not challenging after all. Adapting Ryle's regress argument against intellectualism about intelligent actions is part of the key to this anti-sceptical result. Another part is a conceptual link between knowing actions and knowing.

10.1 Introduction

Epistemological discussions of sceptical arguments about knowledge often treat the arguments as potential threats. Yet exactly what is to be threatened by such arguments? Is it our *having* knowledge? Those sceptical arguments are written as if they are directly and wholly about our chance of having knowledge: 'Imagine being in the following situation …. In that case, you would not know that …. So, *do you* know, *now*, that … ?' But few of us are easily made by these arguments to *feel* that we lack such knowledge. This is so, even when we cannot find a problem within the sceptical reasoning. Nonetheless, even then, what we can readily feel to be lacking is our having adequate *explanations* or *understanding* of ourselves as knowers – of how we know, if we do know. Non-sceptical epistemology strives for explanation or understanding, even when this is not its overt topic. Non-sceptical epistemology can be overtly about the *fact* of whether we know, while also expecting its answers to provide explanations or understanding of that fact.

What would be needed for attaining such an outcome in response to sceptical arguments? First we require understanding of the sceptical arguments themselves – of what they aim to accomplish. So, Section 10.2 will work *within* the viewpoint of some sceptical reasoning. That will clarify the sense of *epistemic priority* at the heart of the sceptical challenge. We will also reflect upon a kind of *ideal* potential knower. In turn, we will reflect upon the idea of knowers as epistemic *agents actively* knowing (not simply as epistemic subjects in states of knowing). Section 10.4 will link those reflections upon active knowing with the sceptical challenge's demands (in Section 10.2) upon would-be knowers. The result will be a Ryle-inspired *metaphysical* undermining of that sceptical challenge. (Then Section 10.5 applies that result in an initially-Moorean way. We will have constructed a setting within which a form of reasoning based initially upon Moore's (1959) 'proof of an external world' no longer begs the question against associated sceptical reasoning.)

10.2 Clarifying sceptical challenges

10.2.1 Explanation or Understanding

Wittgenstein's discussion of some paradigmatic sceptical thinking begins with this distillation of how such thinking might itself start:

> If you do know that *here is one hand*, we'll grant you all the rest'
> (Wittgenstein 1969: sec. 1).

At first glance, Wittgenstein was concerned simply with whether you know. But that appearance is misleading. His focus is also on whether we can *explain* or *understand* you as knowing – even that *here is one hand*. Some sceptical challenges (certainly Cartesian ones) hone in on a specific proposition which, they argue, cannot be known; and Wittgenstein was treating respectfully the sceptical view that this failure to know the specific proposition then prevents, *just like that*, our being able to gain some vast body of further knowledge.[1] For the sceptical reasoning will tell us that no one *can* know that *here is one hand*. No one can know it, at any rate, while 'all the rest' is *still waiting* – knowledge of 'all the rest' not yet being granted. Accordingly, if we lack any adequate story of how one *can* know that *here is one hand* in such a circumstance, we must concede our not understanding or explaining how there can be such knowledge. We should then not *grant* any of this knowledge. As epistemologists, we try to explain or understand how some knowledge is possible. If we fail, we must refrain from granting it – either the knowledge that *here is one hand* or 'all the rest'.

So the sceptical thinking has two strands. There is overt and direct discussion of whether and how you know: *can* you know that *here is one hand*? And that discussion is intended to be such that its adequate answer *is* an explanation, *giving us understanding*, of your knowing: *can* we explain or understand your knowing that *here is one hand*? In what follows, we may intertwine those two strands: we may talk of what is needed to be accurately crediting or according you some particular knowledge, in the course of explaining or understanding your having the knowledge. First, we would counter the sceptical argument as a piece of *epistemology*, by gaining the explanation or understanding. Second, we would escape the sceptical argument's view of us, by explaining or understanding our *having* the knowledge.[2]

Now we may formalise slightly the demand underlying Wittgenstein's distillation:

> Consider any proposition *p* within some epistemic category (such as propositions allegedly about the physical world). In general, *before* you could be credited accurately with knowledge that *p*, it must be possible to credit you accurately with knowledge that not-*q* – for some proposition *q* which, if true, would prevent, for any such *p*, your having knowledge that *p*. (We can therefore call *q* a *sceptical possibility*.)

Here, more concretely, is how that drama is claimed to unfold. The sceptical reasoning challenges your knowing some simple representative *p*. The reasoning describes a putative possibility which is such that if you cannot know it not to obtain, you cannot know even the simple representative *p* – again, *here is one hand* will serve. And if you cannot know even *this* simple a *p*, you cannot know *all the rest*.

But *why* might you not know that *here is one hand*? What sceptical possibility, lurking with intent, must you know not to obtain? The sceptical reasoning highlights a proposition such as *I am dreaming right now*, applied to you. Can you know that this does not obtain? If not, then you do not know that even those of your experiences that feel observational are not actually parts of a state of dreaming. But only somehow *via* those of your experiences that feel observational would you know that *here is one hand* or, indeed, anything else about the physical world at the moment. No such knowledge, therefore, is possible for you.

10.2.2 Priorities

So concludes that Cartesian sceptical reasoning. How should we engage with it in a way that does justice to its potential depth?

We should begin by setting aside, as insufficiently sensitive, what have in recent years become favoured ways of claiming to formulate the sceptical challenge's inferential heart. These days, epistemologists aiming to present sceptical reasoning generally reach for a notion either (i) of *closure* – the closure of knowledge under known entailment – or (ii) of *relevant* alternatives – relevant alternatives to *p*, the initial putative object of knowledge. The former approach attends to what are known by the epistemic agent to be *p*'s logical consequences; and her knowing that *p* could be said (on the sceptical reasoning's behalf) to require her knowing *all* such consequences. The second approach focuses upon what are constituted, perhaps contextually, as genuinely possible competitors to *p*'s obtaining; and the epistemic agent's knowing that *p* is said (again on behalf of the sceptical reasoning) to require her knowing that *no* such alternatives obtain. The second approach can be used to render the first one more realistic: you would be required to know that not-*q*, for any *relevant q*, where you may realistically be deemed to know that not-*q* is at least a logical consequence of *p*. For example, we may be directed to assess a specific case of sceptical thinking as a cast of mind dictated by acceptance of this thesis[3]:

You know that *here is one hand*, only if you know that *you are not dreaming*.

Most likely, that thesis highlights the question of whether *you are not dreaming* because the latter proposition is taken to mean that *you are not merely (and thereby mistakenly) dreaming that here is one hand*. And you are presumed to know that this content is entailed by *here is one hand*.[4]

Yet we should set aside any such approach if we are to understand the sceptical thinking's potential depth. Even when about relevant alternatives, the closure condition is not demanding enough, in a respect which this section will describe. A mark of this problem is that in principle a sceptical demand centred upon something like the modified closure condition mentioned a moment ago could be satisfied in this initially-Moorean way[5]:

> I know that *here is one hand*. Hence (given my having that knowledge), I know that *I am not dreaming*.

It is well-established that this form of response is not one that the sceptical reasoning could accept. (And in this section I am trying only to *understand* sceptical reasoning, not to argue for or against it.) Anyone investigating sympathetically the sceptical reasoning should regard that response as blatantly question-begging.[6] After all, the response advances a premise – 'I know that *here is one hand*' – which the sceptical perspective should not concede to be available as a premise (rather than a supposition) until *after* the response's conclusion – 'I know that *I am not dreaming*' – has been established. Accordingly, that use of '*after*' must be respected when reconstructing the sceptical reasoning.

We therefore need to note the following pivotal aspect of the Cartesian sceptical reasoning. Distinctively, the reasoning assigns elucidatory or explanatory *priorities*. Epistemologists talk of *epistemic* priority. But such talk is not always as clear as it should be. In its attempt to explain or understand how knowledge that *here is one hand* is possible for you, it presumes this knowledge's not being possible for you until you overcome the sceptical challenge, satisfying the sceptical demand by eliminating (either explicitly or implicitly) the sceptical possibility. As I indicated earlier, we may parse the point in terms of accurate knowledge-attributions. The sceptical reasoning relies on the idea that no knowledge that *p* (even a simple representative *p*) can accurately be credited to you *until* you have been accurately credited with satisfying the sceptical demand. Of course, if you *were* to satisfy the sceptical demand, your knowing that *p* and your satisfying that demand could be present at once. In that sense, neither need be *present* prior to the other. Hence, *that* is not the sense in which the sceptical reasoning imposes an epistemic priority upon would-be knowers. Rather, satisfying the sceptical demand is taken by the sceptical reasoning to have an *explanatory* priority: Only once you satisfy the sceptical demand can you be *understood* as having the knowledge that *p*.

Any engagement with the sceptical demand must recognise the role of that sort of priority in the sceptical reasoning's methodology. You are expected to satisfy the sceptical demand in even just one case – without being allowed to do so by satisfying the demand in another *equally* vulnerable case: the simple *p* represents *all* members of some grouping of propositions. For example, if you claim to know that *here is one hand* because you know that *here is one complete body*, the sceptical demand will be re-applied to this new but epistemically interchangeable target. Methodologically, you are able to be accorded knowledge of any such propositions (other things being equal) only once you can be credited with having cleared the sceptical hurdle. If you or anyone else is to *understand* you as knowing *here is one hand*, say, without the sceptical demand's simply being dismissed, then you must *first* be understood as knowing that *I am not dreaming* is not true of you.

10.2.3 Idealisation

In that way, a sceptical argument insists upon a priority of understanding or explanation, applied to alleged epistemic states of affairs. The ordering is correlatively *idealised*. It will be said to be about you and me; only indirectly is it so, though.

We can see this by asking why you would hold yourself *accountable* to the ordering described by the sceptical reasoning. That reasoning talks as if you would not claim the knowledge that *here is one hand* unless you were already able to accord yourself, aptly, the knowledge that *you are not dreaming*. But in what sense is that true of you? In practice, you *will* claim the knowledge that *here is one hand*, without bothering explicitly with whether you know that *you are not dreaming*.

Consider a simple analogy – the idea of a major operator within any complex well-formed formula (wff) of a formal system of logic:

> The major operator is the operator that would be written last, among those operators present in the wff, if we were writing the wff by mirroring the formation rules for wffs in that language. Writing 'A ⊃ (B ∨ C)' from left to right, we will actually write '∨' after '⊃'. But if we were writing the wff by mirroring the formation rules, we would write the '⊃' after the '∨'.

So the idea of a major operator can informally be explained or understood partly in terms of a logically *ideal* writer of wffs. The sceptical challenge, analogously, can be explained or understood partly in terms of an epistemically *ideal* knowledge-claimer or would-be knower. No epistemic agent like that would countenance claiming knowledge that *here is one hand* without having at least decided that she was in position to claim accurately that *I am not dreaming* is true of her. It is that sort of explanatory or elucidatory ordering to which sceptical reasoning adverts when asking *first* for an explanation or understanding of your knowing that *I am not dreaming*.

A moment ago, I imagined your being tempted not to respect that priority: you would claim to know that *here is one hand*, without having already engaged epistemically with whether *I am not dreaming* is true of you. This would reflect your not being epistemically ideal. The sceptical argument describes one way for an epistemic agent to satisfy an ideal explanatory elucidatory account; and in practice you would not proceed like that.

'Fine, but who among us *is* epistemically ideal?' Who, indeed? Is the sceptical challenge thereby inapplicable to us? *If* it is, that is not *how* it is (as we will soon discover). We have noted just now that the sceptical reasoning is directly about an epistemic ideal. Accordingly, it is directly about us only insofar as we *could* be, or *could not* be, epistemically ideal. How is it therefore about us as we *are*? Here is how, at least purportedly.

The sceptical reasoning is modally ambitious. It concludes that no one *could* know that *here is one hand*, say. It does this by talking about actual people – you and me – only *as* (it hypothesises) we might be: insofar as the reasoning imposes a standard apt for someone who is being epistemically ideal, such knowledge (according to the reasoning) is unavailable. An ideal epistemic agent is one who, for a start, always respects proper epistemic ordering. The sceptical reasoning is directly about that sort of epistemic agent. She would not claim to know that *here is one hand*, if she had not *first* accounted for her knowing that *she is not dreaming*. Perhaps a better term than 'ideal epistemic agent', then, is 'fully orderly epistemic agent'. The sceptical argument reflects first upon fully orderly epistemic agents. It questions whether an explanation or understanding is possible even of whether epistemic agents like *that* could know that *here is one hand*.

Then the link with *you* – a non-ideal epistemic agent – is simple. Are you a *less-than-fully orderly epistemic agent*? If so, then *a fortiori* (given that, on the sceptical reasoning, even fully orderly epistemic agents cannot be explained or understood as knowing that *here is one hand*) *you* cannot be explained or understood as having such knowledge. Even if you *were* fully orderly, the point would remain. We may continue understanding the sceptical thinking in modal terms:

> In fact you *could* not know that *here is one hand*, insofar as you *do* not know it *even when* considered as an ideal or fully orderly epistemic agent.

And in failing to know, even possibly, that *here is one hand*, you are unable to know much more besides. Although the sceptical reasoning proceeds in an idealised way, it is not *thereby* irrelevant to you as a less-than-ideal epistemic agent. It seeks to explain or understand you as a potential knower. Initially, it does so in terms of an *idealised* potential knower.[7]

10.3 Knowing actions and intellectualism

10.3.1 Knowing actions introduced

Nonetheless, the sceptical reasoning remains ineffective as a concern about you, *even* when you are considered as an ideal epistemic agent. That reasoning fails even as a conception of what a fully orderly epistemic agent must do if she is to be a knower. The failing is metaphysical. Section 10.4 will describe it in the light of this section's topic: *knowing actions*.

Here are examples of such actions: asserting knowingly, inferring knowingly, moving knowingly, answering knowingly, etc. These are a kind of *intelligent* action. The latter term comes from Gilbert Ryle (1949; 1971). Intelligent actions are those we would describe, pre-theoretically, as exemplifying or manifesting knowledge-*how* – riding a bicycle, writing a letter, cooking dinner, etc. Ryle then asked whether all intelligent actions, in manifesting knowledge-how, manifest knowledge-that. (Section 10.3.2 will consider his answer. First, more taxonomising is needed.)

We might be tempted to think that the following is a further way of asking that question of Ryle's: Are all intelligent actions also what I will call *knowing* actions – actions whose apparent point is to exemplify or manifest knowledge-that? But those questions are not quite identical. This new question differs in one respect from Ryle's. Within the category of intelligent actions, knowing actions are those we would describe *pre*-theoretically as exemplifying or manifesting knowledge-that; whereas other intelligent actions should be so-described only *after* theoretical work. Asserting, inferring, or answering knowingly, for instance, may well be regarded pre-theoretically as actions that 'externalise' the knowledge-that whose *content* is being knowingly asserted, inferred, or answered. Knowing actions are clearly – we would say, pre-theoretically – intended to *convey* knowledge. In this way they are unlike such intelligent actions as riding a bicycle or cooking dinner. Although some philosophers will come to regard the latter actions as exemplifying or manifesting knowledge-that, even those philosophers will not *pre*-theoretically view these actions as intended to *convey* knowledge-that.

With that distinction in mind, we should confront this question. What can we learn about knowledge-*that* from reflecting upon knowing *actions* in particular, given what we have learnt about intelligent actions in general?

10.3.2 Rylean anti-intellectualism

For we *have*, it seems, learnt something about intelligent actions in general. *Intellectualism* deems all manifestations of knowledge-how to be manifestations of knowledge-that: see, for instance, Stanley and Williamson (2001). Famously, however, Ryle argued against intellectualism – the idea of knowledge-that's essentially being involved in knowing-how, needed for producing applications of knowledge-how. Ryle concluded that some actions are performed intelligently (as genuine exemplifications or expressions of knowledge-how) *without* having to be overseen or guided by instances of knowledge-that. These intelligent actions are performed regardless of whether related knowledge-that helps to guide or oversee them into existence.

For example, you could play a specific cricket shot without this manifestation of knowledge-how needing to have been preceded and guided by an associated piece of knowledge-that (such as knowledge that if your left wrist is positioned … just so … just now …, then your timing when playing such a shot will improve). Maybe some knowledge-that was acquired, before being relied upon in practical applications, during the early phase of your cricket education: '*This* is how your body should look, just before hitting that sort of delivery. Now you know'. Possibly, though, later phases of your cricketing development involved improvements in technique that followed *no* such acquiring of knowledge-that. It is possible that you now play the shot skilfully, twiddling your wrist just so, *without* implementing pre-existing knowledge that such a twiddle is needed. The twiddle happens – advantageously, even cleverly. Yet this does not entail that it needed to be overseen or guided by already-existing knowledge that it is the right way to move in this circumstance.[8]

Ryle's argument for that picture was not introspective. He relied on no thinking along these lines: 'I know by introspection that I am acting without calling upon the guiding influence of some knowledge-that. I can know by "looking within" that no prior knowledge-that is being implemented'. Although it might feel like this to the agent, that feeling is hardly conclusive. Instead, Ryle's argument was conceptual. It was an *infinite regress* argument.

The crucial objection to the intellectualist legend is this. The consideration of propositions is itself an operation the execution of which can be more or less intelligent, less or more stupid. But if, for any operation to be intelligently executed, a prior theoretical operation had first to be performed and performed intelligently, it would be a logical impossibility for anyone ever to break into the circle.

Let us consider some salient points at which this regress would arise. According to the legend, whenever an agent does anything intelligently, his act is precededand steered by another internal act of considering a regulative proposition appropriate to his practical problem. But what makes him consider the one maxim which is appropriate rather than any of the thousands which are not? [...] Intelligently reflecting how to act is, among other things, considering what is pertinent and disregarding what is inappropriate. Must we then say that for the hero's reflections how to act to be intelligent he must first reflect how best to reflect how to act? The endlessness of this implied regress shows that the application of the criterion of appropriateness does not entail the occurrence of a process of considering this criterion. (Ryle 1949: 30–1)

10.3.3 Generalising Rylean anti-intellectualism

Ryle's focus was narrower than it would now need to be. Only on an epistemically *internalist* construal of knowledge-that's justificatory component is he showing that knowledge cannot coherently be required as part of what is generating, and thereby constituting the intelligence within, an intelligent action. This is historically understandable: when Ryle was writing, epistemologists had in mind neither the epistemic internalism/externalism distinction nor relevant externalist construals of knowledge-that's epistemic components. In that respect, however, there has been epistemological progress. We can extend Ryle's thinking.[9] His argument is readily generalisable. It possesses a structure that allows us (i) to speak with systematic ambiguity in either internalist or externalist ways about knowledge-that's epistemic portion, as well as (ii) to understand with correlative generality this chapter's talk, on behalf of sceptical reasoning, of explanatory priority.

Here is the generalised Rylean reasoning.

Suppose for *reductio* that any given intelligent action A exists only in part because it has been preceded and overseen (whether with awareness or not) by some already existing instance K of knowledge-that. Notice that such a use of K is an action,[10] presumably an intelligent one.[11] Call that action A_1. Then our initial intellectualist *reductio* assumption applies also to A_1: there needs to have been some instance K_1 of knowledge-that preceding and overseeing the generation of A_1. Yet this use of K_1 is an intelligent action – which we may call A_2. And so on, *ad infinitum*. We confront an unending need for various pertinent actions – $A_1, A_2, A_3, \ldots$ – to have sequentially and jointly contributed to the constituting of A. However, no one *can* have performed an infinitude of such actions – A_1 (= using K to generate A), A_2 (= using K_1 to generate A_1), A_3 (= using K_2 to generate A_2), etc. – as a precursor to performing even a single intelligent action A.[12] Still, intelligent actions are performed. So, that is not *how* they are performed. By *reductio*, in other words, *not every intelligent action, manifesting knowledge-how, needs to have been preceded and overseen* – if it is to exist as an intelligent action – by some knowledge-that.

In that generalised Rylean sense,[13] therefore, intelligent actions can occur *independently* of the influence of knowledge-that: intellectualism about the nature of intelligent actions is false. The alternative is a *practicalism* about what it is to manifest knowledge-how (in this sense, to act intelligently). To deny intellectualism is to endorse such a practicalism. It is to accept that a manifestation of expertise need not involve prior contemplation of the situation. Nor need the manifestation include applying related knowledge-that, only thereby being able to act in that expert or knowing way. This is our generalised Rylean result, then: It is possible to act intelligently or knowingly on a particular occasion without having been guided by some already-existing knowledge-that.[14]

10.3.4 Intellectualism about knowing actions?

What, next, of the relationship between knowledge-that and *knowing* actions in particular – asserting knowingly, inferring knowingly, moving knowingly, answering knowingly, and so on? Even if (for Section 10.3.3's Rylean reasons) intellectualism is not true of intelligent actions more generally, is it true of *these* ones – the knowing actions? For example, when you answer knowingly that p, is your action knowing not merely because you *have* knowledge that p, but because you *use* the knowledge that p in answering that p? Indeed (as Section 10.3.1 mentioned), you are trying to *convey* the knowledge that p. Does this picture support an intellectualist view of the case?

The idea would be that your intelligent action of answering that p is also a *knowing* action because it is guided and overseen by your knowing that p. Several philosophers have recently argued for there being congruent *normative* links between knowing and some sorts of (what I am calling) knowing actions: see, for instance, Williamson (2000: ch. 11) on knowledge and assertion, and Hawthorne and Stanley (2008) on knowledge and action. This section's intellectualist hypothesis is that there is a metaphysical link: knowledge, already present, helps to *constitute* knowing actions, thereby allowing an action to *be* a knowing one.

That intellectualist suggestion tells us this:

(1) Any action is a knowing action only if the agent has knowledge which the action manifests.

That is part of how intellectualism claims to understand or explain an action's *being* a knowing one. But Section 10.2 told us this, on behalf of sceptical reasoning:

(2) Any agent can be understood as having knowledge, only if she is already understandable as having special anti-sceptical knowledge – the extra knowledge highlighted in sceptical demands.

(For instance, you can be understood as knowing that *here is one hand*, only if you are already understandable as knowing that *you are not dreaming*.) Now we should conjoin the intellectualist (1) with the sceptical reasoning's (2):

(3) An action can be understood or explained as a knowing action, only if the action's agent can already be understood or explained as having special anti-sceptical knowledge. [From (1) and (2)]

So far, then, *if* we accept intellectualism about knowing actions (and seemingly most epistemologists would), we commit ourselves to increasing the potential reach of sceptical challenges. Knowledge *and* knowing actions would have to be regarded as being at risk of not being understandable or explicable as such, if knowledge is. Sceptical reasoning, when supplemented by an intellectualism about knowing actions, is claiming that we can explain or understand (i) an action's being knowing and/or (ii) the presence of cognate knowledge, only if we can first explain or understand the epistemic agent as having some special anti-sceptical knowledge.

10.4 Defusing the sceptical challenge

10.4.1 Simultaneity

Yet any such embrace of intellectualism might ultimately damage the sceptical reasoning. *How* would the intellectualism blend with the sceptical reasoning? We need to understand why the special anti-sceptical knowledge needs not merely to be present, but to be part of what is *manifested* in whatever knowledge is itself being manifested in the knowing action.

Section 10.2 noted the following two features of the sceptical reasoning. First, it insists on (2) – the *explanatory* priority of your knowing that *you are not dreaming* over your knowing that *here is one hand*, for instance. Second, the sceptical reasoning does not insist on the former knowledge's being *constitutively* prior to the latter (even for an ideal epistemic agent); for they could *exist* simultaneously. But we may strengthen that non-insistence on behalf of the sceptical reasoning. Far from simply not requiring that constitutive priority, the sceptical reasoning requires a constitutive *simultaneity*, of which (4) is a paradigm example:

(4) If you are to know that *here is one hand*, you must simultaneously know that *you are not dreaming*.

The sceptical reasoning will continue insisting on an associated *explanatory* priority: in order for anyone to understand or explain your knowing that *here is one hand*, it must be possible first to understand or explain how you know simultaneously that *you are not dreaming*. The latter simultaneity is needed, however, because if your knowledge of not dreaming was present prior to – but not also at the same time as – your putative knowledge of a hand's presence, the sceptical challenge would have *been* met without *still* being met. Your knowledge that *you are not dreaming* could have lapsed by the time you are being assessed for whether you know that *here is one hand*.

10.4.2 Part/Whole

Even so, that simultaneity of epistemic presence is more than *mere* simultaneity, if the sceptical challenge is to be satisfied. What more is needed?

Implicit in the picture underlying the sceptical reasoning is the following: part of your knowing that *here is one hand* would be your *manifesting* your knowledge that *you are not dreaming*. Otherwise, there would be a constitutive gap between these two putative instances of knowing; which would suffice for your failing the sceptical reasoning's explanatory demand. If your knowing that *you are not dreaming* is only coexisting with your knowing that *here is one hand*, the latter need not be present, even partly, *because* of the former. Correlatively, the sceptical reasoning leads to this metaphysical conclusion, expanding upon (4):

(5) Your knowing that *you are not dreaming* amounts to *part* of your knowing that *here is one hand*.

It is only a part, not the whole: your knowing that *you are not dreaming* was only claimed by the sceptical reasoning to be necessary, not sufficient, for your knowing that *here is one hand*.

10.4.3 Constituting, Not Merely Enabling

But implicit also in the sceptical reasoning is a view of your knowing that *you are not dreaming* as not *just any* part of your knowing that *here is one hand*. Why does sceptical reasoning highlight the former piece of knowledge in particular as required for your having the latter knowledge? What is special in this setting about your knowing that *you are not dreaming*?

Part of the sceptical reasoning's answer is that if you fail to know that *you are not dreaming*, then there is so much more that you fail to know. Yet this is not the full answer. What is special, in relation merely to your knowing that *here is one hand*, about your not knowing that *you are not dreaming*? The answer is not the holistic one – that so much more potential knowledge is at risk. Instead, there is something more locally special about the putative anti-sceptical knowledge (your knowing that *you are not dreaming*) – even when considered only in relation to your knowing that *here is one hand*.

What is locally special is the constitutive *role* supposedly being played, within your knowing that *here is one hand*, by your knowing that *you are not dreaming*. Underlying the sceptical reasoning is a picture of the latter knowledge, once present, as helping to constitute the former knowledge. And this constitutive assistance is not to be understood in the minimal sense of one thing's being a necessary component of another, let alone an extrinsic enabler of the other. The constitutive role of your knowledge that *you are not dreaming* would be more intimately constructive than that. The sceptical reasoning's idea is that your knowing that *you are not dreaming* is an *internally empowering* part of your knowing that *here is one hand*. It is a part which allows at least some *other* parts to be parts of observational knowledge at all (in particular, of the knowledge that *here is one hand*).

For example, your knowing that *you are not dreaming* helps your apparently observational evidence in support of a hand's presence to be *real* observational evidence. It allays a substantive doubt you could otherwise have about the epistemic quality of your apparently observational evidence. Thus does your knowing that *you are not dreaming* help to constitute your knowing that *here is one hand*. It does this only, as (4) articulated, by remaining present as long as does the knowledge that *here is one hand* – by not 'disappearing' before completing the role of empowering and thereby sustaining the presence of the knowledge that *here is one hand*. But it does not remain present yet apart; all the while, it is *within*. Your knowledge that *you are not dreaming* remains implicit or embodied within your knowledge that *here is one hand*, either implicitly or explicitly overseeing and tending to your apparently observational evidence – a further necessary component of your knowing that *here is one hand*.

And *while* it is within, it empowers. In this respect, contrast your knowing that *you are not dreaming* with, say, your knowing that *someone has assured you of your having a hand*. The latter is good evidence for your belief that *here is one hand*. So, it enables you (all else being equal) to know that *here is one hand*. Nonetheless, it is not knowledge which sceptical reasoning would *require* you to have, if you are to know that *here is one hand*. This is because, even if you do know that *someone has assured you of your having a hand*, this knowledge is not a *constitutive* part of your knowing that *here is one hand*. At most, it is an extrinsic enabler of the knowledge that *here is one hand*. It is not an intrinsic constituent of your knowledge that *here is one hand*, necessary for empowering other constituents to *be* constituents of your knowing that *here is one hand*.

As we have noted, the sceptical reasoning is standardly understood to regard your knowledge that *you are not dreaming* as *explanatorily prior* to your knowing that *here is one hand*. But now we also note that the sceptical reasoning is challenging you to know that *you are not dreaming* – so that this knowledge is *constitutively*, even *actively*, *present within* your knowing that *here is one hand*. The knowledge that *you are not dreaming* would amount to an internal 'safety check' or regulator[15] empowering some other constitutive aspects of your knowledge that *here is one hand* genuinely to be parts of the latter knowledge – parts of real knowledge – rather than parts merely of something feeling as if it is knowledge.[16]

In this way, at the heart of the sceptical reasoning is a presumed picture of your knowledge that *here is one hand* as being metaphysically dependent upon the special anti-sceptical knowledge, your knowledge that *you are not dreaming*.[17]

Now let us conjoin (3), (4), and (5).[18] If we accept intellectualism about knowing actions, we must interpret the sceptical reasoning as being committed to this thesis about such actions:

(6) Any action can be understood as knowing, only if in part it can be understood as manifesting special anti-sceptical knowledge. [From (3), (4), and (5)]

As we have found, the special anti-sceptical knowledge is explanatorily prior but constitutively simultaneous. Its presence must be *understandable* before the action can be understood as a knowing action. But the special anti-sceptical knowledge must *be* present when the action is, insofar as the action is to be the knowing action it supposedly is.

10.4.4 Anti-Intellectualism About Knowing Actions

Given (6)'s application of intellectualism to knowing actions in particular, it is time to revisit Ryle's anti-intellectualism argument. In Section 10.3.4, we asked whether intellectualism could be true of all knowing actions, even if not of intelligent actions in general. Now we have found (in Section 10.4.3) that *if* intellectualism is true of knowing actions, sceptical challenges are even more widely challenging than we may have envisaged: they reflect upon knowing actions, not only knowledge.

Still, we may also take heart from what Section 10.3.3 showed to be the generality in Ryle's regress argument. Sections 10.3.4 and 10.4.3 have supposed for argument's sake that intellectualism is true of knowing actions; and such a supposition seems apt while we seek to model-when-understanding the sceptical reasoning. Otherwise (if that reasoning was to be divorced from intellectualism), we could be confronted by a scepticism about your knowing (e.g. that *here is one hand*); without being confronted equally by a scepticism about there being any actual knowing or knowingness within your putatively knowing *actions* – your answering, inferring, moving, etc., in ways we would pre-theoretically regard as manifesting your knowing that *here is one hand*. Yet that would be a surprising disconnection for sceptical reasoning to allow. A denial that there are any instances of knowing should entail a denial that there are any actions *manifesting* knowing (while seeking to convey some). Sceptical reasoning *should* therefore lead to the more encompassing sceptical way of thinking about both knowing actions and knowing – if to even the narrower view about knowing. Intellectualism effects that link, we have seen, for sceptical reasoning.

So, we should examine the consequences for sceptical reasoning, if it is to remain committed to intellectualism, of intellectualism's likewise being *false* of knowing actions. What would intellectualism's being false in that way reveal about any sceptical reasoning which is (as, we now appreciate, such reasoning should be) *committed* to intellectualism about knowing actions?

10.4.5 Anti-Intellectualism, Knowing Actions, and Scepticism

If intellectualism was to be false in that way, we would find ourselves with this thesis – a denial of (6), Section 10.4.3's sceptical requirement upon knowing actions:

(7) It is possible for there to be actions which can be understood or explained as knowing, *without* first having had to be understood or explained as manifesting special anti-sceptical knowledge.

That thesis, with its talk of special anti-sceptical knowledge, amounts to this one, talking instead of sceptical challenges:

(8) It is possible for there to be actions which can be understood or explained as knowing, *without* first having had to be understood or explained as overcoming a sceptical challenge.

Consequently, the Rylean falsity of intellectualism about knowing actions would offer a *partial* escape from sceptical challenges. These would remain pressing, if at all, only for knowledge-that, not for knowing actions seemingly manifesting the knowledge-that.

Yet even that might be more generous to the sceptical reasoning than is merited. Recall Section 10.4.4's brief argument for the thesis that sceptical reasoning should be applied to knowing actions if to knowing. This suggests that we should more completely *inter-link* knowledge and knowing actions. Here is one possible way of doing so:

(9) Insofar as you can be understood or explained as knowing that *here is one hand*, you can be understood or explained as acting knowingly, either actually or possibly, in some knowing-that-*here-is-one-hand* way.

Is that behaviourist? Not classically so, because the actual or possible actions in question would not need to be externally observable even when occurring. Nor need they actually occur anyway: the link is conceptual, with possible actions sufficing. Even then, there need not be a 'they'; a single possible action would be enough. For example, you could satisfy this requirement simply by being able to infer knowingly and silently, from your belief that *here is one hand*, to *here are five fingers*; or by having been able knowingly to infer your belief that *here is one hand* from your believing that *here is what looks like one hand*. No such inner action need occur; its being possible for you is enough. Notice, accordingly, how minimal is the proposed inter-linking. And how plausible it is: if *no* action, be it outer *or* inner, is understandable or explicable even as *possible* for you, then you cannot be understood or explained as knowing that *here is one hand*. For you cannot be understood or explained as doing anything with that knowledge *or* even as having done anything epistemic to gain the knowledge.[19]

I am only proposing, not claiming to establish, the inter-linking thesis (9). But *if* it is true, it combines profitably with thesis (8) about sceptical challenges and knowing actions. From (8): In general, an action can be understood or explained as knowing, without having had to be understood or explained as overcoming a sceptical challenge. From (9): In general, you can be understood or explained as knowing that *p*, only insofar as some actual or possible action can be understood or explained as a *p*-knowing one for you. Blending those two theses generates this result:

(10) It is possible to be understood or explained as knowing that *here is one hand*, without first needing to be understandable or explicable as having overcome an associated sceptical challenge. (You would not first need to be understandable or explicable as knowing that *you are not dreaming*, for instance.) [From (8) and (9)]

That is a welcome result. The classic Cartesian sceptical challenge, for a start, is no longer a hurdle for you to overcome. An alternative explanatory path beckons. In principle, your knowing that *here is one hand* might now be understandable or explicable in a way that is at least partly action-centred (even if possibly in a minimally active way). At any rate, it would not need to be understandable or explicable in terms that satisfy the Cartesian sceptical challenge – the burden of needing first to know that *you are not dreaming*.

10.5 Initially-Moorean anti-sceptical reasoning, resurrected

That result allows us to recapture now, only now, what Section 10.2.2 discarded on behalf of the sceptical reasoning. We regain the epistemological right to allow you to respond to the sceptical challenge with this initially-Moorean style of reasoning:

I know that *here is one hand*. Hence (given my having that knowledge),
I know that *I am not dreaming*.

Here is why we may now use such reasoning without begging the question badly against the sceptical thinking.

First, by talking of knowing actions and by calling upon a Rylean anti-intellectualism, we have found that you can be understood or explained as knowing that *here is one hand*, without first being able to be understood or explained as knowing that *you are not dreaming*. This is not to deny that there could be independent epistemological complexities, even problems, in understanding or explaining you as knowing that *here is one hand*. (This chapter has not engaged with those further complexities or problems.) I am denying only that *sceptical* reasoning must remain a problem for us when seeking to understand or explain you as knowing that *here is one hand*.

Second, my argument has not restricted the range of people to whom such understanding, or such an explanation, is available in principle. Consequently, we have available the possibility of *you* being the person who is able to have that understanding or that explanation: possibly, *you* can understand or explain your knowing that *here is one hand* without first being able to understand or explain yourself as knowing that *you are not dreaming*.

Thus, you have available the possibility of recreating this chapter's reasoning, *and of applying it to yourself* in this way:

I am able to understand or explain my knowing that *here is one hand*. At any rate (with all else being equal), *this is possible without my first* being able to understand or explain my knowing that *I am not dreaming*. As a result, I am *then* able to understand or explain – on that basis – my knowing that *I am not dreaming*.

The point is that what was previously (as Section 10.2.2 acknowledged) question-begging against the sceptical reasoning is no longer so. The claim to know that *here is one hand* could be made without violating the sceptical demand of the conceptual priority of knowing that *you are not dreaming*; for that demand, you now understand, is metaphysically confused in the first place. Your applying this chapter's argument would allow you to return to this less overtly self-reflective reasoning:

> I know that *here is one hand*. Hence (given my having that knowledge),
> I know that *I am not dreaming*.[20]

And this reasoning by you would no longer be question-begging. We have established that the question at the sceptical thinking's core ('How can you know that *you are not dreaming*?') is not one you must first answer if you are to know that *here is one hand*. Hence, we have shown that *you*, likewise, could have established this. You can do so by calling upon the chapter's reasoning. The self-reflectiveness behind your uses (hypothesised a moment ago) of 'I am able to understand or explain' can realise and reflect this use of the chapter's argument.

Recall why all of that is so – and why we thereby extend our answer to the sceptical reasoning. Given a Rylean anti-intellectualism, the condition which the sceptical reasoning seeks to impose (requiring you to know first that *you are not dreaming*) need not be satisfied even when a *fully orderly* epistemic agent's knowing that *here is one hand* is what is to be understood or explained. *A fortiori*, that condition need not be satisfied if *you* – a *less*-than-fully orderly epistemic agent – are to be understood or explained as knowing that *here is one hand*. And you can be equally aware of this, simply by registering the Rylean anti-intellectualism for yourself.

10.6 Conclusion

H.H. Price mused thus:[21]

> Perhaps it is a pity that the Theory of Knowledge and the Theory of Conduct have fallen into separate compartments. (It certainly was not so in Socrates' time [...].) If we studied them together, perhaps we might have a better understanding of both.
>
> (1975 [1946]: 36)

How might we best do that? Price lamented that epistemologists' focus was too much upon

> cognitive *acts* – acts of sensing, of conceiving, of inferring, &c. – and forget[ting] all about the permanent or standing features of the mind. Or if they do consider them at all, they take account only of innate ones, such as the persistent innate capacity for sensing or for thinking which every normal mind has; whereas those which are acquired in the course of experience, and continue permanently thereafter, are quite as important for our understanding of what a mind is, and acquired but persistent *cognitive* states are for the Theory of Knowledge the most important of all.
>
> (1975 [1946]: 39)

Well, epistemology must have changed in that respect between 1946 and now; for belief – considered as a state, and usually an acquired one – has long been at the conceptual core of epistemological attempts to articulate knowledge's nature. In that way, epistemology's recent focus has not been *enough* upon cognitive acts. Epistemology *should*, as Price advocates, reunite the Theory of Knowledge with the Theory of Conduct. This chapter has some encouraging news: such a reunion would not need to retain a picture of knowing as answerable to *sceptical* challenges like the Cartesian one. Discarding the metaphysics of intellectualism frees us – it frees even ideal epistemic agents – in that respect. It frees *epistemology* in that way.[22]

Notes

1 Wittgenstein's statement also conveys how a non-sceptical foundationalist may aim to *respond* to the sceptical argument: Find a proposition that *can* be known – a success that then renders us able to gain much further knowledge.
2 Pritchard suggests 'recasting the sceptical problem as being directed against understanding rather than knowledge' (2010: 85). He is right to say that understanding is at stake. But this need not be because it is the *epistemic agent's* understanding of the world. It could be because sceptical arguments challenge *us* – who may be epistemological onlookers – to explain or understand the epistemic agent's knowing the world. And if we cannot satisfy that challenge, we should *deny* that the epistemic agent knows the world. So the sceptical thinking can still challenge knowledge indirectly by challenging directly what amounts to epistemological understanding.
3 Epistemology's comparatively new-found tradition, present when sceptical reasoning is being discussed, of doing so in terms of closure and/or relevant alternatives comes mainly from Dretske (1970) and Nozick (1981). For more recent debate, see Dretske (2005) and Hawthorne (2005).
4 The entailment has this simple form: $h \to \text{not-}(d_h \& \text{not-}h)$; that is, $h \to (\text{not-}d_h \vee h)$, where $h =$ *here is one hand* and where $d_h =$ *you are dreaming that here is one hand*. (But what if we do not interpret *you are not dreaming* in that more dramatic way – as *you are not merely (and thereby mistakenly) dreaming that here is one hand*? In that event, we would remove 'not-h' from the possibility's schematic description. The possibility would no longer directly threaten the *truth* of your belief that *here is one hand*.)
5 It is initially-Moorean, in the spirit of G.E. Moore's famous attempt to reason from his knowing that he has a hand – being displayed to his audience – to his knowing that there is an external world. Moore did not claim to know that he was not dreaming. Presumably, Moore-today would admit equally that his reasoning is not giving him knowledge that he is not a brain in a vat, say – let alone that he could *begin* his reasoning here with such knowledge. Perhaps, therefore, it is misleading to call anti-sceptical reasoning neo-*Moorean* when it does begin with 'I know that I am not dreaming'. For that use of that label, see Pritchard (2008: 286). It is not misleading, however, to call this reasoning *initially*-Moorean.
6 But see Section 10.5 for a reappraisal of this initially-Moorean response to the sceptical reasoning. The reappraisal will reflect the chapter's central argument.

7   Incidentally, I have not been characterising sceptical reasoning as needing to apply an *infallibilist* justificatory standard. I am not adverting to *that* sort of idealization by sceptical reasoning. Everything I have said could be understood as being about knowledge-as-infallible and/or knowledge-as-fallible.

8   On the contrary; the knowledge-that's presence could *follow* the knowledge-how's acquisition – as you start noticing, for the first time, that the desired outcome is achieved in this specific skilful way.

9   I am presuming its success, as far as it goes. (And in a moment I will extend its reach.) Stanley and Williamson (2001) criticise it; Hetherington (2011: sec. 2.2) defends it against their criticism.

10 'Why need we describe K as being *used* (so that an action is involved in K's making A an intelligent action)? Why is K not merely present (with the pertinent epistemic agent in a *state* of having K)?' The reason is that intellectualists were never saying simply that some knowledge is *present* with a content apt for overseeing and guiding action A. That would imply only the knowledge's being *in a position* to guide A. What intellectualism should say is that the knowledge K is actively guiding whatever aspects of the epistemic agent suffice, once guided, for A's occurring: *Somehow* there is activity in K's making A an intelligent action. The alternative to this conception of K's role is an analogue of what Kornblith (1980) called the *arguments-on-paper* thesis. According to that thesis, one's belief that p is justified if one has another belief whose content q logically supports p. Kornblith argued that this thesis is false because the belief that q might not have helped to *create* the belief that p. The latter belief is justified only if it is *caused* appropriately, such as via the belief with the supportive content q. This is a naturalised picture of justification as constituted *actively*. And intellectualism relies upon something similar. In this generalised Rylean argument, the intellectualist hypothesis implies that A occurs intelligently only if A is *actively* brought about in a way that involves using K with its apt content.

11 Bengson and Moffett (2011a: secs 2.2, 2.3) deny that intellectualism must always regard intelligent actions as intelligently exercising propositional attitudes. Can an action be intelligent when grounded in a deployment of a propositional attitude – a deployment which is not itself an intelligent action? Bengson and Moffett (2011b) argue so. Accordingly, *if* they are correct, Ryle's reasoning is less powerful than I am presuming. This chapter is enriching our sense of how important Ryle's reasoning is *if* it survives Bengson and Moffett's argument.

12 Moreover, these actions become ever more complex. The sequence begins with your using K to generate A. These are the ensuing required actions:

> your using K_1 to generate your using K to generate A; your using K_2 to generate your using K_1 to generate your using K to generate A; and so on.

Hence, even if the sheer number of actions was not already a conclusive reason to discard our initial *reductio* assumption as an account of your performing A, this infinite complexity of the actions would be. Even if we regard the entirety as a single complex action, *its* complexity would be insuperable.

13 It is also a Wittgensteinian sense – and thereby a Brandomian one. What Ryle most strikingly contributes to this discussion is the distinction between knowledge-that and knowledge-how. But Wittgenstein (1958) and – following his lead – Brandom (1994: 20–3) are no less insistent upon the idea that 'there is a need for a *pragmatist* conception of norms – a notion of primitive correctnesses of performance *implicit* in *practice* that precede and are presupposed by their *explicit* formulation in *rules* and *principles*' (1994: 21). Brandom continues: 'What Wittgenstein shows is that

the intellectualist model will not do as an account of the nature of the normative as such' (1994: 23). The Wittgensteinian argument is a regress argument, fundamentally the same as the generalised Rylean one. It is 'Wittgenstein's master argument for the appropriateness of the pragmatist, rather than the regulist-intellectualist, order of explanation' (1994: 23) – where regulism is the thesis 'that proprieties of *practice* are always and everywhere to be conceived as expressions of the bindingness of underlying principles' (1994: 20).

14 I am not saying that knowledge-that *never* guides our exercises of knowledge-how. Sometimes, this might occur automatically and unconsciously. The point is simply that knowledge-that *need* not do this, either consciously or not.

15 Such knowledge thereby coheres with a detail from Ryle's picture (quoted in Section 10.3.2), according to which intellectualism requires 'a regulative proposition' to be guiding the production of an intelligent action. A regulative proposition is about how to achieve that outcome ('This is how to do X: ... '). And your knowing that *you are not dreaming* can be part of such a story about how you use your apparently observational evidence in support of your belief that *here is one hand*. After all, a fuller rendition of the enabling knowledge portrays it as your knowing that *you are not dreaming your apparent observations of a hand's presence, these being the evidential bases upon which, at least as an ideal epistemic agent, you rely as you seek to know whether here is one hand.*

16 There is an unavoidable simplification within this description. Even if you were to know that *you are not dreaming*, you would not thereby know that *other* specific sceptical possibilities do not obtain – such as that *you are not a brain in a vat*, or that *you are not deeply self-deceptive about your surroundings*, etc. But we may treat the possibility of your dreaming as a colourful way of focusing this more general form of sceptical challenge: the possibility of *somehow your being deceived, as to there being a hand here, by your evidence apparently of there being a hand here*. On that form of challenge, see Hetherington (2009).

17 For more on the idea of knowledge that *p*'s being knowledge of aspects of how it is that *p*, see Hetherington (2011: ch. 5).

18 (4) and (5) are overtly about specific pieces of knowledge; (3) is overtly universal. Nonetheless, (4) and (5) are representative in an epistemologically standard way. We may read them as systematically ambiguous between the stated instances and their implied generalizations.

19 This section's thesis is only a brief hint as to how knowledge-that and knowing actions may be inter-linked. For a fuller account of how we might describe knowledge-that in terms of knowledge-how, see Hetherington (2011: ch. 2). For other recent conceptual inter-linkings of knowledge-that and actions, see Allen (2004: chs 1–2) and Sosa (2011: chs 1–3).

20 That move is possible because – for any *p* – if you can understand or explain your knowing that *p*, you can know that *p*. And we established a moment ago your being able to understand or explain, first, your knowing that *here is one hand* and thereby, second, your knowing that *you are not dreaming*.

21 Thanks to John Bengson for bringing to my attention this lecture by Price.

22 I appreciated helpful comments on drafts of this chapter, by Jonathan Adler, John Bengson, William Lycan, Brent Madison, John McDowell, Anne Newstead, Tim Oakley, and Markos Valaris, along with audience members at the Australian National University, at the 2010 Australasian Association of Philosophy Annual Conference at UNSW, and at CUNY's Graduate Center.

References

Allen, B. (2004), *Knowledge and Civilization*, Boulder, CO: Westview Press.

Bengson, J. and Moffett, M.A. (2011a), 'Two Conceptions of Mind and Action: Knowing How and the Philosophical Theory of Intelligence', in J. Bengson and M.A. Moffett (eds), *Knowing How: Essays on Knowledge, Mind, and Action*, 3–55, New York: Oxford University Press.

Bengson, J. and Moffett, M.A. (2011b), 'Non-propositional Intellectualism', in J. Bengson and M.A. Moffett (eds), *Knowing How: Essays on Knowledge, Mind, and Action*, 161–95, New York: Oxford University Press.

Brandom, R.B. (1994), *Making It Explicit: Reasoning, Representing, and Discursive Commitment*, Cambridge, MA: Harvard University Press.

Dretske, F.I. (1970), 'Epistemic Operators', *The Journal of Philosophy*, 67: 1007–23.

Dretske, F.I. (2005), 'The Case against Closure', in M. Steup and E. Sosa (eds), *Contemporary Debates in Epistemology*, 13–26, Malden, MA: Blackwell.

Hawthorne, J. (2005), 'The Case for Closure', in M. Steup and E. Sosa (eds), *Contemporary Debates in Epistemology*, 26–43, Malden, MA: Blackwell.

Hawthorne, J. and Stanley, J. (2008), 'Knowledge and Action', *The Journal of Philosophy*, 105: 571–90.

Hetherington, S. (2009), 'Sceptical Possibilities? No Worries', *Synthese*, 168: 97–118.

Hetherington, S. (2011), *How to Know: A Practicalist Conception of Knowledge*, Malden, MA: Wiley-Blackwell.

Kornblith, H. (1980), 'Beyond Foundationalism and the Coherence Theory', *The Journal of Philosophy*, 77: 597–612.

Moore, G.E. (1959 [1939]), 'Proof of an External World', in *Philosophical Papers*, 127–50, London: George Allen & Unwin.

Nozick, R. (1981), *Philosophical Explanations*, Cambridge, MA: Harvard University Press.

Price, H.H. (1975 [1946]), *Thinking and Representation*, New York: Haskell House Publishers.

Pritchard, D. (2008), 'McDowellian Neo-Mooreanism', in A. Haddock and F. Macpherson (eds), *Disjunctivism: Perception, Action, Knowledge*, 283–310, New York: Oxford University Press.

Pritchard, D. (2010), 'Knowledge and Understanding', in D. Pritchard, A. Millar and A. Haddock (eds), *The Nature and Value of Knowledge: Three Investigations*, New York: Oxford University Press.

Ryle, G. (1949), *The Concept of Mind*, London: Hutchinson.

Ryle, G. (1971 [1946]), 'Knowing How and Knowing That', in *Collected Papers*, Vol. II, 212–25, London: Hutchinson.

Sosa, E. (2011), *Knowing Full Well*, Princeton: Princeton University Press.

Stanley, J. and Williamson, T. (2001), 'Knowing How', *The Journal of Philosophy*, 98: 411–44.

Williamson, T. (2000), *Knowledge and Its Limits*, Oxford: Clarendon Press.

Wittgenstein, L. (1958), *Philosophical Investigations*, 2nd edn, Oxford: Blackwell.

Wittgenstein, L. (1969), *On Certainty*, Oxford: Blackwell.

11

Some fallibilist knowledge: Questioning knowledge-attributions and open knowledge

We may usefully distinguish between one's having fallible knowledge and having a fallibilist stance on some of one's knowledge. A fallibilist stance could include a concessive knowledge-attribution (CKA). But it might also include a questioning knowledge-attribution (QKA). Attending to the idea of a QKA leads to a distinction between what we may call closed knowledge that *p* and open knowledge that *p*. All of this moves us beyond Elgin's classic tale of the epistemic capacities of Holmes and of Watson, and towards a way of resolving Kripke's puzzle about dogmatism and knowing.

11.1 Elgin: Fallibilism as a stance

Recent epistemology has included welcome discussion of the nature, even the possibility, of *fallible* knowledge.[1] This chapter's emphasis will be on what I will refer to as a form of *fallibilist* knowledge. This is knowledge that might – or might not – be fallible (namely, knowledge satisfying a fallibilist's trademark conception of knowledge). Still, it is fallibil*ist* knowledge, in virtue of being knowledge that (as I will explain) includes a kind of fallibilist perspective on itself. It is somewhat epistemologically self-reflective, self-questioning. More specifically (as I will also explain), it is knowledge that, in a particular way, *asks whether* it is really knowledge.[2] I call it *open* knowledge (in deference to Karl Popper).

It is thereby knowledge that includes what Catherine Elgin would call a fallibilist *stance*:

> Despite the 'ism', I suggest, fallibilism is not primarily a doctrine, but a stance – a stance of intellectual humility. The stance is not a passive concession in the face of epistemic frailty. Rather, it is an active orientation toward a domain of inquiry and our prospects of understanding it.
>
> (Elgin 2017: 298)

This chapter will elaborate on one way of entering into the spirit of some aspects of that suggestion by Elgin.[3]

11.2 Elgin: Holmes, Watson, and knowledge

Elgin is among those who doubt the epistemological centrality of the concept of knowledge.[4] Her views on this are of long standing. In one of contemporary philosophy's wittiest papers, she gave us an extended case study that questions the explanatory power of the traditional philosophical emphasis upon aiming to understand knowledge as being the central exemplar of all things epistemic (Elgin 1988). She did this by scrutinising some imagined epistemic performances from literature's much-loved duo of Sherlock Holmes and Dr. Watson. (Their creator, Arthur Conan Doyle, never portrayed them in quite *this* light.)

Elgin envisaged Holmes and Watson being subjected to the strictures imposed by various representative theories of knowledge – internalist ones and externalist ones alike. Her conclusions are well-known among epistemologists. In the situations she described, Watson was easily able to gain knowledge – albeit uninspiring knowledge bespeaking no intellectual insight, imagination, subtlety, etc. Yet this easy accumulation of knowledge by Watson was partly *because* of his lesser capacity for insight, imagination, subtlety, etc. What of Holmes? In his case, argued Elgin, much less knowledge was forthcoming, partly *because* of his far more interesting intellectual capacities, which – surprisingly – made it more difficult for him to satisfy those epistemic standards that were satisfied so naturally and reflectively by Watson:

> The very limitations on the requirements for knowledge which make it possible for the Watsons of the world to know make knowledge more difficult for individuals like Holmes.
>
> (Elgin 1988: 151)

Here are a few examples.

> The problem is that Holmes is no dummy [...] So Holmes's appreciation of the precariousness of his epistemic situation prevents him from knowing.
>
> Respect for evidence may also inhibit knowledge [...] Watson is credulous; Holmes is not [...] [His] epistemic scruples prevent him from forming the requisite beliefs.
>
> [...] So Watson's obliviousness to the evidence serves him well [in some cases]; it enables him to know.
>
> (Elgin 1988: 142)

> What coheres with a narrow [acceptance] system can fail to cohere with a broader one. So Watson, with his limited purview, knows things that Holmes, burdened with a more comprehensive one, does not [...] [In some situations,] Watson's ignorance thus enables him to know what Holmes cannot. The fact that prevents Holmes from knowing, being external to Watson's acceptance system, cannot undermine Watson's justification.
>
> (Elgin 1988: 145)

> [E]pistemically inaccessible truths are, for the internalist, epistemically inert. It is then his stupidity, not just his ignorance, that enables Watson to know [in some cases] what the more intelligent Holmes cannot.
>
> (Elgin 1988: 147)

What should we infer from this recurring disparity? Elgin's own interpretation was blunt. The fault lay, she claimed, with limitations inherent in the concept of knowledge. She urged epistemologists to enlarge their professional ambit accordingly:

> What Holmes's predicament shows, I believe, is that knowledge, as contemporary theories conceive it, is not and might not be our overriding cognitive objective. For to treat it as such is to devalue cognitive excellences such as conceptual and perceptual sensitivity, logical acumen, breadth and depth of understanding, and the capacity to distinguish important from unimportant truths. Even when Watson knows more than Holmes, he does not appear to be cognitively better off.
>
> This suggests that it is unwise to restrict epistemology to *the* study of what contemporary theories count as knowledge. What is wanted is a wide ranging study of cognitive excellences of all sorts, and of the ways they contribute to or interfere with one another's realization. The fruits of such a study might enable us to understand how Socrates, knowing nothing, could be the wisest of all men.
>
> (Elgin 1988: 152)

I agree wholeheartedly with Elgin's initial sentence. But I disagree with her apparent advice to look so ruthlessly beyond what and how people *know*, if we are to do justice to the epistemic realm of 'cognitive excellences'. Presumably wisdom, as exemplified by Socrates, is a paradigm cognitive excellence. As Elgin interprets the situation, however, wisdom is disconnected from knowing, given her supposedly showing (with her reflections on Holmes and Watson) how easy it is to fail to know while – and even because of – having various cognitive characteristics that we might readily associate with being wise. Nonetheless (even granting Elgin the details of her argument), we need not regard the fault in all of this as lying within the concept of knowledge. The fault might be more with 'what *contemporary* theories count as knowledge' (her phrase above; my emphasis now) – those *conceptions* of knowledge with which contemporary epistemologists have been largely contented, *en route* to seeking an understanding of knowledge's nature. In other words, I suggest, we should remain open to the possibility of the concept of knowledge admitting of some new and more nuanced conceptions, ones that might do much *better* at accommodating Holmes and his superior cognitive abilities. Elgin did not do this. She relied, it seems, upon treating those theories of knowledge that she applied to Holmes and Watson as being sufficiently representative of what theories of knowledge *could* ever be.[5] Yet there *are* further relevant respects in which we might enrich our theory of knowledge. This chapter will describe one such way.

Indeed, in the decades since Elgin wrote about Holmes and Watson, the more general moral behind the possibility I am mentioning – of usefully expanding our shared epistemological conception of forms that knowing can take – *has* been heeded to some extent. After all, those 'cognitive excellences' that Elgin described were what some epistemologists would these days deem to be intellectual *virtues* possessed by Holmes and lacked by Watson; and virtue epistemology has expanded greatly in recent years, partly as a theory of knowledge. This chapter, too, can be regarded as proposing a way to include, within our conception of knowing, what may be seen as a specific intellectual virtue.[6]

11.3 Concessive knowledge-attributions

We can begin by revisiting an existing epistemological debate, regarding knowledge-fallibilism and what are called *concessive knowledge-attributions* (CKAs).[7] These have a distinctive form: 'I know that p, although I could be mistaken as to p.' They have arisen as an epistemological topic because their apparent oddity is often seen as posing a challenge to the possible truth of knowledge-fallibilism.

For knowledge-fallibilism, even minimally construed, is the thesis that at least some knowledge is fallible.[8] And most epistemologists will interpret this thesis as entailing that there are at least some instances of knowledge that p that somehow embody or allow some relevant sort of possibility of believing mistakenly that p. One would not *actually* be mistaken as to p (since one knows that p); in some relevant sense of 'could', however, one *could* be. And most epistemologists will say that *if* that sort of combination is possible (as knowledge-fallibilism allows), then at least some specific concessive knowledge-attributions, too, could be true. In offering a concessive knowledge-attribution, it seems, one claims knowledge, before endorsing some sort of possibility of not actually having the claimed knowledge.[9] Knowledge-fallibilism seems to be committed to accepting that at least some instances of such a combination – some concessive knowledge-attributions – would, if uttered or thought, be true.

Yet many epistemologists regard any attempt to think or give voice to a concessive knowledge-attribution as confrontingly strange. Indeed, many people feel or hear any concessive knowledge-attribution as *inconsistent*. David Lewis, notably, said this:

> If you claim that S knows that P, and yet you grant that S cannot eliminate a certain possibility in which not-P, it certainly seems as if you have granted that S does not know after all that P.
>
> (1996: 549)

Is even a simple instance such as 'I know that it is Tuesday, although I could be mistaken about its being so' too odd to be true? And if no concessive knowledge-attributions could be true, must knowledge-fallibilism be false?

Here I do not attempt to answer that question fully.[10] Still, I provide a *prima facie* reason to doubt that concessive knowledge-attributions show knowledge-fallibilism to be false. Specifically, there is a potential scope ambiguity in the concessive knowledge-attribution's use of 'could'. We can appreciate this by distinguishing (as follows) between two possible disambiguations – in turn, CKA_1 and CKA_2 – of the usual ways of formulating concessive knowledge-attributions.

First, it is clear that an instantiation of CKA_1 – a *wide*-scope reading of the 'could' – is not what a knowledge-fallibilist ever intends to convey with a concessive knowledge-attribution:

CKA_1 It is possible that the following is true: [I know that *p*, although I am mistaken as to *p*].

Almost all epistemologists aver that knowing entails truth.[11] In which case, CKA_1 describes as being possible something – namely, knowing that *p* even though it is not true that *p* – that is clearly impossible. Interpretive charity precludes our attributing CKA_1 to any knowledge-fallibilist.

Consider, instead, CKA_2 – a *narrow*-scope reading of the 'could' in a concessive knowledge-attribution. Any instance of it applies 'could' to an epistemic constituent (either evidence or some other form of justification) *within* the initially claimed knowledge:

CKA_2 I know that *p* – although neither my use of the evidence on the basis of which I believe that *p*,[12] nor any other justificatory means by which I have come to believe that *p*, has guaranteed my thereby forming a true belief (and hence did not guarantee my gaining knowledge) that *p* in forming my belief.[13]

The concessive second half of CKA_2 allows that – in spite of the optimistic first half's claiming knowledge that *p* – there was a possibility of one's being misled by whatever justificatory path one has followed as part of having that claimed knowledge. And this can be a sensible concession by a fallibilist: CKA_2 could readily have instantiations that knowledge-fallibilists will regard as true. Hence, no knowledge-fallibilist needs to regard CKA_2 as a puzzling, let alone clearly false, way of speaking or thinking.

Do we therefore have, at least *prima facie*, a way to defuse the threat that concessive knowledge-attributions have often been thought to pose for knowledge-fallibilism? When a specific concessive knowledge-attribution strikes one as inconsistent, might this be because one is wavering unwittingly between those two ways of reading it – between the wide-scope CKA_1 and the narrow-scope CKA_2. No epistemologist – be she fallibilist or be she not – will allow any concessive knowledge-attribution to be a shorthand for the clearly false CKA_1. On the other hand, any fallibilist epistemologist can sensibly allow any concessive knowledge-attribution to be a shorthand for the internally coherent CKA_2. Correlatively, notice how CKA_2 is talking about knowledge *as such* only epiphenomenally. It talks overtly of the putative knowing that *p* – but only as a shorthand, strictly speaking, for talking more loquaciously of the knowing's justificatory component, along with *its* not having guaranteed the resulting true-belief component of the knowledge.

11.4 Questioning knowledge-attributions

What Section 11.3 noticed about concessive knowledge-attributions can now be adapted, so as to illuminate a further form of claim or thought – one that will help us to model Elgin's schematic suggestion (in Section 11.1) that we should think of fallibilism as a 'stance' that amounts to an 'active orientation toward […] inquiry'. We have not yet done quite enough in that respect. It is true that to utter or think a concessive knowledge-attribution is to take a 'stance' within an epistemic domain: one is expressing and endorsing a thesis about one's knowing that p. It is also true that, in so doing, one is being 'active': one is uttering or thinking that thesis about oneself. Nonetheless, I suggest, *that* kind of blend of stance with activity does not do justice to what Elgin had in mind with her characterisation of fallibilism: even to think or utter a concessive knowledge-attribution is not to be taking the *sort* of stance upon oneself that Elgin, it seems, had in mind when trying to understand fallibilism. Let us therefore see how we can do better in that respect.

We can do so by discussing what I call *questioning* knowledge-attributions (QKAs). The basic form of a questioning knowledge-attribution is this: 'I know that p – although might I be wrong about p?' It begins as a concessive knowledge-attribution does – with a knowledge-claim or -attribution. But then the two forms diverge, although not so diametrically that a person could not say or think both. Insofar as claiming to know that p is compatible with *allowing that there is* some sort of possibility of not-p (the compatibility claimed within a concessive knowledge-attribution), presumably claiming to know that p is no less compatible with *asking whether there is* some sort of possibility of not-p (the compatibility expressed within a questioning knowledge-attribution).

Now, one might proffer a questioning knowledge-attribution before deciding that p *is* true, and indeed that no further questioning of p's being true is appropriate. In that way, one might follow a questioning knowledge-attribution by expressing – uttering or thinking – an *infallibilist* thesis about one's knowledge that p. Nonetheless, there is a striking way (as follows) in which any questioning knowledge-attribution is in itself taking a *fallibilist* stance toward its contained knowledge-claim.

Any questioning knowledge-attribution is, in effect, *asking whether to retain* the knowledge that it begins by claiming; and notice how, in contrast, a concessive knowledge-attribution is *not* doing that. Any concessive knowledge-attribution may be parsed as – overall, taken as a whole – merely *claiming fallible knowledge*: its second half is simply *acknowledging what a fallibilist would regard as an aspect* of the knowing claimed by its first half. (That aspect is the accompanying presence of an epistemically significant *possibility* of mistake.) But that parsing is not available for questioning knowledge-attributions: a questioning knowledge-attribution is *not* – overall, taken as a whole – merely claiming fallible knowledge. One begins the questioning knowledge-attribution by claiming knowledge – before (in almost the same breath) asking whether, perhaps, one should *withdraw* that knowledge-claim. The questioning knowledge-attribution's second half is thus opening the door for a possible *retraction* of the first half, the claim to know that p: if the belief that p is false then it is not knowledge; yet this is the possibility that one is asking, in the second half, to have investigated. In this sense, any questioning knowledge-attribution is *overtly inviting inquiry into whether* one does have the knowledge that *p*. One's questioning knowledge-attribution is *asking whether one does* know that *p* – rather than merely *allowing that one knows fallibly* that *p* (as a concessive knowledge-attribution is doing). In this way, therefore, a questioning knowledge-attribution is a *more* strikingly fallibilist stance than a concessive knowledge-attribution would be at that same moment: a questioning knowledge-attribution is overtly a potentially knowledge-*relinquishing* stance, in a way in which even a concessive knowledge-attribution is not. So, not only is the uttering or thinking of a questioning knowledge-attribution a stance that is actively inviting inquiry (thereby satisfying the basic spirit of Elgin's idea); it is also a more self-*challengingly* – because more *adventurously* – fallibilist stance at a given moment than is the uttering or thinking of a concessive knowledge-attribution.

But is the uttering or thinking of a questioning knowledge-attribution also a *coherent* fallibilist stance, even for a moment? After all, many epistemologists have long treated believing that *p*, let alone knowing that *p*, as akin to according *p* a subjective probability at that time of 1; which bespeaks a view that renders any questioning knowledge-attribution as an incoherent stance. Thankfully, though, questioning knowledge-attributions are at least *prima facie* coherent, in much the same way as Section 11.3 showed that concessive knowledge-attributions can be.

We see this by attending to a distinction akin to that between CKA_1 and CKA_2. The new distinction (as follows) is between two analogous forms of questioning knowledge-attribution.

QKA_1 Might it be that – although I know that *p* – it is not true that *p*?
QKA_2 I know that *p* – although *might* the evidence on the basis of which I believe that *p*, or any other justificatory means by which I have come to believe that *p*, have not lead to my forming a true belief (and hence have not lead to my gaining knowledge) that *p* in forming my belief that *p*?

QKA_1 is a wide-scope reading of the 'might'; and QKA_1 is clearly false in contemplating that, even possibly, although one knows that *p*, it is also not true that *p*: knowing that *p* entails its being true that *p*. On the other hand, instances of QKA_2 (the narrow-scope reading of the 'might') can be unproblematically sensible – and fallibilist in spirit. One is asking either oneself or one's audience whether one might have been misled by the evidence or other justificatory means that has lead to one's forming the belief that *p*. One is asking, in effect, whether the knowledge-claim – the first half of the questioning knowledge-attribution – immediately preceding one's questioning – the second half of the questioning knowledge-attribution – should be *retracted*.

11.5 Open knowledge

Section 11.4 implies that, in principle, one could know that *p* in either a fallible or an infallible way *while also* adopting a fallibilist stance on that knowledge. In that event, though, is there any epistemic significance in adopting that fallibilist stance?

If any instance of knowledge is either fallible or infallible anyway, does one's having a fallibilist stance on some of one's knowledge leave untouched the epistemic nature of this knowledge? In particular, does one's having a (fallibilist) stance expressed by a questioning knowledge-attribution directed at one's having some specific knowledge leave untouched the nature of that knowledge?

I do not believe so. There is, I propose, a distinctive category of knowledge – a way of knowing, beyond the fact of some knowing's being fallible or its being infallible – that is constituted by the presence of a *QKA-fallibilist stance* (as we might term it, still working with Elgin's suggestive view of fallibilism as a special form of stance, 'an active orientation toward a domain of inquiry'). Describing that form of knowledge will be this section's role.[14] The kind of knowledge in question is what I will call *open* knowledge. It is one's knowing that *p* *in a partly self-questioning way* – specifically, a QKA-fallibilist way.

Several years ago, I sketched briefly one possible instantiation of that general idea (Hetherington 2008). My aim was to understand something of what I see as distinctive about *philosophical* knowledge – about knowing philosophically that *p*. I described such knowledge as partly a matter of knowing how to raise various apposite questions pertaining to *p*. I argued that philosophical knowledge is, in part, questioning knowledge. Am I now arguing that open knowledge is therefore a kind of philosophical knowledge? Not at all. Although there is overlap between those categories, they remain distinct, as will soon be clear.

Right now, let us enrich the discussion with an intriguing idea from Jane Friedman (2013). She has argued

> that there is a class of attitudes that have questions as constituents. These attitudes are a class of inquiry-related states and processes [...] The ones that [she – JF] will focus on [...] are: inquiry, investigation, wondering, curiosity and suspension of judgment or agnosticism.
>
> (2013: 145)

This list is not treated by Friedman as exhaustive. Still, she clearly does not intend it to include instances of knowing. Yes, her emphasis is on *wh*-attitudes – those having to do with 'who', 'why', 'when', etc. And yes, there is such a phenomenon as *wh*-knowing – knowing-who, knowing-why, knowing-when, etc. But Friedman would not extend her list to encompass that phenomenon: she takes herself to be 'mark[ing] an important distinction between "questioning" *wh*-attitudes and "answering" ones like knowledge-*wh*' (2013: 162).

But must we likewise halt, in that respect, where Friedman's taxonomising does? Or can we extend her idea, as we explore some possible dimensions of fallibilist thinking? Friedman never discusses incorporating questions into the content of some *knowing* attitudes (such as knowing *wh*-attitudes). Presumably (from the previous paragraph), she would dismiss this idea as conceptually confused, on the epistemologically conventional ground that, at most, questioning can lead *to* knowing – never being part of what knowing *is*. In her view, it seems, although knowing can *answer* questions, it cannot literally *include* questioning.

Yet we are not obliged to embrace that standard partitioning of this epistemic space. A fallibilist, in particular, need not do so. I have indicated how we can regard a questioning knowledge-attribution as expressive of a potentially quite dramatic fallibilist stance upon that knowledge at that shared moment of both attributing and questioning. I also presaged (at the start of this section) that we may introduce an idea of *open* knowledge that p; and here is where I do so. That idea may be understood in partnership with an idea of *closed* knowledge that p.

Those names are inspired by Popper's (1966) justly famous distinction between an open *society* and a closed *society*. His distinction was not epistemological; mine is. But there is an epistemologically useful parallel. Popper's distinction alerted us to the difference between a society that is, and one that is not, actively receptive to a flow of ideas with the potential to question, and even to undermine, its otherwise most treasured and shared beliefs. (There is more to Popper's conception, but that is the basic idea, enough so for immediate purposes.) So, an open society includes, or is ready to receive, resources for self-change, even for radical self-revision. And how, *mutatis mutandis*, might some instances of knowing be like that – thereby being *open* knowledge (as I am calling it)? An initial answer is readily available: *questioning knowledge-attributions point us towards one such form that open knowledge could take*. Someone would claim to know that p, for instance, even while asking whether she might unwittingly be mistaken as to p – and hence mistaken as to whether she really has the knowledge that p that she is taking herself to have.

Now picture that moment being repeated, for a single p. Or, equally, let that moment – that questioning knowledge-attribution – be 'in effect' or 'in place' for an extended 'moment'. One would be continuing to claim the knowledge that p even while asking oneself, or one's wider audience, whether one has the knowledge – more precisely, whether one lacks the knowledge, due to its not being true that p. Again, asking this question while claiming the knowledge does not prejudge whether one will eventually decide, for example, that one has the knowledge in an *in*fallible way. In the meantime, though, one is maintaining a stance – by one's self-questioning – of being actively open to potential inquiry's revealing that what one is claiming as knowledge is *not* knowledge, let alone infallible knowledge. One is standing to one's knowledge-claim as a self-consciously fallibilist inquirer would do – prepared to revisit, even to discard, the claim to knowledge – if one's question is answered with 'yes, you *have* been misled by your justification'.

From knowledge-claims to knowing: how, if at all, is one's *having* knowledge affected, if at all, by one's adopting a fallibilist stance towards it? We have been focusing on the phenomenon of one's claiming knowledge before also asking, in the same breath, whether one really has that knowledge – the combination that amounts to a *questioning knowledge-attribution* (a QKA). Now let us focus on one's *having* knowledge while asking that same question. That is, let us focus on what we might call a *questioning knowledge-state* – a QKS.

On the simplest version of this idea, someone is in a questioning knowledge-state when she knows that p, but when – *regardless* of whether she claims such knowledge – she is asking herself the associated question that is definitive of a questioning knowledge-attribution that p. Thus, she is asking whether her evidence for p, or any other justificatory means by which she came to believe that *p*, guaranteed the truth of that belief – or whether, instead, whatever is justifying her belief might have allowed her to form a false belief. In brief, someone is in a questioning knowledge-*state* when she knows that *p* but she also thinks or utters simply the 'might I not know that *p*?' component of the associated form of questioning knowledge-*attribution*.[15] And then the link with the concept of open knowledge is apparent: namely, *if one is in a questioning knowledge-state, then this is open knowledge* on one's part.

Earlier in this section, I said that I would be indicating how a fallibilist might wish to extend Friedman's idea of there being some 'attitudes that have questions as constituents'. I am now suggesting that there can be questioning knowledge-states. Two details of this suggestion should be mentioned.

First, the *content* of the self-questioning knowledge – the open knowledge – need not be changed by the presence of the questioning: open knowledge that *p* can still be knowledge just of *p*. What changes is the *nature* of the knowing. I am suggesting that one's knowing that *p* can include one's questioning whether one has the knowledge. The knowing as a *state* of the person is, in this way, extended by including the questioning – no matter that the questioning is not itself part of the *content* being known.[16]

Second, the questioning thereby plays a constitutive role that can be categorised in an epistemologically traditional way – once we suitably generalise this 'traditional way'. I am talking here of epistemic *internalism* as an epistemological category. For present purposes, I interpret epistemic internalism in these terms:

> When an internalist conceives of justification as being evidence, say, what she highlights is the evidence's somehow being easily accessible to (or even actually accessed by) the epistemic agent's awareness. And this matters, presumably because the agent therefore can (or does) *use* the evidence accordingly, such as by properly basing her (thereby justified) belief upon it.[17]

Notice (as follows) the breadth and flexibility, in two respects, of that internalist schema.

(i) What forms might be taken by the epistemic agent's actual or possible awareness of her evidence? Importantly, any such awareness need not be a merely passive and/or uncritical and/or unquestioning acceptance of the evidence as pointing her to some specific truth. This is why I used the word 'use' in that internalist schema. Doing so reminds us that the spirit of epistemic internalism is sufficiently broad and flexible to accommodate also the idea of an epistemic agent's accepting her evidence *but* in a deliberatively qualified, cautious, or provisional way. And one possible form that this might take involves the sort of *questioning* – including asking about the strength of one's evidence – that, I am suggesting, could be part of one's knowing. This questioning attitude toward one's evidence would not be part of the *content* that is being known on the basis of the evidence; again, it would be part of the *way* in which the knowing occurs, aided by the (questioning) awareness and use of the evidence.

(ii) With that said, the epistemic agent's questioning *need* not be directly of her evidence. She *might* not even be aware of using evidence. Nonetheless, she believes that *p* (as part of the knowing that is the 'first' half of her questioning knowledge-state). And she can still be asking whether it is possible that *whatever* justificatory path, if any, has lead her to have this belief has misled her, giving her a false belief. Once more, therefore, her awareness of her belief need not amount to a merely passive and/or uncritical and/or unquestioning acceptance of its arising from a process that was guaranteed to point her to truth.

In contrast to all of that, *closed* knowledge lacks the self-questioning element definitive of open knowledge. It is helpful here to reflect again upon Elgin's (1988) tale of Holmes and Watson. Closed knowledge is what Watson would have had, as Elgin described his epistemic efforts. This is partly due to his lack of intelligence and imagination. It would not have occurred to Watson, once it seemed true to him that *p* (hopefully on the basis of apparently adequate evidence of *p*'s being true), to wonder whether – even so – it might be false that *p*. More interestingly, though, closed knowledge could also be what Holmes would have had, when he was able to gain knowledge at all (as Elgin tells the tale). His knowledge's being closed would not clearly be due to Holmes's refined intelligence – part of what, in Elgin's account, at times impedes his gaining knowledge. The point is that Holmes's knowledge, when present, would have been closed because of his intellectual arrogance and self-confidence. What we should therefore realise is that Elgin's charting of the epistemic disparities between the respective characters and capacities of Holmes and of Watson, although usefully suggestive of epistemology's need to cast its net more widely into the epistemic waters, was *not* already charting this chapter's distinction between closed knowledge and open knowledge.

Elgin argued that there is a myopia undermining epistemology's capacity to focus insightfully on the epistemic world. The result, she contended, is epistemology's gazing too much upon knowledge, consequently not noticing and appreciating various epistemic phenomena in which epistemologists *should* be professionally interested. I am arguing for something similar about epistemology and what has been its recurring tendency to focus (even within the category of knowledge) upon *closed* knowledge. At least some of contemporary epistemology's most popular theories of knowledge have therefore been illuminating aspects of the nature of just some possible forms that knowledge might take – by illuminating aspects just of *closed* knowledge. Such knowledge is present when someone has knowledge simply by satisfying any of those theories (if the given theory is true, as far as it goes) – none of which, as they have been developed, discusses any form of *open* knowledge.[18]

Consider, for example, a defeasibility account.[19] Its general approach is to say that a belief is knowledge when true and well supported by evidence overlooking no (current) ultimate defeaters. But any such account is compatible with the belief that *p*'s not being accompanied by an attitude of openness, on the believer's part, towards the possibility of the evidence's having been misleading in its support for *p*'s being true, and hence of the belief's being false in spite of that apparent evidential support. If the belief is not accompanied in that way by such an attitude, this is not a reason for the belief not to *be* knowledge, according to the hypothesized defeasibility account. And I am not disputing that picture, so long as we hold in mind that the knowledge being accounted for along those lines could only be closed knowledge – hence not all possible knowledge.

The situation is no different, if the theory being satisfied by the belief is, for instance, a virtue-theoretic conception of knowledge.[20] I highlight this form of theory because, although Elgin seemingly views her Holmes/Watson tale as an argument for not focusing our epistemological gazes exclusively upon knowledge, her reasoning can also be treated as warning epistemologists not to neglect a wider array of cognitive virtues (such as ones present within Holmes's person but not Watson's) as part of what those epistemologists tell us *about* knowledge. It would just need to be a more *complex* way of knowing than is apparently being described by those currently mainstream forms of theory. Thus, extant virtue-theoretic accounts of knowledge, it seems, have not noticed how easily they could be extended to envisage self-questioning knowledge – open knowledge. Such knowledge would be at least somewhat *more* virtuously justified in virtue of the self-questioning, given that questioning knowledge-attributions (let alone questioning knowledge-states) can be manifesting epistemic humility and epistemic open-mindedness, exemplifying an active receptivity to genuine self-scrutiny. In short, even virtue-theoretic accounts of knowledge seem not to have included an awareness of the possibility of open knowledge; closed knowledge has apparently been the sole *explicandum* of those approaches.

This remains true, even if we call upon Ernest Sosa's evocative distinction (see, e.g., 2009) between animal knowledge and reflective knowledge. We might have suspected that Sosa's distinction would render otiose this chapter's, between closed knowledge and open knowledge. But that would be a mistaken impression. Not even what he calls reflective knowledge need be what I am calling open knowledge. One knows reflectively that p if one's belief that p is accompanied by various kinds of reflection and self-reflection. None of these, however, need involve any overtly fallibilist stance. In particular, none of those Sosa-approved forms of reflection and self-reflection need involve any self-*questioning* – such that, literally, the resulting knowing includes some questioning of the belief's being knowledge at all (such as by questioning whether it is really a true belief, in spite of appearing so in light of the justification supporting it). Reflective knowledge is higher-level knowledge. As Sosa characterizes it, reflective knowledge can be thought of as attained in an epistemological way. Even so, any reflective knowledge, thus characterized, most likely remains *closed* knowledge. The concept of open knowledge is thus distinct from that of reflective knowledge, since both animal knowledge and reflective knowledge can equally well be closed knowledge. Consequently, even when reflective knowledge is *fallible* knowledge, it need not be *fallibilist* knowledge, let alone fallibilist knowledge in the specific way described here – namely, by being *open* knowledge, due to its contained self-questioning.[21]

11.6 The Kripkean dogmatism puzzle

I will close the chapter with an illustrative (even if programmatic) application of our distinction between open knowledge that p and closed knowledge that p. When Elgin (2017) considers the charms or otherwise of fallibilism, she discusses – worriedly – concessive knowledge-attributions, as we saw. On the other hand, when pondering the idea of not adopting a fallibilist stance, she reminds us – again worriedly – of the

Kripkean (2011) puzzle of *dogmatism*.²² For some, the oddity of concessive knowledge-attributions reflects the thought that fallibilism leaves even epistemic agents with knowledge *too* open to counter-evidence. In contrast, the Kripkean puzzle asks whether, if we eschew fallibilism, we find ourselves allowing epistemic agents with knowledge not to be as open as they *should* still be to counter-evidence.

Here is Elgin's formulation of Kripke's argument.

> If an epistemic agent S knows that p, then p is true.
> If p is true, then any evidence against p (its being true) is misleading.
> So, to avoid being misled and to preserve her knowledge that p, S should disregard any evidence against p.
> Therefore, S should in that sense be dogmatic about p's being true.
>
> (2017: 297)

And here is Elgin's gloss on the argument's significance:

> By itself, this is not a paradox [as some have taken it to be]. It is merely an unwelcome conclusion. It becomes a paradox when we connect knowledge with rationality. Since rationality requires responsiveness to evidence, on the recommended approach, knowledge and rationality diverge. Dogmatism requires closing our minds to new evidence, lest knowledge will be lost. Rationality requires keeping an open mind.
>
> (2017: 297)

How might we add to this discussion the distinction between open knowledge and closed knowledge? First, the distinction allows us to interpret the puzzle as falling short at least of showing that *all* knowing risks precluding that sort of open-mindedness (mentioned by Elgin). What the Kripkean argument reflects, we may now appreciate, is the difference between closed knowledge and open knowledge; and the argument is describing a potential problem just for some conceptions of *closed* knowledge. That is because closed knowledge is indeed dogmatic, in this Kripkean sense of being dogmatic: one knows that p; and because (if one's knowledge that p is closed) one need not thereby be asking whether one might actually be mistaken as to p, one is not (other things being equal) knowing that p in a way that actively commits one to seeking and evaluating further evidence if one is to retain one's knowledge that p in an epistemically sound way.

Is this automatically a failing within knowing? Being dogmatic in that way, when holding some knowledge that p, has at least one welcome consequence: it ensures that one will continue having the true belief that p, while this spirit of dogmatism is upon one. Hence (so long as one has the knowledge in a way that is at least consistent with being dogmatic in that way), the dogmatic maintenance of the knowledge is a way of continuing to have the knowledge. Call it dogmatic knowledge if you wish; it is closed knowledge, at any rate. It is probably not everything admirable that we might often want our knowledge to be. Still, insofar as one wishes simply to have and retain some particular knowledge, maybe one is acting as one *should*, by having the knowledge in a closed and thereby dogmatic way. Possibly, then, some knowledge's being closed is sometimes quite apposite.

Open knowledge, on the other hand, has the potential to evade the Kripkean puzzle. For a moment, at any rate, it achieves that escape. One knows that p even while being manifestly open to receiving evidence that would destroy the knowledge. One knows that p even while being actively open to this outcome, by questioning whether one really has the knowledge. This does not ensure that one will not then *revert* to knowing that p in a closed and thereby dogmatic way; and, again, perhaps this would have some epistemic benefits. The immediate point is that open knowledge – if it exists – is in principle a way of evading the Kripkean puzzle (at first for a moment; then maybe for longer – or not). Accordingly, the puzzle need not have *such* a strong grip upon knowledge-fallibilists – if knowledge *can* be open, as has been hypothesized in this chapter.

My proposal is thus that Kripke's argument looks like a paradox only once we neglect the distinction – introduced here – between open knowledge and closed knowledge. Once we accept that distinction, we may interpret Kripke as alerting us to a feature of only some knowledge – closed knowledge. Now, perhaps in practise *most* knowledge is like that, if most of us mostly do not adopt the sort of self-directed fallibilist stance that would turn our knowledge into open knowledge. Even if that is so, though, we now see what – if we are troubled by the Kripkean implication of dogmatism – *would* suffice as an escape: we would need only to adopt, at least increasingly, a fallibilist stance on ourselves that (with all else remaining equal) will turn more of our knowledge into open knowledge.

Notes

1   See, for Reed (2002, 2012), Fantl and McGrath (2009: 7–15), Dougherty (2011), and Hetherington (1999, 2005, 2016b, 2018).
2   Pasnau argues that even God's knowledge would at best be fallible, since God could not help but ask whether His knowledge really is knowledge (Pasnau 2017: 121–6). In this chapter's terms, this might be better interpreted as God's knowledge being fallibilist – thanks to His viewing his knowledge in some fallibilist terms.
3   This will not involve entering into *all* of the suggestion's aspects. Elgin discusses mainly *understanding* a *domain* of inquiry, rather than (as will be this chapter's topic) *knowledge* of a *single* state of affairs. The concept of knowledge cannot do justice to the reality of scientific progress, argues Elgin: for a start, knowledge entails truth, whereas scientific understanding does not. Actually, as I explain elsewhere, knowledge and understanding might not be so far apart in nature (Hetherington 2011: sec. 5.15). But none of this matters for my argument here. Nor will I be arguing for the *correctness* of fallibilism as a stance. My aim is to expand upon this basic idea of Elgin's (describing fallibilism as 'a stance' – in the sense of 'an active orientation toward […] inquiry') by investigating one associated explicative path that a fallibilist might follow. I have offered defences of fallibilist thinking elsewhere: see Hetherington (2001, 2002, 2013).
4   Others who do so include Kaplan (1985) and Johnsen (2017).

5   Just to remind ourselves: Elgin discussed causal theories of knowledge (Goldman 1967, 1976) and reliabilist theories (Dretske 1971; Nozick 1981), along with (internalistic) coherence (Lehrer 1974, 1986) and defeasibility theories, including social defeasibility theories (Harman 1973; Cohen 1986).

6   It is perhaps a virtue that Holmes himself would have scorned, since (as we will find) it involves self-questioning, and since Doyle, his literary creator, left us in no doubt as to Holmes's intellectual arrogance. As I mentioned, Elgin regarded Holmes's epistemic superiority – other than as a knower (given, she argued, how this was being conceived of by various representative forms of epistemological theory) – as reflecting significant deficiencies in knowledge's nature, rather than in Holmes. As Elgin was interpreting the case, if Holmes lacks knowledge because he has various epistemic qualities not viewed by those epistemological theories as constitutive of knowing, then epistemology should be altered to be *about* such qualities, instead of remaining so much about knowledge; and, in any event, knowledge is thereby an attainment that is itself lessened in stature, given its ready availability to Watson and not Holmes. Even without engaging directly with Elgin's Holmes/Watson argument, then, if we wish to maintain an epistemological focus on knowledge we should take from her argument this potentially useful challenge: namely, conceive of knowledge in a more subtle way, a way that *can* do justice to Holmes's superior intellect (if we could prevail upon him to set aside his intellectual arrogance). The conception to be presented in this chapter should help in that respect.

7   For some discussions of concessive knowledge-attributions and fallibilism, see Stanley (2005), Dougherty and Rysiew (2009), and Dodd (2010).

8   We might ultimately want to defend a stronger – non-minimal – conception, such as '*All* knowledge is fallible' or even '*Necessarily*, all knowledge is fallible'. This chapter's discussion does not need to engage directly with any such stronger conceptions.

9   How often do people *actually* utter or think concessive knowledge-attributions? I do not know. Nor does it matter, for our immediate purposes. Epistemologists discuss concessive knowledge-attributions with another question in mind: *if* a concessive knowledge-attribution was to be offered, would it be a coherent thought or utterance? If it can be, then knowledge-fallibilism passes at least this *test* of its own coherence – hence of its at least possibly being true.

10 But see Hetherington (2013) for an extended discussion of concessive knowledge-attributions.

11 What is the nature of this entailment? Is it conceptual? Is it metaphysical? Is it logical? I will treat it as conceptual, given how readily epistemologists characterize their project of understanding knowledge's nature as being an exercise in conceptual analysis. And I will take it that conceptual entailments include a clarity component, rendering any denial of such an entailment clearly mistaken – clearly enough that the denial would cause conceptual confusion or consternation, for a start.

12 I talk here of 'evidence' to reflect (generically) an *internalist* focus, and of 'any other justificatory means' to do (generic) justice to an *externalist*'s approach. So, my aim is to be discussing (albeit generically) all kinds of justificatory component within the initially claimed knowledge. On the difference between epistemic internalism and epistemic externalism, see Conee and Feldman (2001), Bergmann (2006), Coppenger and Bergmann (2016), and Hetherington (1996: chs 14–15, 2020).

13 Incidentally, this lack of a guarantee does not depend on p's being only contingently true. Even a necessarily true p can be known fallibly. When this occurs, it reflects something of the means by which the (true) belief has been formed: for example,

a false belief could have been formed instead of the (necessarily) true one that has actually been formed. Even one's attending and responding only to one's evidence, say, *need not* have resulted in one's forming the true belief that *p*.

14   Moreover, recognising this previously unnoticed category of knowledge has epistemological benefits. Section 11.6 will describe one of them.

15   Does this make a questioning knowledge-state a higher-order knowledge-state? I do not think of it in quite that way. It is knowing while also asking whether one knows. So, this is not one's knowing that one knows, for instance – a paradigmatic higher-order knowledge-state. It need not even be an awareness of one's knowing. As far as the knower is concerned, it could amount simply to her asking whether she knows; it just so happens that she does this while in fact she does know.

16   On the general idea of an extended knowing-state, see Hetherington (2012).

17   For more on the proper basing relation, see Hetherington (2019).

18   I realise that this not a problem if we do not need to accept that there could be both open knowledge that *p* and closed knowledge that *p*. At this stage of the chapter, I am relying on the foregoing (if programmatic) motivation for adding that distinction to our epistemology.

19   For the initial such account, see Lehrer and Paxson (1969). For some refinements, see Pollock (1986). For a recent version, see De Almeida and Fett (2016).

20   For prominent such conceptions, see Zagzebski (1996), Sosa (2007), and Greco (2010).

21   It might be asked whether I am being too dismissive too quickly of too much contemporary epistemology; after all, not all prominent sorts of theory of knowledge have been considered in this section's argument. But I am not being 'too dismissive', because I am not arguing that existing theories *could not* be expanded to encompass this chapter's suggestion. I am not advocating an overthrow of traditional epistemology; I am noting simply some respects in which epistemology can be modified. Still, for arguments that do develop reasons to be more deeply suspicious of some key aspects of contemporary epistemology, see Hetherington (2011, 2016a). Moreover, I do not claim to have discussed here all currently prominent sorts of theory of knowledge. Like Elgin's, my approach is programmatic, talking about just some representative sorts of theory of knowledge.

22   It was through Harman (1973: 147–9) that most epistemologists first became aware of this Kripkean puzzle.

References

Bergmann, M. (2006), *Justification without Awareness: A Defense of Epistemic Externalism*, Oxford: Clarendon Press.

Cohen, S. (1986), 'Knowledge and Context', *The Journal of Philosophy*, 83: 574–85.

Conee, E. and Feldman, R. (2001), 'Internalism Defended', in H. Kornblith (ed.), *Epistemology: Internalism and Externalism*, 231–60, Malden, MA: Blackwell.

Coppenger, B. and Bergmann, M. (eds) (2016), *Intellectual Assurance: Essays on Traditional Epistemic Internalism*, Oxford: Oxford University Press.

De Almeida, C. and Fett, J.R. (2016), 'Defeasibility and Gettierization: A Reminder', *Australasian Journal of Philosophy*, 94: 152–69.

Dodd, D. (2010), 'Confusion about Concessive Knowledge Attributions', *Synthese*, 172: 381–96.
Dougherty, T. (2011), 'Fallibilism', in S. Bernecker and D. Pritchard (eds), *The Routledge Companion to Epistemology*, 131–43, New York: Routledge.
Dougherty, T. and Rysiew, P. (2009), 'Fallibilism, Epistemic Possibility, and Concessive Knowledge Attributions', *Philosophy and Phenomenological Research*, 78: 123–32.
Dretske, F.I. (1971), 'Conclusive Reasons', *Australasian Journal of Philosophy*, 49: 1–22.
Elgin, C.Z. (1988), 'The Epistemic Efficacy of Stupidity', *Synthese*, 74: 297–311. (Reprinted in N. Goodman and C.Z. Elgin (1988), *Reconceptions in Philosophy and Other Arts and Sciences*, 135–52, Indianapolis: Hackett.) (Page references in this chapter are to that reprinting.)
Elgin, C.Z. (2017), *True Enough*, Cambridge, MA: The MIT Press.
Fantl, J. and McGrath, M. (2009), *Knowledge in an Uncertain World*, New York: Oxford University Press.
Friedman, J. (2013), 'Question-Directed Attitudes', *Philosophical Perspectives*, 27: 145–74.
Goldman, A.I. (1967), 'A Causal Theory of Knowing' *The Journal of Philosophy*, 64: 357–72.
Goldman, A.I. (1976), 'Discrimination and Perceptual Knowledge', *The Journal of Philosophy*, 73: 771–91.
Greco, J. (2010), *Achieving Knowledge: A Virtue-Theoretic Account of Epistemic Normativity*, Cambridge: Cambridge University Press.
Harman, G. (1973), *Thought*, Princeton: Princeton University Press.
Hetherington, S. (1996), *Knowledge Puzzles: An Introduction to Epistemology*, Boulder, CO: Westview Press.
Hetherington, S. (1999), 'Knowing Failably', *The Journal of Philosophy*, 96: 565–87.
Hetherington, S. (2001), *Good Knowledge, Bad Knowledge: On Two Dogmas of Epistemology*, Oxford: Clarendon Press.
Hetherington, S. (2002), 'Fallibilism and Knowing that One Is Not Dreaming', *Canadian Journal of Philosophy*, 32: 83–102.
Hetherington, S. (2005), 'Fallibilism', *The Internet Encyclopedia of Philosophy*, URL: http://www.iep.utm.edu/f/fallibil.htm.
Hetherington, S. (2008), 'Knowing-That, Knowing-How, and Knowing Philosophically', *Grazer Philosophische Studien*, 77: 307–24.
Hetherington, S. (2011), *How to Know: A Practicalist Conception of Knowledge*, Malden, MA: Wiley-Blackwell.
Hetherington, S. (2012), 'The Extended Knower', *Philosophical Explorations*, 15: 207–18.
Hetherington, S. (2013), 'Concessive Knowledge-Attributions: Fallibilism and Gradualism', *Synthese*, 190: 2835–51.
Hetherington, S. (2016a), *Knowledge and the Gettier Problem*, Cambridge: Cambridge University Press.
Hetherington, S. (2016b), 'Understanding Fallible Warrant and Fallible Knowledge: Three Proposals', *Pacific Philosophical Quarterly*, 97: 270–82.
Hetherington, S. (2018), 'Skepticism and Fallibilism', in D. Machuca and B. Reed (eds), *Skepticism: From Antiquity to the Present*, 609–19, London: Bloomsbury.
Hetherington, S. (2019), 'The Epistemic Basing Relation, and Knowledge-That as Knowledge-How', in P. Bondy and J.A. Carter (eds), *Well-Founded Belief: New Essays on the Epistemic Basing Relation*, 305–24, New York: Routledge.

Hetherington, S. (2020), 'The Grounds of Knowledge Need Not Be Accessible', in S. Cowan (ed.), *Problems in Epistemology and Metaphysics: An Introduction to Contemporary Debates*, 107–18, London: Bloomsbury.

Johnsen, B. (2017), *Righting Epistemology: Hume's Revolution*, New York: Oxford University Press.

Kaplan, M. (1985), 'It's Not What You Know that Counts', *The Journal of Philosophy*, 82: 350–63.

Kripke, S.A. (2011), *Philosophical Troubles: Collected Papers*, Vol I, New York: Oxford University Press.

Lehrer, K. (1974), *Knowledge*, Oxford: Clarendon Press.

Lehrer, K. (1986), 'The Coherence Theory of Knowledge', *Philosophical Topics*, 14: 5–25.

Lehrer, K. and Paxson, T.D. (1969), 'Knowledge: Undefeated Justified True Belief', *The Journal of Philosophy*, 66: 225–37.

Lewis, D. (1996), 'Elusive Knowledge', *Australasian Journal of Philosophy*, 74: 549–67.

Nozick, R. (1981), *Philosophical Explanations*, Cambridge, MA: Harvard University Press.

Pasnau, R. (2017), *After Certainty: A History of Our Epistemic Ideals and Illusions*, Oxford: Oxford University Press.

Pollock, J.L. (1986), *Contemporary Theories of Knowledge*, Totowa, NJ: Rowman & Littlefield.

Popper, K.R. (1966 [1945]), *The Open Society and Its Enemies*, Vol. I: *The Spell of Plato*, 5th edn, London: Routledge.

Reed, B. (2002), 'How to Think about Fallibilism', *Philosophical Studies*, 107: 143–57.

Reed, B. (2012), 'Fallibilism', *Philosophy Compass*, 7: 585–96.

Sosa, E. (2007), *A Virtue Epistemology: Apt Belief and Reflective Knowledge*, Vol. I, Oxford: Clarendon Press.

Sosa, E. (2009), *Reflective Knowledge: Apt Belief and Reflective Knowledge*, Vol. II, Oxford: Clarendon Press.

Stanley, J. (2005), 'Fallibilism and Concessive Knowledge Attributions', *Analysis*, 65: 126–31.

Zagzebski, L.T. (1996), *Virtues of the Mind: An Inquiry into the Nature of Virtue and the Ethical Foundations of Knowledge*, Cambridge: Cambridge University Press.

12

The luck/knowledge incompatibility thesis

Epistemologists have long argued that an opinion or belief being correct is not enough for its being knowledge. Most contemporary epistemologists also argue that even being correct and well supported by evidence is not enough to make an opinion or belief an instance of knowledge. Recent epistemology, in particular, has sought to do justice to these standard views by describing forms of luck that preclude a particular opinion or belief from being knowledge. This chapter motivates – and critically evaluates – that epistemologically widespread picture.

12.1 An older luck/knowledge incompatibility thesis

Much modern epistemological reflection on the nature of knowledge is still being shaped by its ancient roots. In particular, these words – from Socrates in Plato's dialogue *Meno* (97e–98a) – continue to influence epistemology:

> To acquire an untied work of Daedalus is not worth much, […] for it does not remain, but it is worth much if tied down, for his works are very beautiful. What am I thinking of when I say this? True opinions. For true opinions, as long as they remain, are a fine thing and all they do is good, but they are not willing to remain long, and they escape from a man's mind, so that they are not worth much until one ties them down by (giving) an account of the reason why. And that, Meno my friend, is recollection, as we previously agreed. After they are tied down, in the first place they become knowledge, and then they remain in place. That is why knowledge is prized higher than correct opinion, and knowledge differs from correct opinion in being tied down.[1]

Socrates' picture is metaphorical, somewhat generic, and very programmatic. It is metaphorical, with its invocation of Daedalus' statues – famous for their ability, and indeed tendency, to run away when not tethered. In this respect, these statues are being said to be like our true beliefs.[2] They have the potential to be distinctively valuable, as does a true belief. But this potential is realised only once they are tied down (and thereby held in place) – a process and result that is claimed to mirror a true belief's becoming *knowledge*. Thus, it seems, we are meant to infer that knowing includes an element akin to that tethering. And in this respect Socrates' picture is less generic than it might have been. For he suggests that what thereby needs to be present, as part of the knowing, is a *logos* – which is present, he also suggests, through *recollection*. In that way, the believer would bring to mind an *account* (this being the translation here of '*logos*') of how her belief is true. We might describe this as her *understanding*, well enough, that the belief is true; which could be a matter of her understanding, well enough, *how* the belief is true. Even this is a quite programmatic description, though: Socrates is proposing just one from among the possible ways in which we might claim to understand his metaphor.

Was epistemological progress thereby made by Socrates? Most post-1963 epistemologists will say that most pre-1963 epistemologists would have taken from that Platonic portrayal this seemingly Socratic moral (a moral emerging from Socrates' words):

> A belief is not knowledge simply in virtue of being true (its being accurate). The belief's being knowledge requires also its being *tethered* for the believer, such as by her having good evidence for the belief's being true. This good evidence might include an account of *how* the belief is true.

What else might epistemologists claim to learn from Plato's account? Socrates and Meno were discussing whether, in undertaking a journey to Larissa, one needs only a *true belief* as to the correct direction, or whether something relevantly stronger – specifically, *knowledge* – is needed. The two of them agree that knowledge is preferable; why, though? For example, was Socrates telling Meno that a true belief is knowledge only if, by possessing an associated account of the belief's being true, the believer would not be relying upon *luck*, in travelling to Larissa? Not in those words. But others – contemporary *anti-luck* theorists of knowledge – could well wish to place that interpretive sheen upon Socrates' words. They might claim to see an *incompatibility* thesis about knowing and luck as being embedded, even if inchoately, within his words. Accordingly, their accompanying interpretive thinking could proceed along the following lines.

> Even a true belief is not knowledge if the believer has not done enough to eliminate some significant element of *luck* in the presence of that true belief. This could encompass both the true belief's coming to exist in the first place and its then staying in place (its being maintained). The true belief's merely *happening* to stay in place, for instance, would not be enough for it still to be knowledge, because even its continued presence might be due merely to luck; in which event, the belief – regardless of its being true and regardless of how non-luckily it originally came into existence – is not as *dependable* a guide as is needed, if it is to be knowledge.

12.2 A newer luck/knowledge incompatibility thesis

Recent epistemology has not rested content with Section 12.1's version of a luck/knowledge incompatibility thesis – a Socratic one. Epistemologists have enriched that thinking, largely as a move within what is often called *post-Gettier* epistemology.

Edmund Gettier (1963) made his mark within contemporary philosophy with a challenge to what he saw (1963: 121 fn. 1) as 'perhaps' a version of the Socratic account of knowing. Because Gettier's challenge has attained the status of epistemological orthodoxy, I will not repeat or evaluate it here in detail.[3] But I will outline the basic idea, with an eye on how this has led to a newer luck/knowledge incompatibility thesis than the one prompted by the Socratic thinking in the *Meno*.

Gettier directed our attention to a putative philosophical *definition* of knowledge. It was a definition that he thought of as encompassing Section 12.1's Socratic picture of knowing's nature. Should we regard that picture as relevantly *complete* – albeit generic and programmatic – in its portrayal of the state of having some knowledge? Is knowledge *nothing beyond* how it is portrayed by Plato – namely, as a true belief that is well supported (epistemically justified, to use the usual epistemological jargon), such as by good or even excellent evidence for its being true? In short, is knowledge *definable* – albeit generically and programmatically – as a justified true belief?

Not if Gettier was right; and, according to most epistemologists, he *was* right in his key move. He gave us two imagined *counterexamples* to the knowledge-equals-justified-true-belief definition. These counterexamples are descriptions of possible situations where someone has a justified true belief that falls short of being knowledge – and hence is *not* equal to justified-true-belief. So said Gettier, in interpreting his imagined situations. Other philosophers immediately concurred with him; and thus began a vast post-1963 epistemological enterprise – post-Gettier epistemology.

Gettier's own two counterexamples, along with the many similar ones that have since been imagined, are generally called *Gettier cases*. And such cases have seemed to many recent epistemologists to be describable in anti-luck terms. Those descriptions have taken two forms – sometimes being offered simply as *intuitive*, sometimes receiving more *technical* treatments.

I will explain all of that in a moment. For specificity, here is a famous and representative Gettier case.

> *The sheep-in-the-field*. Looking on at a field, you see what looks like a sheep. You form the belief, 'There is a sheep in that field'. You are correct – yet not because what you are seeing is a sheep. Rather, it is a disguised dog. But there is a sheep in the field anyway, feeding peacefully behind a slight hill, hidden from your gaze. Your belief is therefore true. So, it is a belief that is true and supported by evidence with many features that good evidence typically has. Is the belief knowledge? Presumably not.[4]

Yet why would that belief not be knowledge? Here is a supposedly *intuitive* anti-luck answer.

> *Only luckily* is your belief true, given its being guided into existence by that particular sensory evidence (which makes no mention of the actual sheep, whose existence is why your belief is actually true).

And here is a more *technical* anti-luck answer.

> Your belief is true only in a *veritically* lucky way. In order to understand this failing, consider the possible worlds most like this one from among those where again you form a belief as you do here within that same perceptual situation – standing outside that field, using your senses as you do here, being guided by seemingly identical sensory evidence to what you have used here. In many of those possible worlds, we assume, your belief is false; for the *actual* sheep (or its counterparts within those worlds) not being in the field is not precluded by what your senses are telling you. Hence, even though your belief is true within this world, *only luckily* is it true within this world.[5]

12.3 Epistemological significance

Gettier's challenge has thus prompted increased acceptance among epistemologists of some form of luck/knowledge incompatibility thesis. In Gettier cases (we are told by epistemologists in general), the central belief – the Gettiered belief – is not knowledge; and this (we are told by anti-luck epistemologists) is *because* the Gettiered belief is true only luckily, in spite of its being supported by good evidence. The claim that no Gettiered belief is knowledge has been widely embraced by epistemologists. This claim has attracted such attention due to the epistemologically widespread belief that it provides real insight into knowledge's nature, by taking us forensically into the heart of an otherwise perplexing piece of philosophy.

So, if a luck/knowledge incompatibility thesis can unravel the complexities – as epistemologists have long taken to be latent – within Gettier's challenge, then the thesis is not only true but *helpfully* true. It is standardly proffered, therefore, as a thesis that assists us in *understanding* something important about knowledge – something close to the centre of the web of features that are constitutive of whatever knowing is, most fundamentally characterized. In that respect, we are being enjoined to treat any luck/knowledge incompatibility thesis as epistemologically significant because it has purportedly *explicative* import, revealing something significant about knowledge's nature.

The post-Gettier version of the luck/knowledge incompatibility thesis is thus said to point to the luck present within any Gettier case as sufficing to *explain why* the case's central belief, although true and well justified, fails to be knowledge. The more general moral thereby being grounded is that any true belief – even when well justified – fails to be knowledge *if* there is significant luck in how it has come into existence, or in how it is being maintained, as a true belief. The latter luck would be taken to explain the former failure.

12.4 Critical evaluation

How should we approach the challenge of evaluating the truth and explanatory potential of a luck/knowledge incompatibility thesis? First, for simplicity we can talk of *the* luck/knowledge incompatibility thesis, allowing it to be Section 12.2's newer version, which in the following sense incorporates Section 12.1's older version. If there can be knowledge-precluding luck even when a belief is true *and* justified, then – *a fortiori* – there can be knowledge-precluding luck when a belief is true without also being justified.

So, how are we to decide whether (Section 12.2's version of) the luck/knowledge incompatibility thesis is true, let alone true and explanatorily useful? We will make little if any epistemological progress with this issue by simply exchanging supposed intuitions (even if these are in agreement with each other).[6] Equally, insofar as there is intuitive support for the thesis, our relying too much upon a specific technical formulation of it will risk our not doing justice to the thesis, especially if that formulation has its own problems. Accordingly, we should seek a middle evaluative path: the language used in the rest of this section will therefore be only slightly technical. (Yet, even thus constrained, we will uncover a simple reason why the luck/knowledge incompatibility thesis – *even* if true – cannot play the explicative role, described in Section 12.3, of helping us to understand knowledge's nature.)[7]

Consider, then, a generic version of the luck/knowledge incompatibility thesis. We may avoid any very specific assumptions about the nature of the luck being discussed.[8] Nonetheless, one general feature must be mentioned, since it would be part of any specific version of the thesis. We need to note that, whenever the luck/knowledge incompatibility thesis alerts us to a particular belief's being luckily true, the thesis is saying that, somehow and somewhere in that belief's coming into existence or being maintained as a true belief, there was a significant and marked possibility of this particular combination of belief-plus-truth *not* coming into existence or being maintained. Because the belief *is* true, that particular combination *has* in fact eventuated, perhaps due to a role played by some supportive evidence; even so (as at least a minimal aspect of the luck pertaining to how that belief is both present and true), that particular combination *might well not* have eventuated.

We could also parse that point in the following way.

> Even when what could otherwise be some *good* luck is bringing about or maintaining the belief – in that the belief is present or maintained as a *true* belief – a correlative kind of bad luck instead *could easily* (even with all else being equal) have been bringing about or maintaining a belief – so that a false belief would instead have been present or maintained (even with all else being equal). The latter luck – the bad luck, that 'could easily' have been the only luck operative in the situation – is enough to prevent the former luck – the good luck – from crowning the resulting true belief as an instance of knowledge.

Thus, we can appreciate an essential element of the spirit underlying the luck/knowledge incompatibility thesis. But that reasoning in support of that thesis also directs us (as the rest of this section will show) towards a reason why the luck/knowledge incompatibility thesis *cannot* ever help us to understand or explicate knowledge's absence from a situation.

From Section 12.3, the luck/knowledge incompatibility thesis purports to be *explicating* a way – specifically, due to the presence of a pertinent form of luck – in which even a true belief that is evidentially supported (let alone a true belief lacking such support) can fail to be knowledge. This failure to be knowledge is supposedly being *explained* by the former state of affairs – that is, by the true, and perhaps justified, belief's being present only in a relevantly lucky way, which prevents even the belief's being true and justified from sufficing to make the belief knowledge.

Yet already we may begin to appreciate why this explicative aim will never be satisfied. Consider the following exchange.

[spoken by me, S.H.] *Within* any possible situation where a given true belief is present only luckily, there is no accompanying failure of the belief – due to the luck – in the sense of its also being false within that possible situation. (This is trivially so: in no possible situation is a belief both true and false.)

[spoken by a proponent of the luck/knowledge incompatibility thesis] That trivially true point is irrelevant. A given true belief can be present luckily in *this* world – and is therefore not knowledge in this world – in part because that same belief (with all else being equal) is false in various *other* relevant possible worlds. In those *further* possible worlds, the belief is false, hence immediately not knowledge in those worlds. (I say 'immediately' because it is manifest that, in any possible world, if a belief is knowledge then it is true.) And the belief is thereby – even if not immediately – also not knowledge in this world (because, given the relevance of those other worlds, the belief is *thereby only luckily* true in this world).

[spoken by me, S.H.] But that reasoning by a proponent of the luck/knowledge incompatibility thesis, although epistemologically familiar, remains irrelevant to her explicative challenge – a challenge to which my first point in this exchange, although trivially true, *is* relevant. The luck/knowledge incompatibility thesis envisages a modal state of affairs – constituted by those further possible worlds, in which the belief reappears, although not always as a true belief. But that envisaged modal state of affairs literally constitutes only *the belief* – but not therefore *the luckily true belief* – being *tracked* or *re-identified across* those various possible worlds. Accordingly, the modality that is literally being *constituted* by that envisaged state of affairs – the modality, after all, *is* that pattern of possible worlds and their contents – is at most *about* the recurring belief as such that is present within each of those worlds. It is not thereby *about* the (luckily, and perhaps justified) true belief as such – since this true (and perhaps justified) belief as such is *not* reappearing within all of those possible worlds. For we are explicitly told that the belief is not true within all of those worlds; hence, we are *im*plicitly told that those worlds are not jointly constituting a modal state of affairs including the justified and (luckily) true belief as such. However (from Section 12.3), our guiding epistemological challenge right now is that of understanding how *even a true* belief could fail – even when supported by good evidence – to be knowledge, due to some kind and degree of luck in how that combination of truth and belief (and perhaps evidence) is present or maintained. Correlatively, the challenge right now is not to understand merely how *a belief* could fail to be knowledge, in virtue of the fact that, although it is true, it need not have been (even with all else being equal). Yet *that* understanding is the most that could be articulated by talking in that standardly proposed way of that range of worlds, in some of which the belief is false.

This does not prove immediately that the luck/knowledge incompatibility thesis is false. But it *does* tell us that this pessimistic view of the thesis should be considered seriously – now, all the more so. What we have found so far is that the thesis – even *if* true – lacks the explicative power attributed to it by its proponents. And perhaps this is at least partly because the thesis is *not* true. How might that be so? Here is a stark thought: perhaps the thesis is not true, because each and any true belief *is* knowledge – regardless, therefore, of whether or not it is luckily true.[9] If so, then accompanying luck even in how a given true belief is true would never be a reason why that true belief – let alone if it is also justified – is *not* knowledge.

12.5 Examples

Section 12.4's line of thought is epistemologically heterodox. It is rather abstract, too. So, we might usefully test it on our two earlier examples – each of which is taken by many epistemologists to motivate some version of a luck/knowledge incompatibility thesis.

First, let us rejoin Socrates and Meno (in Section 12.1) as they contemplate that journey to Larissa. If we wish to parse their conversation in terms of a concern about some pertinent kind of luck, it is clear what the luck in question would be. If they set out on the journey equipped only with a *true belief* as to the correct direction to follow – thus lacking anything epistemically stronger than that true belief – then it seems that Socrates and Meno would regard it as lucky if the true belief is *maintained* along the way. They agree that the true belief is no less helpful than knowledge would be, *provided* that the true belief stays in place. But will it do so? Tethering is therefore proposed by Socrates as a way of accomplishing that outcome. Tethering thereby sets aside any *need* for there to be continued good luck in the true belief's somehow being maintained.

Notice, though, how tethering is thus *not* an action or state of affairs with independent merit – an action or state of affairs possessing a point in this setting *beyond* its setting aside that need for continuing good luck. Hence, the thinking by Socrates and Meno falls short of establishing as strong a commitment about knowledge's nature as is expressed by the luck/knowledge incompatibility thesis. Seemingly, Socrates and Meno's thinking tells us that if we *could* maintain the true belief, this would be enough also to maintain all of the relevant merits that are being expected of the corresponding instance of knowledge over that same time period (insofar as a conception of knowledge's nature is to be motivated by this discussion between Socrates and Meno). Significantly, however, this in turn suggests that the true belief on its own is *already* an instance of that knowledge *at* a time: if *maintaining* the true belief is enough to accomplish whatever it is that the knowledge would be expected to accomplish over that period, then perhaps *having* the true belief now is sufficient for already having the knowledge – having it *now*, at any rate.[10]

Of course, having the true belief now is no guarantee that the true belief *will* be maintained. Yet even that cautionary observation does not entail that the true belief is *not* knowledge now. Such an entailment obtains only if the belief's being knowledge now awaits, or at least ensures, its continuing to be knowledge. No wonder, then, that tethers are envisaged by Socrates as being needed from the outset: the tether is supposedly what, by its being present now, will maintain the true belief in place.

But that view – of all synchronic knowledge (knowledge-at-a-particular-time) as needing to be diachronic knowledge (knowledge-held-from-one-time-to-the-next) – is highly questionable:[11] knowing now does *not* await or ensure knowing later, for example. Nor is that entailment guaranteed by tethers anyway; for tethers can slip or be damaged. To put the same point less metaphorically: having evidence in support of a true belief as to the direction to follow in undertaking a journey will not guarantee a successful arrival, even with all else being equal. Like the belief in question, the supportive evidence *itself* must be maintained – alongside the belief, just as firmly present *as* the belief. Holding it, too, in place could even *distract* one from holding in place the initial true belief: now there is *more* material – there are *more* beliefs – that must be maintained, rather than merely the initial true belief. In practical terms – remember that we are talking about an *action* of travelling to Larissa – what matters most is the maintenance of the true belief. Having a back-up power supply or generator – which is what the evidence or tether amounts to – is thus not *essential*. It might be helpful. Then again, it might not. So, it should not be assumed to be *needed* as an essential condition or part of the pertinent knowledge's being present.

Let us revisit also Section 12.2's Gettier case – the field containing that dog disguised as a sheep (along with a real but hidden sheep). As ever, there are different ways of trying to explicate the supposedly knowledge-precluding luck present within this situation. But each of them will instantiate a more generic and underlying idea – to the effect that there was a *real possibility of you not* forming a true belief (as you have actually done), relevantly restricted as you are in responding to the evidence with which you are being presented while standing outside that field. We will be assured (as part of telling us why your belief, although true and justified, is not knowledge) that there are many possible variations on the case, in enough of which various important aspects of your epistemic perspective are being maintained – yet where there is *no* sheep in that field.

Now, along some such lines, maybe there is indeed luck in your sheep-in-the-field belief's being present and true. Yet even to understand this is not to understand, in addition, how the true belief is too luckily present to be knowledge. Basically, in order to have the former understanding, we need to imagine simply a range of possibilities where *the belief* reappears, presumably sometimes true, definitely sometimes not. Even basically, however, in order to have the latter understanding we need to imagine a range of possibilities where *the true belief* reappears, at least sometimes failing to be knowledge (in spite of never also failing to be true).

And *is* the latter imaginable? Whether it is depends ultimately on how we should evaluate the previous test case – the philosophically famous journey to Larissa. And that case, we have seen just now, might *not* be providing good support even for the older and simpler – Section 12.1's Socratic – luck/knowledge incompatibility thesis. In any event, we face the new point (from the previous paragraph) that we should not react to the sheep-in-the-field case by confusing (i) the question of whether *the belief* is luckily *true*, with (ii) the question of whether *the true belief*, by being *luckily* true-or-false-or-whatever, is not *knowledge*.

12.6 An objection and a reply

Sections 12.4 and 12.5 imply that to describe a belief as luckily true is never a way of explicating its not being knowledge. For a necessary condition of having that sort of understanding is failed, perhaps surprisingly so, by any attempt to apply the luck/knowledge incompatibility thesis.

Let us now consider an objection to that way of doubting the explanatory power of that thesis. This objection asks (as follows) whether a focus on belief-forming or belief-maintaining *methods* can restore the standardly claimed explanatory power to that thesis.

> Above, we have talked of evaluating a particular belief – the one that is claimed to be true only luckily – across possible situations or worlds. But we need not apply the luck/knowledge incompatibility thesis in that way. We can evaluate instead a belief-forming or -maintaining *method*. A particular belief could then be deemed only luckily true, because it is present and true only as the product of a *generally* poor belief-forming or -maintaining method – so that one has formed or maintained the particular true belief via a method that would *most likely* have given one a false belief instead. Using a method like that is no way to gain or maintain knowledge: the belief is true only luckily, hence is not knowledge.

Yet such reasoning is weaker than would standardly be believed by epistemologists. Here is an alternative interpretation of the epistemic impact of using an unreliable belief-forming or -maintaining method to form or maintain a true belief.

A method's being generally poor (unreliable in this world and/or across possible worlds) entails at least that it is not *inherently* knowledge-producing or knowledge-maintaining – because it is not inherently at-least-true-belief-producing or -maintaining. This tells us that citing the use of that method is at least not enough in itself to stamp, as being knowledge, a belief produced or maintained via the method. Accordingly, we may also grant that one could well need to be lucky if one is to gain or maintain even a true belief by using such a method. Yet this concession need not then be interpreted as entailing that one *never* gains or maintains knowledge in that way – unless, of course, we have independently shown that a true belief produced or maintained in a lucky way is not knowledge. And this, from earlier sections, is not something that we have already shown. Perhaps, therefore, we have the interpretive licence to say the following.

> Suppose that the method is far from reliable at producing or maintaining true beliefs. Suppose that this is at least a lack of reliability in producing or maintaining knowledge: whenever it does produce or maintain a false belief, it is thereby *manifesting* that unreliability (given that any instance of knowledge needs to be true). Even so, that lack of reliability in producing or maintaining knowledge – manifested in those actual or possible failures to produce or maintain a true belief – might be because knowledge *is nothing more than* true belief.

Again, until this is independently shown not to be so, we should not assume that the former unreliability is *in itself* a reason to deem – as falling short of being knowledge – even any true belief that is produced or maintained by the belief-forming or -maintaining method.[12]

12.7 A luck/knowledge compatibility thesis?

We have found that epistemologists might be unable to call upon the luck/knowledge incompatibility thesis to *explicate* there being a sense of 'luckily' in which a belief's being formed or maintained luckily precludes its being knowledge. Sections 12.4 and 12.6 ended by suggesting briefly the possibility that a belief's being luckily true is in fact *not* a barrier to its being knowledge: perhaps any true belief, let alone any justified true belief, *is* knowledge. That suggestion amounts to the idea of replacing the luck/knowledge incompatibility thesis with a more heterodox luck/knowledge *compatibility* thesis.

Unlike the luck/knowledge incompatibility thesis, which would point to luck's presence to explain why some particular belief, although true and even justified, is not knowledge, a luck/knowledge compatibility thesis need only be saying that the luck's presence does not *prevent* a belief (all else being equal) from being knowledge. This compatibility thesis would regard the luck as being explanatorily epiphenomenal in that respect. By all means (the thesis might continue), tell us what makes a belief luckily true, since this might be a feature with some significance for how we could wish to view that belief's epistemic dimensions. Yet do not assume (we will then be advised) that the significance has to include the belief's *thereby failing* to be knowledge.

Could we even talk usefully – and still in a compatibilist vein – of a belief's *luckily being* knowledge? At the very least, we could do so by applying Duncan Pritchard's (2005) notion of *evidential* luck, whereby a person can be lucky to gain some specific evidence in the first place, only then to use it aptly – and luckily – in forming what is thereby a well justified true belief and even perhaps knowledge. As this chapter's discussion has exemplified, however, evidential luck is not what epistemologists have in mind when endorsing the luck/knowledge incompatibility thesis. They generally have in mind something like Pritchard's concept of *veritic* luck (mentioned in Section 12.2). Yet even the presence of this sort of luck, we have seen (in Sections 12.4 through 12.6), cannot be *shown* – and hence should not be *assumed* – to be incompatible with a true belief's being knowledge. Again, therefore, the question arises of whether it is possible that a belief *could* be knowledge even while being true in a veritically lucky way, for example. Can we make sense of this idea, at least in an initial or *prima facie* way? I believe so, although here I will offer only a few programmatic remarks in support of this view.

Recall our discussion of Socrates and Meno – their pondering the respective merits of a true opinion that is, and a true opinion that is not, knowledge. We might take from their discussion a pragmatist moral about what knowledge can be enough for (as in: what must we expect *of* knowledge?) – and hence what can be enough for knowledge (as in: what must we expect if there is to *be* knowledge?). The point of contention between Socrates and Meno concerned what would hold in place a particular true opinion, enabling it to guide its holder through to Larissa. If a tether is added, this guidance will indeed be accomplished, we are told by Socrates. But even if we grant the claimed need for guidance if there is to be knowledge, and even if we interpret such guidance via the Socratic metaphor of a sustained tether, we should acknowledge that a tether with this pragmatic power need not be *evidential*. More generally, it need not even be epistemic – in the sense of being a feature with a special link to truth as such.[13] Rather, it might be merely *psychological*: for instance, it need not be anything beyond an effective state of one's being *determined* to hold in place what seems to one to be a true opinion worth holding in place. Once an opinion is true, what matters most in a tether is simply *that* it hold the opinion in place. What is less important is *how* this is achieved. For example, what is not also needed is that the tether allow the person to *explain, to herself or others, why* she has and is maintaining that opinion. Such an ability could well be *welcome* in many a piece of knowledge: clearly, there are settings where this *is* expected of knowledge. (Philosophical settings themselves come readily to mind here.) That capacity, however, is not always *needed* in a piece of knowledge – needed, that is, simply in order *for there to be* the piece of knowledge at all. Indeed, this discussion between Socrates and Meno is itself one that should help us to see – along the lines outlined just now – why knowledge *per se* does not have that need. That is so, in spite – ironically – of the fact that this classic discussion between Socrates and Meno has often been cited by epistemologists as an argument *for* knowledge's needing to include something of an evidential, but at least of an epistemic, nature.

We should thereby be encouraged to think more broadly about knowledge's nature. And then the encouraging thought might occur to us that even a true belief's being luckily maintained *is* a tether. This tether *can* possess all of the power that Socrates and Meno would ask it to have, if it is to guide one effectively onwards to Larissa. A true belief is being maintained *simpliciter*, after all, if it is being luckily maintained. And what holds in that way of a true belief's being maintained holds also of its being formed in the first place: if one is to head towards Larissa, then forming a belief that represents accurately – even if luckily so – the direction to follow is all that one could want of knowledge *at that initial time* as to the direction to follow. Obviously, one could be concerned that, without an evidential tether, one might forget the path to take. (And so we find Socrates stressing the potential importance of recollection.) But in that respect there is nothing special about having an *epistemic* tether, such as evidence pointing to the pertinent truth that is being represented. All that is needed is *any* sort of tether, including one that is a tie simply to the belief's staying – once the belief is present, once it is representing what is true. And luck can be just such a tether. Truth-directed luck in particular can be so.

We thus return to a compatibilist conjecture. Perhaps it is possible to know luckily, even in a veritically lucky way. Perhaps it is possible, similarly, to know dogmatically, as one remains tethered by one's obstinacy to what is in fact a true opinion. And so on. In this structurally allowed sense, there might be many ways to know – more of them than epistemologists usually acknowledge. We should at least not cast aside such possibilities prematurely; what might well be a mistaken allegiance to the luck/knowledge *in*compatibility thesis could incline us towards performing that dismissive action.

Notes

1   The translation here is from Grube (1981: 86).
2   Although Socrates talks, in this translation, of *opinions*, I will follow contemporary epistemological practice by writing mainly of *beliefs*, as being the identifiable units within, or aspects of, a person, some of which might collectively be all of her knowledge.
3   For extensive discussion of it, see Shope (1983), Lycan (2006), and Hetherington (2016).
4   This comes from Chisholm (1966: 23 fn. 22, 1977: 105, 1989: 93), although I am not using Chisholm's own words in presenting it.
5   This technical way of thinking originates with Engel (1992, 2011). In recent years, it has been associated especially with Pritchard (e.g. 2005).
6   In fact, many epistemologists have claimed – and still claim – to be accepting the thesis on the basis of an intuition that it is true. Nonetheless, the epistemic strength of any such reliance upon appeals to intuition has been questioned increasingly in recent years, particularly with the rise of experimental philosophy – a development initiated especially by Weinberg, Nichols, and Stich (2001). For further discussion of this issue, see Deutsch (2015) and Hetherington (2016: ch. 6).
7   Elsewhere, I show in detail why the concept of veritic luck (mentioned above in Section 12.2) – like its close cousin, the concept of epistemic safety (e.g. Sosa 1999) – provides no explicative insight into why the epistemologically standard interpretation of Gettier cases is true, if indeed it is (Hetherington 2016: ch. 3). The argument that I am about to present is a more general one. For a still-fuller version, see Hetherington (2016: ch. 2).
8   For some extended discussions of this, see Levy (2011) and Coffman (2015).
9   Have any epistemologists not only hypothesized, but actually argued for, this view of knowledge? How *could* it be that any true belief is knowledge? Generically, two paths have been followed towards that view. Either (i) we argue that all and only instances of true belief are instances of knowledge (e.g. Sartwell 1991, 1992; Hetherington 2018). Or (ii) we argue just that all true beliefs are knowledge – leaving open whether there are or might be instances of knowledge that also have something more, such as evidence, within them (Hetherington 2001, 2011; Foley 2012). This 'something

more' might *improve* an instance of knowledge as knowledge (e.g. in accord with how strong the included evidence is), even without having been part of what *makes* that instance of knowledge knowledge at all. Section 12.7 will comment further upon alternative (i).
10 I should note that this is my interpretive suggestion. It is not the interpretation of this passage that is standardly offered by epistemologists.
11 For a more detailed critical discussion of it, see Hetherington (2011: ch. 4).
12 For more on this reasoning, see Hetherington (1998, 2013).
13 Talk of a tether can be evidential – as pre-1963, pre-Gettier, epistemology would presumably have taken it to be. It can equally well be more generally epistemic, by being about what Plantinga (1993a, 1993b) calls *warrant*. Inspired especially by post-Gettier epistemology, Plantinga was designating *whatever* else is (epistemic and) needed if a true belief is to be knowledge, see Hetherington (2016: 153–4).

References

Chisholm, R.M. (1966), *Theory of Knowledge*, Englewood Cliffs, NJ: Prentice-Hall.
Chisholm, R.M. (1977), *Theory of Knowledge*, 2nd edn, Englewood Cliffs, NJ: Prentice-Hall.
Chisholm, R.M. (1989), *Theory of Knowledge*, 3rd edn, Englewood Cliffs, NJ: Prentice-Hall.
Coffman, E.J. (2015), *Luck: Its Nature and Significance for Human Knowledge and Agency*, Basingstoke: Palgrave Macmillan.
Deutsch, M. (2015), *The Myth of the Intuitive: Experimental Philosophy and Philosophical Method*, Cambridge, MA: The MIT Press.
Engel, M. (1992), 'Is Epistemic Luck Compatible with Knowledge?' *The Southern Journal of Philosophy*, 30: 59–75.
Engel, M. (2011), 'Epistemic Luck', *The Internet Encyclopedia of Philosophy*, URL: http://www.iep.utm.edu/epi-luck
Foley, R. (2012), *When Is True Belief Knowledge?* Princeton: Princeton University Press.
Gettier, E.L. (1963), 'Is Justified True Belief Knowledge?' *Analysis*, 23: 121–3.
Grube, G.M.A. (trans.) (1981), *Plato: Five Dialogues*, Indianapolis: Hackett Publishing.
Hetherington, S. (1998), 'Actually Knowing', *The Philosophical Quarterly*, 48: 453–69.
Hetherington, S. (2001), *Good Knowledge, Bad Knowledge: On Two Dogmas of Epistemology*, Oxford: Clarendon Press.
Hetherington, S. (2011), *How to Know: A Practicalist Conception of Knowledge*, Malden, MA: Wiley-Blackwell.
Hetherington, S. (2013), 'Knowledge Can Be Lucky', in M. Steup, J. Turri, and E. Sosa (eds), *Contemporary Debates in Epistemology*, 2nd edn, Malden, MA: Wiley Blackwell.
Hetherington, S. (2016), *Knowledge and the Gettier Problem*, Cambridge: Cambridge University Press.
Hetherington, S. (2018), 'The Redundancy Problem: From Knowledge-Infallibilism to Knowledge-Minimalism', *Synthese*, 195: 4683–702.
Levy, N. (2011), *Hard Luck: How Luck Undermines Free Will and Moral Responsibility*, New York: Oxford University Press.
Lycan, W.G. (2006), 'On the Gettier Problem Problem', in S. Hetherington (ed.), *Epistemology Futures*, 148–68, Oxford: Clarendon Press.

Plantinga, A. (1993a), *Warrant: The Current Debate*, New York: Oxford University Press.
Plantinga, A. (1993b), *Warrant and Proper Function*, New York: Oxford University Press.
Pritchard, D. (2005), *Epistemic Luck*, Oxford: Clarendon Press.
Sartwell, C. (1991), 'Knowledge Is Merely True Belief', *American Philosophical Quarterly*, 28: 157–65.
Sartwell, C. (1992), 'Why Knowledge Is Merely True Belief', *The Journal of Philosophy*, 89: 167–80.
Shope, R.K. (1983), *The Analysis of Knowing: A Decade of Research*, Princeton: Princeton University Press.
Sosa, E. (1999), 'How Must Knowledge Be Modally Related to What Is Known?' *Philosophical Topics*, 26: 373–84.
Weinberg, J.M., Nichols, S., and Stich, S. (2001), 'Normativity and Epistemic Intuitions', *Philosophical Topics*, 29: 429–60.

13

The redundancy problem: From knowledge-infallibilism to knowledge-minimalism

Among the epistemological ideas commonly associated with the Descartes of the *Meditations*, at any rate, is a knowledge-infallibilism. Such an idea was seemingly a vital element in Descartes's search for truth within that investigative setting: only a true belief gained infallibly (as we would now describe it) could be knowledge, as the *Meditations* conceived of this. Contemporary epistemologists are less likely than Descartes was to advocate our ever seeking knowledge-infallibility, if only because most are doubtful as to its ever being available. Still, they would agree – in a seemingly Cartesian spirit – that *if* infallible knowledge was available then it would be a stronger link to truth than fallible knowledge ever manages to be. But this chapter argues that infallible knowledge lacks that supposed advantage over fallible knowledge. Indeed, we will see why we should move even further away from the epistemological model at the heart of the *Meditations*: we should adopt knowledge-*minimalism*, by conceiving of a belief's being true as always sufficient for its being knowledge – this, for any belief.

13.1 Introduction

There is no more Cartesian an idea within epistemology than knowledge-infallibilism (as a contemporary philosopher might call it). At least within his *Meditations on First Philosophy*, Descartes sought truth by seeking known-by-him truth; and he deemed himself to know a truth only when the associated idea had been gained by him in such a way as to eliminate even the possibility of his mistaking the idea as being true when it is not.[1] In contemporary terms, the Descartes of the *Meditations* was thus a knowledge-infallibilist.

But should he have been so? More strongly, should anyone be so? This chapter will argue against one of the more seemingly excellent reasons for conceiving of knowledge in infallibilist terms. Initially, the chapter will thereby be advocating a knowledge-fallibilism. Of course, whether there can be fallible knowledge – or whether instead knowledge must somehow incorporate infallibility – depends first on what fallibility is.[2] What would infallibility give us that fallibility does not, when we are functioning as knowers? In this chapter, I discuss one apparent epistemic advantage that infallible knowledge would routinely be taken to have over fallible knowledge. That appearance is badly misleading, I will contend.

13.2 Distinguishing knowledge-fallibilism from knowledge-infallibilism

Let knowledge-fallibilism and knowledge-infallibilism, at their most generic, be the following theses.[3]

> *Knowledge-fallibilism* It is possible for at least some knowledge to be fallible.
> *Knowledge-infallibilism* It is impossible for there ever to be fallible knowledge, because knowledge could only ever be infallible.

And what would the difference be between knowledge's being fallible and its being infallible? This difference has traditionally been construed as a function of at least the truth-directedness strength of the justification component within, respectively, any instance of fallible knowledge and any instance of infallible knowledge. Truth-directedness is not the only epistemologically significant possible aspect of epistemic justification, of course. But it has long been the most salient aspect to mention when trying to distinguish just between a fallibilist and an infallibilist sense of justification and thereby knowledge. The central question over which those two approaches differ has typically been one of whether the belief's being *true* would be entailed or, more generally, somehow ensured or guaranteed by the justification, or whether – even though the belief is true – its being false was in some way allowed by the justification (Hetherington 2005, 2016b, 2018).

Upon epistemological analysis, that central question readily becomes more complicated, such as by asking about whether the belief is *accidentally* true, relative to the justification (Reed 2000, 2002, 2012), or about whether the belief is *failably* knowledge (Hetherington 1999, 2001: ch. 2), for example.[4] Still, throughout all such variations on knowledge-fallibilism's central theme, the following minimal component recurs – the idea that there is some sort of compatibility (whatever form, more exactly, that compatibility takes) between (i) the justification within the knowledge (whatever form, more exactly, that justification takes) and (ii) the belief's not being true (no matter that it is actually true).

And that recurring minimal component, talking as it does of compatibility and truth, admits of being parsed modally. Doing so produces, I will assume, a characterisation that includes something relevantly like the following.

> Within at least one possible world from within whatever group of possible worlds is most apt for modelling the fallibility or otherwise of a particular true belief's being justified, the belief is false – no matter that the belief is in fact knowledge.

The generality in that formulation will enable the chapter's argument to be adverting, with systematic ambiguity, either to metaphysically possible worlds or, more narrowly, to epistemically possible ones – without our needing to choose in this setting between these respective ideas as ways of understanding the fallibility or otherwise of some knowledge.[5] That difference will be immaterial to the argument. In *either* case, the point is still this: we have ready to hand a philosophically congenial means of taking at least a first step – even if a schematic and programmatic one – towards parsing modally the epistemologically traditional idea of there being a difference of justificatory *strength* between any instance of fallible knowledge that p and any instance of infallible knowledge that p. Specifically, the modal translation of that sort of claim about a difference of justificatory strength will tell us this:

> There is at least some salient not-p possibility that any fallible knowledge that p's justification does – while no infallible knowledge that p's justification does – *fall short* of eliminating.

In effect, we are being told that, for any given instance of knowledge that p (and so long as all else is equal), *at least one more group* of possibilities – from among all of the relevant not-p ones – is eliminated if the justification within the knowledge that p is infallible than if the justification within the knowledge that p is fallible.

The availability of some such line of thought matters, because it is seemingly an epistemological truism – a claim accepted without hesitation by epistemologists – that infallible knowledge that p would somehow be a stronger justificatory link to the truth that p than fallible knowledge that p would be. Let us parse the core of that standard idea more fully and precisely, still in terms of possible worlds, in this way.[6]

> *KInF > KF* For any given proposition p, consider both (i) any possible *fallible* justification $_pJ_F$ within this world α for a belief that p and (ii) any possible *infallible* justification $_pJ_I$ within α for a belief that p. For any such $_pJ_F$, let the $_pJ_F$-*worlds* be those where the belief that p is formed on the same fallible justificatory basis $_pJ_F$ (the same justifying evidence and in the same justifying circumstances that jointly constitute $_pJ_F$) as does or could occur for that belief within α. For any $_pJ_I$, too, let the $_pJ_I$-worlds stand analogously to $_pJ_I$: that is, they stand to $_pJ_I$ as, for any $_pJ_F$, the $_pJ_F$-worlds stand to $_pJ_F$. Let $_p\%T_F$ be the proportion of accessible p-worlds (those where it is *true* that p) among those $_pJ_F$-worlds; and, analogously, let $_p\%T_I$ be the proportion of accessible p-worlds among those $_pJ_I$-worlds. Then $_p\%T_I > _p\%T_F$ – because $_p\%T_I = 100\%$ while $_p\%T_F < 100\%$. Next, assume that any fallible *knowledge* that p would include some $_pJ_F$ and that any infallible *knowledge* that p would include some $_pJ_I$. Then we may infer that no fallible knowledge that p includes within itself as strong a justificatory link to the truth that p as does any infallible knowledge that p – again, because $_p\%T_I > _p\%T_F$.

13.3 The redundancy argument

But is that epistemological truism – *KInF > KF* – actually true? Here is an argument against its being so. Let FJTB be the property of being a fallibly justified true belief, and let InFJTB be the property of being an infallibly justified true belief. Included within each of those complex properties is the property T, the property of being true. Hence, in no possible world is there an instance either of FJTB or of InFJTB that is not an instance of T. Obviously there are worlds where neither of those two complex properties – FJTB and InFJTB – is instantiated, either for a given belief that p or even at all. Yet in no possible world where InFJTB *is* instantiated is the belief in question not true. And, likewise, in no possible world where FJTB is instantiated is the belief in question not true. So (for a given p), $_p\%T_I = 100\%$ *and* $_p\%T_F = 100\%$. In short, $_p\%T_I = {_p\%T_F}$. And thus thesis *KInF > KF* is false: the justificatory support for p even within some infallible knowledge that p is *not* a stronger link to its being true that p than is the justificatory support for p within some fallible knowledge that p.

I call that *the redundancy problem*. It identifies a respect in which infallible justification for a true belief is always redundant, once there is fallible justification for that true belief. Initially, we are encountering this as a potential problem for infallibilist conceptions of knowledge.[7] It tells us that *no* higher a proportion of relevant possibilities of falsity is eliminated by infallible justificatory support for a true belief than is eliminated by fallible justificatory support for that same true belief. In that sense, fallible justificatory support for a true belief *may as well remain* fallible: no proportional improvement in justificatory strength could be achieved by replacing the fallible support for that true belief with infallible support for that same true belief. Apparently, therefore, this is a sense in which infallible justificatory support for a true belief would be no stronger than fallible justificatory support for that true belief. And so – given knowledge's needing to include justificatory support that is either fallible or infallible – we find that even infallible knowledge that p would be no stronger a justificatory link than fallible knowledge that p would be to the truth that p.

13.4 The swamping problem

Section 13.3's redundancy problem is a close cousin of what epistemologists call the *swamping* problem.[8] The latter arose initially as a putative objection to process-reliabilist accounts of knowledge. In that form, the swamping problem talks of epistemic value, and it denies that there is any added epistemic value in having a reliably acquired true belief that p, beyond whatever epistemic value there is in having a true belief that p. The thinking behind the problem is as follows.

> The process-reliability of which many epistemologists speak so favourably is a truth-directed reliability: it is a matter of how reliable a given belief-forming process or method is in generating true beliefs, at least within actual situations but perhaps also within alternative possible ones. Now, imagine a person's *having* a true belief via a reliable belief-forming process. How is that true belief's presence epistemically better because the process – due to its reliability – could easily have produced *further* true beliefs, say? It is not. (Nor is the true belief's reliable pedigree to be respected purely for its *own* sake.)

Clearly, there is a similarity between that line of thought and Section 13.3's reasoning for the redundancy problem. Nevertheless, they remain distinct problems.

First, the reasoning for the redundancy problem does not rely upon the thesis that generates the swamping problem and that Olsson (2011: 175), following Goldman

(1999), calls *Veritism*: 'All that matters in inquiry is the acquisition of true belief.' Section 13.3's argument was about $KInF > KF$. What was being discussed there was a comparison that concerned just the supposed *increase in justificatory strength* between, respectively, fallible knowledge and infallible knowledge. That there would be such an increase between those two states will not be considered epistemologically controversial. It is far less controversial, at any rate, than Veritism's claim that the *only possible epistemic value* involved in inquiry is that a true belief is gained. The 'justificatory increase hypothesis' (which I adopt here for the sake of argument, since others adopt it) reflects the epistemologically standard view that – regardless of whatever will not change between knowing fallibly that p and knowing infallibly that p – there has to be *some* sort of epistemic strengthening of a believer's standing in relation to p, whenever she knows infallibly rather than fallibly that p. The usual way to explicate this epistemic strengthening does not need to talk of epistemic values as such; and hence Section 13.3's reasoning for the redundancy problem has not done so. All that has entered the reasoning is a modal way of modelling – not of valuing – that difference of epistemic strength, a difference that epistemologists would typically think is at least part of what is involved in the difference between knowing fallibly and knowing infallibly.

Second, as the next section will explain, the argument for the redundancy problem need not be regarded as being about how the true belief has been *formed* or *produced* (such as in a reliable way).

13.5 The justificatory link to truth

I have presented the redundancy problem as telling us that no stronger a justificatory link to a belief's being true is constituted by having infallible, rather than fallible, justificatory support for the belief's truth. Yet how could such a thesis about justification and truth be correct? For a start, it clashes with the usual view that infallible justificatory support is a perfect justificatory link to the particular truth, while fallible justificatory support is only an imperfect link to that truth.

That usual view, however, might be overlooking the following distinction.

(1) *Active justificatory linking.* This is a process of justifying. It is one's *gaining* a true belief, or at least one's *trying* to do so, by the use of what would *then* – if one was to proceed to gain that belief – constitute one's justification for the belief's being true. Here, we are asking whether one's justification – be it fallible or be it infallible – *will* lead one to a true belief.

(2) *The state of being justificatorily linked.* This is one's *having* a true belief, perhaps – but not necessarily – as a result of a prior (and, in the sense described just now by (1), an active) justificatory linking. Here, we are asking whether one's justification – be it fallible or be it infallible – *has* led one to a true belief.

Presumably, an active justificatory linking to a truth is what an inquirer seeks, as she moves to and fro between data, observations, stray thoughts, hypotheses, beliefs, etc. – with all of this being intended to lead her to a state in which she is linked justificatorily to a pertinent truth. In contrast, however, the state of being justificatorily linked to a truth is what needs to be at least our initial focus as we analyse epistemologically what knowledge *is* – which is to say, what it is *to be in* a state of knowing. The redundancy problem arises just for the latter – that is, for the state of knowing, and thereby for the state of having a true belief that has been justified either fallibly or infallibly. The redundancy problem's question is then the following one. *Once one has* some knowledge that p – or, equally, *in having* that knowledge – how could infallible justification within that knowledge ever be contributing a stronger justificatory link, beyond what fallible justification within the knowledge would be contributing, to the truth that p?

I am not thereby asking whether, given the redundancy problem, fallible justification and infallible justification are equally good in all epistemic respects – even in all justificatory respects. In particular, I acknowledge, they are not equally good *active* justificatory links to truth. If an inquirer gains evidence that infallibly justifies p's being true, whereupon she forms the belief that p, then she has been actively linked to a true belief in a way that guaranteed her belief's being true once formed. An inquirer actively relying instead upon fallible justification for p's being true has no such guarantee, as she contemplates whether to proceed to believe that p. Perhaps her active justificatory linking will in fact be to that truth; right now, though, there is no guarantee that this will occur. No matter: we have begun to see why this sort of justificatory disparity is in any case not the sort of situation that is being discussed by Section 13.3's argument for the redundancy problem.

Let me expand upon that point. A corollary of the redundancy problem is that whatever increased truth-likelihood there is in an infallibly justified belief (as compared with a fallibly justified belief) could only have been present at an *earlier* stage of the belief-forming process, not insofar as we are comparing the two relevant *completed* states with each other – the states of being a fallibly justified true belief and being an infallibly justified true belief. Hence, if we insist on there being a stronger link to the truth that p in having an infallibly justified true belief that p, then – given the redundancy problem – we are pointing only to what would have been the greater likelihood, given some infallibilist justificatory support at an *earlier* moment of the overall justifying process, of a true belief that p's *proceeding to come into* existence. And this increased truth-likelihood is part only of an *active* justificatory linking, relative to that particular belief. So, it cannot still be present once the true belief *has* eventuated: after all, at that stage the potential for a true belief to eventuate – again, a potential that would have been stronger, in advance, within any infallible justification than within any fallible justification for that potential belief – has been *realised*. At which stage, however, the resulting state – the justified true belief – must be assessed against a *different* kind of criterion for strength-of-justificatory-link-to-truth. Specifically, at that stage it has to be assessed as a *static* (rather than an active) justificatory link to the truth that p. And the verdict, according to the redundancy problem, is that in this respect the resulting state *may as well* have been produced in an infallible way. Yes, this is an assessment 'after the event'. But the point is that the justificatory link being assessed at that stage is itself the *state* that has *been* produced, not the *process* that, earlier, might – or might not – *proceed to* produce that state.

13.6 Unsafety and veritic luck

We can apply Section 13.5's general point to a case study. Recent epistemology has included much discussion of the concept of epistemic safety, including the idea that a belief is not knowledge if it has been formed in an epistemically unsafe way.[9] This approach amounts to suggesting (as Mylan Engel and Duncan Pritchard, notably, have done) that even a true belief is not knowledge if it is true only in a *veritically (epistemically) lucky way*;[10] which is to suggest a condition along these lines:

> A belief is not knowledge if it is false within too many of the closest possible worlds where the belief is formed in the same way (hence, in particular, on the basis of the same evidence) as it is within this world.[11] (For convenience, I will call those worlds *justification-mirroring truth-failure* possible worlds for the belief in question.)

I mention this sort of condition because seemingly it describes a truth-linked justificatory respect in which, many epistemologists would presume, a fallibly justified true belief that p – but not also an infallibly justified true belief that p – *could* be less strong as a link to p's being true. That comparative weakness would be explicable in modal terms. Most epistemologists will allow that whenever a true belief is justified only fallibly – in contrast to when it is justified infallibly – there was also at least a chance of its being formed unsafely; in which event, it would have been true only in a veritically lucky way.[12] Thus, let W be one of those justification-mirroring truth-failure possible worlds, for a given belief that p:

> W is a not-p world, and its existence is (in accord with the generic account of veritic luck mentioned just now) part of the modal dimension of the given belief that p's being true in *this* world α in a veritically lucky way.

Within W, the fallibly justified belief that p reappears, formed in the same (mirroring) way as within α, where it is likewise fallibly justified. Within W, however, the belief is false – unlike in α. I expect that many epistemologists would then accept the following thesis:

> If the belief that p had instead been justified *in*fallibly within α, there would be no such W, where it is not true that p. So, at least *that* additional truth-directed justificatory strength – a modally explicable form of strength – is part of a true belief's having been infallibly rather than fallibly justified.

However, that reasoning would be invalid, as I will now explain.

The reasoning begins by positing a justification-mirroring truth-failure world W where the pertinent way of forming a belief (let us call that way WAY) has led to a false belief that *p* – instead of a true one, as has happened in α. We are asked to consider the existence of W as being, in that respect, a modal manifestation of the truth-directedness weakness within the (fallible) justificatory link that is constituted within α by the use of the fallible WAY. Now, within α, WAY has in fact led to a true belief that *p* – whereas, within W, the result of using WAY is a false belief that *p*. The proposed (standard) reasoning then takes into account *both* of those worldly points about WAY, in deciding that WAY has led only unsafely within α to the true belief that *p*. That is, WAY is being considered in a *trans*world manner, even as part of evaluating its justificatory strength just within *this* world. That much is epistemologically familiar fare.

But that epistemologically familiar line of thought can show only that WAY's modally explicable weakness as a justificatory link to the truth that *p* is a weakness within it as a fallible *and active* linking to any given true belief that *p*. This point is less familiar, but it is easily seen (as follows). The transworld explicative structure that is being portrayed reveals only WAY's being a modally less-than-wholly-reliable means of *coming* to have a true belief that *p* within various worlds: in using WAY, one will *come* to form a belief that *p*; and, in doing so, one might (as within α) – but also one need not (as within W) – come to have a *true* belief that *p*. (It is precisely the fact that within W the belief being formed is not true that reveals this evaluation of WAY as not succeeding in being an evaluation of WAY *after* WAY has produced the true belief within α.) That sort of truth-directedness modal weakness is absent, of course, when the relevant way of proceeding to form a belief is an *in*fallible and active link to the truth that *p*. Yet the existence of that sort of disparity was already conceded in Section 13.5, where we observed its doing nothing to undermine the impact of the redundancy problem. For that problem, we noticed, applies only to justification as a *static* link to truth, not as a means of *coming* to have a belief (which might turn out to be a true belief).

Correlatively, nothing in that standard thinking about WAY and its potential to be used actively both within this world α and within a justification-mirroring truth-failure world W shows that, *once the active justificatory linking by WAY has been completed within α* (with a true belief that *p* now being in place), *the resulting state* – the fallibly justified true belief that *p* – is a modally weaker justificatory link to the truth that *p* than would obtain if an infallible active linking had instead been the cause within α of the true belief that *p*'s coming to be. After all, the fact remains that in no possible world is a fallibly justified true belief not true – *just as* there is no possible world where an infallibly justified true belief is not true. This fact remains, as a fact about *being in* those respective (completed) states.

Once more, therefore, we meet the redundancy problem. When an advocate (such as Pritchard) of the explanatory efficacy of the concepts of epistemic safety and veritic luck asks us to consider a *not-p* world W where the belief that *p* has been formed in the same way – WAY – as within α (a *p*-world), this amounts to asking us to be using W as part of our evaluating WAY's strength as a justificatory link to the truth that *p* only insofar as WAY has not yet resulted (within any given world, such as α or such as *W*) in a true belief that *p*. (The hypothesized advocate is asking, in effect, whether using WAY *will* produce a true belief; and we proceed to say that in W it has not done so.) Correlatively, the usual epistemological thinking on behalf of that evaluation of WAY can amount (even if unwittingly) only to highlighting the fact that, *considered in this active respect*, the use of WAY might – but need not – proceed to generate a true belief that *p*: in α it does so, whereas in *W* it does not. Along such lines, therefore, the epistemologically standard thinking amounts only to evaluating WAY as a putative *active* justificatory link to truth; which, we saw in Section 13.5, is beside the point that is being made by the redundancy problem. Consequently, that problem survives the proposed (and epistemologically standard form of) counter-argument that this section began by proposing.

13.7 The Gettier problem

Upon being confronted by the redundancy problem, a further objection that would occur readily to many epistemologists is this.

> Whenever a true belief is justified only fallibly, the justificatory door remains open for it to be part of a *Gettier case* – that is, to be *Gettiered* (and thereby not knowledge).[13] Even if in fact the belief is not Gettiered, the *potential* for its being so was present, since there was fallibility in the justification on the basis of which the belief has been formed. Conversely, whenever a true belief is justified infallibly, that door has been closed, since there are no infallibly justified Gettiered beliefs.[14] This difference may readily be thought of as just one further reflection of the fact that infallible justificatory support is a stronger link to truth than fallible justificatory support manages to be.

Such a suggestion calls upon the widespread epistemological conviction that a belief's being Gettiered precludes its being knowledge. Nevertheless, as I will now explain, what is described by the suggestion is *not* the existence of a stronger justificatory link to a truth that *p* within the state of being an infallibly justified true belief that *p*. This is because the redundancy problem reappears (*mutatis mutandis*, and as follows) for Gettier cases and the suggested way of thinking about them.

> Let G be the property of being Gettiered, a property categorially applicable to beliefs.[15] G is a complex property. It includes at least FJTB – the complex property of being a fallibly justified true belief[16] – and hence the property T (of being true). Consequently, because G includes T, there is no possible world where a belief is Gettiered without being true. Yet – via the following reasoning – this also renders the relationship between G and T relevantly like that between InFJ (the property of being *in*fallibly justified) and T:
>> Let b_p – a particular belief that *p* – be infallibly justified. Then b_p's being justified in the way it is entails b_p's being true: InFJ includes T.

Let b_p be Gettiered. Then b_p's being justified in the situation it is in (that is, within the surrounding Gettier case as such) entails b's being true: G includes T.

Following Gettier (1963: 121), epistemologists say that the justification within a Gettier case is providing only *fallible* support: the property G includes the property FJ, just as it includes the properties T and B. Even so, that standard way of speaking could mislead us into thinking that fallible justification is a *weaker* link than infallible justification is to truth (with Gettier cases being an exemplification of this moral). Yes, the justification for b_p, considered in itself, is instantiating FJ – and does not thereby include T. Even so, G includes T; and hence no belief can instantiate G (thereby instantiating FJ, too) without instantiating T. Consequently, G *may as well* be including InFJ rather than FJ, insofar as the enclosed (static) justificatory link to the truth that *p* is concerned. Perhaps surprisingly, then, we find that being Gettiered – and thereby being fallibly justified in that notorious way – is *not* a state with a weaker justificatory link to the relevant truth than a state built around infallible justification would be.

The point, more simply, is this. The redundancy problem (as it has been generalised in this section) tells us that, once the state of being Gettiered is present *as a whole* – that is, once a belief *is* Gettiered – the justificatory link within that completed state may as well be reflecting the Gettiered belief's having instead been justified infallibly within that circumstance. The justificatory link between *being* Gettiered – that is, the state of being Gettiered, of *now being in* that complex state as a whole – and being true is as strong as that.[17]

13.8 Knowledge-minimalism

So far, we might regard the redundancy problem as amounting to an argument for a kind of knowledge-*fallibilism*, since it aims to undermine what would, for many, be a potential motivation for seeking to be a knowledge-*in*fallibilist in preference to being a knowledge-fallibilist. Even so, we have not yet confronted the redundancy problem's full potential significance. We now need to notice how an instance of it arises also for knowledge-fallibilism.

Thus, compare a fallibly justified true belief that *p* (this being at least part of what is described in any standard knowledge-fallibilist conceptions of knowledge that *p*) with what epistemologists call a mere true belief that *p*. More precisely, compare *instantiating the property FJTB* with *instantiating the property TB*. It is no more possible to instantiate TB without instantiating the property T than it is to instantiate FJTB without instantiating T: in neither case is it possible at all. Accordingly, there is the same sort of redundancy relationship between FJTB and TB as that which was described earlier as obtaining between InFJTB and FJTB. And so, if there is a redundancy problem for InFJTB in relation to FJTB, there is one likewise for FJTB in relation to

TB. Previously, the redundancy problem told us that any *infallible* justification as such that is present as part of an instantiation of InFJTB is redundant – in the sense of providing no extra strength – as a link to truth. Now, the redundancy problem has become broader in its thinking: now, it delivers the same verdict even for the *fallible* justification within any instantiation of FJTB.[18]

Most epistemologists, I expect, will wish to treat such a verdict as a *reductio* of the reasoning behind the redundancy problem. They will say that, if anything is clear within epistemology, it is that any belief that p is less strongly linked to the truth that p insofar as it is a *true* belief than insofar as it is a *true and justified* belief. After all, this conviction is why we require justification at all within knowledge. Is the redundancy problem's thinking therefore mistaken?

I do not believe so, because I regard that standard epistemological reaction as being needlessly restrictive in its conception of the relationship between knowledge and justification. Obviously we may readily allow that there is a *justificatory* strength in having some justification for one's true belief, and hence within any instance of knowing that includes some justification. But that is hardly surprising: justification is justification, regardless of whatever else it is. Beyond acknowledging that triviality, though, we should wish to ascertain more substantively what further kind of truth-linked strength, if any, there is in the justification's presence. Epistemologists have had much to say about this. Still, we need not engage here with that body of writing, because there is a conceptually prior issue to be confronted – as follows – about the metaphysics of knowing.

I assume that we are standardly being told that, whenever there is fallible knowledge that p, the associated justificatory strength (1) would be within, or part of, the knowledge (because the fallible justification is literally a component or part of the fallible knowledge), and (2) would be explicable as a correlatively stronger link to the truth in question (stronger than the link that would be present if the true belief was present without also being justified). But the redundancy problem (as it has been generalised further in this section) may then be interpreted as questioning whether that combination of (1) and (2) is how we *need* to understand the location and role of the justificatory strength associated with an instance of knowledge.

First, here is the relevant application of the generalised redundancy problem:

The presence of the justification – be it fallible or be it infallible – within some knowledge that p serves no purpose towards the knowledge's being a stronger link to the truth that p than would be served by the presence simply of the true belief that p. As regards being a state, or part of a state, that is linked to the particular truth that p, the true belief that p *may as well* be accompanied by its being unjustified as by its being justified.

Next, notice that even this need not lead (as would standardly be assumed to follow from the redundancy problem's thinking) to our *dismissing* the importance, for knowing that p, of having justification for the belief that p. For there is a structurally available escape from that conclusion. Specifically, we may discard thesis (1), as the price to be paid for retaining thesis (2); *and we may come to understand why it is not so high a price*. More fully: we may react to this further application of the redundancy problem by recognising that there *is* still a way for knowledge that *p* to be associated, via justification, with a stronger link to the truth that *p*. Our first step towards this alternative interpretive framework is to *cease requiring that justificatory link to satisfy (1)*. What would this mean, as a resulting view of knowledge? By discarding (1), we would be conceiving of each instance of knowledge in such a way as to allow us to place any associated justificatory link *outside* the knowledge (which would itself be interpreted as at least a true belief). This would allow us to bypass the redundancy problem, which is generated by (1)-plus-(2). And then – this is our second interpretive step here – we will be able to retain (2): we will be able to *return* to accommodating – even if non-standardly (as we are about to see) – the justification's functioning as a stronger link to truth.

How would that be so? Can we interpret that suggested combination – not-(1) plus (2) – less schematically? Indeed so: we need only to call upon Section 13.5's distinction between two ways of being linked to a truth. The present interpretive aim is to accommodate, in a constructive way, this implication of the redundancy problem:

> If the justification associated with a case of knowledge that *p* is somehow to be a further and stronger link to the truth that *p* (a stronger link beyond what is effected by the true belief that *p*) – so that the redundancy problem is to be bypassed – then the justification needs to be playing that role *not* from within the knowledge that *p* as such – that is, not as *part* of the knowledge that *p*.

This is because – as we have found – some knowledge's having a stronger justificatory link to truth is not a circumstance that obtains once the justification is *a static link in place within the knowledge as a whole*. When suitably generalised, the redundancy problem shows, we saw, that a fallibly justified true belief that *p* is not a stronger static link to the truth that *p* than is the mere true belief that *p*. Correlatively, if there is to be a stronger link to the truth that *p* due to the presence of supportive justification, this needs instead to be an *active* justificatory linking to truth. In other words, its linking to the truth that *p* would be achieved *not* by the justification's being a part of the (completed) state that is the knowledge that *p*. Rather, we might treat an active linking along such lines as more of a preparatory link, one that could help us to *proceed* to reach the knowledge – yet without its thereby becoming a *part* of the knowledge.

That interpretive prospect coheres with Section13.5's acknowledgement that the redundancy problem leaves untouched the uncontentious-because-trivial idea that infallible justification *per se* is stronger *as* justification than is fallible justification *per se*; and, of course, it is equally uncontentious-because-trivial that fallible justification *per se* is stronger as justification than is a complete absence of justification. Even the redundancy problem allows that, whenever you have infallible rather than fallible justificatory support for believing that *p*, you have justificatory support which – purely *as* justification *per se* – is stronger. But we should not infer that there is thereby a stronger link to *truth*. The redundancy problem implies that whenever such justification is included within knowledge – so that now we are considering at least a justified true belief as a completed combination – this resulting combination does *not* possess such an increased strength as a link to truth. The redundancy problem enters the epistemological story when we are comparing instantiations of the property InFJTB with ones of the property FJTB, or (in this section) instantiations of FJTB with ones of TB. However, what the redundancy problem does not impugn is the capacity for justification *per se* – let alone for stronger rather than weaker justification (for example, instantiations of InFJ rather than of FJ) – to lead a person, actively, *to* the state of having a true belief. The redundancy problem does not bar that *active* linking to truth from being more, or less, literally *effective* in a truth-linked way: it could well be stronger, or indeed less so, in that active way in accord with the justification's being more, or indeed less, strong.

All of that leads us constructively towards an unorthodox picture – which we may call knowledge-*minimalism* – that was advanced memorably by Sartwell (1991, 1992), in particular. He argued that knowledge *is* simply true belief: nothing more, nothing less. His picture has attracted few adherents, seemingly because it weakens the conceptual link between knowing that *p* and having justification for a true belief that *p* (that is, for the true belief that, according to knowledge-minimalism, is *ipso facto* her knowledge that *p*). But might that standard reaction – that wariness about knowledge-minimalism – be *needlessly* worried about knowledge-minimalism's prospect of doing justice to how knowledge and justification are to be linked within our conceptual theorizing? Even a minimalist conception of knowledge need not deny that knowledge does, or at least can, have *something* important to do with justification; what, though? Sartwell's answer was that, always, the justification is 'a *criterion*, though not a logically necessary condition, of knowledge' (1991: 161). This is not the epistemologically traditional view. Is it at least coherent, though?

Indeed so, especially given this chapter's argument. For knowledge-minimalism can be conjoined smoothly with one or another coherent way of recognising the epistemic contribution being made by some evidence, for instance, to one's knowing on a given occasion. One such form of conjunction opens the conceptual door to the idea of there being *different epistemic strengths* of knowledge, even for knowledge of a single *p*. On that gradualist approach (as it has been termed), any instance of knowledge that *p* is itself better or worse – possessing *some* epistemic grade – as knowledge that *p*. Goldman (1999: 23–6) allows there to be weak knowledge, strong knowledge, and superstrong knowledge. For Goldman, weak knowledge is mere true belief (this being, for Sartwell, what *all* knowledge is). I have elsewhere envisaged a more *extended* acceptance of possible strengths of knowledge that *p*, for a specific *p* (Hetherington 2001). I allowed – as a limiting case for the concept of knowledge – the minimalist possibility that some knowledge that *p* might be merely a true belief that *p*. But then I allowed that further instances of knowledge that *p* could include increasingly strong justificatory support, with the knowledge that *p* being correlatively strengthened itself as knowledge that *p* – that is, being improved epistemically as knowledge of that specific *p*. In principle, then, I allowed that there can be both minimal knowledge that *p* and many possible grades of improved knowledge that *p*.[19] Foley's (2012) view of knowledge is also apposite here. He conceives of knowledge (almost) purely as mere true belief. I say '(almost)' because he conceives of knowledge as true belief plus enough important information (where information is also true belief); yet this further condition required by Foley could be viewed as a form of epistemic justification, a point noted by Warenski (2014: 896). And so perhaps he, too, could – although in fact he does not – talk in terms of there being minimal knowledge that p and improved knowledge that *p*.[20]

Those views from Goldman, Foley, and me are not clearly *pure* forms of knowledge-minimalism, because each, it seems, allows that, for a given *p*, there could be knowledge that *p* that literally includes some justification. In contrast, Sartwell's view – like this chapter's – is more *starkly* knowledge-minimalist. For, again, this view says that knowledge is *only ever*, in itself, a true belief – and hence that, even if there is justification for a given such instance of knowledge, this does not literally affect or change the epistemic nature of that knowledge. Instead, the knowledge, *as* knowledge, remains only the true belief; any justification for that belief's being true – even though the justification is thereby *supporting* the knowledge – is not also literally a *part* of the knowledge. How, then, is this stark knowledge-minimalism to accommodate the fact that justification often *is* present with – indeed, because it has often generated – a particular instance of knowledge? We should ask whether all knowledge is only *barely* knowledge, according to this strict form of knowledge-minimalism.

And the answer to that pressing question would be that in one sense all knowledge *is* barely knowledge, even while in another sense it need not be so. *Yes*: on this chapter's knowledge-minimalism, all knowledge is barely knowledge, in the sense that something's being knowledge *consists merely in* its being a true belief – with its being this true belief thus being considered independently of whatever, if any, further justification for it might also be present. On the other hand, *no*: an instance of knowledge need not barely be knowledge, in the sense that it might not have to *function epistemically on its own merely as* a true belief. For it could function as part of a larger epistemic 'package', one that at least often includes some justification supporting and supplementing the knowledge in the ways that justification does this. In that sense, a given instance of knowledge (a true belief) might actually be justified quite well, thereby enjoying all of the epistemic and psychological security that would typically attend the presence of that justification. But even this would not change the knowledge's *being* knowledge only insofar as it is a true belief.

Accordingly, here is how we could synthesize the previous paragraph's combination (that 'in one sense all knowledge *is* barely knowledge, even while in another sense it need not be so').

> Any instance of knowledge is simply a true belief: that is, the belief's *being* knowledge is nothing beyond its being true. Even so, in principle an instance of knowledge could be justified, to some or another extent; maybe all or most knowledge will in fact be justified. Hence, in principle there can be justified knowledge, perhaps a lot of it. But my main point has been that to describe an instance of knowledge as being justified is not to speak emptily, because in principle any instance of knowledge could also *fail* to be justified. So, even when – as might in fact always happen – an instance of knowledge *is* justified, this does not entail that the true belief in question would not have been knowledge *until* it was

justified. Any instance of justified knowledge is thereby a justified true belief – but not because the knowledge *in itself* is at least a justified true belief.

Even on knowledge-minimalism, therefore, justification can continue to be accorded epistemic roles that accord with its traditionally being so closely associated with knowing. The redundancy problem described in this chapter – along with our distinction between two ways of being linked by justification to truth – provides a conceptual framework within which we may usefully regard the basic idea behind knowledge-minimalism more favourably in that respect than most epistemologists have done. Again, as I indicated just now, we may continue to expect that justification might well in fact play one or more roles in how we know. But the moral that we should hold in mind is that the main such role would remain a metaphysically *extrinsic* role – a role that is not metaphysically *constitutive* of knowing. The contribution would instead be one of being merely *causally* constitutive of some knowing's coming to exist.[21] That causal contribution might admit of grades, too: we will at least hope that (with all else being equal) better justification is better at *giving* us knowledge, at *getting* us knowledge.

I am proposing, then, that the redundancy problem supports the following picture.

Whenever a person has a true belief that p, this is knowledge that p. If the person also has (and has used aptly)[22] some pertinent justificatory support for p's being the case, this justification has, or at least could have, been what *brought* the person to, or at least towards, the state of having that knowledge.

That would be an *active* justificatory linking of the person to a true belief – to the knowledge. We may then distinguish between at least these two kinds of way in which such a link might be effected.

Internalist. The linking could be a process of self-aware guidance, such as by involving the deliberate gathering and assessment of evidence prior to forming what one hopes will be a true belief, indeed knowledge. (This would be an internalist paradigm of an active justificatory genesis for the true belief.)

Externalist. The justificatory process might be the instantiation of a reliable belief-forming process, with the reliability as such being metaphysically constitutive of the justification's presence. (This would be an externalist paradigm of an active justificatory genesis for the true belief.)[23]

In either of those kinds of case, the following conceptual option emerges for us as epistemological interpreters.

In general, some justification might have been causally constitutive (in either an internalist or an externalist way) of some knowledge's coming to exist – without the justification's thereby being a *part* of the resulting knowledge. In any given case of knowing, perhaps that knowledge would not in fact have come to exist, if not for the justification's existing and functioning aptly. Yet even this would not entail the justification's being literally a part of the knowledge that would have now (at least partly by way of the active use of the justification) come to exist.

Nothing in that picture is at odds with the possibility that in fact all instances of our knowledge are accompanied, or even generated, by some justification. Whether that does occur depends on what justification is, for a start; and what justification is constrains also how we would try to ascertain whether in fact all of our knowledge is accompanied or generated by justification. (Maybe it is an empirical matter; maybe it is a transcendental need; etc.) Regardless, however, of what the outcome would be of any such investigation (be it empirical or be it otherwise), my basic conceptual point remains:

> If we wish to view a person's justification for believing that p as strengthening her link as a knower to the truth that p, we would do well to regard that justification as not literally being *part* of that (completed state of) knowledge. We would do better to regard that justification as instead a causal precursor to the knowledge as such – so that the justification's role is that of actively linking the person to the truth that p by helping to *produce* the true belief that p that is *ipso facto* her knowledge that p.

The redundancy problem has thus opened the door to this alternative conceptual prospect within the metaphysics of knowledge.

And that prospect deserves a name of its own. I have been calling it knowledge-minimalism. And I have explained how it is the thesis that knowledge as such is merely a true belief. Once more, I stress, this is not thereby a complete rejection of the epistemic significance of epistemic justification. Knowledge-minimalism is compatible with such justification's having many forms of epistemic significance, such as by being a guide at any given moment to *further* knowledge – that is, to knowledge not-as-yet acquired. It is also compatible with all knowledge's in fact being productively supported by justification, so that wherever and whenever there is knowledge there either is or has been justification, playing a relevantly active role in the knowledge's coming to be. But knowledge-minimalism distinguishes between that form of relationship (even when the relationship does obtain) and knowledge's ever needing to *include within* itself that causally associated justification. We saw that good evidence or strong reliability, say, can help you to know that p – by being good *sources*, in their respective ways and with all else being equal, of the actively generated true belief that p – without their having to be literally a *part* of the resulting knowledge that p.

Maybe our lives will never actually include some knowledge that is completely unsupported by justification: maybe any knowledge that in fact we will ever have will be supported by justification that we will also have. Even if that is what transpires, however, there will remain a need for epistemologists not to confuse such a *conjunction* of circumstances or, more strongly, such a circumstantial *progression* with a *metaphysically constitutive inclusion* – by inferring that therefore the justification is a part, rather than merely a helpful generator, of the knowledge. And the redundancy problem, I suggest, should make us more alert to this possible conceptual refinement of some standard epistemological thinking. We have this opportunity to travel far – even further than we might well have set out to travel – from a Cartesian knowledge-infallibilism.[24]

Notes

1 Perhaps Descartes in other guises did not constrain himself in this way. I take the *Meditations* to have been portraying a quest for metaphysical truth in particular. On whether Descartes was content to settle for satisfying a probabilistic standard when seeking truth in general, especially within empirical science, see Clarke (2012).
2 On some details that arise for this issue, see Reed (2000, 2002, 2012), Fantl and McGrath (2009), Dougherty (2011), and Hetherington (2016b).
3 Non-modalized versions of these two theses are also available. They would say only that there *is*, or there *is not*, some fallible knowledge. But I take the modalized versions to fit better with the metaphysical, rather than empirical, road to be followed in this chapter. (I call that road metaphysical, not conceptual, because the chapter's project is not the traditional one of seeking necessary and sufficient conditions for the satisfaction of a concept. The emphasis will instead be on what is involved, essentially versus accidentally, or inherently versus extrinsically, in a given belief's being an instance of knowledge.)
4 Incidentally, these ideas are general enough to accommodate either *internalist* or *externalist* accounts of justification. For a formulation of this epistemologically significant distinction, see Hetherington (1996: chs 14–15). On an internalist account, the question is one of whether the person's *evidence* – where, contrary to Williamson (2000), I do not presume this to be knowledge – has a content that entails the truth of the belief. On an externalist account, the question is one of whether the obtaining of some further *circumstance* – such as the belief's having been formed in a truth-conditionally reliable way – is compatible with the belief's nonetheless being false.
5 In using the term 'epistemically possible', I am not presuming any specific full conception of epistemic possibility. For example, suppose that we use the term as Hintikka (1962) did, to mean 'compatible with what one knows'. A world W would thus be epistemically possible, relative to one's knowledge within this world, if and only if whatever obtains in W is compatible with whatever one knows within this world. But that conception will not tell us about fallible knowledge's difference from infallible knowledge. It implies that if in this world one knows either fallibly *or* infallibly that p, then no epistemically possible world for one is a world where not-p obtains. Yet – on the core commitment (mentioned above) behind the traditional idea of fallible knowledge that p – *somewhere* there is at least one *somehow* relevantly possible world where, when one's knowledge that p is fallible but not when it is infallible, not-p obtains. This remains so if we think of epistemic possibility in other ways. (i) For instance, suppose that not-p is said to be epistemically possible for one even when one knows that p in case one does not know that not-p is not compatible with what one knows. This still allows not-p to obtain in at least one world that would help to model such a possibility; for not-p is being said to be compatible with one's *bi*-level epistemic stance on p at that time. Hintikka (1962: ch. 5) argues that knowing entails knowing that one knows, and so would not allow this possibility. (ii)

Or suppose that, like Chalmers (2002), we say that not-p is epistemically possible, even when one knows that p, if it is not ruled out *a priori*: it is not known *a priori* that p. Explicating this, too, will call upon the existence of at least *some* relevant not-p world(s). For more on how to conceive of fallible knowledge in terms of possible worlds, see Hetherington (2016b).

6   Doing so does not preclude the possibility that the disparity between those respective justificatory strengths would be better articulated without mentioning possible worlds at all. But in this respect the explicative onus, I suggest, is upon those who would seek to evade this approach. The difference in justificatory strength has been explicated above in modal terms, by talking of the presence of a *possibility* – a compatibility – that accompanies fallible but not infallible justification. Accordingly, until I am aware of a better way of modelling possibilities, I will continue speaking of possible worlds in this setting. In this respect, too, I take heart from Pritchard's (2016) argument that we should conceive in modal terms of the related aspects of knowledge.

7   In Section 13.8, however, we will extend this section's argument, by investigating how the redundancy may be generalised so as to pose a challenge also to knowledge-fallibilism.

8   For some of the swamping problem's history, see Riggs (2002), Kvanvig (2003), Zagzebski (2003), Olsson (2011), Davis and Jäger (2012), Bates (2013), and Dutant (2013).

9   For seminal advocacy of this conception, see Sosa (1999, 2007).

10 See Engel (1992, 2011) for the initial such use of the term 'veritic', and Pritchard (2005, 2007, 2009, 2013) for refinements of the concept. Pritchard (2016) now argues that we should focus epistemologically on veritic (epistemic) *risk* rather than veritic (epistemic) luck. Even so, I will present this section's discussion in terms of veritic (epistemic) luck since, at this stage, it has become such an epistemologically familiar topic. But in any case I believe that the section's discussion will also apply, *mutatis mutandis*, to the concept of veritic risk.

11 Perhaps more generally, here is an alternative version of that condition:

> A belief is not knowledge if it is false within too many of the closest possible worlds where the belief is formed in the same way and within the same circumstances as it is within this world.

The argument I am about to present will not rely upon any specific version of the general idea behind this condition.

12 Sosa has also argued *against* conceiving of knowledge in terms of safety, in favour perhaps of letting aptness – '*manifestation of competence*' – be the pertinent explicative phenomenon (Sosa 2011: 84–5). He also allows that '[a]ptness comes in degrees' (2011: 10) and hence that a belief could manifest a less-than-wholly reliable competence, thereby being formed aptly yet fallibly. This apt formation of the belief could be *fully* apt, too, by manifesting meta-aptness (such as a competence in choosing to exercise the competence that has been manifested aptly in the belief's formation). Nonetheless, I am not sure that this recourse to talk of competence-manifestation *will* accomplish that explanatory goal in a way that allows knowledge still to be fallible. For detailed discussion of this point, see Hetherington (2016a: sec. 5.4).

13 See Gettier (1963) for the original instances of this phenomenon – the first two *Gettier cases* (as they speedily became known). A belief is *Gettiered* when it is the

central belief within a situation saliently similar to the ones described by Gettier. Any such belief is true and justified fallibly; yet it is also, according to most epistemologists, not knowledge. For overviews of the history of epistemological engagement with the challenges for understanding knowledge that were spawned by Gettier, see Shope (1983) and Hetherington (2011). For extended critical discussion of that history, see Hetherington (2016a).

14   For elaboration of this point, see Zagzebski (1994) and Howard-Snyder *et al.* (2003).
15   This is the conceptually *primary* range of applicability for G. Secondary applications of it are as follows. A *person* is Gettiered insofar as she has a Gettiered belief. A situation is a Gettier *case* insofar as it is centred upon a Gettiered belief (and thereby upon a thereby Gettiered person).
16   FJTB would routinely be assumed to include more besides, if only as details *within* those individual components F, J, T, and B. Many of those possible details attract continuing epistemological debate. (For example, this is where a requirement of the belief's being formed *safely* – the condition described in Section 13.6 above – would be held by some epistemologists to enter the story in an explicative role.) Epistemologists also standardly claim that instantiating G precludes being knowledge, so that G cannot be even partly coextensive with the property K.
17   Perhaps this can help us to understand an epistemologically *disjunctivist* line of thought that has recently been advocated, in particular by McDowell (2011). For example, he says that one can gain '*indefeasible* warrant for perceptual beliefs' (2011: 38). Suppose that you seem to be confronted by something green. In that event, your 'perceptual state leaves no possibility that [the thing] is not green' (2011), *given* that your perceptual state has resulted from 'a non-defective exercise' (2011: 39) of your 'capacity to tell whether things in [your] field of vision are green' (2011: 38). In other words, once there *has been* an exercise of the relevant perceptual capacity, what amounts to a kind of infallibility is present – a kind that fits with the picture I am drawing here. In that respect, it is significant that McDowell regards himself as having provided a *fallibilist* picture; for, he says, although capacities can misfire, his focus is on those times when they do not. Notice how this account is like the way in which, just now, I have described Gettier cases: even while there is fallible justification within them – in the sense of a fallible *active* justificatory link having been used by the person who forms the Gettiered belief – the *resulting* state, of the belief's *now* being in the state of being Gettiered, is itself a watertight static link to the truth in question. (But I will not develop this comparison any further in this chapter.)
18   Strictly, this verdict is gained by a *limiting* case of the relevant form of thinking, since TB's link to T is not justificatory at all. Nonetheless, modally speaking, it is still the same form of (static) link to T as was the (static) justificatory link from FJTB and from InFJTB. In order to avoid confusion, I will now talk more simply of a (static) link to truth – without still using the term 'justificatory'.
19   These grades of potential improvement in one's knowledge that *p* are purely epistemic, in accord with any justificatory improvement within the knowledge. That sort of improvement must be distinguished from mere *psychological* strengthening in believing that *p*, such as when one is hypnotised into holding a true belief that *p* more doggedly. After all, that psychological strengthening need not be accompanied by any epistemic strengthening; and so a belief that is held with more conviction is *not* thereby improved as knowledge that *p*, on that account of mine. Note, though, that my earlier approach was general enough to accommodate different conceptions

of purely epistemic improvement. Congruently, for instance, Pritchard (2016) argues that our assessments of the sort of luck or risk that – he also argues – most of us think is incompatible with knowing should be understood in modal rather than probabilistic terms, and that such terms are gradational, allowing a knowledge-precluding false belief, say, to be *more or less* modally close to our actual world.

20 Lycan (1994) and Kvanvig (2003) argue against the cogency of Sartwell's position; and I would expect them to apply their arguments likewise against these further forms of knowledge-minimalism. For criticism of their arguments, however, along with some experimental support for at least part of Sartwell's position, see Sackris and Beebe (2014).

21 The justification's being possessed could also be causally constitutive of mere *attempts* – including unsuccessful ones – to bring into existence some instance of knowing. And of course the causal constitutiveness of which I am talking need not be the *only* causal contributor to the existence of the attempt or the knowing. In that respect, then, I am simplifying the story. My immediate aim is to note simply the broad categorial point – namely, that we may wish to regard justification as a part of our epistemic lives (including our coming to know) that is never literally a part of the knowledge produced at least partly via the justification. (Some justification might itself include knowledge. That is a distinct point.) Theory-of-knowledge would thus be conceptually distinct from theory-of-justification – a distinction long embraced by Foley (1987).

22 Many epistemologists have remarked on the need for evidence to be used aptly, not merely to be present (even if thereby *able* to be used aptly). For example, Kornblith (1980) noted as much on behalf of a (reliabilist) grounding condition. Elsewhere (Hetherington 2013), I have described in detail the importance of an 'activist' conception of evidence within sceptical arguments.

23 This conception of the distinction between epistemic internalism and epistemic externalism was introduced above, in fn. 4.

24 I am grateful to Dick Foley and Brent Madison for comments on some earlier drafts of this chapter.

References

Bates, J. (2013), 'Damming the Swamping Problem, Reliably', *Dialectica*, 67: 103–16.
Chalmers, D.C. (2002), 'Does Conceivability Entail Possibility?' in T.S. Gendler and J. Hawthorne (eds), *Conceivability and Possibility*, 145–200, Oxford: Oxford University Press.
Clarke, D.M. (2012), 'The Epistemology of Descartes', in S. Hetherington (ed.), *Epistemology: The Key Thinkers*, 90–110, London: Continuum.
Davis, W.A. and Jäger, C. (2012), 'Reliabilism and the Extra Value of Knowledge', *Philosophical Studies*, 157: 93–105.
Dougherty, T. (2011), 'Fallibilism', in S. Bernecker and D. Pritchard (eds), *The Routledge Companion to Epistemology*, 131–43, New York: Routledge.
Dutant, J. (2013), 'In Defence of Swamping', *Thought*, 2: 357–66.
Engel, M. (1992), 'Is Epistemic Luck Compatible with Knowledge?' *The Southern Journal of Philosophy*, 30: 59–75.

Engel, M. (2011), 'Epistemic Luck', *The Internet Encyclopedia of Philosophy*, URL: http://www.iep.utm.edu/epi-luck.
Fantl, J. and McGrath, M. (2009), *Knowledge in an Uncertain World*, New York: Oxford University Press.
Foley, R. (1987), *The Theory of Epistemic Rationality*, Cambridge, MA: Harvard University Press.
Foley, R. (2012), *When Is True Belief Knowledge?* Princeton: Princeton University Press.
Gettier, E.L. (1963), 'Is Justified True Belief Knowledge?' *Analysis*, 23: 121-3.
Goldman, A.I. (1999), *Knowledge in a Social World*, Oxford: Clarendon Press.
Hetherington, S. (1996), *Knowledge Puzzles: An Introduction to Epistemology*, Boulder, CO: Westview Press.
Hetherington, S. (1999), 'Knowing Failably', *The Journal of Philosophy*, 96: 565-87.
Hetherington, S. (2001), *Good Knowledge, Bad Knowledge: On Two Dogmas of Epistemology*, Oxford: Clarendon Press.
Hetherington, S. (2005), 'Fallibilism', *The Internet Encyclopedia of Philosophy*, URL: http://www.iep.utm.edu/f/fallibil.htm.
Hetherington, S. (2011), 'The Gettier Problem', in S. Bernecker and D. Pritchard (eds), *The Routledge Companion to Epistemology*, 119-30, New York: Routledge.
Hetherington, S. (2013), 'Skeptical Challenges and Knowing Actions', *Philosophical Issues*, 23: 18-39.
Hetherington, S. (2016a), *Knowledge and the Gettier Problem*, Cambridge: Cambridge University Press.
Hetherington, S. (2016b), 'Understanding Fallible Warrant and Fallible Knowledge: Three Proposals', *Pacific Philosophical Quarterly*, 97: 270-82.
Hetherington, S. (2018), 'Skepticism and Fallibilism', in D. Machuca and B. Reed (eds), *Skepticism: From Antiquity to the Present*, 609-19, London: Bloomsbury.
Hintikka, J. (1962), *Knowledge and Belief: An Introduction to the Logic of the Two Notions*, Ithaca, NY: Cornell University Press.
Howard-Snyder, D., Howard-Snyder, F., and Feit, N. (2003), 'Infallibilism and Gettier's Legacy', *Philosophy and Phenomenological Research*, 66: 304-27.
Kornblith, H. (1980), 'Beyond Foundationalism and the Coherence Theory', *The Journal of Philosophy*, 77: 597-612.
Kvanvig, J.L. (2003), *The Value of Knowledge and the Pursuit of Understanding*, Cambridge: Cambridge University Press.
Lycan, W.G. (1994), 'Sartwell's Minimalist Analysis of Knowing', *Philosophical Studies*, 73: 1-3.
McDowell, J. (2011), *Perception as a Capacity for Knowledge*, Milwaukee, WI: Marquette University Press.
Olsson, E.J. (2011), 'Reply to Kvanvig on the Swamping Problem', *Social Epistemology*, 25: 173-82.
Pritchard, D. (2005), *Epistemic Luck*, Oxford: Clarendon Press.
Pritchard, D. (2007), 'Anti-Luck Epistemology', *Synthese*, 158: 277-97.
Pritchard, D. (2009), *Knowledge*, Basingstoke: Palgrave Macmillan.
Pritchard, D. (2013), 'Knowledge Cannot Be Lucky', in M. Steup, J. Turri and E. Sosa (eds), *Contemporary Debates in Epistemology*, 2nd edn, 152-64, Malden, MA: Wiley Blackwell.
Pritchard, D. (2016), 'Epistemic Risk', *The Journal of Philosophy*, 113: 550-71.
Reed, B. (2000), 'Accidental Truth and Accidental Justification', *The Philosophical Quarterly*, 50: 57-67.

Reed, B. (2002), 'How to Think about Fallibilism', *Philosophical Studies*, 107: 143–57.
Reed, B. (2012), 'Fallibilism', *Philosophy Compass*, 7: 585–96.
Riggs, W. (2002), 'Reliability and the Value of Knowledge', *Philosophy and Phenomenological Research*, 64: 79–96.
Sackris, D., and Beebe, J.R. (2014), 'Is Justification Necessary for Knowledge?' in J.R. Beebe (ed.), *Advances in Experimental Epistemology*, 175–92, London: Bloomsbury.
Sartwell, C. (1991), 'Knowledge Is Merely True Belief', *American Philosophical Quarterly*, 28: 157–65.
Sartwell, C. (1992), 'Why Knowledge Is Merely True Belief', *The Journal of Philosophy*, 89: 167–80.
Shope, R.K. (1983), *The Analysis of Knowing: A Decade of Research*. Princeton: Princeton University Press.
Sosa, E. (1999), 'How Must Knowledge Be Modally Related to What Is Known?' *Philosophical Topics*, 26: 373–84.
Sosa, E. (2007), *A Virtue Epistemology: Apt Belief and Reflective Knowledge*, Vol. I, Oxford: Clarendon Press.
Sosa, E. (2011), *Knowing Full Well*, Princeton: Princeton University Press.
Warenski, L. (2014), 'Review of Foley (2012)', *Mind*, 123: 894–8.
Williamson, T. (2000), *Knowledge and Its Limits*, Oxford: Clarendon Press.
Zagzebski, L.T. (1994), 'The Inescapability of Gettier Problems', *The Philosophical Quarterly*, 44: 65–73.
Zagzebski, L.T. (2003), 'The Search for the Source of Epistemic Good', *Metaphilosophy*, 34: 12–28.

14

And next?

14.1 Progressing beyond Gettierism

The term 'post-Gettier epistemology' is capacious, encompassing many attempts to say what knowledge is, or is not, in light of Edmund Gettier's (1963) supposed result. Those myriad attempts include disagreements over details. But they converge too, upon what I call *Gettierism*, a 'bare' statement of which is this:

> A belief's being true and well justified (epistemically justified) is not enough to make it knowledge.

Epistemologists in general insist that this – *bare*-Gettierism – is true. But can they know that it is? The initial justification standardly offered is this: 'We know it by intuition! *Obviously* Smith within Gettier's job/coins case, for example, does not know that the person who will get the job has ten coins in his pocket. Ask even beginning epistemology students. They will say this, too. I see this uniformity in class after class, year after year.'[1]

With which assurance, philosophers proceed to *expand epistemologically* upon that 'intuitive' verdict, offering putatively explicative principles or theories of *how* their verdict is correct. They seek, in other words, to turn bare-Gettierism into *explicated*-Gettierism, telling us what has gone awry – and hence *how* it is that knowledge is absent – whenever a belief is 'Gettiered'. We find a range of such specifications within 'post-Gettier epistemology' (so-called, because bare-Gettierism is being presumed to be true, with a correlatively restricted range of consequences being 'in play' for what we should aim to say about knowledge's nature). We gain a sense of that range, by envisaging (as follows, albeit schematically) how such specifications are formed, aiming to formulate an explicated-Gettierism.

First, we seek to make explicit that what is involved is not a merely accidental correlation. The point, we accept, is that any belief's being Gettiered *precludes* its being knowledge. There is something *in* being Gettiered that precludes knowing.

Second, in order to understand such preclusion, we aim to instantiate this schematic form (finding illuminating values for 'X' and 'Y'):

> Any belief's being Gettiered precludes its being knowledge – *because* being Gettiered includes X, which – due to Y – precludes being knowledge.

Here, epistemologists talk of epistemically cognate or enriched versions of such phenomena as reliability, causality, defeat (evidential or circumstantial), safety, sensitivity, virtuous belief-formation and veritic luck. Professionally notable careers have been (and still are) built around such approaches. We might be told, for example, that no Gettiered belief has been formed in a way that is epistemically virtuous (this is a value of 'X') – and maybe that this reflects a deficiency of epistemic agency (this is a value of 'Y'), entailing that any Gettiered belief is thereby precluded from being knowledge.

That should be familiar to anyone seeking to move beyond bare-Gettierism, onwards to an adequate explicated-Gettierism. But the news from my *Knowledge and the Gettier Problem* (2016) is that no such attempts have succeeded. I did not reach this conclusion by working through each kind of theory, noting specific flaws. No, I developed detailed arguments of principle. I argued that post-Gettier epistemology, centred upon at least a bare-Getterism and often striving for an explicated-Gettierism, has been misleading itself – fundamentally so. I accept that it has included engaging and potentially fruitful descriptions of aspects of the epistemic world. But basic changes are needed, even so. We should *revisit* what was at stake in, let alone established by, Gettier's challenge.[2]

Here is a brief sense of how that book's main worry begins.[3]

- Each value of 'X' that has been offered depends, somewhere within its thinking (in its specification of 'Y'), on the view that, whenever a belief is Gettiered, *some form of significant (and perhaps abnormal) susceptibility to falsity* was present, given some aspect of the circumstance C in which the belief has been formed.[4]
- But a belief's *being Gettiered* includes its *being true*. (This is definitionally so.)
- Hence, there is no possible situation or world where a belief, *while being Gettiered*, is false.
- But any instance of explicated-Gettierism is, or entails, this:

    Any belief's being Gettiered precludes its being knowledge – because it is impossible for a belief to *be* Gettiered *while* being knowledge.

- So, if an instance of explicated-Gettierism is to be true, at least one possible situation or world includes a belief that, *while* being Gettiered, is not knowledge.
- But there is no possible situation or world where a belief, *while* being Gettiered, is not knowledge *because* it is false.
- Consider all of the possible situations or worlds as like this world, say, as possible, *given* that, within each, the belief in question is Gettiered (as it is within this world). Within *none* of them is that belief Gettiered and thereby not knowledge because of falsity.
- So, there is *no* relevantly possible situation or world where a belief, *while being* Gettiered, is not knowledge due to falsity.
- Hence, it is impossible to justify a completed statement of explicated-Gettierism, insofar as that statement needs there to be at least some possible situation or world where a belief, while being Gettiered, is not knowledge due to falsity.

- That is an excellent reason, for any epistemologist seeking such explicative insight, to discard bare-Gettierism (even if 'intuition' supports it).[5]

For example, when B is a specific Gettiered belief, we might be encouraged to ask whether, given circumstance C (maybe along with a would-be explication's favoured 'X'), producing B might easily have resulted in a false belief. Suppose that this *is* so: for instance, in *many* possible worlds where C obtains and B results, B is false. (This is plausible, given the oddity present within any Gettier case.) On my argument from above, however, this point about C and B fails to justify an explicated-Gettierism. For the very fact of B's being false in those possible situations entails that none of them is a situation where B's *being Gettiered* is present. So, none is a possible situation where B *is Gettiered and thereby* fails (due to being false there) to be knowledge.

To that reasoning, Gettieristic epistemologists might reply in this way.

Those situations are possible ways in which being in C is *already* enough for B's failing to be knowledge. B is Gettiered within C (since C *is* the Gettier-odd aspect of the situation). This is because of how easily a false belief could have resulted, *given C*. We might model this by envisaging possible situations where B and C appear, and where (unsurprisingly) B is false – *without* B needing also to be Gettiered within those other situations. Because of those *other* situations (where B is not still being Gettiered), B is not knowledge within its *actual* situation, where it *is* being Gettiered.

But this, although 'textbook' thinking, is beside the point.[6] It amounts only to how easily *being in C* might preclude a belief's being knowledge. It does not, however, amount to how easily *being Gettiered* (which might include being in C, but definitely includes being true) precludes a belief's being knowledge. Being in C might be a danger to knowing, even if being in C and forming a true B is not. But only with the *latter* pairing (C plus a true B) are we in a Gettier case. Being Gettiered is more than being true, of course; it does include some circumstance such as C; and this is where, we can agree, the threat lies to being knowledge. The nature of that threat, however, is not where we are being told it is. Yes, there are circumstances C within a Gettier case that lower dramatically the chance of forming a true belief that is knowledge. Yet this is at least partly because the circumstances lower dramatically the chance of forming a true belief *at all*. I concede that this – thanks to those circumstances – is a weakness in one's epistemic situation within a Gettier case. But even this, I argue, does not entail that, when a true belief *has* been formed, that weakness persists: the danger has *passed*, at least within a Gettier situation. It has not been *realized*. The circumstance that *was* the danger is still present; no matter, though, once we are asking only the second of the following questions:

- Given C, is there a danger that B, if formed, will not be knowledge? (After all, it is likely not to be true.)
- Even given C, is B, now that it is formed and is true, not knowledge?

To provide an explicated-Gettierism would be to answer the second question. But standard epistemological discussions proceed as if unable to move beyond the first question.

My argument, sketched above, respects that choice. We must adjust epistemologically to the fact that, in spite of the danger posed by the case's odd circumstance, a true belief *has* arisen. This aspect of the case, once in place, *cannot be set aside* when we are examining alternative possible situations. That is, it cannot be set aside once we are trying to model whether *being Gettiered* precludes being knowledge. I accept that, given C, a true B might easily not have arisen. But this entails, too, that a *Gettiered* B might easily not have arisen. It is therefore *not* a way of modelling how, *given B's being Gettiered*, B is failing to be knowledge. Since B is true, if we ask whether it is knowledge, given *its being true but also formed within C*, we must examine alternative possible situations where, again, *it is true but also formed within C*. Although those textbook accounts describe alternative possible situations where B is formed within C, they set aside its being true. They thereby set aside *the fact of its being Gettiered* – which needed *not* to be set aside, if we were to be justifying an explicated-Gettierism.

This anti-textbook thinking easily defuses what is probably the standard Gettieristic approach. We are often advised to focus on *the way W in which* a Gettiered belief B has been formed. Think of how easily W might have led to a false belief, rather than to the true belief arising in the specific Gettier case. But everything that I said a moment ago about C applies equally to W. For (depending on how we describe the particular way of forming B, and how we describe the particular C) W *is simply an instance of* C, as C has featured in the past few paragraphs.

In which event, epistemologists are not only mistaken, but badly so, in how they have sought, year upon year, a satisfactory explicated-Gettierism. How could this be so?

I have two diagnostic comments. One is about methodology and metaphysics. The other concerns 'intuitions' and knowledge assessments.

Metaphysics enters because I believe that epistemologists are not directing their would-be explicative efforts at the appropriate *explanandum*. The correct challenge is not to explain why *B the belief* (that happens to be Gettiered) is not knowledge. The correct challenge is to explain why *B's being Gettiered* is not knowledge. We need to be told why B is not knowledge *due to* being Gettiered – more precisely, *while and in* being Gettiered. And the latter is a state of affairs – not an individual (such as B) *within* that state of affairs.

In *Knowledge and the Gettier Problem* (2016: 13–14), I posed the explicative challenge in terms of the following distinction.

> *Individual-Gettierism.* For any belief, it is necessarily true that, if the belief is Gettiered, it is not knowledge.
>
>> More formally, for any belief B and any accessible possible world W, within W this is true: <B is Gettiered ⊃ B is not knowledge>.
>
> *Instantiated-property Gettierism.*[7] Necessarily, instantiating the property of being Gettiered precludes instantiating the property of being knowledge.

More formally, for any belief B and any accessible possible world W ∈ {w: B is Gettiered within w}, W ∉ {w: B is knowledge within w}.

Or, equally, for any belief B and any accessible possible world W ∈ {w: B instantiates, within w, the property of being Gettiered}, W ∉ {w: B instantiates, within w, the property of being knowledge}.

A property's being instantiated amounts to a *state of affairs*. And identifying a state of affairs across alternative possible situations is clearly different to identifying, across such situations, some *element* from within that state of affairs. We are not identifying *B's being Gettiered* across possible worlds if we are identifying merely B, or even B plus C/W, across possible worlds. As soon as we set aside B's *being true*, when identifying just B, or even B plus C/W, across possible worlds, *we are no longer identifying B's-being-Gettiered* across those worlds. Hence, we are not (i) focusing *on* B's being Gettiered, and (ii) charting what further properties (such as being knowledge) must, or must not, be *accompanying* that focus (B's being Gettiered). Yet this combination *is* what is needed if we are to reach a satisfactory explicated-Gettierism.

What, then, of bare-Gettierism? How much weight should epistemologists give to their 'intuitive' assessments of Gettiered beliefs as failing to be knowledge? Presumably, we are to welcome the 'speed' with which 'intuition' delivers its insights, along with the lack of supporting argument needed in moments of 'intuition'. In a correlative spirit, then, I will raise a few 'speedy' questions about how compelling we should find our professionally entrenched 'Gettier intuitions'.[8]

- How can one know that one *is* being genuinely 'intuitive' when responding to a Gettier case?
- Even if one is being so, what does this achieve? How can one know that one is thereby likely to be *accurate* in one's view of the case?
- Relatedly, how can one know that one is applying appropriate *criteria* in evaluating the case? *Knowledge and the Gettier Problem* examined (in Chapter 6) whether standard 'intuitive' responses to Getter cases are applying the *fallibilist* standard that – given how Gettier (1963: 121) framed his cases – is apt.

That final question is telling. For that chapter's conclusion (2016: ch. 6) was that, if epistemologists really are being 'intuitive', this is already reason to believe that they are being unwittingly *in*fallibilist. In which case, they have moved too far away from how Gettier framed his cases. They might well be unwittingly – 'intuitively' – deeming any Gettiered belief not to be knowledge, *merely because*, when all is said and done, the belief is justified *only fallibly*. If so, then philosophers have been responding confusedly to Gettier's cases from the very outset of post-Gettier epistemology.[9]

14.2 Knowing as burrowing

Before *Knowledge and the Gettier Problem* (2016) did battle with post-Gettier epistemology, *How to Know* (2011) questioned several distinctive marks of 'the standard analytic conception of knowledge' (2011: 1). It also suggested ways in which we might conceive *anew* of knowledge. One of those proposals (in Chapter 5) was the idea of *how-knowledge*. What is this? What might it contribute to epistemology?

First, we must distinguish it from knowledge-how (at least initially). The latter is knowledge-how-*to* – knowledge how *to do* some action, or kind of action. We might call how-knowledge knowledge-how-*is*, except that the difference between this and knowledge-how-to would inevitably be lost in practice. How-knowledge that *p* is knowledge *of how it is that p*.

Here is an example of what I had in mind:

> in knowing that you are looking at a goldfinch, most likely you know not only the truth that you are looking at a goldfinch. Probably, you also know truths that report *elements* or *parts* of the truth-with-some-complexity that is your looking at a goldfinch. You could know something of the animal's plumage, its size, its movements, its call, and so on. You may well know aspects of what makes the animal a goldfinch rather than something else [...]
>
> (2011: 170)

More recently, I have conveyed the idea slightly differently:

> When someone claims to know 'That's a barn', for instance, she claims knowledge of an aspect of reality. She *sums up* this knowledge with words apparently reporting a single fact: 'That's a barn.' But this fact is constituted by further facts, its 'contained' details. That is a barn; *how* is it a barn? Specific pieces of wood are arranged thus-and-so; particular nails are used, etc. 'Deeper' facts underlie those ones, interlinking them, such as laws of woodwork, of engineering, even of physics. Perhaps social facts contribute, so that this is a barn and not an art installation. All of these are facts 'within' that first fact, collectively summed up as 'That's a barn.' A fact can thus include further facts, as a topic can include facts. [...] This *metaphysical* complexity within a fact suggests part of an *epistemological* picture of knowing that fact: one might know the fact by knowing facts 'within' it. In knowing that an object is a barn, one might know some of those further facts mentioned a moment ago – because they are 'within' the fact being known (the fact that the object is a barn).
>
> (2019: 92–3)

And once we adopt such a picture, inviting epistemological possibilities are soon flowering, including some that might allow us to reframe some familiar debates. I will mention just a few.

Metaphysics. When someone claims to know that *p*, are they really saying that they have a cognitive relationship to ... a proposition? We can *represent* their knowledge by using a sentence with a propositional form. But that is not the knowing's *being* a relationship to a proposition. I suggest that how-knowledge is a relationship to a fact, or a state of affairs. Is that a step towards epistemological truth? It is at least an implicit invitation for epistemologists to revisit some apposite metaphysical questions that used to be treated as more pressing.[10]

Depths. Although I know that the earth is not flat, many people know this fact *much more deeply* than I do. This is easily modelled with the idea of how-knowledge. The earth's not being flat is composed of many *further* facts. And any relevant scientist knows many more of these than I do. We might regard her as knowing more 'hidden depths' within the fact of the earth's not being flat. She knows *more deeply into* the fact in question:

> knowing is always more or less detailed and full in its engagement with a fact F. Any knowing of F 'burrows' more, or less, deeply into the range of facts 'within' F (whatever facts are joining together to constitute F). So, F is being known more – or less – deeply, depending on *how many of the constituently significant facts within* F *are being known*.
> (Hetherington 2019: 94)

(For now, I call this a *burrowing* conception of knowing.)

Grades. That picture points to the possibility of there being better, or worse, knowledge even of a specific fact. Each of those scientists knows *much better* than I do the fact of the earth's not being flat. They know *far more* of what is 'inside' that fact, helping to constitute it as this specific fact. There is hope, though. Maybe years of study will *improve* my knowledge of the fact that the earth is not flat.[11]

Scepticism. At least some traditional sceptical arguments can fade away once we conceive of knowing as burrowing.

Consider a Cartesian dreaming argument for external world scepticism. You are asked to know that you are not dreaming that p (where 'p' is ostensibly about the physical world), as a necessary precondition of knowing that p. This knowing that p is said to depend on your ostensibly sensory evidence of p – evidence that could, however, be present merely as part of your being in a state of *dreaming*.

But here is some counter-reasoning.

- Let 'p' be 'This is a barn.' Let 'd' be 'I am dreaming its seeming to me that this is a barn.'
- On the burrowing conception, to know that p is *literally* to know enough of whatever other factors, such as further facts, are *literally* constituting the fact that p.[12]
- But not-d is not one of those further facts.
- Hence, your knowing that p would *not itself be literally constituted by*, even in part, the knowledge that not-d.
- Hence, it is metaphysically misplaced to insist that knowing that p requires knowing that not-d.

The burrowing account also helps to show where the sceptic's demand *does* have a role.

- Your knowing that not-*d* *would* be literally a (needed) part of knowing that your *ostensibly* sensory evidence for *p is really* sensory evidence for *p*.
- For the fact of not-*d* would be literally a (needed) part of the fact of your ostensibly sensory evidence for *p* being really sensory evidence for *p*.
- Hence, if we insist on your knowing that not-*d*, this demand is readily interpreted as insisting on your knowing something further *of which not-d is a needed part*.
- And this, we see, is *your ostensibly sensory evidence really being sensory*.
- So, we are insisting on your knowing that not-*d*, as part of insisting on your knowing that *your ostensibly sensory evidence really is sensory*.
- But then we may repeat that style of reasoning, applying it to that newly mentioned knowledge: of what further knowledge is *that* knowledge (about your ostensibly sensory evidence's *bona fides*) a needed part?
- It is perhaps most easily interpreted as a needed part of your *knowing that* you know that *p*.

There it is: the classic Cartesian dreaming challenge is perhaps best directed at *knowing that* one knows that *p* – not at knowing that *p*. Yet the latter (for any external world '*p*') was the challenge's claimed target. The burrowing conception of knowledge thus allows a simple reinterpretation, indeed a dissolution, of that challenge.

Knowing-first. Maybe surprisingly, the burrowing conception accommodates one of the main ideas behind a 'knowledge-first epistemology', the programme associated closely with Williamson (2000). I say 'surprisingly' as a comment on myself: I am not drawn to that programme. So, let me frame this immediate discussion differently: it is to the credit of knowledge-first epistemology that, whatever other shortcomings it has,[13] one of its main ideas could be accommodated within a burrowing conception of knowledge.

This is because a burrowing conception allows there to be knowledge 'all the way down', a point able to be supplemented in interesting ways.

- It might be that, for some fact or state of affairs, you know it by *knowing* many of its constituent facts or states of affairs. And, in some epistemological discussions, this guiding way of talking might be enough for making whatever explanatory progress is being sought (as occurred a moment ago, regarding Cartesian dreaming scepticism). This, I take it, is in the spirit of one of the main ideas behind the knowledge-first programme.
- That idea's scope can be increased, if not all knowledge is directed at facts or states of affairs (these being what I have mentioned so far). In knowing that the object in front of you is a barn, you know a fact, part of which might be argued to be *the object* itself. Do you know *it* as part of knowing the fact? If so, this probably involves knowing further facts, about it. But even if your knowing the object is not thereby your knowing only facts (such as if some form of knowledge-by-acquaintance is involved), this complexity can be accommodated by the burrowing conception, which allows any instance of knowing that X to encompass knowing *whatever* aspects of reality are part of *how X is actually constituted*

(whatever X is). These aspects can include facts, but might also include objects, events, and more besides.
- We might even expand the scope of the burrowing conception's guiding idea by letting it include knowing-how – one's knowing *how to* perform various associated actions, such as perceptual ones, inferential ones, linguistic ones, communicative ones, etc. For example, maybe your knowing that the object in front of you is a barn includes some instances of knowledge-how, such as your knowing how to answer questions about what you are seeing.

So, I suggest that the burrowing conception can accommodate (while possibly moving beyond) that idea from the knowledge-first programme. It can also embrace some of that programme's other ideas. For example, on both knowledge-first and knowledge-as-burrowing, we *need not* be talking about anything more than knowledge, in populating our epistemic world. Equally, if (as Williamson argues) knowledge is a normative standard for believing, or for action, say, this is equally true on a knowledge-as-burrowing account. Still, to what extent *should* we hold knowledge-as-burrowing answerable to the further elements of Williamson's knowledge-first programme? Here I cannot improve on McGlynn (2014):

> Like all promises to end politics as usual, knowledge first philosophy's promise has proved empty. If the pattern of counterexamples found in the post-Gettier literature were a symptom of the pursuit of a bad research programme – the pursuit of analyses – then we would expect to find that abandoning that research programme would result in a break in the pattern. [But] this hasn't happened. On the contrary, the approach has been plagued by apparent counterexamples, often running into problems with the very examples that cropped up in the Gettier literature.
>
> (2014: 172–3)

The knowledge-first programme's initial motivation, too, was uncompelling. (And here we meet the programme's other main idea, which I am *not* accommodating.) Williamson cited the supposed failure of post-Gettier epistemology's collective effort to find a conceptual analysis of knowledge. He thereupon turned his back upon a previously dominant programme – the quest for that conceptual analysis, exemplified by those post-Gettier efforts. As McGlynn says: 'Perhaps the one nonnegotiable commitment for a proponent of knowledge first philosophy is that knowledge is not analysable, in anything like the sense proposed in the literature generated by Gettier' (2014: 15). However, we are not obliged to join Williamson in inferring, from those repeated failures, that conceptual analysis was the culprit.[14] For a start, before drawing dramatic conclusions from those failures, we should be sure that epistemologists have actually been engaging with Gettier's challenge as well as was *needed*, if a real analysis was to be attained of why being Gettiered preclude being knowledge. But Section 14.1 points to a strong reason for *doubting* that epistemologists have been guiltless in that respect.[15] Correlatively, we have strong reason to stay with conceptual analysis, at least for a while – using it *better*, though, as we seek to understand Gettier's challenge. The key failing in post-Gettier epistemology has never, if I am correct, been the use of conceptual analysis as such. The key failings have long been in *how* it is used, as well as in the Gettieristic *expectations* that have propelled and sustained it since 1963.

Notes

1. I still encounter this form of comment, in spite of the growth of experimental philosophy, with its origins in Weinberg *et al.*'s (2001) paper that included a significant percentage of respondents *not* providing this sort of initial verdict on the 'Gettier cases' with which they were presented. Soon, I will comment briefly on 'intuitions' and post-Gettier epistemology.
2. Some will reply thus: 'Yes, which is why Williamson's (2000) *knowledge-first* programme is energising.' I comment below on how we might retain something of a knowledge-first epistemology, if that is our wont, without following Williamson's lead.
3. For the full argument, see Hetherington (2016: chs 2–4).
4. For details underlying this claim, see Hetherington (2016: sec. 2.2). See Zagzebski (1994) for a simpler version of this point. The significant chance of falsity need not be what is *highlighted* by a given epistemologist. It is a necessary element, though, possibly being taken for granted when we are being encouraged to appreciate the conceptual richness of a suggested value of 'X' and its associated 'Y'.
5. Soon I will say more about the power, or otherwise, of 'intuition' in this context.
6. If I am right, those epistemology textbooks *are* mistaken, no matter how many of them repeat their shared mistake. There is professional safety, but not always truth, in such numbers.
7. Earlier, I called this, slightly less helpfully, 'property-Gettierism' (Hetherington 2016: 14).
8. For a 'slower' discussion of this, see Hetherington (2016: ch. 6).
9. All of this makes *Knowledge and the Gettier Problem* sound purely critical. Mostly, it is. But it ends with a compatibilist proposal for an improved post-post-Gettier epistemological future. I show how to blend (i) the usual assessment of any Gettiered belief (as not being knowledge) with (ii) a *non-reductive* view of knowledge as only ever justified-true-belief.
10. On the idea that knowledge is a relation to a state of affairs, and that belief is not (because it is a relation to a proposition), see Vendler (1972: ch. V) and Sayre (1997: ch. 5), for example.
11. For more on the basic idea of better, or worse, knowledge of a specific *p*, see Hetherington (2001).
12. This is obviously a somewhat vague formulation (although precise enough for the immediate setting). For more details, see Hetherington (2011: ch. 5).
13. For critical discussion, see the non-Williamson contributions to Greenough and Pritchard (2009) and McGlynn (2014).
14. See Hetherington (2022: sec. 6.3). I should also note that Williamson did not rely only on the supposed failures of post-Gettier epistemologists to agree on a conceptual analysis of knowledge. He also discussed (2000: ch. 1) conceptual analysis *per se*, why even in principle it would not be able to help us to understand the nature of knowing, and why (by thinking of knowledge purely as a kind of mental state) he

would be able to bypass it in providing just such an understanding. Nonetheless, here I bypass that discussion, since I accept Cassam's (2009) criticisms of Williamson on these points.
15 And Williamson has been no less guilty of this failing. He has not improved on epistemological orthodoxy in this respect (Hetherington 2011: sec. 3.16).

References

Cassam, Q. (2009), 'Can the Concept of Knowledge Be Analysed?' in Greenough and Pritchard (2009), 12–30.
Gettier, E.L. (1963), 'Is Justified True Belief Knowledge?', *Analysis*, 23: 121–3.
Greenough, P. and Pritchard, D. (eds) (2009), *Williamson on Knowledge*, Oxford: Oxford University Press.
Hetherington, S. (2001), *Good Knowledge, Bad Knowledge: On Two Dogmas of Epistemology*, Oxford: Clarendon Press.
Hetherington, S. (2011), *How to Know: A Practicalist Conception of Knowledge*, Malden, MA: Wiley-Blackwell.
Hetherington, S. (2016), *Knowledge and the Gettier Problem*, Cambridge: Cambridge University Press.
Hetherington, S. (2019), *What Is Epistemology?* Cambridge: Polity Press.
Hetherington, S. (2021), 'Gettier's *Actual* Challenge: Methodology and Metaphysics', in E. Alves, J.R. Fett and K. Etcheverry (eds), *Socratically: A Festschrift in Honor of Claudio de Almeida*, 583–611, Porto Alegre: EDIPUCRS.
Hetherington, S. (2022), *Defining Knowledge: Method and Metaphysics*, Cambridge: Cambridge University Press.
McGlynn, A. (2014), *Knowledge First?* Basingstoke: Palgrave Macmillan.
Sayre, K.M. (1997), *Belief and Knowledge: Mapping the Cognitive Landscape*, Lanham, MD: Rowman & Littlefield.
Vendler, Z. (1972), *Res Cogitans: An Essay in Rational Psychology*, Ithaca, NY: Cornell University Press.
Weinberg, J.M., Nichols, S. and Stich, S. (2001), 'Normativity and Epistemic Intuitions', *Philosophical Topics*, 29: 429–60.
Williamson, T. (2000), *Knowledge and Its Limits*, Oxford: Clarendon Press.
Zagzebski, L.T. (1994), 'The Inescapability of Gettier Problems', *Philosophical Quarterly*, 44: 65–73.

15

A life in philosophy

We close this collection with a candid discussion we had with Stephen Hetherington about his early life, his work as a philosopher, the motivations that led him to pursue epistemology and the original ideas he contributed in this field of philosophy. Readers may find the autobiographical nature of this chapter helpful in understanding the development of Stephen's overall philosophical outlook.

1. Where were you born and raised? What was your childhood like? Did you have an inkling about getting into philosophy early on?

Ah, we begin with the difficult questions!
Born and raised in Sydney, I lived close to native bushland and beautiful Sydney Harbour. I could easily find quiet places to sit alone, bush behind me, water before me, climbing around rocky foreshores at low tide. Living also near Sydney's main zoo, on cloudy days I could hear lions roaring and hyenas calling. So, distinctive silences *and* sounds.

My childhood was slightly unusual, for a few family reasons.
My father – Norman Hetherington (1921–2010) – was a puppeteer. For forty years, his main character Mr Squiggle, a marionette, was a constant on Australian TV (on the ABC, the national public broadcaster). Dad *was* Mr Squiggle. He created, voiced, and manipulated Mr Squiggle, along with the show's other puppet characters. Mr Squiggle was beloved around Australia, turning children's 'squiggles' into cartoons, right there on screen, even 'live' in the early days. He used his nose, which was a large pencil, by moving his head this way and that, thanks to a bendy and extendable neck. Almost no one could have done this with a puppet, certainly not as well as Dad did it. He had been a successful political cartoonist before becoming a puppeteer. Those early skills found a surprising home on TV, in the 'person' of Mr Squiggle. The show ran from 1959 through 1999, covering my entire childhood (and more). Mr Squiggle was (as they say) world-famous within Australia. Dad's 2010 death was a news headline around the country.

The show's fame meant that, during my school years, I was often known as 'the son of Mr Squiggle'. This was generally enjoyable, given how much everyone liked Squiggle. Unlike my friends, though, I could not complain about my family, especially my father. Everyone knew who he was. Everyone assumed that he must be lovable. Everyone thought that it had to be great fun, 'having Mr Squiggle as your father'. But Dad and I clashed a lot, which I suffered in silent loyalty to my family's public face. Dad was talented, creative, hard-working – and an alpha-male. Thankfully, I am not an alpha-male.

I went to an academically renowned high school, the one that Dad attended – Fort Street. It was Australia's first public (= state) high school, from 1849. Entry was highly selective. I won many academic prizes there. (But I also spent a *lot* of time running frenetically around the playground, typically chasing a ball. I was obsessed with cricket for a few years and continued – no longer obsessively – playing it at Sydney University and Oxford.) My intellectual tastes and abilities developed early. Perhaps the main influence was my reading widely and precociously among my mother's extensive collection of classic and obscure literature, poetry and essays. Some of that reading had philosophical elements. Yet I had no idea of the existence of philosophy as such. My favourite author then – as now – was P.G. Wodehouse, the twentieth century's greatest English-language humourist. (How did he not win the Nobel Prize for Literature? A disgrace! His best book? *Joy in the Morning*, in my view.) I enjoyed school and my friends. School took me away from my family, allowing me to be cheerful, chatty, and jokey

My mother (1923–2022) had some relevantly interesting qualities when I was young.

Dad and she wrote the scripts for Mr Squiggle. (As a child, I would often sit beside them during the writing.) In later years, however, Mum took full public credit for the scripts (and Dad, to keep peace at home, let her do so). For many years, Australian journalists have routinely repeated that falsehood.

Mum was serious about studying and practising astrology, having friends among Sydney's professional astrologers. As a boy, I attended several of their meetings, which were intriguing. Philosophers unhesitatingly dismiss astrology as wholly irrational; what I observed was more intellectually respectable than some other supposedly rational settings that I have experienced.

Mum was also involved in local environmental battles. Living where we did (Mosman), threats to native bushland were a constant, from 'developers' and rich homeowners 'improving their views' over Sydney Harbour. I was introduced early to the world of local government and 'green' issues. I have never lost those sympathies.

2. How did you get into philosophy? Who were your teachers? Who had the most philosophical impact on you?

I am grateful to my mother for two main things that bore upon my studying philosophy.

First, my studying *anything* at university was non-trivially helped by her. Astoundingly (given my academic record at school), Dad was resistant to my attending university. To him, I was perfectly capable of getting a job – hence of not 'lounging around at home' while he worked hard, earning money! It was Mum who encouraged me to take on a part-time job as a puppeteer, taking some pressure off

Dad. I did this for my four years at Sydney University. Dad was appeased (and later was proud of my academic achievements, insofar as he understood them).

Second, my mother said to the seventeen-year-old me, 'You might find philosophy interesting.' I was heading to Sydney University as an Arts/Law student. The Law subjects would be mandated. The Arts subjects were my choice. With no idea of what philosophy was, I headed towards the 'philosophy desk' in the enrolment area because of Mum's comment. I liked the philosophy tutor, who helped me to choose my subjects. (She turned out to be the sister of an ABC TV producer who had worked on *Mr Squiggle* a few years earlier.) Prior to Mum's comment, I had drawn a pencil line through 'Philosophy', in the list of Arts departments. I never asked Mum why she made that comment. It probably reflected how easily (and well) I wrote school essays, especially on comparatively abstract intellectual books, poems and plays. I had even, when told to write a sonnet for the school magazine, created 'The Hetheringtonian Sonnet' – which mainly explained why it was not any existing form of sonnet. Youthful confidence!

Anyway, having begun my university studies, I was lucky to have outstanding philosophy teachers, initially at Sydney, later at Oxford and Pittsburgh.

At Sydney, my main teachers were David Stove, D.M. Armstrong, Keith Campbell, Michael Devitt, William Lycan (visiting) and John Bacon. At Oxford, I was taught by P.F. Strawson, Christopher Peacocke, John McDowell and Simon Blackburn (who supervised my B Phil Thesis). At Pitt, my teachers included Wilfrid Sellars, Mary Louise Gill, Shelly Kagan, Nicholas Rescher, Richmond Thomason, Gerald Massey, Carl Hempel, Wesley Salmon, Alexander Nehamas, Annette Baier (audited) and Joseph Camp (who supervised my PhD Dissertation). I was Nuel Belnap's research assistant for a year. I doubt that I could have had a more impressive range of teachers.

Who among my teachers had the strongest impact? The early impacts were probably the most vital. Stove and Armstrong were outstanding exemplars of clarity, abstractness and rigour. They also treated me with respect, Stove particularly. This gave me philosophical and personal confidence.

Lycan introduced me, in 1978, to 'the Gettier problem'. Visiting from Ohio State, his energy and enthusiasm, plus the sense of witnessing professional philosophical back-and-forth on something important unfolding 'in real time', made me eager for each week's class meeting. Unprompted, I began formulating and writing ideas of my own about self-justifying theories of justification.

Another undergraduate incident is worth mentioning. Armstrong, commenting on an essay of mine (on Locke, in 1978, my year 2), said 'Stephen, I do hope that you are not going to be one of those philosophers who puts their most interesting material in footnotes.' At times, I have followed this advice; at other times, not so much. But I valued Armstrong's attention and respect.

My enthusiasm for philosophy began early, in year 1 at Sydney University. Stove and Armstrong, among the teachers; Plato, logic and Berkeley, among the topics. My main essay for the year was a sustained defence of Berkeley's account of material objects. I never felt intellectual or emotional barriers when reading philosophy. I was 'at home' from the outset. During that first year, learning of the existence of Honours degrees, I set my sights on that. My Law studies continued, dutifully and dully, without enthusiasm. Then, in 1980, my philosophy Honours year was a joy. I wrote a Thesis on sentential non-significance – category mistakes – with John Bacon as an attentive and precise supervisor. (And although he was not my teacher, I should mention Richard Routley at ANU, whose writing on my Thesis topic I loved.) A whole year on philosophy! It was great. (It was also 'pre-professionally' profitable. Two of my Honours essays became my first two publications, in *Canadian Journal of Philosophy* and *Australasian Journal of Philosophy*. Many years later, feeling gratitude, excitement, and responsibility, I became Editor-in-Chief of the latter journal.)

In 1981, I happily suspended my Law degree, staying with philosophy. Whereupon, a few weeks later – a miracle! I was awarded a Travelling Scholarship by Sydney University; several months later, I was indeed travelling – to Oxford. (The scholarship was endowed in 1876/88/89, in the university's beginning years.) I could not have been happier. That changed my life. Without the scholarship, without Oxford and its wealth of powerful philosophy and friendly people, I might *easily* have drifted away from philosophy, early in the 1980s. Thankfully, my Oxford experience was fantastic. I was at New College, one of the prettiest and grandest colleges; and – please indulge my mentioning this – I had my best-ever bowling figures, 8/32, playing cricket for the college.

But soon I was leaving behind cricket and Oxford, heading to Pittsburgh. This was an exciting opportunity, especially given my main interests at the time in philosophy of language, philosophical logic and metaphysics – all strengths of Pitt's. (David Lewis, in letters encouraging me to enrol at Princeton, acknowledged that Pitt was also good for me, given those interests. The Pitt/Princeton choice was difficult.) After reaching Pitt, however, it did not take long to confront, once more, the real possibility of a life-not-in-philosophy. I almost limped away from Pitt after my first year (1983–4). In that year's second semester, I had glandular fever (mononucleosis), which led swiftly to chronic fatigue syndrome. My teachers did not know this. As my second year approached, in 1984, I was considering leaving the programme, given how exhausted and weak I was. I had to tell John Haugeland (Director of Graduate Studies), and – sympathetically – he helped ease me into my second year. I managed to stay, albeit affected by tiredness and 'brain fog' for the rest of my time at Pitt. I moved quickly through the programme, while never – alas – having the mental energy or sharpness with which I had entered it. I went 'on the job market' earlier than would be normal (at least a year early, in late 1986). It had been a stressful and physically debilitating period. I was tired of being a student. I wanted to leave.

I had a few job offers. One was tenure-track, at West Virginia University. I was very grateful for that opportunity and I enjoyed Morgantown. Virginia Klenk, my WVU department chairperson, was extremely supportive, a lovely person, an excellent 'boss'. I gained much confidence as a teacher at WVU, especially with upper-level classes. Even so, I was still struggling with the chronic fatigue, often becoming quite ill. It took me years to overcome some of those physical susceptibilities. They began easing only after I returned to Australia.

For yes, early in my third year at WVU, my mother alerted me to an advertisement in a Sydney newspaper. The University of New South Wales (UNSW) wanted a new philosophy lecturer. Finally! A substantial Australian philosophy position. This was at the close of 1989, after a decade in which, as far as I know, Australia offered no new continuing (tenure-track) philosophy jobs. I often felt homesick for Sydney and Australia, when living in the United States. This was pre-internet, meaning that, in practice, I was living fully as an American, since my country had almost no existence in American news reports. A year could pass without Australia being mentioned – anywhere, by anyone. This was understandable; I am not being critical of the United States. I willingly lived in a 'normal American' way. But I missed my homeland. I applied to UNSW – and, luckily, was offered the position.

I saw out that academic year with WVU, before leaving for Sydney in mid-1990, newly married and eager to be returning to Australia. Slowly, my health stabilized in what was, for me, a more congenial climate. (I do not like even Sydney winters. Yet they are mild, by world standards.) Slowly, I settled into being a philosopher within Australia.

And that is where my career took shape. I never thought about leaving Australia for philosophy study until, in year 2 at Sydney University, Lycan volunteered to me that the only philosophy jobs in the world (this was the late 1970s) were in the United States; that American departments favoured American PhDs; that Pitt and Princeton had the top two programmes; but that one foreign degree was highly regarded – Oxford's B Phil. From then onwards, I dreamed of following that path. I have always been thankful to Lycan for that advice and encouragement. I knew almost nothing about the wider world of philosophy study, or philosophy as a potential profession. Over the next several years, however, I was fortunate enough to travel – walking, crawling, limping, and dashing – along that path described for me by Lycan.

3. Lycan's influence must have been strong, since much of your work (as evidenced by this collection) is on topics related to Gettier's problem. But what do you think the Gettier problem is really about? Could you discuss what you think is wrong with the supposed solutions given to it throughout the years?

As I mentioned earlier, Lycan did implant within me, in 1978, a sense of urgency and enthusiasm about the Getter problem. But I did not remain focused on Gettier. I returned to this topic several years later, at Pitt, for a chapter of my PhD dissertation. That dissertation was titled – provocatively (without intending any disrespect) – *Narcissistic Epistemology*. I argued for much epistemological thinking's being too 'inward-looking', in various ways.

My motivating question was simple. Have some debates about knowledge and justification been framed in ways that amount to epistemologists *projecting* their ways of thinking onto their epistemic subjects? Is this why various debates look as they do? Think of internalism vs externalism. Think of knowing vs knowing that one knows. Think perhaps of foundations vs coherence. Think of regress, and various classic sceptical challenges. How reflective, how self-aware, how context-aware, must one be, when knowledge or justification is at stake? How aware must one be of epistemic standards, even their applying to one? And (a little later, as contextualism entered the epistemological room) how high should those standards be? It seemed to me that epistemologists might well be unwittingly reading their own standards, at those moments of being epistemological, *into* the situations about which they were being epistemological.

I viewed the Gettier problem, too, as possibly instantiating that general idea. Might epistemologists think that 'Gettiered beliefs' are not knowledge, because those beliefs fail an epistemic standard to which epistemologists would want to hold *themselves* as potential knowers? Could epistemologists have responded to 'Gettier cases' by reading into the cases their own epistemically fuller and more reflective perspectives on the cases? Those epistemological perspectives include an awareness, of the case's details, that is unavailable, *within* the case, to the epistemic subject whose belief is being 'Gettiered'. Might a less demanding epistemic standard be apt for her? Mark Kaplan (*Journal of Philosophy*, 1985) asked something similar, without framing the worry in terms of epistemological onlookers and non-epistemological epistemic subjects – as I proceeded to do.

I even wondered whether an epistemic subject within a 'Gettier case' might *have* knowledge – albeit not what an epistemological perspective on the case would accept as knowledge. It would be a different form or level of knowledge – non-epistemological knowledge. Even so, ….

I realized – the evidence was all around me! – that epistemological onlookers were not regarding any 'Gettiered belief' as knowledge. But could this be a (professionally reinforced) projection, reflecting what any such epistemologist would expect of her *own* knowledge? The non-epistemological participant within the case *would* regard her belief as knowledge. *And why must the epistemological perspective on her (denying such knowledge's presence) be correct?*

So, my general question was at least this: do we have good reason to expand our epistemic-logical space by talking of epistemological knowledge and epistemic subjects, vs non-epistemological knowledge and epistemic subjects?

My initial engagement with that question was in my dissertation, followed by my first book (*Epistemology's Paradox*, Rowman & Littlefield, 1992). The book expanded the dissertation's target: the book's subtitle was *Is a Theory of Knowledge Possible?* (See Chapter 2 here for a brief sense of that book's thinking.) Thus far, then, my epistemological writing was mostly *meta-epistemological*. It was an epistemology *of being epistemological*. It was not akin to meta-ethics, where we 'analyse' moral ideas or terms. I was *evaluating*, epistemically, *the 'analysing' itself of* epistemic ideas or terms. And I was being meta-epistemologically quite sceptical.

After writing that book, I did not engage critically with Gettier for several years. I engaged, but not critically (see, for example, Chapter 4). But that changed when some of my previous worrying emerged from hibernation.

A 1998 paper, 'Actually Knowing' (*Philosophical Quarterly*) asked whether we might sensibly regard 'Gettiered beliefs' as knowledge, or at least whether we have conclusive reasons for deeming them not to be knowledge.

Of course, epistemologists assure us that any Gettiered belief 'is clearly not knowledge'. But how does a given epistemologist know that she is not confusing knowledge with something similar? Or even confusing an exceptionally high grade of knowing, such as infallible knowledge, with what would be knowing in a slightly-less-impressive way?

'No, there are no grades of knowing. We all know that!' Or do we? My questioning of what (since 2016) I call 'Gettierism' (on which all 'Gettiered beliefs' must fail to be knowledge) probably began, in the mid-1990s, when asking whether knowing can admit of grades, perhaps degrees. (I comment further on this in a moment; and see Chapter 6.)

The link with Gettier was direct. One reason why knowing might not admit of grades would be its needing to be infallible. Whether knowing is like that is at the core of the Gettier problem. Here is how.

Gettier introduced his challenge in fallibilist terms: the justificatory standard that he put in place before spinning his yarns asked only that justification-within-knowing (on the definition being tested by him) be fallibly good. Yet was Gettier, by the end of his paper, merely expressing an unacknowledged *infallibilism* about justification-within-knowing?

Methodologically, that should be a worrying question. Is Gettierism ultimately *nothing more than* an expression of an infallibilism about what is needed within knowing? This is not how Gettier's challenge is 'sold' to students and philosophers in general. If it amounts only to a colourful way of giving voice to an infallibilism, *is* it really a challenge? *Would* it have been a distinctive powerful insight?

We may thus appositely ask epistemologists how they know that their so-called 'intuitive' reactions to Gettier cases are not merely infallibilist. Indeed, Chapter 6 of my *Knowledge and the Gettier Problem* (Cambridge University Press, 2016) argues that if epistemologists are being 'intuitive' in their usual Gettierist reactions, they *are* being infallibilist. This would make their reactions unfair to the terms with which Gettier claimed to be framing his cases.

I should expand on that point, given how embedded is the sort of professional reflex that I am questioning. Where, in their routine responses to Gettier cases, do epistemologists display any awareness of that methodological danger? They do not. How do they ensure that they are assessing Gettiered beliefs fairly – in particular, against a fallibilist standard? They do not. Where does this needed 'quality control' enter the usual story? It does not.

Obviously, exposing that methodological carelessness does not prove that Gettiered beliefs are knowledge – even fallible knowledge. But it is a reason to relinquish the usual *unswerving* allegiance to Gettierism – its view of Gettiered beliefs as failing to be knowledge. (When experimental philosophy began, officially in 2001 with a paper by Weinberg, Nichols, and Stich, I was unsurprised by its suggesting that untutored responses to 'Gettier cases' need not be as epistemologists had routinely claimed them to be.)

All of that should already be disquieting for standard epistemology. Yet the problems for Gettierism run even deeper. If we ask epistemologists to explain how any Gettiered belief fails to be knowledge, they will fail – for reasons previously overlooked. This is shown at length in Chapters 2 and 3 of *Knowledge and the Gettier Problem*. Here is a tiny hint as to those lengthy reasons.

Central to Gettierism is the thesis that being Gettiered precludes being knowledge. Ask any Getteristic epistemologist what 'being Gettiered' includes, and she may say that this is a matter for extended debate. At the very least, however, a belief's being Gettiered includes its being true. There is no possible way for a belief to be Gettiered and not true. Hence, no explanation can be given of why any Gettiered belief fails, *due to the belief's being (in the state of being) Gettiered*, to be knowledge – *so long as* that explanation has to point, somehow, to a possibility involving that belief's falsity. Why so? Perhaps *the belief* could be false, in some worlds. But it cannot be false *while still being* Gettiered. This is a vital distinction. For what we must reidentify and chart across possible worlds, say, is the belief *in its state of being Gettiered*. As it happens (and as I explain in *Knowledge and the Gettier Problem*), mainstream Gettieristic explanations do rely, at *some* point, on the possibility of a false belief's being produced. All of them therefore fail.

To that quick initial argument, as I know well from experience, many will object (as follows) that I am overlooking a simple fact.

Accounts such as 'anti-luck' ones locate the supposed fault in *how* the Gettiered belief *has arisen*, for example. The *method* is the problem. And the possibility of false beliefs being produced by that method need not include – *per impossibile* – *the Gettiered belief itself* possibly being false (while being Gettiered).

So, how do I reply to that professionally entrenched line of thought? (I mentioned 'anti-luck' because it is 'catchy'. The same kind of Gettieristic defence is offered by safety accounts in general, and modalized accounts even more generally.)

Knowledge and the Gettier Problem explains how that standard thinking flows from a fundamental methodological mistake, arising from metaphysical carelessness. The mistake concerns how the Gettier problem is standardly *framed*, using an irrelevant *explicandum*. We can gain a sense of this through Bertrand Russell's stopped-clock case, treating it as a pre-Gettier Gettier case.

Suppose that we want to explain the lack of knowledge in his famous case by adverting to *the way* in which the relevant belief was formed. We offer the following attempted explanation.

> The person looks at the clock, which is stopped, and she forms a belief as to the time. Doing this in response to a stopped clock is not a good (such as a reliable) way to form a true belief as to the time. So, the belief is not knowledge.

Even that usual description is beside the explanatory point. It cannot explain why a belief as to the time, formed from a stopped clock, is not knowledge *even when true*: it is apparently seeking only to explain how forming-a-belief-as-to-the-time – a *belief*, not a *true belief* – is not knowledge in this setting. Yet if we wish to think of this as a Gettier case, then the belief's not being knowledge *even when true* is the *explicandum* crying out for attention. If we are to explain it, we must be talking initially along the following lines.

The person looks at the clock, which is stopped, and she forms a true belief as to the time.

And once we begin like that ('keeping hold of' the fact that the belief formed was true), we cannot coherently continue, as we did in the initially attempted explanation, with 'Doing this in response to a stopped clock is not a good (such as a reliable) way to form a true belief as to the time. So, the belief is not knowledge.' Why not? The reason is simplicity itself: what the person did *was* a good – a *wholly* reliable – way to form a true belief as to the time. Thus, the usual kind of ground for denying that this philosophically memorable Gettiered belief is knowledge is removed.

That moral applies to post-Russell Gettier cases, too. My key point is that Gettierists need to explain how a belief, *even when Gettiered* (hence *even when true*), is not knowledge. Why is a Gettiered belief, *in being* Gettiered, not knowledge? They fail in that respect when, in seeking to describe how a belief (which happens to be Gettiered) is not knowledge, they direct us to worlds containing *only some* of what is *essentially* involved in the belief's being Gettiered. As it happens, and inappropriately, their metaphysical focus is standardly on the (*object* that is the) belief and some of its properties – not (as would be appropriate) on the *state of affairs* that is the belief's being Gettiered.

Unfortunately, that mistake in attempted explication (and, for more on it, see Chapters 12 and 14 here) has become an epistemological norm. The result is a failure of philosophical methodology, reflecting a flawed metaphysical focus. The reason behind it is … who knows? I can speculate – which brings us to the next question, I see.

4. Your main contribution to philosophy, especially to epistemology, can perhaps be viewed as a series of arguments for fallibilism. Could you describe what that view is – and why we should adopt it?

Fallibilism is among those central epistemological ideas from which so much flows.

Take Gettier cases, for example (which we were discussing a moment ago). Why have philosophers reacted to those cases as they do? I gestured at a few philosophical mistakes that have helped to shape post-Gettier epistemology. Here is a more psychological speculation.

When people relaxedly say something like 'We are all fallible, even as inquirers, seeking to know', they can be sincere. But they might be meaning only that we do not always know, even when thinking we do. That is compatible with expecting that knowledge, once it *does* arise, is infallible.

Some will reply that, no, they accept that knowing is itself fallible. But I am unsure of their always applying that thesis properly. Often, it seems, people overreact to *manifestations* of fallibility, instead of accepting simply that they are witnessing what fallibility can produce in practice. Maybe what they are encountering *feels* worrying, like a manifestation of something *more*-than-merely-fallible. So, might people sometimes not 'correct' for being 'up close' to the expressing of the fallibility?

Presumably a fallibly good person could make an unexpectedly bad mistake. 'No, only someone with a dark soul would do that. She must not be good!' Not necessarily. Maybe the lapse looks worse 'up close' than it really is – *in the larger picture*. The person remains a good person. Her glaring lapse is simply what fallibility at times can 'do'.

I cannot prove that this is why, in my view, epistemologists overreact to Gettier cases. Still, I do wonder. Those cases are odd ways of gaining a true belief. If that is a possible way for fallibility (or something similar, as I explain in a moment) to be 'played out' in practice, please give me more of it! What would I choose, between (i) a life of being Gettiered, and (ii) a life of forming beliefs in ways that meet with approval from epistemologists who deem Gettiered beliefs not to be knowledge? I would choose the life of being Gettiered.

Would that be a life of not gaining knowledge? Contemporary epistemologists would think so. But *must* we regard this as a strong reason for thinking so?

I begin answering that question, by revisiting probably my first fallibilist proposal – my knowledge-*gradualism*. This arose in a 1998 paper (in *Philosophical Papers*), and, in a different form, a 1999 *Journal of Philosophy* paper (part of which is in Chapter 6) – before being expanded in my book *Good Knowledge, Bad Knowledge* (Clarendon Press, 2001, two sections of which are also in Chapter 6). That book's main idea was that any instance of knowing that *p* can be better, or worse, even *as* knowledge of that particular *p*. Perhaps there are *degrees* of such knowledge that *p*. Perhaps there are *grades* of it. Either way, this is a knowledge-fallibilism, by allowing there to be improvable knowledge that *p*, imperfect knowledge that *p*, good-but-potentially-better knowledge that *p*. One might know that *p* while falling short of infallibility, enjoying a lesser grade of fallibility.

Knowledge-gradualism rejects knowledge-*absolutism*, which seems to be treated by many philosophers as a 'given'. I did not show that they must discard such absolutism; I sought just to show that knowledge-gradualism is coherent and useful. After that book, I offered two further versions.

They appear in *How to Know* (Wiley-Blackwell, 2011). The main one was an implication of the knowledge-*practicalism* first assayed in an earlier paper – 'How to Know (That Knowledge-That Is Knowledge-How)', in *Epistemology Futures* (edited by me: Clarendon Press, 2006). Since then, my knowledge-practicalism has taken shape in several publications (see Chapters 8–10 here). It arose when I was reflecting on *why* there could be grades of knowing. Knowing is always a matter of having various skills or abilities (I hypothesized): knowing-*that* is a form of knowing-*how*. And skills and abilities can be more, or less, good. If my knowing that it is Thursday *is* my having various abilities or skills, say, in principle I could have more, or fewer, of these; and those that I have could themselves, in principle, be more, or less, fully developed.

How to Know's Chapter 5 described another schema for knowledge-gradualism. The idea behind that approach is gestured at here, in Chapter 14. Think of knowing a fact as knowing more, or fewer, of its 'inner' *constituent* facts. Again we can have a conception of improvable knowledge, imperfect knowledge. As ever, I do not find that idea concerning. Knowing is knowing, no matter its 'contained' potential for not having been knowledge.

What does that mean? I described that kind of potential in my 1999 *Journal of Philosophy* discussion. That paper *generalized* the idea of fallible knowledge. It began, though, by proposing that knowledge is fallible when, in a specific respect, it *includes the potential for not* being that knowledge. Maybe it never had to come into existence as knowledge; maybe it still has the potential to go out of existence as knowledge. It carries *within* itself this weakness or fragility, this potential not to be or to have been the knowledge that, in fact, it is.

The specific respect making some knowing *fallible*, on that general conception, is the potential for its *truth* component not to have been present, even once the rest of the knowing's components or constitutive aspects were in place. (That is how fallibility is a possibility of *mistake*.)

I generalized that conception by talking of *failable* knowledge. Insofar as knowledge also has other components or constitutive aspects (beyond truth), if any one or more of *those* could be absent while the knowing's other components or constitutive aspects are present, then the knowing is failable in associated ways. (Belief could depart. Justification could depart. So could any other favoured aspect of knowing.) Thus, fallibility is a *species* of failability.

And in principle there could be *degrees* or *grades* of failability. Any instance of knowledge is failable, in one or another way(s), and to some or another extent(s), depending on various modal niceties. Knowledge-*gradualism* returns to centre stage (and in Chapter 6 here).

We are used to hearing that justification can be better or worse. It might be surprising to hear knowledge described similarly. But, once more, if we are fallibilists about knowing, we should open our epistemological hearts and minds to some ways of talking and thinking that could momentarily feel odd. (Some philosophers do this more readily. In 1995 or so, when first thinking along these lines, I sent a draft version of my knowledge-gradualism to David Lewis. He was writing 'Elusive Knowledge', subsequently in 1996's *Australasian Journal of Philosophy*. Lewis apparently liked the general idea, adding a gradualist wrinkle to his picture of knowing: see his footnote 20. Almost no one comments on that element of his account!)

But should I affix this warning label to what I have been saying just now?

Being a knowledge-fallibilist could lead to being a knowledge-*minimalist*. (I introduced this possible linking in Chapter 4 of *Good Knowledge, Bad Knowledge*; then in Chapter 4 of *How to Know*; in Chapter 13 here; most recently in *Defining Knowledge*, Cambridge University Press, 2022.)

Knowledge-fallibilists should envisage possible boundaries for knowing: how will we demarcate not-knowing from what might be a range of grades of knowing? But what, then, would be the *worst possible* grade of knowing? Could it even be *mere true belief*?

The latter highlighted phrase is a conventional shorthand among epistemologists for something like 'a true belief, or whatever else of that ilk is involved in knowing, *sans* epistemically justificatory support, such as good evidence or a truth-conditionally good pedigree'. *Could* some knowing be like that?

Of course, if anything is a 'truism' among epistemologists (other than Gettierism!), it is the denial of knowledge-minimalism: '*Obviously* knowing includes more than true belief. This has been a philosophical given since Plato's *Meno*.'

Well, I am unsure about that. I have never argued that there *is* some knowledge-as-mere-true-belief. What I have done, however, is to take seriously – as a fallibilist – the idea of this being *possible*. I have done so on theoretical grounds, eschewing 'appeals to intuition'.

We might think of it in this way: even if in fact every instance of knowledge involves epistemic justification, this does not entail the justification's being *essential* to the knowing. In that strict sense, the justification might not be *part* of the knowledge. The justification could be like clothes for us – practically useful but constitutively inessential. We always wear them, especially for social purposes. But this association could be metaphysically accidental. Similarly, the *essence* of the knowing might be nothing beyond *being correct in what one thinks* – with justification playing associated causal-practical roles, such as helping us, even reliably, to reach the knowledge. A few others (notably, Crispin Sartwell and Richard Foley) have also defended this sort of view; it should receive wider consideration.

Why has it not done so? Suffice it to repeat that I was pleased when experimental philosophy arrived, pricking one bubble of philosophical methodology as possibly having been too *ad hoc* for ultimate philosophical purposes. (I worry that experimental philosophy is itself becoming an unilluminating methodology, being used beyond its real purpose. But that is another story.)

A further reason, I suspect, why knowledge-minimalism receives almost no love from epistemologists is that many have strayed too far from *metaphysics*. What is knowledge? That should be treated as a metaphysical question. What is knowledge, in itself? What is its metaphysical essence? *True belief*, I say (in this mode, setting aside some details from knowledge-practicalism, described above). What are knowing's metaphysical accidents? Maybe *epistemic justification*, I reply.

I do not say this on the basis of 'intuitions' (or anything similar, I hope). How much could they help here? It is easy to recall someone's saying that they cannot imagine according someone knowledge when she apparently has no evidence in support of her admittedly true belief. But this is *so* inconclusive. 'Intuitions' even about Gettier cases, as I explained above, are far from decisive. Why should we expect them to be incisive on knowledge's nature? They might reflect mere social expectations, for example. And how can they discern the difference between justification's being essential to knowing and its happening always to accompany knowing?

In short, I welcome theoretical discussions, not people's reporting 'intuitions'. If metaphysics is available with which to enrich an epistemologically theoretical discussion, so much the better, all else being equal. (I considered writing my PhD Dissertation on the metaphysics of modality, not on epistemology. Who knew, back then, that those two topics would someday and somewhat merge for me?)

Why should we be fallibilists about knowing? Why not? Is epistemological talk of infallibility merely aspirational? Or helpfully descriptive? (See Chapter 5 above on this issue.) I doubt that it is the latter: in which, if any, aspects of our lives are we infallible? Think – micro-think – of how many everyday movements are consequences or manifestations of fallibility. Think of how many simple movements are needed due to forgetting an action's detail, or to dropping something, or not making a movement so well, or not thinking through the best path to follow, or …. I notice – too often! – my making a movement only because I did not do something else, even a moment earlier, as well as I could or should have done it. And knowing is simply one kind of thing that we do, even if it is possibly implicated in almost everything that we do. Personally, I expect *everything* we do to be done fallibly. (Or, more generally, to be done *failably* – see above.)

This is not to say that our actions are failures, or must be felt as being so. Even if they are not quite what I would have done if I was less fallible, they can be performed competently. Most are normal actions. It is just that they can be given a fallibilist interpretive overlay. I feel no philosophical temptation to step away from that general picture, seeking an interpretation on which, in knowing, one transcends that general limit on the quality of everything else that we do. Humans are fallible in all that we are and do, I believe. In which case, knowing is also something that we do fallibly, if at all.

Little wonder, then, that I have taken so many steps – fallibly! – towards a *theory* of the nature of fallible knowledge. (Chapter 11 above is one recent step.)

All of that is why this book has the subtitle that it has (*Knowing, More or Less*), and the cover picture that it has. I see knowing *as* a matter of 'more or less' – even while still *being* knowing. It can look vague; it can be messy; it can be better or worse; yet somehow it stays in place, useful and recognisable. And that is what the cover's picture, 'Going, Going' – by my artist wife, Parveen Seehra – conveys to me.

5. Have any of your main epistemological views changed over the years, since they were first published?

I will mention two candidates: (i) my initial meta-epistemological scepticism and (ii) some of my early writing on Gettier.

(i) It is not that I have fashioned a later argument undermining that early view. But what *if* I had been mistaken? It was a bold stance, seemingly confrontational. Since then, therefore, I have mostly written *as if* that meta-epistemological scepticism is not true. ('Mostly', because Chapter 3 in this book aims to *reinforce* that scepticism, especially after Chapter 2 explains it briefly.) I have offered ideas as *possibly* true. I regard them as describing *models*, as *hypotheses*. What further epistemic status should I assign to them? I hope to revisit this in the next few years.

Maybe that is partly why I have been drawn to some *epistemically forgiving* models and hypotheses – such as knowledge-minimalism, knowledge-fallibilism, knowledge-gradualism, and knowledge-practicalism. Knowing is a matter of acting and being able to act. Knowing can be done more, or less, well. It can even be done poorly. All of this (including my theorizing about it) is fallibly performed.

Or so I am hypothesizing. If any of those hypotheses are true, and if I have good arguments for them, then maybe my meta-epistemological scepticism should at best be adopted in a less (youthfully!) confident spirit than animated 1992's *Epistemology's Paradox*.

(ii) As I explained earlier, my initial meta-epistemological scepticism included doubts about Gettier cases posing real challenges. I set aside those worries for a few years, publishing some papers (such as Chapter 4) that presumed the usual Gettieristic reading of such cases. Then I resumed being doubtful about Gettier cases. Were they being read correctly, in some basic respects? Could they coherently and usefully be read as stories where a person *has* knowledge? The knowledge in question would have *a lower standard, even as knowledge*. That might sound odd; must it be false, though? Once I opened the door to this idea, further interesting epistemological ideas soon appeared on the doorstep. I welcomed them at the time – as I have done ever since, along with their kinfolk.

6. You have spent many years writing on epistemology. At this stage (and in a fallibilist spirit!), what do you see as its future direction?

There are paths along which I would like epistemology to wander. There are paths along which at present it seems likely to walk. I am unsure how large the overlap is between those two groups. I am loath to be too critical.

Still, I do hope for a day when epistemologists cease being Gettierists. Some will hear that remark as saying just that they should 'move on' from trying to *define* knowledge in light of Gettier's challenge – a move that, many insist, they have already made. Some will cite, with approval, Timothy Williamson's knowledge-first rejection of 'conceptual analyses' of knowledge. Some regard his move as a deep insight into what was wrong with 'that whole tradition'. In my view, it is not so. May I direct readers again to *Defining Knowledge: Method and Metaphysics* (Cambridge University Press, 2022)? It includes (as Chapter 14 above indicates) some of my reasons for being underwhelmed by that current chorus within epistemology.

Actually, my concern for the future of epistemology extends further. There are a few associated trends within current epistemology (generally instances of modalized epistemology, highly influential since at least Robert Nozick in 1981) that many of its practitioners apparently see as part of epistemology's future. I hope that it will not be so, since (as I also explain in *Defining Knowledge*) I believe that such epistemology has been built upon, and is energetically entrenching, some serious flaws, both methodological and metaphysical.

My preference for future epistemologists no longer to be Gettierists reflects some answers already given in this interview. I do not believe that Gettier established what, ever more habitually, he is credited with having established. The sooner that we cease taking his supposed insight for granted, the better. Epistemologists have absorbed a *false* sense of having in hand, thanks to Gettier, some genuine progress. For just a start, it is not 'simply obvious' that Gettiered beliefs fail to be knowledge. Theories of knowledge are abounding that repeat and reinforce the basic mistakes underlying Gettierism. But will this professionalized

Gettierism ever be corrected? That would mean casting aside a *lot* of professionally respected writing – a challenge in itself for many.

I have long cared about epistemology's future and its potential progress. So much so that, in 2006, I edited *Epistemology Futures* (OUP; now – 2023 – in Chinese). That was partly an attempt to encourage diverse searches for fresh epistemological paths.

One path that was not explored in that book, but that I hope will be increasingly followed by epistemologists, involves *retracing* some steps – large ones. I am talking here of the *history* of philosophy. Epistemological revisiting of it is starting to occur – a little. For example, some have asked '*Was* there really a justified-true-belief definition implicitly in place within philosophy, prior to Gettier, with his challenge thereby gaining added import?' That is one possible instance. Forwards into the past? Further steps are available. I general-edited the four-volume *The Philosophy of Knowledge: A History* (Bloomsbury, 2019). And I co-edited, with Nicholas D. Smith, *What the Ancients Offer to Contemporary Epistemology* (Routledge, 2020). Have epistemologists always chosen the best options available at a time? I doubt it. Is epistemological activity perennially helping to produce epistemological progress? I doubt this, too. We should never ignore the possibility even of going backwards in our epistemological thinking. Meta-epistemological humility matters if we are not to regress in that respect.

7. Finally, let us talk about legacy, particularly your legacy in philosophy. How will the philosophers of the future remember you? How would you like to be remembered?

I do not think of myself as potentially having a legacy. The most that I hope for is that my more recent writing on Gettier can, one of these days, awaken some epistemologists from what seems to have become a dogmatic doze. But I do not expect to live to see this happen.

If I was to be remembered at all, I would welcome its being for a few odd epistemological ideas – and for having defended these in interesting and strongly argued ways. Who needs philosophers to tell them (even with added technical flourishes) what they are already confident of knowing? Why do philosophers need other philosophers to tell them variants (even with added technical flourishes) of what they already believe with professionally buttressed confidence?

Sometimes I wish that various peers would find epistemology more deeply, perhaps inescapably, questioning and puzzling than they apparently do. Chapter 11 above introduces the ideas of *open* knowledge (rather than closed knowledge) and *questioning* knowledge-attributions (beyond concessive knowledge-attributions). These feel to me like fallibilist ideas that should always be close to our philosophical hearts. Whenever I have felt spurred to write as an epistemologist, my motivation has not been to find a preferred place within a professionally circumscribed debate. Who needs to hear whether I share their views? At times, however, I have felt prompted to test a debate's *resilience*. Is it a debate worth having? What potentially significant ideas has it already ruled out as not worth considering? How well-formed a formula of a debate is it? (Thus, for example, witness Chapters 7–9 here, on some classic attempts to embroil us in sceptical debates.)

So, if I have taken seriously and even defended a few ideas that others thought were indefensible, that sounds fine to me. I think of this as philosophical theory-testing – conjecturing and risking. Although it can be messy work, someone needs to do it. In fact, *many* of us need to do it, now and far into the future. Thankfully, they do. Hopefully, they will.

Index

Allen, B. 159 n. 19
Alston, W. 12 n. 1, 19 n. 3, 37 n. 21
Annas, J. 112–13
Annis, D. 37 n. 20
Anscombe, G.E.M. 136 n. 3
Audi, R. 12 n. 1, 12 n. 6
Ayer, A.J. 8, 11, 79–80

Baker, G. 13 n. 11
Bates, J. 210 n. 8
Bergmann, M. 175 n. 12
BonJour, L.
    and coherence 57–8, 60
    and internalism 8, 12 n. 3
Brandom, R. 158 n. 13

Campbell, R. 135
Carrier, L. 73 n. 2
Cartesian scepticism *see* Descartes, R., and scepticism
Cassam, Q. 225 n. 14
Chalmers, D. 117 n. 2, 210 n. 5
Chisholm, R. 8, 31, 37 n. 24, 37 n. 26, 47, 111, 190 n. 4
Chrisman, M. 133
Coffman, E.J. 190 n. 8
Cohen, L.J. 138 n. 14
Cohen, S. 62 n. 10, 73 n. 1, 175 n. 5
coherentism 37 n. 26; *see also* BonJour, L., and coherence; Cross, C.
Conee, E. 175 n. 12
contexts, epistemological 17–19; *see also* contextualism; epistemic subjects/agents, epistemological; meta-epistemology
contextualism 17, 37 n. 20, 232; *see also* contexts, epistemological; Lewis, D.
Craig, E. 138 n. 22
Cross, C. 57–61

Davis, W. 210 n. 8
De Almeida, C. 176 n. 19

Descartes, R. 6, 20 n. 7, 112–15, 121, 124, 135
    and infallibilism 193, 209
    and scepticism 41–53, 69, 77–8, 80, 83–6, 95 n. 1, 98 n. 24, 102, 104, 108, 141, 142–4, 155, 157, 221–2
Deutsch, E. 190 n. 6
Dodd, D. 175 n. 7
dogmatism 74 n. 7, 161, 172–4; *see also* knowledge, as fallible; Kripke, S.
doubt *see* scepticism
Dougherty, T. 174 n. 1, 175 n. 7, 209 n. 2
dreams *see* Descartes, R., and scepticism; scepticism, external world
Dretske, F. 52, 96 n. 8, 157 n. 3
Dutant, J. 210 n. 8

Elgin, C. 161–4, 166–7, 168, 171–3
Engel, M. 190 n. 5, 199
epistemic principles *see* epistemic subjects/agents
epistemic subjects/agents 37 n. 23, 58–60, 78, 82, 85, 141, 143, 145–6, 150, 156, 157 n. 2, 158 n. 10, 159 n. 15, 173; *see also* knowledge-practicalism
    epistemological 16–17, 19, 26, 29–30, 31, 32, 232; *see also* meta-epistemology
    non-epistemological (standard) 17, 19, 26, 30, 31, 32, 231, 232
experimental philosophy 131, 212 n. 20, 224 n. 1, 233, 238
externalism, epistemic 5, 7, 36 n. 16, 38 n. 27, 59–60, 61 n. 3, 148, 162, 207, 209 n. 4
    see also internalism, epistemic; justification, epistemic; reflectivism

fallibilism 73 n. 2, 74 n. 7, 118 n. 27, 138 n. 21, 161, 164–73, 194, 202, 235, 239; *see also* knowledge, as failable; knowledge, as fallible; knowledge, as imperfect

Fantl, J. 36 n. 15, 36 n. 17, 174 n. 1, 209 n. 2
Feldman, R. 62 n. 9, 175 n. 12
Fett, J.R. 176 n. 19
Fogelin, R. 13 n. 11
Foley, R. 190 n. 9, 205–6, 212 n. 21, 238; see also knowledge, as minimal
Frances, B. 98 n. 19
Friedman, J. 168, 170
Fumerton, R. 12 n. 1

Gettier cases 15, 49, 102–3, 111–12, 117 n. 14, 181, 182, 190 n. 7, 201–2, 210 n. 13, 215–16, 224 n. 1, 232–6, 238, 240
  and intuitions 15–16, 111, 118 n. 22, 218–19, 224 n. 1
  see also experimental philosophy; Gettier problem; Gettierism; luck, and knowledge; post-Gettier epistemology; scepticism, Gettieristic
Gettier problem 19 n. 1, 49, 121, 117 n. 8, 181–2, 201–2, 215–16, 218, 219, 220, 223–4, 229, 231–4, 240; see also Gettier cases; Gettierism; knowledge, and conceptual analysis; post-Gettier epistemology; Williamson, T.
Gettier's challenge see Gettier problem
Gettierism 233–4, 238, 240–1
  bare- 215–17, 219
  explicated- 215–19
  see also Gettier cases; Gettier problem; post-Gettier epistemology
Glick, E. 137 n. 8
Goldman, A.I. 5, 50, 175 n. 5, 196–7, 205–6
Greco, J. 86, 176 n. 20

Haack, S. 73 n. 2, 74 n. 7
Hacker, P. 13 n. 11
Harman, G. 175 n. 5, 176 n. 22
Hawthorne, J. 96 n. 8, 99 n. 35, 149, 157 n. 3
Hintikka, J. 209 n. 5
how-knowledge 220–1
Hume, D. 24, 86, 121, 123–4, 125, 135, 136 n. 5

infallibilism see Descartes, R., and infallibilism; fallibilism; knowledge, as fallible
intellectualism see knowledge-practicalism; Ryle, G., on intellectualism
internalism, epistemic 5–8, 10, 11, 36 n. 16, 38 n. 27, 58–60, 148, 162–3, 170, 175 n. 12, 207, 209 n. 4; see also BonJour, L., and internalism; Descartes, R.; externalism, epistemic; justification, epistemic; reflectivism

Jacquette, D. 107
Jäger, C. 210 n. 8
Johnsen, B. 174 n. 4
justification, epistemic
  as epistemological 20 n. 3, 26–30
  as infallible 60–1, 158 n. 7, 196–8, 201–4, 210 n. 6
  see also coherentism; contexts, epistemological; epistemic subjects/agents; fallibilism; internalism, epistemic; knowledge, as fallible; knowledge, as imperfect; knowledge-gradualism; scepticism, and possibilities; scepticism, external world
justified true belief see Gettier cases; Gettier problem; knowledge, and conceptual analysis

Kaplan, M. 19 n. 1, 174 n. 4, 232
Kim, K. 61 n. 3
Klein, P. 36 n. 17, 57–61
knowledge
  and conceptual analysis 134, 175 n. 11, 223–4
  and intuitions 116, 183, 238; see also Gettier cases, and intuitions
  as ability see knowledge-practicalism
  as failable 64–73, 117 n. 11, 194, 239
  as fallible 63–6, 104, 106, 111, 114, 115, 158 n. 7, 161, 166, 167–8, 193–7, 202, 203, 209 n. 5, 233, 237, 239; see also fallibilism
  as imperfect 69–72, 105, 197, 236

as infallible 71, 104, 115, 138 n. 21, 158 n. 7, 166–8, 169, 193–8, 200, 202, 209 n. 5, 233, 235, 239
as knowledge-how *see* knowledge-practicalism
as minimal 186–7, 193, 202, 205–8, 238, 239
-first 223–4, 224 n. 2, 240
-gradualism 108–9, 110, 114, 118 n. 19, 118 n. 21, 205–6, 236–7, 239; *see also* knowledge-practicalism
-practicalism 121, 130–3, 134, 149, 236, 238, 239
see also Ryle, G. *see also* contextualism; fallibilism; Gettier cases; Gettier problem; Gettierism; how-knowledge; justification, as infallible; Lewis, D.; luck, and knowledge; modality, and knowledge; post-Gettier epistemology; scepticism, external world; scepticism, Gettieristic; Williamson, T.
Kornblith. H. 61, 158 n. 10, 212 n. 22
Kremer, M. 137 n. 13, 138 n. 15
Kripke, S. 9, 13 n. 11, 172–4
Kvanvig, J. 210 n. 8, 212 n. 20

Lehrer, K. 175 n. 5, 176 n. 19
Levy, N. 190 n. 8
Lewis, C.I. 133–4
Lewis, D. 17–19, 23, 74 n. 8, 74 n. 10, 118 n. 17, 164 n. 26, 230, 237
luck, and knowledge 111–12, 179–90, 199–200, 210 n. 10, 212 n. 19, 216, 234; *see also* Gettier cases; Gettierism
Lycan. W. 136 n. 1, 212 n. 20

Macarthur, D. 99 n. 34
Makinson, D. 97 n. 13
McDowell, J. 211 n. 17
McGinn, C. 9, 13 n. 11
McGlynn, A. 223, 224 n. 13
Merricks, T. 61 n. 1
meta-epistemology 23, 27, 33, 36 n. 15, 232, 239–40, 241; *see also* epistemic subjects/agents, epistemological; justification, epistemic, as epistemological
Mill, J.S. 121, 135–6

modality, and knowledge 135–6, 145–6, 197, 212 n. 19, 237; *see also* knowledge, as failable; knowledge, as fallible; luck, and knowledge; Gettierism; post-Gettier epistemology; scepticism, and possibilities
Moore, G.E. 118 n. 19, 141–2, 144, 155, 157 n. 5; *see also* scepticism, external world
Myers-Schulz, B. 123, 131–2, 138 n. 15

Nagel, T. 72–3
Nichols, S. 190 n. 6, 224 n. 1, 233
non-reflectivism 29, 38 n. 27; *see also* epistemic subjects/agents, non-epistemological (standard); externalism, epistemic; reflectivism
Nozick, R. 52, 96 n. 8, 157 n. 3, 175 n. 5, 240

Olsson, E. 196, 210 n. 8

Pasnau, R. 174 n. 2
Paxson, T. 176 n. 19
Pears, D. 10
Peirce, C.S. 121, 125, 135
Plantinga, A. 191 n. 13
Plato 112–13, 123, 181
Pollock, J. 176 n. 19
Popkin, R. 118 n. 24, 118 n. 26
Popper, K. 108, 161, 169
post-Gettier epistemology 45, 121, 180–2, 191 n. 13, 215–16, 219–20, 223–4, 235; *see also* Gettier cases; Gettier problem; Gettierism
pragmatism 121, 134; *see also* knowledge-practicalism
Price, H.H. 156–7
Pritchard, D. 224 n. 13
and epistemic luck 190 n. 5, 199–200, 212 n. 19; *see also* Gettier problem; Gettierism; luck, and knowledge; post-Gettier epistemology
and scepticism 157 n. 2, 157 n. 5
Pryor, J. 79, 90–1

Radford, C. 131
Reed, B. 138 n. 18, 138 n. 19, 174 n. 1, 194, 209 n. 2

reflectivism 29–30, 37 n. 20, 38 n. 27;
    see also epistemic subjects/agents,
    epistemological; internalism,
    epistemic; justification,
    epistemological
Riggs, W. 210 n. 8
Russell, B. 8, 9–10, 237
Ryle, G. 121, 131, 135, 137 n. 13, 138 n.
    15, 141
    on intellectualism 126–8, 146–8
Rysiew, P. 175 n. 7

safety, epistemic see luck, and knowledge;
    modality, and knowledge
Sartwell, C. 190 n. 9, 205, 238; see also
    knowledge, as minimal
Sayre, K. 224 n. 10
scepticism
    and objectivity 72–3
    and possibilities 17–18, 35 n. 8, 49,
        67–9, 77–80, 81, 82–8, 101–2, 103,
        104, 107, 108–9, 112, 159 n. 16; see
        also contextualism
    external world 41–53, 77–93, 116 n.
        1, 119 n. 28, 157 n. 5, 221–2; see
        also Descartes, R., and scepticism;
        knowledge, as failable; knowledge,
        as fallible; knowledge, as imperfect;
        knowledge-gradualism; knowledge-
        practicalism; Moore, G.E.
    Gettieristic 41–53; see also Gettier
        cases
    Humean 41
    meta-epistemological see meta-
        epistemology
    Pyrrhonist 41, 98 n. 22
    rule 41
Scheffler, I. 138 n. 15

Schwitzgebel, E. 123, 131–2, 138 n. 15
Sellars, W. 8, 10–11, 229
Shope, R. 117 n. 4, 136 n. 1, 190 n. 3, 211
    n. 13
Sosa, E. 172, 176 n. 20
    and epistemic action 133, 159 n. 19,
        210 n. 12
    and epistemic safety 190 n. 7, 210 n. 9
    and scepticism 78, 90–1
Stanley, J. 126, 136 n. 2, 137 n. 7, 147, 149,
    158 n. 9, 175 n. 7
Stich, S. 190 n. 6, 224 n. 1, 233
Stroud, B. 54 n. 7, 78, 80, 85, 90, 102
swamping problem 196–7

Vendler, Z. 224 n. 10
veritic luck see luck, and knowledge;
    modality, and knowledge
veritism 197
virtue epistemology 121, 132, 138 n. 19,
    164, 172; see also Elgin, C.;
    Sosa, E., and epistemic action;
    Zagzebski, L.

Warenski, L. 206
Warfield, T. 57–61
Weatherson, B. 117 n. 5
Weinberg, J. 190 n. 6, 224 n. 1, 233
Williams, M. 37 n. 20
Williamson, T. 38 n. 30, 136 n. 2, 147,
    149, 158 n. 9, 209 n. 4, 222–4; see
    also knowledge, and conceptual
    analysis; knowledge-first
Wittgenstein, L. 8–9, 137 n. 9, 142, 158
    n. 13

Zagzebski, L. 176 n. 20, 210 n. 8, 211 n. 14,
    224 n. 4

www.ingramcontent.com/pod-product-compliance
Lightning Source LLC
Chambersburg PA
CBHW071824300426
44116CB00009B/1420